Samuel Richardson

Samuel Richardson, Author of Clarissa

Samuel Richardson
A Man of Letters

CAROL HOULIHAN FLYNN

Princeton University Press
Princeton, New Jersey

PR
3667
.F5
1982

Copyright © 1982 by Princeton University Press
Published by Princeton University Press, 41 William Street,
Princeton, New Jersey
In the United Kingdom: Princeton University Press, Guildford, Surrey

All Rights Reserved
Library of Congress Cataloging in Publication Data will be
found on the last printed page of this book

Publication of this book has been aided by a grant from the
Paul Mellon Fund of Princeton University Press

Designed by Barbara Werden

This book has been composed in Linotron Caslon

Clothbound editions of Princeton University Press books
are printed on acid-free paper, and binding materials are
chosen for strength and durability

Printed in the United States of America by Princeton
University Press, Princeton, New Jersey

Frontispiece: Portrait of Samuel Richardson by
J. Highmore (1750). Courtesy of the
National Portrait Gallery, London.

For
Dennis Patrick Aloysius Flynn
Patrick Houlihan Flynn
Molly Maureen Flynn

with love and admiration

Contents

Preface

"What a world is this! What is there in it desirable?" Clarissa wonders. "The good we hope for, so strangely mixed, that one knows not what to wish for! And one half of mankind tormenting the other, and being tormented themselves in tormenting!" (II, 38) [I, 265] Her complaint reveals much about Samuel Richardson's world as well as her own, a world strangely mixed, offering possibilities of self-creation and annihilation, joy and torment. In his finest novel, Richardson explored the tension between absolute and relative moral values as he considered the possibility of Clarissa's purity surviving its compromising circumstances. Even as he offered his readers rules of conduct to protect and perfect the self, Richardson undermined the possibility of such simple maxims ever succeeding in Clarissa's personal arena of torment. "I don't know what to wish," she recognizes, "without a sin," acknowledging that her dilemma can never be resolved on earth.

Even while he placed his favorite heroine into a world so strangely mixed, where every moral choice is, in some vital sense, the wrong choice, Richardson still regarded himself as a moralist first, committed to the social as well as spiritual reformation of his readers. His early work, *Vade Mecum*, a conduct manual for apprentices, and his collection of epistolary and moral models, the *Familiar Letters*, demonstrate Richardson's faith in an idealized world of reciprocal relationships and moral absolutes, a faith, however, that changed significantly when the author investigated his moral assumptions dramatically in his novels. In *Pamela*, Richardson turned to the novel to make his moral, reasoning that fallen times called for stronger measures than conduct manuals. Disguised as an entertainer as well as a moralist, Richardson discovered that he could "steal in" doctrines of Christianity "under the fashionable guise of an amusement." (VIII, 308) [IV, 553] But once he began to develop characters as well as morals, personality complicated proselytizing. In his novels, Richardson examines the social and moral conventions that he endorsed so automatically in his earlier work, transforming the simple aphorisms of his conduct guides into richly complex fiction.

Richardson possessed a positive genius for the commonplace, but always the commonplace transformed. We can see in his early *Familiar Letters* as well as in his last work, a ponderous collection of moral sentiments, that he was a great receptor of popular wisdom, a compulsive hoarder of moral aphorisms. But Richardson had no commonplace mind. He could both accept conventional morality and analyze it, relentlessly, disturbingly, taking its measure in spite of the nasty contradictions he would uncover along the way. In *Clarissa*, he was brave enough to let the contradictions stand, but in *Sir Charles Grandison* he retreated to cover up the inconsistencies he had exposed.

For even the most conventional reader, the moral of *Clarissa* can certainly be puzzling. In her introduction to Richardson's correspondence, Mrs. Barbauld asks an important question: "That Clarissa is a highly moral work has been always allowed; but what is the moral?" Her answer is less striking: "That virtue is triumphant in every situation." She goes on, however, to qualify this moral in a most unsettling way: "It is immaterial what particular maxim is selected under the name of a moral, while such are the reader's feelings. If our feelings are in favour of virtue, the novel is virtuous; if of vice, the novel is vicious."[1] Exactly the problem and the strength of Richardson's greatest novel. Ostensibly promoting principles of absolute morality, Richardson creates a world of infinite complexity and ambiguity where commonplace maxims have little effect on real situations.

Richardson's commitment to perfect and redeem his reader

freed him to create fictional characters and situations that
threaten to burst the moral framework of his novels. Only
in his simplest, early work could he maintain the morally
absolute world of idealized reciprocal relationships. Once
he turned to the novel, he left moral certainties to create
characters acting independently in a complicated world,
following the dictates of their own consciences rather than
the simple rules of a conduct manual. His aesthetic commitment to his characters subverted his moral intention.
We must not forget, however, that Richardson could never
have followed the fates of his characters to their logical
ends without the certainty his moral license granted him.

Richardson himself held a double view of himself and
his writing. On the one hand, he was "a plain writer: a
sincere well-wisher; an undesigning scribbler; who admire
none but the natural and easy beauties of the pen." But this
"plain writer" could also portray himself (with tongue in
portly cheek) as a "sly sinner, creeping along the very
edges of the walks, getting behind benches: one hand in
his bosom, the other held up to his chin, as if to keep it
in its place: afraid of being seen, as a thief of detection."[2]
The perfect man to "steal in" to investigate moral precepts
"under the fashionable guise of an amusement." Richardson's double view of himself reflects his own self-conscious
awareness of the difference between intention and result, a
difference repressed altogether in his final work, *Sir Charles
Grandison*, where the moral intention reigns.

This study will examine the tension between Richardson's moral and aesthetic principles in his novels and letters. I do not propose to discuss a "divided" Richardson
working against himself, nor do I present the author as an
unconscious artist creating in spite of himself. Richardson
knew what he was doing in his novels, recognizing, even
while he suppressed, the inconsistencies in his final work.
I am interested in uncovering the conscious conflict in
Richardson's best work between stated moral and expressed
art, the tension between the artistic and moral principles

that energizes his novels. Richardson's reluctant compulsion to present a world of torment and sexual conflict, a world so strangely mixed, overcame his understandable attraction to a unified, morally absolute world where things are as they should be. *Clarissa* bears witness to Richardson's recognition of such a mixed universe, just as *Grandison* signals a retreat to a morally comprehensible society where Sir Charles, who always does as he ought to do, reigns, firmly suppressing the passions.

We shall first look at the deliberate ways in which Richardson set out to perfect his readers, in his conduct manuals and through the use of moral exemplars like Pamela, Clarissa, and Grandison. As the artist developed his characters, he transformed his moral, turning his secular saints into impassioned characters of complexity and ambiguity, characters who literally create themselves in their letters. To perfect his readers, Richardson created a fictional world that may appear commonplace, but is in fact fantastic—a prosaic nightmare of violent, sexual conflict. To redeem his readers, the author first had to catch them, luring them in with the promise of a sensational romantic world, yet one seeming "realistic" enough to satisfy his moral censor. In his novels, Richardson authenticated his fairy tales, investing the commonplace with menace and wonder, to present a world of fantasy made concrete. He deliberately chose commonplace feminine models, adopting the sexual stereotypes of his age, but he transformed them in his fiction. Sentimental misses became heroines of integrity, often at odds with conventional morality. Ostensibly upholding the traditionally feminine virtues of submission, obedience, filial piety, and chastity, Richardson actually celebrates a personal purity that transcends all rules of decorum, exalting a raped runaway as his most spotless saint, most inviolate when most violated. In *Clarissa*, Richardson reverses the sentimental formula of "marriage heals all," presenting a heroine who elevates herself, enriching sentimentality with the integrity of the tragic imperatives of her personality.

Speaking through his characters, rebels like Lovelace and Clarissa (less obvious but no less effective in her subversive attack on society), Richardson articulates a tension between sincerity and artifice, morality and art, compulsion and freedom. For the artist is both compelled and freed to work out the complexities of the fictional world of his own invention. Disguised in his novels and letters, and licensed by his moral imperative, Richardson could invent a bolder, freer personality. Lovelace especially offered great possibilities for personal freedom. Richardson's rake defines himself through his imagination, wildly inventing new schemes as old ones fail, eventually losing himself in the very fantasy he creates. Richardson both valued and feared this terrible freedom, recognizing its possibilities not only for self-realization but also for madness and self-damnation. We can see Richardson's ambivalence towards Lovelace in his authorial intrusions and footnotes to the novel, where he alternately attacks and defends his creation. By officially damning Lovelace, Richardson was then free to construct his creation's rich fantasy world without assuming moral responsibility for its results.

Letters offered Richardson a similar freedom to express himself with impunity. In letters to young girls, coy matrons, and bluestockings, Richardson became a teasing tyrant, familiar and audacious, taking liberties with his correspondents and himself. "I write," he told Miss Mulso, "to carry myself out of myself; and am not quite so happy, when, tired with my peregrinations, I am obliged to return home." (*Correspondence*, vol. III, pp. 190-91) In his novels, Richardson carried himself out of himself, and paradoxically deeper into himself, into the true self unbound by commonplace conventions, where personal integrity can stand outside social morality. The freedom he gained from his characters and his letters expanded and completed both his fiction and himself.

Students of Richardson have all been fortunate in their

instruction. From McKillop, Sale, Eaves and Kimpel, Kearney, Watt, Golden, Traugott, Preston, Kinkead-Weekes, and Doody, as well as from the many others I have tried to acknowledge in this book,[3] I have gained many insights and been directed towards important areas of investigation. Such insights remain the property of critics before me; any errors become mine. I have differed from many of my predecessors, perhaps, in insisting on a certain bleakness of vision in Richardson's novels. His fictional subversion of his moral seems to me to upset the balance others have been able to find in his work. It will, in fact, soon become obvious that this particular study is decidedly off balance: *Sir Charles Grandison* gets short shrift, *Pamela* more serious attention, *Clarissa* the lion's share.[4] And it is in *Clarissa* that Richardson calls into question his own perfectionism, as self-improvement becomes self-annihilation and the transformed self creates itself out of its own ashes.

The creation of this book was hardly such a phoenixlike feat; it depended greatly upon the support of friends and advisors. John Traugott, who introduced me to Richardson so long ago, has stayed with the book from its inception until its end. His brilliantly practical approach to criticism, his insistence on its being, at its best, a conversation between thinking people, is one I greatly admire. I want to thank him for his constant friendship and advice. Gardner Stout's humane and searching criticism has been invaluable. Without his encouragement, perceptive readings, and unflagging aid, and his insistence that I make connections, this book would have been greatly diminished. Charles Leahy, always filled with new ideas to pursue, an endless source of richly historical anecdotes, gave many sound and searching readings of the manuscript. Dustin Griffin, my teacher, colleague, and friend, offered helpful and welcome advice on several chapters as well as encouragement at a time when it was sorely needed. And Ann Van Sant was with me throughout the writing of the book. I thank them all for their help and encouragement.

The staffs of the London Library, the British Library, the New York Public Library, and the libraries of the University of California and New York University were all very helpful to me. For their able assistance I am most grateful.

I would also like to thank Marjorie Sherwood, my editor, for her sympathetic interest, encouragement, and commitment. My copy editor, Alida Becker, took pains, gently and generously, in the finishing of the book. And Marilyn Campbell has been both efficient and considerate in the production of this book. The careful, perceptive readings of Judith Wilt, Peter Sabor, and especially Margaret Doody (who suggested important links between the traditions of fairy tale and romance) added greatly to the formation of this book. Elaine Gould, Charles Morris, and J. L. Lewis also provided appreciated close readings.

Finally, I want to thank my husband Denny, whose love and endurance supported me through the years of my work on this book (which he has still managed not to read), and my children, Patrick and Molly, who grew along with the manuscript and share my scepticism about the sublime.

A Note on the Texts

Since there is no definitive standard edition of Richardson's works, I have followed the usual practice of citing volume and page numbers from the Shakespeare Head editions, edited by William King and Adrian Bott (Oxford, 1929-30), of *Pamela* and *Clarissa*, while adding references to the more easily accessible editions in Everyman's Library (1914, 1932) in brackets. I regret not using T. C. Duncan Eaves' and Ben D. Kimpel's excellent edition of *Pamela* (Boston, 1971), but since I quote extensively from the second part of *Pamela*, I decided to stay with the Shakespeare Head and Everyman editions for both parts of *Pamela* rather than confuse the reader with an escalating series of brackets and parentheses. All references to *Sir Charles Grandison* are from the three-volume edition, edited by Jocelyn Harris (London, 1972). The volume and letter numbers correlating to the first edition of *Grandison*, 1753-54, can be found in brackets.

Letters from *The Selected Letters of Samuel Richardson*, edited by John Carroll (Oxford, 1964), are cited in the text as *Letters*. Letters edited by Anna Laetitia Barbauld in *The Correspondence of Samuel Richardson*, 6 volumes (London, 1804), are cited as *Correspondence*. *The Apprentice's Vade Mecum: or Young Man's Pocket Companion*, edited by A. D. McKillop for the Augustan Reprint Society, nos. 169-70 (Los Angeles, 1975) is cited as *Vade Mecum*. Finally, Richardson's *Familiar Letters on Important Occasions*, edited by Brian W. Downs (London, 1928), is cited in the text as *Familiar Letters*.

Samuel Richardson

ONE • The Self-Made Saint: Richardson's Perfectionism in His Life & Art

Yet, what can be expected of an angel under twenty?
LOVELACE (V, 122) [III, 64]

IN 1753, obviously enjoying his literary fame, Samuel Richardson let it be known that he was to dine with Ralph Allen, the good man of Bath, at Prior Park, proudly adding that "twenty years ago, I was the most obscure man in Great Britain; and now I am admitted to the company of the first characters in the kingdom."[1] The author's delight in his self-importance is touching or embarrassing, depending upon the degree of sympathy the reader has for the heady triumphs of the self-made man. Richardson's former obscurity explains much of his well-known diffidence, his need for praise (Johnson suggested that he died for want of change among his flatterers),[2] and his own belief in the possibility, indeed the duty, of self-improvement.

Throughout his writing career Richardson explored the possibilities of the created self. Beginning with his advice to apprentices and closing with his portrait of the perfect man, Sir Charles Grandison, Richardson investigated the ways in which man can determine his fate. The apprentice he addresses in his *Vade Mecum* will, if he follows Richardson's advice, become something more—a master. The epistolary models of the *Familiar Letters* offer advice to people in a state of transition, people attempting to become something better: young girls being courted, widows considering proposals for second marriages, fathers investigating professions for their sons. Central to these early works is a faith in reciprocal roles and relationships. If the apprentice treats his master with respect and diligence, he will prosper. If a "young miss" cheerfully follows the advice of her guardians and friends (who, unlike the Harlowes, are always benevolent), she will succeed in her prescribed role as dutiful daughter and eventually as dutiful wife. Richardson offers little possibility for ambiguous relationships in his predictable world, only correct models for writing and living.

In his novels, however, Richardson leaves the predictable world of moral aphorism to create characters who function independently, following the dictates of their own consciences rather than the rules published in a *Vade Mecum*. Pamela, who at first may appear to be just another self-improver, the servant who becomes a lady, is also a compelling character in her own right, humorous, naive, candid, and, above all, ambiguous. Her conduct, in fact, contradicts Richardson's own rules of behavior. She acts as a person, not a model, in disobeying her querulous parents to remain on at Mr. B.'s in spite of their suspicions about his unseemly advances. In *Clarissa*, Richardson creates an even more complicated world. Moral aphorisms can hardly apply to the tangled, obscured circumstances facing his heroine. As Pamela becomes a lady, Clarissa becomes a saint, but at the expense of her sense of self. Her progress is less sure and more complicated. The subtle snares of Lovelace's invention cut across her simple, narrow path of virtue. After her rape, Clarissa creates a new self invulnerable to Lovelace's penetration, but it is a most ambiguous self, saintly and human, forgiving and vengeful. For Clarissa, self-creation is also self-annihilation. Her death creates a profound sense of loss for the reader as well as the spiritual elevation Richardson wanted to elicit, a state of mind "strangely mixed." In his final novel, Richardson retreats to surer ground, leaving the disturbing martyrdom of Clarissa behind to create his good man, Sir Charles

Grandison. Sir Charles has created himself, pruning his passions and cultivating his benevolence before the book has begun. We see the finished product, a self-possessed paragon in control not only of his own nature but of the situations and souls of the other characters as well. The complexity of *Clarissa* has vanished.

From the start, Richardson wrote with an obvious moral intention—to perfect his readers. Following St. Matthew's command, "Be ye therefore Perfect,"[3] Richardson offered patterns of moral behavior to save his reader. Highly conscious of his vocation, he once suggested to Lady Bradshaigh that she place her copy of *Clarissa* next to Jeremy Taylor's *Holy Living* and *Holy Dying*, "Practice of Piety, and Nelson's Fast and Festivals," in the better company of the graver writers. (*Letters*, p. 117) Yet Richardson was also a highly conscious artist, honest enough to preserve the integrity of his artistic creations, even at the expense of his moral. However, without the confidence his overt intentions provided, Richardson would have found it difficult, perhaps impossible, to write his novels. Assured that he was working legitimately as a moralist, not one of the "low company" of the less serious novelists, he could allow his inventions to come forth. Richardson's moral license freed his creative imagination.

Most readers of Richardson's *Familiar Letters* or of his later *Collection of Moral Sentiments*, a modest tome of sententious epithets culled from the novels, would agree that on its own, Richardson's morality is neither original nor exceptional. His moral gentleman honors his parents, pays his bills on time, writes thank-you notes promptly, bewares of young widows with children, and stays away from dissenters, blasphemers, and bottle companions. His moral young miss rises early to begin her day of good deeds, obeys her parents, eschews mannish clothing, and avoids the company of mantua-makers.

These moral concerns, commonplace on their own, provided him with the necessary base from which to begin his most uncommon work. To improve his readers, literally to perfect them, Richardson provided them with moral exemplars, living saints. To Richardson's credit as a moralist, his saints turn into characters. And once he began to create characters, Richardson's straightforward interest in moral improvement led him to a complex and subtle exploration of fundamental problems of personality, problems that could not be remedied by a quick and easy application of a moral maxim. In this first chapter, we shall look at the way Richardson's moral perfectionism influenced his creation of fictional characters and situations. Paradoxically, to present living saints to perfect his readers, Richardson created characters who act outside the boundaries of their limited moral spheres. And to establish a "more perfect" world governed by absolute moral principles, Richardson invented sensational, violent situations in an arena of relative, not absolute, values.

With the guiding principles of *The Apprentice's Vade Mecum* firmly in hand, Richardson set out to create the perfect apprentice. The very nature of the apprentice suited his goal, for the apprentice is always preparing to become someone different, something more. Richardson remembered the position well: he served seven years "to a Master who grudged every Hour to me, that tended not to his Profit." Even young Samuel's candle was "of [his] own purchasing, that [he] might not in the most trifling Instance make [his] Master a Sufferer." To improve his mind (for the successful apprentice is always embarked on a strict course of self-improvement), Richardson was "engaged in a Correspondence with a Gentleman greatly my superior in Degree, and / of ample / Fortunes, who, had he lived, intended high things" for him. The gentleman, alas, died, but Richardson, "The Pillar" of his master's house, rose to become a master printer.[4] *Vade Mecum* expresses his own faith in self-improvement and the possibilities of worldly success.

Apprentices traditionally dreamt of worldly success. Chapbooks, such as *The Famous History of the Valiant London Prentice*, catered to those dreams, showing the rise of apprentices not through cheese paring and candle saving but through swashbuckling adventures with pirates and Turks: "Noble Exploits at Home and Abroad." Such tales, "Very Pleasant and Delightful," were written "for the Encouragement of Youth." The *Valiant Prentice* ending with "His Love and Great Success," satisfies the most fantastic longings for power: at one point, thrown to the lions, the apprentice squeezes the beasts, forces out their hearts, and lays the steaming organs at the Turkish king's feet. The startled king rewards the apprentice with his beautiful daughter, "who for his Sake became a Christian."⁵ Richardson surely read and even invented these sorts of stories to amuse his school friends. He told Johannes Stinstra, his Dutch translator, that since he was "early noted for having Invention," schoolmates frequently asked for his stories. "One of them, particularly, I remember, was for putting me to write a History, as he called it, on the Model of Tommy Potts; I now forget what it was; only, that it was of a Servant-Man preferred by a fine young Lady (for his Goodness) to a Lord, who was a Libertine. All my Stories carried with them, I am bold to say, an useful Moral."⁶ They also carried with them a useful libertine, always an inspiring character for Richardson.

The useful moral dominates *Vade Mecum*. "The present Depravity of Servants" and "the Degeneracy of the Times," compelled Richardson to "endeavour" to reform the servant and, through the servant, who will someday be master, "to amend the Age,"⁷ a modest task for a beginning writer. His manual solemnly lists temptations to be avoided and lessons to be learned. His apprentice cannot expect entertainment of any sort, save the heady treat of attending the playhouse once a year to see Lillo's history of George Barnwell, *The London Merchant*, the "One Play only calculated for the Benefit of City-Youth." All other theatrical entertainment is dangerously inappropriate, "calculated for Persons in high Life." (*Vade Mecum*, p. 16) Richardson complains that "even in the best Plays, the Moral lies so deep and hidden, as if the Play were not written for the Sake of it." (*Vade Mecum*, p. 11) We have no problem looking for a "deep and hidden" moral in *Vade Mecum*, for Richardson offers little art to disguise it. Only in an occasional caricature does he suggest his artistic talent. In one of his liveliest portraits, he presents the effeminate gentleman apprentice, a foppish creature mincing about in his absurd wig, "*plaister'd* rather than *powder'd*, and appearing like the *Twigs* of a *Goosebury-Bush* in a *deep Snow*; his Shoulders also crusted or iced over with White, as thick as a *Twelf-Cake*; with a plaited Shirt, ruffled at Hands and Bosom; a Coat, with a Cape reaching like an *old Wife's Tippet*, half way down his Back . . . Spanish-Leather Pumps (without Heels) and the burnish'd peeked Toes, seeming to stare the Wearer in the Face." He goes on in this vein for some time, wildly inventing and expanding his ludicrous picture, closing with the wish that "the ingenious Mr. *Hogarth* would finish the Portrait" to "shame such Foplings into Reformation." (*Vade Mecum*, pp. 34-35) For the moment, at least, Richardson leaves "art" to the artist, and is happy to return to his drier moral instruction.

The world of *Vade Mecum* is a predictable one of rewards and punishments. The good apprentice will prosper, the negligent fail. There are no bad masters in this ideal world, only bad apprentices. The apprentice must guard against the usual pitfalls: gaming, fornicating, drinking, play-going, and idle prating—Deism offers the worst temptation of all. But if the apprentice holds firm, like the young Samuel Richardson, pillar of his master's house, he will find his reward. This faith in well-defined, reciprocal roles breaks down in Richardson's later work, but in *Vade Mecum* clearly a young man who knows his place and works diligently in it will rise.

The image of the worthy, well-rewarded apprentice was

attractive to the eighteenth century. Hogarth expressed his own faith in an orderly world of rewarded virtue in his influential and well-received series of prints, *Industry* and *Idleness*, published in 1747, which show the progress of two apprentice boys, one working busily at his loom, the other vacantly daydreaming. Appropriately, the industrious lad steadily advances, marrying his master's daughter and finally becoming lord mayor of London. His idle friend ends up on the gallows, paying for a life of negligence and crime. Derek Jarrett questions the usefulness of Hogarth's illustrated moral, "calculated for the use and instruction of youth," pointing out that the industrious apprentice's meteoric rise was not entirely owing to industry, but also to "studied sycophancy and a calculated marriage: and few masters in London had as many daughters as they had apprentices." Hogarth, he reminds us, had married Sir James Thornhill's daughter while he was a student— "though scarcely an apprentice"—at the Thornhill academy. Hogarth should have known that "very few apprentices made good, marriage or no marriage, and that even fewer became lord mayor of London." Jarrett cites the observation of Francis Place, who had been a member of a club of apprentices in the 1780s, that "apart from himself there was only one lad who was at all successful—and he had married his master's daughter."[8] (It is worth noting that Richardson was also one of the luckier apprentices who managed to marry his master's daughter.)[9]

The real world of the London apprentice was far less simple than the ideal world both Richardson and Hogarth portrayed. When Dorothy George investigated the condition of the London apprentice, particularly the parish apprentices bound over to the most menial tasks, she found it impossible to read of "the many instances of hardship, cruelty and misfortune recorded in the appeals to Quarter Sessions" and the reports of Old Bailey without "coming to the conclusion that, generally speaking, the relationship between master and apprentice was an unsatisfactory one."[10] In the real world, bad masters prospered.

In 1767, Mrs. Brownrigg was convicted of the murder of her apprentice, Mary Clifford, and sentenced to be hanged. At her trial, Mary Mitchell, another Brownrigg apprentice fortunate enough to survive, testified that Mrs. Brownrigg often tied both girls up naked in the cellar, where she starved them and beat them with the stump of a riding whip. Mary Clifford died of her wounds, "her Back and Shoulders cut in a very shocking Manner." Brownrigg's dutiful son testified that "once, when his Mother had whipped her till she was tired, he, by her Orders, took the Whip, and gave her about twenty Lashes more."[11] Sarah Metyard and her daughter Sarah were also convicted for the murder of their apprentice. They tied the thirteen-year-old girl to the door, binding her hands and waist with cord to make it impossible for her to sit or lie down. The girl spent three days in this position until she died of starvation.[12] In the previous century, Elizabeth Wigenton was found guilty of whipping her apprentice to death. She beat her with a bundle of rods, "so unmercifully, that the blood ran down like rain, yet she could not be persuaded to desist till the girl fainted away with crying, and of her unmerciful usage in a short time dyed. Upon her tryal she pleaded little in her defence, only saying that she did not think to kill her."[13]

The cases of Mrs. Brownrigg and Mrs. Metyard, both tried in the same decade, "roused public horror." But equally horrible cases of brutality went unpunished in the earlier half of the eighteenth century. In 1748, for instance, Elizabeth Dickens murdered her apprentice, a girl with "dirty habits." In spite of evidence given that she had sworn to kill the girl, Mrs. Dickens was acquitted. And in 1736 James Durant, a ribbon weaver, was tried for the murder of his apprentice, "whom he had brutally beaten with a mop-stick." He was also acquitted. Dorothy George suggests that such atrocities, far from being isolated, sensational cases, represent "an infinitesimal proportion of the little apprentices who were beaten, starved and neglected, still less of those who ran away to become beggars and vagrants." The victims were usually apprentices for labor, "the start in life of the majority of children" in London. Poverty had forced these children into their situations: "The poorer, younger, and more friendless the child, the greater of course were the dangers and miseries of apprenticeship."[14]

Apprentices such as the young Richardson and Hogarth's industrious model, bound over for professional training, were treated more like pupils than drudges. In theory, that is. In practice, there were still dangers for the more affluent apprentice who paid a fee for his seven years of training. His progress depended upon the skill and interest of his master, variable qualities at best. A pamphlet written in 1687 argued for the "Relief of Apprentices wronged by their Masters," complaining that too many apprentices failed to exercise their chosen trade "through the carelessness and negligence or the harshness and unreasonableness (or which too often happens) through the ill-designs and practices of their masters."[15] Apprentices who paid for their instruction frequently asked the courts to discharge their bonds. Francis le Strange, bound for £21 to a stationer, complained of receiving insufficient food, "and that often unwholesome and not fit for any Christian," sleeping three in a bed, and being forced to round up his drunken master at the public house at four in the morning. John Edleston, bound to a tin-plate worker for £15, charged that his master horsewhipped him, "knocking him down with his fist and striking him with other blunt weapons that first came to hand."[16]

In his *Vade Mecum*, Richardson offers little comfort to the unlucky apprentice who complains of severe treatment, warning that "the young Man [must] make it a Rule to himself, to shun, at the *very first* Acquaintance, the Company of all such as would inspire him with a *mean* or *dis-*

respectful Opinion of his *Master* or his *Family*, or who express themselves undutifully of *their own.*" The servant with the audacity to complain is "the *Spy-fault*, the *Backbiter*, the *Detractor*, the *Ingrateful*, the *Betrayer of Secrets.*" The apprentice must "draw the veil" over his master's faults: were they "ever so flagrant," the master still "is not accountable for them to the Insolence of a Servant." It is the servant's duty to endure, regardless of his master's severity. "If you should happen to be bound to an unkind, a severe, or morose Master, your Duty to him and obliging Behaviour will have the greater Merit; and 'twill be but for a *Time*, and for that Portion of Time too, when 'tis needful that you should be curb'd and held in, and wherein Severity may perhaps be of far greater Service to you than a milder sort of Usage." (*Vade Mecum*, pp. 45, 47, 50) Presumably Richardson would not have advised the trussed-up, "curb'd and held in," apprentice of Sarah Metyard to be patient "but for a *Time*." Richardson himself was a kind master, known to hide a half crown among his letters for the first journeyman arriving at work to find,[17] but a master who chose to avoid confronting the unhappier aspects of the apprentice system. "The Art of Tormenting," so important in the world of *Clarissa*, did not interest him at this time. The atrocities of the Brownriggs and Metyards have no place in the well-regulated world of his *Vade Mecum*.

The world of the *Familiar Letters* is equally comfortable and predictable. In his preface to the letter manual, Richardson expresses his rather complacent faith in the power of language: by presenting epistolary models, he will be able to promote moral behavior. He means to *"mend the heart and improve the understanding"* of his readers, "to inculcate the principle of virtue and benevolence; to describe properly, and recommend strongly, the social and relative duties; and to place them in such practical lights, that the letters may serve for rules to think and act by, as well as forms to write after."[18] Richardson's rules offer numerous situations bristling with moral import. A reader encountering the letter "Against a Second Marriage, where there are Children on *both* Sides," (*Familiar Letters*, p. 171) learns how to think as well as write on so prickly a subject. For Richardson, good living and good writing are one and the same. Later, in his novels, his most contemptible characters are shown to be even more odious because they cannot write proper letters. The poor spelling of Solmes and the illiteracy of Charlotte Grandison's deceitful lover reveal the baseness of their characters.

If he follows the "rules to think and act by," man can perfect himself, but Richardson is careful to add that this can only be accomplished by recognizing the limitations of an individual's ability. His first letter warns a father against putting his son, "a Youth of but moderate Parts in a Profession that requires more extensive Abilities." Young Will, "a well-inclined lad of moderate passions, great natural modesty, and no soaring genius," is advised to stay out of the legal profession and keep to the lower, more mechanical trades. (*Familiar Letters*, pp. 1-4) But once personal limitations are recognized, there must be no holding back. It is always man's duty to improve himself. "Study," commands an uncle to his straying nephew who persists in keeping bad company. "Study to *improve*, not *divert* your faculties." (*Familiar Letters*, p. 7) Nothing can be left to nature; even "agreeable Conversation" must be learned. To sparkle in conversation, one must avoid silly disgressions,[19] "which are the great cause of a story's seeming tedious." (*Familiar Letters*, p. 16) Always sensitive to his own "sheepishness" in polite society, Richardson insists that the "art of rendering yourself agreeable in conversation is worth your serious study." (*Familiar Letters*, pp. 14-16)

The *Familiar Letters* provide models of moral as well as social correctness. One must be ever vigilant to avoid the snares of "keeping a horse," establishing "sudden intimacies," or entertaining a relationship with a flighty woman. Certain of these directives seem ludicrously simplistic in light of Richardson's later work. To provide such inflexible examples to promote a standard morality is to assume that the world of experience is absolute and unvarying. The early Richardson dispensed his advice in the simplest of terms. Filial piety, for instance, could not be debated. Children were to obey their parents and guardians—absolutely. When a young lady requests that her guardians be changed, Richardson demonstrates the inflexibility of his position. His young lady simply has no right to make such a request. Her guardians were trusted friends of her father: "Will you reflect upon his judgment? . . . what room have you, to suppose yourself better to judge of the consequences of what you desire, than they?" (*Familiar Letters*, pp. 58-60) Mr. Harlowe would applaud such high-flying Tory sentiments, but surely his daughter Clarissa would question them.

Richardson does occasionally relax his control over his readers, offering them three different forms of "An Excuse to a Person who wants to borrow money" and two types of thank-you letters: "To a Person of Note, in Acknowledgment of great Benefits received" and "Another for Favours of not so high, yet of a generous Nature." (*Familiar Letters*, pp. 140-42) He also provides a list of instructions to "young Orphan Ladies, as well as others, how to judge of Proposals of Marriage made to them without their Guardians or Friends Consent, by their Milaners, Mantua-Makers, or other Go-betweens." After warning the young orphan of the dangers of clandestine proposals, he offers several ways of dealing with the offending proposer, depending upon the degree of his offense. If a go-between makes the proposal, the young orphan may directly write her definite dismissal to the proposer. But if the young man "takes upon himself to send letters to teaze a young lady to encourage her address," a direct response would compromise her. She must "get some friend to write to him . . . for even a denial, if given in *writing* under *her own hand*, will encourage some

presumptuous men." Life is becoming more complicated
for the young orphan. Richardson offers several more responses in varying tones: "To a young Fellow who makes
Love in a romantic manner. By the Hand of a Friend;
Another less affronting on the same Occasion; Another still
less severe, but not encouraging"; and finally, the most
delicate and subtle response of all, "To rebuke an irregular
Address, when it is not thought proper wholly to discour-
age it." (*Familiar Letters*, pp. 124-31) An irregular address that might be encouraged introduces an element of
relativity in Richardson's world of clearly and absolutely
defined roles and relationships.

In general, however, the *Familiar Letters* provide inflexible models: apprentices must serve their masters; children must obey their parents; debtors must pay their debts.
But in Letters 138 and 139, Richardson unexpectedly leaves
the clearly defined boundaries of his moral maxims, presenting us with an unfamiliar figure, the bad master. The
scoundrel actually makes an attempt on his servant's virtue.
The girl's father advises her to "come directly away," (*Familiar Letters*, pp. 165-66) indicating that the reciprocal
relationship between servant and master has broken down.
The servant can disobey her master, not "draw the veil"
over his faults. Although the two letters in themselves are
an unadorned and unexciting account of a seduction attempt, they signal a great change in Richardson's work.
His first novel explores the consequences of the seduction
attempt, the fate of the bad master and the virtuous servant. Significantly, his own serving girl, Pamela, acts independently as a character rather than as an epistolary model.
In fact, instead of following her own father's advice to
"come directly away," she stays on, depending not upon
the moral bromides of the *Familiar Letters* but upon herself, to become Mrs. B., the self-made lady, while Richardson, the self-made printer, becomes a writer.

To mend the heart and improve the understanding,

Richardson turned to the novel, choosing characters rather than models to reach his reader's heart. "It is," says Belford to Lovelace, "my design to make thee *feel*. It gives me pleasure to find my intention answered. And I congratulate thee, that thou has not lost that sense." (VIII, 35) [IV, 367] Richardson had the same design for his reader— to restore his sensibility by making him feel the assorted sentiments of his fictional world. But feelings are difficult to fix, as Richardson sadly learned when even the most carefully tutored of Richardson's female coterie confessed to "conditional liking" of Lovelace well after their mentor had blackened his "villain's" image with slurs. In his novels, Richardson powerfully presented "warm" scenes of rape, seduction, dueling, suicide, and murder attempts, justifying the sensational nature of his fiction with his moral intention. "Instruction, Madam, is the Pill; Amusement is the Gilding," he informed Lady Echlin: "Writings that do not touch the Passions of the Light and Airy, will hardly ever reach the Heart. . . . Your Ladyship wishes a Widow might drop from my Pen; but were not this Widow to have been a Lover too, she would lose more than half her Merit." (*Letters*, p. 322) The widow would also lose half her market; her author was always highly conscious of what would sell. He predicted to his friend and physician George Cheyne that Pamela would "catch young and airy Minds . . . when Passions run high in them. . . . And if I were to be too spiritual, I doubt I should catch none but the Grandmothers, for the Granddaughters would put my Girl indeed in better Company, such as that of the graver Writers, and *there* they would leave her." (*Letters*, pp. 46-47)[20] It appears that Richardson would not have been entirely comfortable in the spot he coveted on Lady Bradshaigh's bookshelf, next to Taylor and *The Practice of Piety* in the better company of the graver writers. To insure a wider audience of girls as well as grandmothers, Richardson needed to affect the feelings. Ideally, his reader properly responds to the heady stimuli Richardson provides the "young and

airy Minds": rape, suicide, and violent death are prescribed for therapeutic use only.

With a keen understanding of the attractive nature of
pain, Richardson deliberately exploited the sensationalism
and sentimentalism of his novels. Virtue in distress was the
most affecting picture he could present. How else could
Clarissa shine? As Anna Howe explains to Clarissa, "AD-
VERSITY *is your* SHINING-TIME," calling "forth graces and
beauties which could not have been brought to light." (IV,
67) [II, 282] To promote feeling, Richardson places his
heroines in situations of great extremity, exercising his
reader's emotions to the fullest. We all "shine" together,
the heroines directly, the reader vicariously. The possibility that the reader might enjoy the victim's suffering presents a problem that Richardson apparently chose to ignore.[21]

Although he deliberately manipulated his reader's feelings, Richardson hotly denounced other writers who tamp-
ered with the passions. Matron Pamela disapproves of the
"Rant and Fury" of *The Distressed Mother*: "Half of it is
a tempestuous, cruel, ungovern'd Rant of Passion, and ends
in Cruelty, Bloodshed, and Desolation, which the Truth
of the Story not warranting." Indeed, most plays have "too
much of Love in [them], as that Passion is generally treated.
How unnatural in some, how inflaming in others, are the
Descriptions of it!—In most, rather Rant and Fury . . .
than the soft, sighing, fearfully-hopeful Murmurs, that
swell the Bosoms of our gentler Sex; and the respectful,
timorous, submissive Complainings of the other, when the
Truth of the Passion humanizes, as one may say, their
more rugged Hearts." (IV, 58-59) [II, 253]

How much of gentle Pamela's own courtship was filled
with "soft, sighing, fearfully-hopeful Murmurs"? Has she
already forgotten the "Rant and Fury" of Mr. B., hardly
a "respectful, timorous, submissive" lover as he lunged for
his "saucy slut's" bosom? All of Richardson's important
characters act and react with violence and passion: Pamela

scales walls and contemplates suicide; Clementina goes mad; Clarissa is abducted and raped; Harriet Byron barely escapes rape; Olivia tries to stab Sir Charles Grandison with a poinard. Two of Richardson's most effective "familiar letters"²² describe Bedlam and a public execution, where "all was hurry and confusion, racket and noise, praying and oaths, swearing and singing psalms." (*Familiar Letters*, pp. 219-20)

Richardson's constant defense of his "warm scenes" ("Perhaps I have in mine, been too copious on that Subject") indicates his uneasiness about the sensational nature of his fiction. (*Letters*, p. 322) Directing passions can be dangerous work. In his postscript to *Clarissa* he compares himself to a thief who, "in an age given up to diversion and entertainment . . . could *steal in*, as may be said, and investigate the great doctrines of Christianity under the fashionable guise of an amusement." (VIII, 308) [IV, 553] Rationalizing his license with a moral goal, Richardson freed his imagination, not just for "warm scenes," but for the creation of impassioned and believable characters and situations that often threaten to burst through the moral framework of his fiction. Richardson himself held a double view of his writing. On the one hand, he was a "plain writer: a sincere well-wisher: an undesigning scribbler; who admire none but the natural and easy beauties of the pen: no carper." (*Letters*, p. 66) But, as we have seen, this plain scribbler is also a "sly sinner," creeping along the edges of the walks at Tunbridge Wells, "one hand in his bosom, the other held up to his chin, as if to keep it in its place: afraid of being seen, as a thief of detection . . . stealing in and out of the bookseller's shop, as if he had one of their glass-cases under his coat." (*Letters*, p. 88) The very man, we might say, to steal in the gilded pill of moral improvement under the fashionable guise of amusement. A writer for all situations.

The subtitle of Richardson's first novel gives it all away:

"Virtue Rewarded." I shall not repeat the countless arguments against Richardson's moral; they are too well known and, for the most part, too well taken. Perhaps one of the most glaring problems of the novel is the static nature of the virtue Richardson rewards. Pamela's sainthood, obvious from the first pages of the book, is ideally suited to the secular world, where white hands, passable French, expertise at carving, and an encyclopedic knowledge of both the Bible and tragicomedy are valued equally. Although her personality develops throughout the novel, her golden virtues are with her from the start. Her chronicle finally closes with a treacly tale of her own making to amuse her children and ward: the fortunes of "Four pretty Ladies," Coquetilla, Prudiana, Profusiana, and Prudentia, "their several Names denoting their respective Qualities." (IV, 442) [II, 465] And as Miss Godfrey, the illegitimate daughter of Mr. B., recognizes, "Prudentia" is Pamela. "It *can* be nobody else!—O teach me, good GOD! to follow *Your* Example, and I shall be a SECOND PRUDENTIA— Indeed I shall!" (IV, 452) [II, 471]

Good luck, Miss Godfrey. All signs indicate that there shall never be another Pamela. She is, indeed, an exemplary model, but one impossible to follow, as B. points out to scoffers who accuse him of setting a leveling example throughout the countryside. Let another, he dares his critics, find a paragon like Pamela, and he may marry her. The paradox: there can be no other creature. (III, 323-30) [II, 168-71]

Yet in spite of his heroine's obvious excellencies, Richardson never can stop advertising her quality. He catalogs her virtues almost obsessively, as though he were preparing an application for sainthood to bring before the heavenly board. And the novel suffers accordingly, groaning under its unnatural weight. Cynthia Griffin Wolff's study of Richardson's use of Puritan characters can help to explain some of the author's reasons for devoting so much time to Pamela's static virtue at the expense of his dramatic action. She argues that Richardson employed two basic eighteenth-century Puritan ego models in his novels, the sinful self-examiner, minutely recording his faults in his diary, and the virtuous exemplar, celebrated posthumously in his saint's life, a public record of the exemplar's social virtues. From the start Pamela is a living saint, a being who has achieved as much perfection as possible in an imperfect world. Her virtue is spelled out literally in wordly, social terms. She is also, however, a self-examining sinner, minutely recording her innermost thoughts in her letters to her parents and later in her journal. But it is impossible to mix the two roles successfully in one novel: "The tone of the first would be unsure and self-condemnatory while the tone of the second would presume success and a degree of superiority. When Richardson permits his novel to become an exemplum, with Pamela the embodiment of successful virtue, the tensions created by her efforts at self-examination are destroyed."[23] As soon as the suspense of the seduction plot is relieved, the novel gives itself over entirely to incessant celebration of Pamela's virtue. She shines: as forgiving wife who learns to curb her jealousy, as gracious stepmother of B.'s illegitimate child, as loving mother, and as bountiful lady of the manor.

Mrs. Pamela even converts her stiff-necked sister-in-law. Lady Davers demands that Pamela correspond with her regularly: "Not that I will promise to answer every Letter: No, you must not expect that.—Your Part will be a kind of Narrative, purposely designed to entertain us here; and I hope to receive Six, Seven, Eight, or Ten letters, as it may happen, before I return One." Lady Davers, one of the sorriest examples of Richardson's peculiarly rude notions of what passed for manners among the upper classes, argues that it is Pamela's duty to instruct through letters. "But consider, Child," she rebukes, checking any feeble excuses Pamela might make to avoid such a time-consuming epistolary task, "the Station you are raised to, does not require you to be quite a domestick Animal.

You are lifted up to the Rank of a Lady, and you must act up to it, and not think of setting such an Example, as will draw upon you the Ill-will and Censure of other Ladies." (III, 40-41) [II, 24-25] Pamela is to be a model for her sex, "the perfectest Character . . . ever heard or read of." Lady Davers and company agree to this in chorus: Mrs. B. must be "quite perfect," says Lady Jenny, says her Brother Lord John, says the Earl their Father, confirms Lord Davers. "And *Jackey swore* to it." Certain as they are that "there cannot be such a Character in this Life, as has not one Fault, altho' we could not tell where to fix it," the company asks Pamela, knowing herself "better than any-body else can do," to acquaint them "with some of those secret Foibles, that leave room for her to be still more perfect." (IV, 41-42) [II, 243-44] Be ye perfect, said St. Matthew. Be ye even more perfect, adds Richardson for good measure, in spite of the grammatical and metaphysical impossibility of such a command.

As Pamela becomes a paragon on earth, Clarissa becomes a saint, but a saint peculiarly unsuited for earthly triumphs. Although Richardson ostensibly presents Clarissa as a useful moral exemplar, the ultimate self-improver, he is really presenting his reader with an anguished saint who lives and dies for herself alone, not for the good of others. His Clarissa becomes a social pariah, defying society as she rejects public censure, withdrawing to perfect her private self. No one could or should follow her example; the effect would be disastrous.[24] Lovelace thinks she is a bit cracked: "Dost think she is not a little touched at times? I am afraid she is," he anxiously asks Belford. Her example, he insists, should be avoided: "What would become of the peace of the world, if all women should take it into their heads to follow her example?" (VII, 16-17) [IV, 40-41] If Clarissa is to be evaluated only in terms of the efficacy of her example, she will be found wanting. But she is far more important as a character of complexity than as an exemplary type. As Richardson explores the mysteries of her personality, he allows the imperative of Clarissa's individual conscience to break through the moral framework of his novel. Richardson transforms the simple convention of virtue in distress even while he is helping to popularize it. The simple becomes the complex as he questions the nature of identity and personality, setting down absolute rules of behavior inapplicable in a world where there are no absolutes.

From the start, Richardson consciously designed his Clarissa to be a saint among women, an example for her sex. "I laid indeed an heavy hand on the good Clarissa," he admitted to Miss Mulso. "But I had begun with her, with a view to the future saint in her character: and could she, but by sufferings, shine as she does?" (*Letters*, p. 190) Richardson charges his saint's life with emotional power and psychological complexity. Her sainthood profoundly reflects her integrity, courage, and (perhaps most interestingly) her ambivalence.

In the first letter of the first volume of *Clarissa*, Miss Howe points to the exemplary nature of her friend. Always desirous of "sliding through life to the end of it un-noted," always preferring to be considered "*rather useful than glaring*," Clarissa has been "pushed into blaze." "You see what you draw upon yourself by excelling all your Sex. Every individual of it who knows you, or has heard of you, seems to think you answerable to *her* for your conduct in points so very delicate and concerning. Every eye, in short, is upon you with the expectation of an example." (I, 2-4) [I, 2-3] With every eye upon her, including the reader's, Clarissa is surely more glaring than useful. She may wish to slide through life unnoticed, but her friends and relations will never allow her to retreat to her solitary noble consciousness. And by assuming her exemplary role, passing judgment on her friends' behavior, even offering unsolicited advice in an anonymous letter to a friend's Mama, Clarissa seeks her position of authority.

Clarissa accepts her exemplary role because she has faith in the power of her goodness. The world, she believes, is an accommodating place. Petted for years by her family, the favorite of her doting grandfather, and heiress to a large estate, she rests secure in her power. "Upon my word, I am sometimes tempted to think that we may make the world allow for and respect us as we please, if we can but be sturdy in our wills, and set out accordingly," she confides. (I, 32-33) [I, 22] Ideally, the world "is but one great family." (I, 49) [I, 34] Anna Howe, another doughty believer in the will, encourages Clarissa to trust her powers. Although Clarissa never can "penetrate" the mysterious Lovelace, Miss Howe predicts that "were he deep, and ever so deep, you would soon penetrate him, if they would leave you to yourself." (I, 75) [I, 51] The evil nature of her own brother and sister shakes Clarissa's confidence in the ideal world. For if the world is one great family, what does that make her own family? Repressive, vindictive, and cruel? And what does that make the world? Anna Howe can sagely suggest that Arabella envies Clarissa's beauty and James covets her grandfather's estate, but she can never explain the original cause of such jealousy. Clarissa questions their hatred on a more fundamental level: "Children of the same parents, how came they by their cruelty?—Do they get it by travel? Do they get it by conversation with one another?—Or how do they get it?" (II, 216) [I, 386] Material reasons like beauty and fat estates cannot completely account for evil. Shakespeare knew this when he created Iago, and Richardson knew this when he created Clarissa's unnatural "friends."

Clarissa would rather avoid facing the evil of her family. Approaching it countless times, provoking Miss Howe to rage and bellow at the Harlovian atrocities freshly committed, she always demurs at the end, insisting that her "friends" will come around at last. She would also rather avoid facing her own passions. She assures Miss Howe of her emotional immunity: "Indeed I would not be *in Love*

with him, as it is called, for the world." Miss Howe chides
her presumption on "being the first of our Sex that ever I
heard of, who has been able to turn that Lion, Love, at
her own pleasure, into a Lap-dog." (I, 68-71) [I, 47-49]
Clarissa recalls this image after her rape in her allegory of
the lady and the lion. The lady tamed her beast through
love, "so that, like a Lap-dog, it would follow her all over
the house." But the beast resumed its nature, suddenly fell
upon her "and tore her in pieces." And who was to blame?
"The Lady, surely.—For what *she* did, was *out* of character, at least: what *it* did, was *in* its own nature." (V,
329) [III, 206] Clarissa has a lot to learn about her own
character here. And conduct books will be of no use.

Lovelace immediately recognizes that Clarissa's mis-
placed confidence in the power of her goodness is fatal.
When "satisfied with her own worthiness," she refuses to
justify herself to the women at Hampstead, Lovelace exults
in her naïveté: "A dear silly Soul, thought I at the time,
to depend upon the goodness of her heart, when the heart
cannot be seen into but by its actions; and she, to appearance, a Runaway, an Eloper, from a tender, a most indulgent Husband!—To neglect to cultivate the opinions of
individuals, when the whole world is governed by appearance! Yet what can be expected of an angel under Twenty?"
(V, 122) [III, 64] An angel lives not in the world of
appearances but in the world of eternal truths. Richardson
manages to hold both positions at once: Clarissa is a silly
goose for trusting the Lovelacian world of appearances,
but she is also divine, untouched by Lovelace's deception.
The rape only affects her person, not her soul.

Anna Howe, on the other hand, firmly grounded in the
real world where one marries or prosecutes her seducer,
cannot be content with Clarissa's expectations of heavenly
justification. She tries to salvage her friend's earthly reputation, which is a great deal more valuable to her than it
is to Clarissa, and finally rationalizes that Clarissa can still
serve as a useful example—of ruined innocence. "For who

is it that will not infer, That if a person of your fortune, character, and merit could not escape ruin, after she had put herself into the power of her *hyaena*, what can a thoughtless, fond, giddy creature expect?" (VII, 357) [IV, 269] An important point, and a disturbing one. Logically, Clarissa's warning should deter the thoughtless, giddy creatures. But if Clarissa, with all of her virtues, could not escape putting herself in her hyaena's power, what hope has the giddy creature? This nice point is appreciated by the hyaena Lovelace, who swears that if Clarissa's virtue can be corrupted there is no virtue in the whole sex. "Is not then the whole Sex concerned that this trial should be made?" (III, 92) [II, 40] The trial of Clarissa, the trial of a saint, dominates the book.

Years of training produced Saint Clarissa. Anna Howe's post-mortem description of her friend's rigidly scheduled life indicates a highly disciplined code of behavior. Miss Howe takes great pains to demonstrate "that *precept* and *example* always went hand in hand with her." (VIII, 227) [IV, 497] Allowing only six hours for rest, Clarissa carefully audited her waking hours: "She had calculated according to the practice of *too many*, she had actually lived more years at *Sixteen* than *they* had at *Twenty-six*." (VIII, 240) [IV, 506] All work hours were accountable: "Once a week she used to reckon with herself: when, if within the 144 hours, contained in the six days, she had made her account even, she noted it accordingly: if otherwise, she carried the debit to the next week's account; as thus: *Debtor to the article of benevolent visits, so many hours.* And so of the rest." Cynthia Griffin Wolff explains that Miss Howe's account should be seen as her funeral oration, "an almost classic delineation of a member of the Elect . . . an unabashedly admiring third-person description of the heroine's daily activities and habits." But Miss Howe's evaluation, even if "it has the virtue of being traditionally 'correct,' "[25] barely succeeds in smoothing over the loose ends Richardson worked so hard to unravel throughout most of the novel. Miss Howe describes a martyr without passion, while Clarissa, in her letters to that same Miss Howe, reveals powerful, tangled passions that drive her to her martyr's death. Paradoxically, the martyr willingly embraces her fate as the culmination of her self-denial and her self-assertion, the last significant article in her weekly account.

When Richardson told Miss Mulso that he laid a heavy hand on Clarissa with a view of her *future* sainthood, he reminded her that Miss Harlowe, cynosure of the neighborhood, must *become* a saint. She labors to perfect herself, showing a Pelagian faith in the power of good works: the self can perfect itself through benevolent actions. Through her sturdy will, allotting so many hours to charitable visits and so many hours to meditation, she prepares herself for heaven. Her perfectionism, a softened version of the Puritan progression towards sainthood, comes out of the latitudinarian tradition, an eighteenth-century form of perfectionism that John Passmore defines as the "daily practice of morality."[26] Be ye perfect, gradually. However, Clarissa's well-planned progress towards sainthood suddenly changes pace. Lovelace dramatically alters her in his rape, assaulting her latitudinarian optimism and abruptly, not gradually, forcing her to change her notion of herself and her salvation. Purified through her sufferings, "like gold in a crucible,"[27] she emerges a saint in the mystic, not the Pelagian, tradition.

In her symbolic preparation for death, with her carefully selected coffin and black-bordered book of meditations, Clarissa connects herself to the seventeenth-century tradition of poetic meditation. Her coffin, Margaret Doody argues, "reminds us abruptly of the seventeenth-century use of the *memento mori*, of John Donne wearing his winding sheet." Doody sees Clarissa as the last in a literary tradition of the contemplation of death that had been initiated by the spiritual exercises of the Counter Reformation taken up by John Donne, George Herbert, and Richard Crashaw and would end in the works of Jeremy Taylor and Samuel Richardson.[28] We can go even further in this direction, for Richardson's development of the mystical and devotional elements of Clarissa seems to transcend one single tradition. Wolff argues that the Puritan saint, having achieved "as much perfection on earth as an imperfect being is capable of . . . differed greatly from the medieval Catholic notion; Catholicism tended to emphasize the miraculous, and the legends of the Church of Rome hint at a struggle between good and evil so dark and mysterious that man can only fear and marvel." For the Puritan saint, God's grace would be manifested through worldly actions in everyday life; the social, not the mystical, aspects of sainthood were emphasized.[29] When seen in this light, Clarissa, emerging triumphantly from her struggle "so dark and mysterious that man can only fear and marvel," is a most Catholic saint, literally reincarnating the spiritual perfectionism of the mystical saints. Her progress towards sainthood recalls the spiritual journeys of Teresa of Avila and John of the Cross. Without any apparent familiarity with the histories of Teresa and John,[30] Richardson managed to transcend his own tradition to create a mystic saint who recreates the Catholic saints' experiences and meditations in their own language. Clarissa even uses the same metaphors as Teresa and John, looking to the books of the Psalms and Job for inspiration.

In their writings, Teresa and John both emphasize the painful suffering necessary to one who would know God. Their God is the bridegroom who chastises before he comforts, the bridegroom Clarissa so eagerly awaits. God punishes those he loves, forcing them into the dark night of the soul, into the dryness of the desert, where they suffer what John calls the "aridities of this sensory night."[31] Clarissa has also been in the desert, as she laments in her meditations: "*I am like a pelican of the wilderness. I am like an owl of the desart.*" (VII, 165) [IV, 140]

The saint must suffer alienation, feeling, as John warns, "forsaken and despised by creatures, particularly by his friends." John adds the words of Psalm 87 to his warning: *"You have withdrawn my friends and acquaintances far from me; they have considered me an abomination."*[32] In her own dark night of the soul, Clarissa also feels forsaken by everyone, even by Miss Howe. She bitterly writes to her faithless friend: "But what have *I*, sunk in my fortunes; my character forfeited; my honour lost [While *I* know it, I care not *who* knows it]; destitute of friends, and even of hope; what have *I* to do to show a spirit of repining and expostulation to a dear friend, because she is not *more* kind than a Sister?" Forsaken by all, Clarissa still retains her pride, archly apologizing for her bitter tone: "I find by the rising bitterness which will mingle with the gall in my ink, that I am not yet subdued enough to my condition." (VI, 160) [III, 350-51] Clarissa never does subdue her pride completely, finding the saintly virtue of humility most difficult to attain.

The saint not only expects but seeks out alienation. Warning that "much that is worldly will stick to us," St. Teresa describes her own temptation to love her sister more than she loved other people. Although Teresa "remained alone as much as I could . . . I found that I was much more affected when she was distressed than when my neighbours were, and that I was quite concerned about her."[33] For Teresa, excessive sisterly love is a sin, calling her to the entangling pleasures of the world. Clarissa demonstrates a similar fear of social concerns as she deliberately detaches herself from the world. Clarissa prefers to die alone, apart from her old friends: *"God will have no rivals in the hearts of those he sanctifies.* By various methods he deadens all other sensations, or rather absorbs them all in the love of Him. . . . I am now above the quick sense of those pleasures, which once most delighted me: and once more I say, that I do not wish to see objects so dear to me, which might bring me back again into sense, and rival my *Supreme Love.*" (VII, 404-405) [IV, 302]

The loneliness that both Teresa and Clarissa suffer brings them closer to God. In one of her meditations, Clarissa speaks of herself as "*a sparrow alone upon the house-top,*" watching and waiting for deliverance. (VII, 165) [IV, 140] Teresa uses the same metaphor, taken from Psalm 102, when she describes the extreme loneliness of her soul: "There comes a distress so subtle and piercing that, placed as it is in this desert, the soul can, I think, say literally with the Royal Prophet: 'I watch, and am as a sparrow alone upon the housetop.' "[34] Forcing them into the desolation and dryness, God annihilates those who would be saints. St. John also goes to the Psalms to describe his sense of dissolution: "*I was brought to nothing and annihilated, and I knew not.*"[35] Clarissa expresses her own sense of annihilation most fully in the cryptic fragments she composes after her rape. She recognizes that she is "no longer what I was in any one thing." (V, 327) [III, 205] "My head is gone," (V, 334) [III, 210] and with it her sense of herself. She assures Anna Howe that God will soon dissolve her substance and bring her to death. (VI, 412) [III, 523] Only in dissolution and annihilation can she find freedom.

For Teresa and John, the divine bridegroom exists in a physical as well as a metaphorical sense. God assaults them with his love, raping their very souls. In "The Living Flame of Love," celebrating "the intimate union" of the soul with God, "its beloved Bridegroom," John begs the bridegroom to tear through the veil of his secular life:

O living flame of love
That tenderly wounds my soul
In its deepest center! Since
Now you are not oppressive,
Now Consummate! if it be Your will:
Tear through the veil of this sweet encounter![36]

John explains that the veil represents the union between

the spirit and flesh that separates the soul from God. "Tearing," he finds, is "more proper to this encounter than cutting or destroying, . . . because love is the friend of the power of love and of the strong and impetuous touch, exercised more in tearing, than in cutting or destroying."[37] John is the bride (for "if it is to commune with God," the soul must learn that "its role can only be that of the bride, it must play the woman"),[38] and the veil is his maidenhood. His "enamoured soul" begs to be torn "by a supernatural encounter and impetus of love."[39]

Teresa's vision of the bridegroom, made famous by Bernini's statue, *Santa Teresa in Estasi,* is explicitly sexual as well as spiritual. In his study of the relationship between Teresa, Bernini, and Crashaw, Robert Petersson warns against explaining Teresa's vision in completely erotic terms, but does not deny the sensuality so central to an understanding of her raptures: "Many have taken her character to be completely erotic and her spiritual passion to be sexual sublimation. Indeed she is erotic. The error is to limit that quality to the physical instead of realizing that God is the object of her love and her love is total and indivisible, including the body."[40] In her vision, as Bernini emphasizes in his sculpture, both the body and the soul of Teresa are being ravished by God. He has sent her an angel, "in bodily form, such as I am not in the habit of seeing except very rarely." His face aflame, the beautiful angel appeared holding a "great golden Spear" tipped in fire. He plunged the spear into Teresa's heart several times, "so that it penetrated to my entrails":

When he pulled it out, I felt that he took them with it, and left me utterly consumed by the great love of God. The pain was so severe that it made me utter several moans. The sweetness caused by this intense pain is so extreme that one cannot possibly wish it to cease, nor is one's soul then content with anything but God. This is not a physical, but a spiritual pain, though the body has some share in it—even a considerable share. So gentle is this wooing which takes place between God and the soul that if anyone thinks I am lying, I pray God, in His goodness, to grant him some experience of it. Throughout the days that this lasted I went about in a kind of stupor. I had no wish to look or to speak, only to embrace my pain, which was a greater bliss than all created things could give me.[41]

"Now Consummate! if it be Your will," pleads John. Both Teresa and John are "utterly consumed by the great love of God," consumed both in spirit and in body. As Teresa admits, the body has some share in this consummation, "even a considerable share."

Clarissa is also ravished, but by man, not by God. Lovelace, the "machine" of the Harlowes, as Belford calls him (IV, 123) [II, 320], also serves as the "engine" of God, penetrating Clarissa's body and forcing her to alter her entire sense of herself. The physical violence of Lovelace's rape paradoxically creates the conditions of Clarissa's sainthood. John of the Cross understood the necessity of violent grace acting upon the soul when he prayed for supernatural love to "tear" the veil of his secular life. Lovelace's violent assault of love and revenge tears the secular veil of Clarissa's life, the veil that separates her from God. Forced out of her complacent, benevolent self into the wilderness of her madness, she emerges, purified and sanctified. Lovelace, ironically, is the first to claim credit for the creation of the divine Clarissa: "But it is owing to the uncommon occasions she has met with that she blazes out upon us with such a meridian lustre. How, but for those occasions, could her noble sentiments, her prudent consideration, her forgiving spirit, her exalted benevolence, and her equanimity in view of the most shocking prospects (which set her in a light so superior to all her Sex, and even to the philosophers of antiquity), have been manifested?" (VII, 345) [IV, 261]

Clarissa's terrible dream about Lovelace is an inverted vision of heavenly assault. As the flaming cherub pierced Teresa's heart with his golden spear, Lovelace stabs Clarissa "to the heart," despite her pleas of innocence. Then, Clarissa recalls, Lovelace "tumbled me into a deep grave ready dug, among two or three half-dissolved carcases; throwing in the dirt and earth upon me with his hands, and trampling it down with his feet." (II, 283) [I, 433] There is no glory in Clarissa's dream, only dirt, earth, and half-dissolved carcasses.

The flaming light of Teresa's vision of divine annihilation can be found in another dream, Lovelace's vision of a beatified Clarissa. Lovelace dreams that Morden, brandishing a sword, attempts to kill him, but is stopped by Clarissa's intercession: "The most angelic form I had ever beheld, all clad in transparent white, descended in a cloud, which, opening, discovered a firmament above it, crouded with golden Cherubs and glittering Seraphs, all addressing her with: Welcome, welcome, welcome! and, encircling my charmer, ascended with her to the region of Seraphims; and instantly the opened cloud closing, I lost sight of her, and of the bright form together." Clutching her azure robe, Lovelace falls into a hole "without view of a bottom," to awaken "in a panic . . . as effectually disordered for half an hour, as if my dream had been a reality." (VII, 159-60) [IV, 136]

Lovelace's "visionary stuff" troubles him one more time, on his deathbed, where Clarissa appears, at first (it seems) as a frightful specter. "Take her away!" he cries, but "name[s] nobody." His French valet reports that he deliriously called out to "some Lady" as "Sweet Excellence! Divine Creature! Fair Sufferer!—And once he said, Look down, blessed Spirit, look down!" Lifting his eyes to heaven, "in a seeming ejaculation," Lovelace "spoke inwardly so as not to be understood: At last, he distinctly pronounced these three words, LET THIS EXPIATE!" (VIII, 276-77) [IV, 530]

We never know if Lovelace achieves communion with

the divine Clarissa in this final inward vision. Clarissa's death is equally mysterious. She hints of *"foretastes"* and *"assurances"* of a blessed death, looking up "as if in a thankful rapture, sweetly smiling." Holding up her hands, she calls out "O come—Blessed Lord—JESUS! And with these words, the last but half-pronounced, expired: Such a smile, such a charming serenity overspreading her sweet face at the instant, as seemed to manifest her eternal happiness already begun." (VIII, 3-5) [IV, 346-47] We are not allowed to learn of the nature of Clarissa's raptures, but must trust the testimony of outsiders like Belford, who bear witness to her sainthood. Richardson comes tantalizingly close to a psychological analysis of the mystical experience, the raptures that Teresa describes so precisely and movingly. Approaching Clarissa's mystical union with her heavenly bridegroom through a detailed presentation of her sufferings, her dark night of the soul, Richardson abruptly withdraws at the end, unwilling or unable to enter into Clarissa's experience of death. His saint's purification through her suffering interests him far more than her final beatification.

Indeed, suffering always fascinated Richardson. "Calamity," he told Miss Grainger, "is the *test* of virtue, and often the *parent* of it, in minds that prosperity would ruin. What is meant, think you, Madam, by the whole Christian doctrine of the Cross?" (*Letters*, p. 151) Physical as well as mental pain must have a reason. Richardson's physician and friend, George Cheyne, treated Richardson's own melancholy with his peculiarly perfectionist therapy, prescribing a regimen of milk and seed diets, thumb vomits, tarwater tonics, and frequent purges. Cheyne believed that "Pain, punishment, and *Suffering* then would seem to be a natural, necessary and (as it were) a *mechanical* Mean [*sic*] of Expiation, Purification, and Perfection, to all sentient and intelligent Beings in this Present State of Existence."[42] Perhaps Richardson's own personal sufferings encouraged his belief in the redemptive nature of pain. He told Lady

Bradshaigh that "no less than Eleven concerning Deaths attacked me in two years. My nerves were so affected with these repeated Blows that I have been for seven Years past forced, after repeated labouring thro the whole Medical Process by Direction of eminent Physicians, to go into a Regimen, not a Cure to be expected, but merely as a Palliative; and for Seven Years past, have forborn Wine, Flesh, and Fish." To bear the pain of life, one must not expect a cure, but a palliative. Clarissa's noble end ("O that my own last Hour, and the last Hour of those I love may be such as that I have drawn for my amiable Girl!" he prayed) may have served to palliate, not cure, Richardson's own pain. (*Letters*, pp. 110-11)

Saintly zeal always disturbs the secular world; Clarissa, always zealous, becomes a most disturbing saint. As we have seen, Clarissa had been preparing for sainthood for many years. Even when she fears that she is being "punished, as I frequently think, for my vanity in hoping to be an *Example* to young persons of my Sex," she still refuses to relinquish her exemplary role. "Let me be but a *Warning*, and I will now be contented." (III, 141) [II, 73] Clarissa's inability to separate herself from her exemplary self-image restricts her behavior and impels her towards martyrdom. If she must "warn," let her warn all the way, to death. "Let my Ruin, said she, lifting up her eyes, be LARGE! Let it be COMPLETE, *in this life!*—For a *composition*, let it be COMPLETE."(VI, 292) [III, 441] Preparing her papers, her truly large and complete composition of self-vindication, Clarissa regards herself as pattern more than person. Yet in these moments of spiritual pride, she seems the most human and the most interesting.

In her desire for her large and complete composition, Clarissa seeks out her earthly trial. A pattern of anticipated judgment and persecution develops early in the book. At first her family acts as judge and jailer, imprisoning her until she accepts its authority. Self-consciously, almost eagerly, Clarissa accepts the role of prisoner at the bar. While she plays the part of "the poor prisoner," her family constitutes an "awful Court. . . . so venerable a judicature . . . such a tribunal." (II, 291-92) [I, 439] Harlowe House, the Widow Sinclair's, and Hampstead all serve as arenas for Clarissa's trial. The prostitutes, in their scabrous unity, and the genteel women, in their meddlesome curiosity, form as "venerable a judicature," as the Harlowe family. Only in her rented room, surrounded by strangers and her cryptic coffin, can Clarissa find freedom.

Clarissa helps to create the conditions of her martyrdom, making it almost too easy for Lovelace to overcome her. She staunchly resists his advances, yet lets down her guard at crucial moments. For instance, when she flees Mrs. Sinclair's after the fire scare, she makes her recapture ludicrously simple. As she tells Miss Howe, "I am present at one Mrs. Moore's at Hamstead. My heart misgave me at coming to this village because I had been here with him more than once; But the coach hither was so ready a convenience that I knew not what to do better." Lovelace less generously interprets her actions: "A silly dear novice, to be heard to tell the coach man whither to carry her!—And to go to *Hamstead*, of all the villages about London!—The place where we had been together more than once! Methinks I am sorry she managed no better! I shall find the recovery of her too easy a task, I fear!" (V, 54-58) [III, 18-21]

Clarissa's complicity in her own rape is also disturbing. Despite the "antipathy" she had taken to the "vile house," she allows herself to be carried into Mrs. Sinclair's. Her entry is a nightmare: crowds press, people whisper, all observe Clarissa's fate. "And thus pressed and gazed at (for then I looked about me) the women so richly dressed, people whispering; in an evil moment, out stepped I, trembling, forced to lean with both my hands (frighted too much for ceremony) on the pretended Lady Betty's arm— O that I had dropped down dead upon the guilty threshold!" (VI, 183-85) [III, 366-68] Disregarding the ominous signs, Clarissa steps through the door. Inside the house, Clarissa "was made" to drink drugged tea. She "thought, *transiently* thought, that the tea, the last dish particularly, had an odd taste," but accepts the ladies' excuse that it is tea with "*London Milk*; far short in goodness of what they were accustomed to from their own dairies." Clarissa has encountered London milk before in Mrs. Sinclair's dining room; surely it never tasted so odd. Now she tastes a different sort, the mother's milk of a brothel.[43]

Clarissa cannot, or will not, recognize the signs of her dilemma: "Ill before, I found myself still more and more disordered in my head; a heavy torpid pain encreasing fast upon me. But I imputed it to my terror. Nevertheless, at the pretended lady's motion, I went upstairs." As she qualifies her resistance, Clarissa qualifies her tale. She does not want to enter the house, but she enters; she does not want to drink her tea, but she drinks it; she feels ill, but still goes upstairs.

After the rape, Clarissa makes no attempt to conceal her shame; her ambivalence has vanished. She tells Mama Norton that she is not to blame: "For what need had the cruel Spoiler to have had recourse to unprecedented arts— I will speak out plainer still (but you must not at present report it) to stupefying potions, and to the most brutal and outrageous force; had I been wanting in my duty?" (VI, 144-45) [III, 341] She hides her rape from no one. "Why," she asks the "real" Lady Betty, "should I seek to conceal that disgrace from others, which I cannot hide from myself?" (VI, 138) [III, 336] Until her death, Clarissa glories in her martyr's crown of thorns.

Clarissa's candor horrifies Lovelace, who has depended upon his victim's silence. She is breaking the code. Nowhere do Lovelace's worldly ethics conflict with Clarissa's spiritual concerns more violently. If other women followed her example, Lovelace incredulously predicts, "the whole world would either be a scene of confusion; or cuckoldom." In Lovelace's world, such honesty is insane. When

Clarissa is openly selling her clothes, visible tokens of her poverty and shame, Lovelace asks, "Dost think she is not a little touched at times? I am afraid she is. A little spice of that insanity, I doubt, runs thro' her, what she had in stronger degree, in the first week of my operations. Her contempt of life; her proclamations; her refusal of matrimony; and now of money from her most intimate friends; are sprinklings of this kind, and no other way, I think, to be accounted for." (VII, 16-17) [IV, 40-41] Clarissa's "contempt of life"—Lovelace's version of life—is insane, unless Clarissa is judged by a different standard. Clarissa's madness is the madness of a martyr: she refuses to accommodate herself to the world any longer.

Clarissa's refusal to accommodate ends in her death, which on at least one level must be seen as suicide.[44] The orthodox Richardson naturally condemned suicide. In his analysis of *The Fair Penitent*, Belford, Richardson's moral spokesman, ridicules the stage tradition of violence and suicide: "But indeed, our poets hardly know how to create a distress without horror, murder, and suicide; and must shock your soul to bring tears from your eyes." (VII, 134) [IV, 117]

According to foreign visitors at the time of Belford's complaint, the poets were only imitating life. Suffering from their native malady, melancholia, the English were notorious for being hellbent to do away with themselves. Self-murders were reputed to occur "almost daily," as people cut their throats, shot, or stabbed themselves "upon mature deliberation." Voltaire mused that so many people killed themselves "par humeur," out of a mysterious urge to get their names in the newspapers.[45] Desperate measures were suspected to have been taken to protect the English from themselves. Monsieur Grosley reports his difficulty in discovering a "fine prospect" of the Thames from the city, explaining sagely that because of the "natural bent" of the English to suicide, the river banks in London were deliberately blocked off by factories and docks.[46]

Richardson was not alone in his public criticism of self-destruction. Edward Young, Richardson's friend and admirer, rebuked the populace in his *Night Thoughts*, guaranteed to feed his reader's appetite for melancholy even as he attempted to correct it:

O Britain, infamous for suicide!
An island in thy manners! far disjoin'd
From the whole world of rationals beside!
In ambient waves plunge thy polluted head,
Wash the dire stain nor shock the Continent.[47]

Pamela at least appears to be considering Young's advice in a most literal way when she contemplates plunging her own "polluted head" into Mr. B.'s pond: "What to do, but to throw myself into the pond, and put a Period to all my Griefs in this World!" (I, 232) [I, 149]

Suicide fascinated Richardson even as it appalled him. After her rape, his Clarissa, "in a perfect frenzy," seeks death in any form, begging Lovelace to do away with her: " 'Twill be a mercy, said she, the highest act of mercy you can do, to kill me outright upon this spot—This happy spot, as I will, in my last moments, call it!—Then baring, with a still more frantic violence, part of her enchanting neck, Here, here, said the soul-harrowing Beauty, let thy pointed mercy enter!" (V, 375) [III, 238] Lovelace places his "soul-harrowing beauty" within the Christian tradition of martyrdom, for like Christ, Clarissa harrows the hell of the Sinclair brothel, seeking death, "thy pointed mercy." After her rape, Clarissa gains a spiritual freedom, a detachment from her own body, which allows her to concentrate on her salvation. Suicide offers her a way out of the body altogether. In one of the novel's most powerfully melodramatic scenes, Clarissa defiantly threatens to kill herself, holding "a penknife in her hand, the point to her own bosom." (VI, 67) [III, 288-89]

Although Richardson toyed obsessively with suicide, he rejected it as the final solution. Pamela "escapes herself" to live a long and prosperous life as Mrs. B. Clarissa's fate, however, is more questionable. Never has a dying heroine been so scrupulously mysterious, so candidly discreet. After Mr. Goddard, her apothecary, warns Clarissa that "so much watching, so little nourishment, and so much grief, as you seem to indulge, is enough to impair the most vigorous health," she strongly protests his implication of self-destruction: "I have engaged sir . . . to avoid all wilful neglects." (VI, 436) [IV, 13] But what is the will? After nineteen years of excellent health, hardy Clarissa sickens and dies.[48] We never learn the nature of her illness, only its unavoidable fatality. Clarissa continually makes sure that she cannot be accused of suicide: "So, Doctor, tell me truly, May I stay here, and be clear of any imputations of curtailing, thro' wilfulness or impatiency, or thro' resentments which I hope I am got above, a life that might otherwise be prolonged?" (VII, 277) [IV, 216] Samuel Johnson's trenchant judgment of Clarissa, that "there is always something which she prefers to truth,"[49] can apply here.

Clarissa has been preparing for death from the beginning. "I have sometimes wished," she tells Anna Howe in her first letter, "that it had pleased God to have taken me in my last fever, when I had every-body's love and good opinion." (I, 5) [I, 4] Much later, Mama Norton concurs, expressing the wish that Clarissa had died at the age of nine, of her "dangerous fever." "What a much more desirable event, both for you, and for us, would it have been, had we *then* lost you! (VI, 30) [IV, 49] "A sad thing to say," she adds. Hard words, but listen to Clarissa's mother: "Should they lose you, which God forbid! the scene would then indeed be sadly changed; for then those who now most resented, would be most grieved; all your fine qualities would rise to their remembrance, and your unhappy error would be quite forgotten." (VII, 380) [IV, 285] Clarissa, wise girl, knows what is expected of her.

Clarissa seeks death not only to please her family but to please herself, to escape from the demands of life. Instead

of marrying Solmes, she would "rather be buried alive."
(I, 127) [I, 87] "O that they did but know my heart!—
It shall sooner burst, than voluntarily, uncompelled, un-
driven, dictate a measure that shall cast a slur either upon
Them, or upon my Sex." (I, 209) [I, 143] Death offers
a way out of an odious marriage, indeed out of any marriage, which is a state both attractive and repellent to Clarissa. She admits to Miss Howe that she would rather marry
her shroud than "any man on earth!" (III, 291) [II, 176]
Later, Clarissa realizes her wish. Her shroud awaits her:
"And tho' not fine or gawdy to the sight . . . yet will they
be the easiest, the *happiest* suit, that ever bridal maiden
wore—for they are such as carry with them a security against
all those anxieties, pains and perturbations which sometimes succeed to the most promising outsettings." (VII,
406) [IV, 303] Even when she considers the possibility of
marrying Lovelace instead of her shroud, she grimly anticipates martyrdom: "I will content myself to be a *suffering
person* through the State to the end of my life.—A long
one it cannot be!" (IV, 112-13) [II, 313] On her coffin,
Clarissa inscribes April 10 as the date of her "death," as
the "fatal day of her leaving her Father's house." (VII,
339) [IV, 257] While insisting upon her desire to prolong
her life, Clarissa steadily seeks death as the only solution
to her distress.

   If we apply Emile Durkheim's definition of suicide to
Clarissa's death, we can understand her motives even more
clearly. According to Durkheim, "any death which is the
direct or indirect result of a positive or negative act accomplished by the victim himself. . . . When resolution entails
certain sacrifice of life" is suicide.[50] Durkheim separates
suicidal types into three main groups: (1) egoistic, when
the individual fails to integrate himself into his society; (2)
altruistic, when the individual's life is rigorously governed
by custom, causing the individual to take his life because
of a higher commitment to a religious, political, or social
ideal; and (3) anomic, when the social regulation of the

individual is expanded, because of sudden wealth or success, for instance, or contracted, because of a calamity such as war, death, or divorce, beyond what he can endure.

Clarissa's suicide is both egoistic and altruistic, befitting her strangely mixed personality. Her egoistic, protestant individualism compels her to reject familial and social demands. "Marry Lovelace," urges Anna Howe, society's spokeswoman. "I should sooner marry my shroud," answers Clarissa. Yet Clarissa's death is also altruistic. Committed to spiritual truths, Clarissa impersonally detaches herself from the material world. Durkheim is familiar with such behavior: the altruistic individual seeks to "strip himself of his personal being in order to be engulfed in something which he regards as his true essence. . . . He must therefore consider that he has no life of his own. Impersonality is here carried to its highest pitch." In her rented room, comforted by strangers, turning herself into a symbol of purity and denying herself personal contact with friends and family, Clarissa methodically erases her personal self. "Yet this body clings!—How it incumbers," she complains. (VII, 254) [IV, 201] Only in death, detached at last from her violated body, will she discover her "true essence."

Both the egoist and the altruist experience melancholy before committing suicide, but in different ways. The egoist suffers weariness and depression, while the altruist's melancholy, like Clarissa's, is more energetic, springing "from hope; for it depends on the belief in beautiful perspectives beyond this life." The altruist eagerly seeks death, "affirming itself by acts of extreme energy."[51] Zealous Clarissa, preparing her will, writing endless post-mortem letters, ordering her coffin and supervising its carved detail, affirms her own faith in the "beautiful perspectives beyond this life." She denies her physical self—"this vile self," as she calls it—to prepare to meet God with enthusiastic joy.

Yet, curiously, Clarissa's elaborate preparations for heaven seem unconnected to the world of formal religion. Clarissa, after all, saves herself by her own sturdy will. She experiences St. John's dark night of the soul and the mystical assault of grace, but she recreates these mystical experiences in her own terms, defined by her own sense of self in a world notably empty of Christian emissaries. No guidance comes from the clergy. Reverend Lewen impotently watches Clarissa's family force her into marriage with the obviously unacceptable Solmes; later, finally ready to intervene on her behalf, he sickens and dies. Reverend Brand's petty and pedantic malice actually helps to destroy Clarissa's hopes for a reconciliation with her family. Without help from the church, Clarissa saves herself by herself, becoming a self-made saint.

In his study of the puritan family, Levin Schucking discusses the absence of the "religious factor" in *Clarissa*, arguing that the Harlowe family would surely have used "religious arguments" to persuade Clarissa to marry Solmes. "She would have been prayed for at family prayers. She would have had the Bible quoted at her and all moral means available to the family theocracy would have been used to break her obstinacy." He also notices that Clarissa, "in that particular world of ideas," would have naturally "prayed God to help and guide her so that the conflict in which she had been caught up might be resolved."[52] Perhaps Richardson's sensitivity to the critical attacks upon his Pamela's overly zealous piety caused him to modulate the religious tone of *Clarissa*. Pamela, always ready to say the Lord's Prayer at the very moment Mr. B.'s hand probes her bosom, was attacked for hypocrisy. Richardson, diffident and always sensitive to his critics' charges, may have suppressed Clarissa's religiosity on aesthetic grounds.

Paul Parnell suggests another possible reason for the oddly irreligious tone of the novel. He examines the motivations of the "sentimental Christian," who takes on the burdens of Christ, suffering the sins of others. By assuming the Christ-like mask of humility and suffering, the sentimental Christian gains the power to forgive and condemn. Richardson places Clarissa in just such a position: all characters in her story meet their rewards or punishments directly because of their treatment of her. Parnell argues that the wearer of the Christ-like mask is motivated by egoism, rather than by spiritual commitment: "Ostensibly there is no more loyal supporter of religion. After all, if he patterns his life on Christ, what more can we ask? But if this emulation of Christ is only a self-deception for primarily egoistic reasons, then his attitude is presumptuous rather than admirable. And in that case, sentimentalism might be said to make a distinct step away from traditional Christianity."[53]

Certainly we cannot avoid questioning the nature of Clarissa's "forgiving" spirit. Saints should forgive their enemies. Clarissa makes the attempt, but her forgiveness is more infernal than divine. It is here that she behaves least like a pattern and most like a person. After the fire scare, Lovelace begs her forgiveness. Her answer: "I will—I do forgive you—Wretch that you are." (IV, 396) [II, 505] The "wretch" never receives an unqualified pardon. (Not that he should, but Clarissa *is* assuming the mantle of sainthood.) Understandably, Clarissa refuses to see her seducer after her imprisonment. The very thought of the man's presence causes her to flee her room to wander the streets of London, carried in a chair when she is too weak to walk. But Clarissa still insists that she forgives him, wretch that he is. Nevertheless, she arranges to revenge herself on Lovelace's encroaching curiosity after her death. In her will, she instructs that if Lovelace should insist upon viewing "*her dead* whom he ONCE before saw in a manner dead, let his gay curiosity be gratified." While he beholds and triumphs over her "wretched remains," let "some good person," give the wretch a piece of paper, "containing these few words only: 'Gay, cruel heart! behold here the Remains of the once ruined, yet now happy, Clarissa Harlowe!—See what thou thyself must quickly be;—and RE-PENT.' " She follows her morbidly nasty scenario with a statement of forgiveness most difficult to believe: "Yet, to shew that I die in perfect charity with *all the world*, I do most sincerely forgive Mr. Lovelace the wrongs he has done me." (VIII, 107-108) [IV, 416-17] "Yet." Clarissa's conjunction betrays her true feelings. Her reference to Lovelace's "viewing *her dead* whom he ONCE before saw in a manner dead" prods Cousin Morden into action. Inspired by Clarissa's hint, he kills Lovelace in a duel, carrying out the spirit of Clarissa's "forgiveness."

On one level, Clarissa is conscious of her vengeful forgiveness. Preparing to die, she exults in her power over Lovelace: "The man whom once I could have loved, I have been enabled to despise: And shall not *Charity* complete my triumph? And shall I not *enjoy* it?—And where would be my triumph if he *deserved* my forgiveness?—Poor man! He has had a loss in losing me! I have the pride to think so, because I think I know my own heart. I have had none in losing him!" (VII, 232) [IV, 186] Some of Clarissa's delight stems from a pride in her self-control ("I have had none in losing him!"), but more comes from pure revenge: "Poor man! He has had a loss in losing me!" In her death, Clarissa lives out the child's fantasy of revenge through suicide, the fantasy of the grieving parents mourning the child they have mistreated. Richardson brilliantly depicts Clarissa's "strangely mixed" feelings towards Lovelace. She forgives and hates him at the same time. As Lovelace recognizes, "her charming Body is not equally organized. The unequal partners pull two ways; and the divinity within her tears her silken frame." (IV, 217) [II, 384] Lovelace also recognizes the revenge mixed with Clarissa's forgiveness: "So this Lady, as I suppose, intended only at first to vex and plague me; and finding she could do it to purpose, her desire of revenge insensibly became stronger in her than the desire of life; And now she is willing to die as an event which she thinks will cut my heart-strings asunder. And still, the *more* to be revenged, puts on the Christian, and forgives me." (VII, 440) [IV, 326] When Clarissa "puts on the Christian," the Christ-like mask of sentimentality, she curses as well as forgives.

The forgiven Harlowe family does not fare any better with Clarissa's mixed blessings. Her memory, made vivid through her posthumous letters, haunts them. Morden reports the family remorse to Belford: the Harlowes, hanging their pensive heads, mope about, shunning one another. Their memories of her "excellences" will "for a long time make their very blessings a curse to them!" (VIII, 180) [IV, 465-66] Clarissa's forgiveness reproaches her family. They can never find relief from her "charity." When they read her "comforting" posthumous letters, their "intelligences and recollections" become "perpetual subjects of recrimination to them." Their guilt "not seldom made them shun each other (at the times they were accustomed to meet together) that they might avoid the mutual reproaches of Eyes that spoke when Tongues were silent—Their stings also sharpened by time; what an unhappy family was This!" (VIII, 281) [IV, 534] Exerting her "will" posthumously, Clarissa punished the family that had punished her in life. We remember "the times they were accustomed to meet together in the family way," times to judge Clarissa and determine new ways to punish, times to force the odious Solmes upon her. Breakfast, tea time, and dinner—all became nightmares for Clarissa. Now, wearing the Christ-like mask of forgiveness, Clarissa can make such occasions nightmares for her family. As John Dussinger suggests, Clarissa's perfectionist quest has a "double edge." In positive terms, "it is justified by Christian tradition as the spiritual striving for transcendence and beautification [*sic*]; but in negative terms her desire for the heavenly father's blessing and for marriage to the heavenly bridegroom is a grandiose scheme to prevail over the world of mortals."[54] And Saint Clarissa does prevail, triumphing in her death over those mortals who thwarted her in life.

The History of Sir Charles Grandison is a classic saint's

life. Unfortunately, the corpse walks among his admiring mourners, complacently accepting their choruses of praise. He has been awarded sainthood by popular acclaim before the novel even opens. His goodness blazes, dazzling rivals, converting villains, and redeeming hardened old sinners. And, as in so many posthumous saints' lives, all of his public virtues (and there are no private) become flattened out. In Anna Howe's account of Saint Clarissa, her friend's appearance ("In her dress she was elegant beyond imitation") takes on the same significance as her acts of charity, while the "neat and free cut of her letters (like her mind, solid, and above all *flourish*)" becomes one with her "sacred regard to truth." (VIII, 218-23) [IV, 491-94] In ending her account with an awe-inspiring description of Miss Harlowe's bookkeeping methods, her panegyrist inadvertently turns an impassioned saint into a moral accountant.

This same leveling occurs throughout *Grandison*. Sir Charles bustles about self-importantly in all directions— flying off to Bath, up to London, out to Italy; saving Harriet from a fate worse than death; teaching Milton to Italians; paying off relict mistresses of old relatives; settling elderly friends' tangled estates; granting doweries; and lecturing on the evils of dueling. As Leslie Stephen observes, Sir Charles:

> is one of those solemn beings who can't shave themselves without implicitly asserting a great moral principle. He finds sermons in his horses' tails; he could give an excellent reason for the quantity of lace on his coat, which was due, it seems, to a sentiment of filial reverence; and he could not fix his hour for dinner without an eye to the reformation of society. In short, he was a prig of the first water: self-conscious to the last degree; and so crammed with little moral aphorisms that they drop out of his mouth whenever he opens his lips. . . . As he carries his solemnity into the pettiest trifles of life, so he

considers religious duties to be simply the most important part of social etiquette. He would shrink from blasphemy even more than from keeping on his hat in the presence of ladies; but the respect which he owes in one case is of the same order with that due in the other: it is only a degree more important.[55]

His saintliness becomes predictably commonplace, ultimately banal.

Conflict plays an essential part in Richardson's best work. Pamela's personality develops under stress; Clarissa's virtues shine because of, not in spite of, her great distress. Suffering distills the spirit, polishes and perfects the soul. But we never once see Sir Charles suffer—never, at any rate, convincingly. For one thing, he is always certain that he is doing the right thing, the only thing possible for him to do, and he never suffers remorse. Torn between Harriet and Clementina, he trusts his moral sense to see him through. Even then, there can be no struggle, only a passive waiting game as Sir Charles watches to see whether Clementina will withdraw her claim or not. Back in England, Harriet loses flesh and spirit as she suffers from the protracted suspense, but not Sir Charles. He's too busy overseeing the rest of the Poretta family, always in need of his English good sense.

In *Pamela* and *Clarissa*, Richardson made his heroines suffer, in part, to elicit an emotional response from his reader. In *Grandison*, the author subverts the sentimental ethic, presenting as his hero a man of feeling who truly cannot be said to feel. Although he keeps warning the reader about his dangerous passions, they remain relentlessly held in check; we have only the good man's word for their repressed presence. While Pamela's Mr. B. is brought to a point of moral sensibility, guided by her letters and journals depicting the pathos of her plight, Sir Charles needs no such tutelage in proper feelings: he is already perfect. Lovelace, unlike B., is not moved by Clarissa's letters; he takes a peculiar pleasure in forging the pathetic missives. But in spite of Lovelace's heartlessness, Richardson does not overturn the sentimental assumptions underlying his novel. Clarissa triumphs in the end, just as the promptings of heart over head, conscience over social mores, triumph over Lovelace's empty cynicism. In *Grandison*, however, the public triumphs over the private, as Sir Charles exercises his sense rather than his sensibility.

In *Grandison*, Richardson attempts to socialize Clarissa's virtue. Although Clarissa, the private saint, cannot exist in the real world, Sir Charles, the public saint, must. Manners matter in Sir Charles's world, not meditation. While Richardson allowed Clarissa to escape into heaven, leaving her black-bordered meditations and her will behind for others to admire, he forces the characters in Sir Charles's world to remain in the public arena. Clementina is not allowed to escape into her nunnery, nor to remain isolated and protected in her madness. Sir Charles drives her back into the world of familial and social expectations. The public spirit of reason and right thinking triumphs over the private promptings of the heart.

Richardson's biographers, Eaves and Kimpel, make an interesting suggestion for the failure of Sir Charles's history. Citing a "little book" of Richardson's preserved by his daughters after his death, they speculate that there must have been earlier notes to a novel Richardson never wrote, possibly a chronicle of a younger, rakish gentleman who becomes involved with at least two women and loves both. Later he apparently substituted his "good man" for the rake. "Some such history might account for the rather uneasy relationship between the story of the novel and the character of its hero, who is never credible in his double love—or in any love."[56] Eaves and Kimpel are the first to admit that this argument is very tenuous, but it can be an attractive one. It is at least certain that the deadly weighted character of Sir Charles stifles the dramatic action of the book.

In their important studies of Richardson, both Mark Kinkead-Weekes and Margaret Doody seem to share a generous appreciation of *Grandison*.[57] While recognizing the novel's drawbacks, they demand that the reader attend to its significance as an expression of Richardson's desire for a moral community and his longing to refine and nurture the passions. Their interpretations, in accord with their more optimistic readings of Richardson, lead us to a greater understanding of the scope of Richardson's moral vision. But, sadly, the aesthetic and dramatic inferiority of *Grandison* remains. Clarissa's sainthood emerges from her own suffering, from the tragic imperatives of her own character, her willful, relentless drive for perfection. Sir Charles's sainthood is pasted onto him from the start, by fiat. We must only wonder at his perfection, never at his anguish. If, that is, we can stay awake.

An old lady of Sir Walter Scott's acquaintance explained why she enjoyed hearing *Sir Charles Grandison* read aloud: "Should I drop asleep in course of the reading, I am sure, when I awake, I shall have lost none of the story, but shall find the party, where I left them, *conversing in the cedar-parlour*."[58] And they will, to be sure, be conversing on the virtuous excellencies of Sir Charles, never changing in a static, self-enclosed universe.

It is ironic that Richardson's perfectionist quest should end so complacently. In *Clarissa*, the author's peculiar angle of vision, his probing of the tangled passions of a saint, allowed him to uncover essential truths about the human personality. But in *Grandison*, external rather than internal, perfect goodness glitters on the surface, promising spiritual health and happiness to all who follow the good man's exemplary pattern (if they dare). Morris Golden remarks that *Grandison* is an old man's book.[59] I would only add that it is just the sort of thing one would expect from a self-improver, a fitting extension of *The Apprentice's Vade Mecum*.

TWO • A Delicate Balance: Richardson's Treatment of the Sentimental Woman

You must see that the Tendency of all I have written is to exalt the Sex.

RICHARDSON to LADY BRADSHAIGH (*Letters*, p. 112)

But, Madam, be so good as to consider, that man, at the time woman was formed out of his rib, was in a state of innocence. He had not fallen. The devil had need of a helper: he soon found one in Eve. But, if I may be forgiven for a kind of pun, you seem to think, madam, that the faults of men lie in the flesh; the faults of women are deeper—they lie in the bone.

RICHARDSON to LADY BRADSHAIGH
(*Correspondence*, vol. VI, p. 165)

ONE THING IS CERTAIN: Richardson thought a great deal about women. As John Traugott points out, "What is obvious from everything he wrote is that he almost exclusively was interested, outside his printing business, in the sexual gauntlets young women of his circle ran or were said to run."[1] His biographers are more discreet about their subject's obsession, couching it in polite, sociological terms: "The ideas he loved to discuss were not about politics, religion, or philosophy, but about the family, the relations between women and men, the position and proper conduct of women."[2] Rakes and virgins, virgins and rakes.

Richardson's interest in the fortunes of young maidens corresponds to his perfectionism. For who promises more than the tender virgin, teetering on the brink of womanhood, neither burdened by domestic responsibilities nor soiled by worldly encounters? With so much to give and, equally important, so much to lose, the young virgin, in Richardson's imagination, offers and risks the most. She is Eve before the fall. Should she waver, paradise escapes us once again, and she will have brought it all down upon herself. Women's faults lie ever so deep—in the bone.

Of course, wherever there's a virgin, a rake's not far behind, wetting his lips appreciatively over the tea table. The rake, the snake in the garden, always threatens, foiling the best-laid schemes for human perfectibility. No matter how many conduct manuals and avuncular letter guides Richardson can write warning young misses of the dangers lurking in the world outside the nursery, the fall repeats itself, locking us mortals out of paradise. The conflict between innocence and experience, good and evil, fills Richardson's mind and books. Indeed, the fall interests him as much as the paradise lost. As much as he loved virtue, he loved virtue in distress the more. We can see this in his novels, where once the conflict ends the author's (and the reader's) sense of engagement ends as well.

In the next two chapters, we shall investigate the objects of Richardson's major obsession—women, both innocent and fallen. As Richardson received, explored, and transformed commonplace notions of human perfectibility in his novels, so did he transform popular conceptions of sexual roles. This chapter will discuss his treatment of the sentimental woman,[3] first examining the way women were depicted in the history and literature of the eighteenth century. We shall then look at the ways Richardson accepted and transformed social conventions in his novels, and examine the importance of sexual conflict in his work. Although he ostensibly places his heroines in stress-filled situations to reveal their shining virtues, Richardson often appears more concerned with the sensations he is eliciting than with the moral he is drawing. The conflict, appropriately enough in the work of a man obsessed with seduction, is sexual. Incestuous fantasies haunt Harlowe House, while rape fantasies dominate the outside world beyond the

Harlowe garden gate. In his novels, Richardson presents a brutal world of sexual warfare in which men and women torment each other, battling for supremacy by virtue of their own natures.

In his novels and letters, Richardson reveals a view of women common to his age: they were purer than men, sublime in nature, yet at the same time more susceptible to temptation. Through a careful program of checks and balances, "punctilio" Richardson called it, society insured the purity of its women.[4] Not without reason, for women, by nature of their inherent frailty, the evil that lies in the bone, were ever in danger of sliding down to their naturally low level. The sentimental woman, the artificial product of sublimation and repression, had to be guarded by her family and husband, matronized by her children, bound in by hoops and rules, to keep social morality properly fixed.

Richardson recognized and applauded such moral commonplaces, carefully presenting portraits of matronized hoydens like Charlotte Grandison as he sagely warned his own young misses Highmore, Westcomb, and Mulso about the snakes coiled throughout the borders of their own gardens. Yet, as always, Richardson managed to have it both ways, both supporting and subverting his moral. In his finest work, he overturns the conventions he appears to be endorsing, creating heroines of independence and integrity who stand outside social boundaries to elevate themselves.

In Chapter Three, we will continue our discussion of women, looking at the fallen woman, that "natural woman" Richardson and his society so greatly feared. By looking at the ways the fallen woman was treated in fact and fiction, we can better understand the way all women were both degraded and (in the luckier cases) elevated once again as vessels for society's moral conventions. Although he reflects many of the ideas of his own age, in his best work Richardson refuses to follow the sentimental formula of degradation and elevation. His Clarissa transcends her sentimental tradition to follow the dictates of her conscience and to answer the tragic imperatives of her own personality.

Sir Charles Grandison, like his creator, thinks often on the nature of women. When Lady G. pertly asks her brother if there is a natural inferiority in the faculties of the one sex, he answers evasively at first. In general, yes, but on an individual level, surrounded by such superior women, Sir Charles demurs. But not for long. Soon he warms to his subject, asking hard questions: "Why has nature made a difference in the beauty, proportion, and symmetry, in the *persons* of the two Sexes? Why gave it delicacy, softness, grace to that of the woman—as in the Ladies before me; strength, firmness, to men; a capacity to bear labour and fatigue; and courage, to protect the other? Why gave it a distinction, both in qualities and plumage to the different sexes of the feathered race? Why in the courage of the male and female animals?—the surly bull, the meek, the beneficent cow, for one instance? We looked upon one another." (III, 247) [VI, LV] Well might the women look upon one another, mouths agape in bovine wonder. Eleven pages earlier, the matronized Lady G. had employed the same "beneficent cow" metaphor to describe Harriet's wedding day: "We women, dressed out in ribbands and in gaudy trappings, and in Virgin-white, on our Wedding days, seem but like milk-white heifers led to the sacrifice." (III, 236) [VI, LIII] Intellectually, Richardson is able to see the problem of women both ways. Speaking through his mouthpiece, Sir Charles, he espouses conventional views of the sexual roles: women are cows, men surly bulls. But even as he is deliberately employing sexual stereotypes, Richardson can also attack the traditional ideas about the sexual roles. Speaking through Lady G., who mourns the sacrifice of the virgin heifer, he extends sympathy to the "inferior" sex, but always a qualified sympathy. Richardson can never completely forget the "natural" difference between men and women, the chilling and titillating awareness that the faults of women "lie in the bone." Lady G. and Anna Howe are allowed their say, but after airing their dissatisfaction, they are expected to assume their proper female roles, Miss Howe as the wife of the colorless Hickman and Lady G. as the matronized mama, nursing her "Marmouset" at her breast.

Although in general, and especially when he is expressing aphoristic truisms, Richardson sees women as weaker creatures, dependent on men for guidance and protection, in his novels, he creates heroines of great strength who unconventionally follow the dictates of their own consciences. Pamela wins Mr. B. because she regards herself as a person, not as an accommodating wench. Clarissa refuses to compromise herself to the demands of society, a position Richardson both warns against and glorifies. In his novels, Richardson uses conventional stereotypes of women, and then transforms them as he explores them. In the previous chapter, I discussed the conflict between Richardson's moral and aesthetic intentions: in his art Richardson actually contradicted the perfectionist premises of his novels; the moral maxims he so easily dispensed could not apply to Clarissa's complex and tragic plight. The same thing happens to Richardson's attitudes towards women. Even as he upholds the traditional virtues of submission and obedience, he creates heroines who deny these virtues and make their own fates.

In his *Familiar Letters*, Richardson insisted upon a definite separation of sexual roles: women were always to keep to their proper places. The letter "Against a Young Lady's affecting manly airs; and also censuring the modern Riding-Habits" sets out the boundaries. A "tender uncle" admonishes his niece for "imitating the manners of the other sex, and appearing more masculine than either the amiable softness of your person or sex can justify." Like Sir Charles, the uncle draws strong distinctions between the "intrepid,

free, and in a prudent degree bold," nature of man and
the "soft, tender, and modest" nature of woman.

In all of his work, Richardson demonstrates his dislike
of the "*masculine woman* . . . a character as little creditable
as becoming." (*Familiar Letters*, pp. 113-14) Both Mrs.
Jewkes and Mrs. Sinclair, hired to break in their charges,
frighten Pamela and Clarissa with their masculine airs:
Mrs. Jewkes, who teases Pamela with her "Impertinence,
and bold Way," (I, 142) [I, 91] has a "huge Hand, and
an Arm as thick as my Waist. . . . She has a hoarse, man-
like Voice, and is as thick as she's long; and yet looks so
deadly strong, that I am afraid she would dash me at her
Foot in an Instant, if I was to vex her." (I, 151) [I, 97]
Mother Sinclair's "mannish airs" ("Oh, she is a frightful
woman! If she *be* a woman! She needed not to put on that
fearful mask to scare me out of my poor wits.") terrify
Clarissa. (V, 335) [III, 211] In *Grandison*, Miss Barnevelt, a horsewoman, is "sneeringly spoken of rather as a
young fellow, than as a woman; and who will one day look
out for a *wife* for herself!"[5] Harriet Byron disapproves of
her fellow creature: "But see what women get by going out
of character. Like the Bats in the fable, they are look'd
upon as mortals of a doubtful species, hardly owned by
either, and laugh'd at by both." (I, 43) [I, X] Harriet
especially dislikes Barnevelt's lesbian manner, and reports
that "Miss Barnevelt said, she had from the moment I first
enter'd beheld me with the eye of a Lover. And freely
taking my hand, squeezed it." (I, 43) [I, X] Such freedom rankles. Later in the evening, Miss Barnevelt is even
bolder: "But what extremely disconcerted me was a freedom of Miss Barnevelt's. . . . She profess'd that I was
able to bring *her own sex* into reputation with her. Wisdom, as I call it, said she, notwithstanding what you have
modestly alleged to depreciate your own, proceeding thro'
teeth of ivory, and lips of coral, give a grace to every
word. And then clasping one of her mannish arms around
me, she kissed my cheek." (I, 57) [I, XIII] Miss Barne-

velt's mannish assault is more offensive than similar freedoms taken by Mr. Greville because it is out of nature; the woman is not acting her proper part and is calling her sexual identity into question.[6]

Richardson's insistence upon well-defined feminine roles reflects commonplace fears of the eighteenth century. Women were becoming too bold; the age was out of joint. In *An Estimate of the Manners and Principles of the Times*, John Brown complained that "the Sexes have now little other apparent Distinction, beyond that of Person and Dress: Their peculiar and characteristic Manners Are confounded and lost: The one Sex having advanced into *Boldness*, as the other have sunk into *Effeminacy*."[7] Brown's fears were echoed by other detractors of the effeminate fop and the bold woman. Foreign visitors frequently noted the unusual freedoms of the English woman. An Italian traveler, Gemelli, reported that English women "do whatsoever they please, and do so generally wear the breeches (as we used to say) that it is now become a proverb that England is the hell of horses and the paradise of women; and if there were a bridge from the island to the continent, all the women in Europe would run thither."[8] Another visitor, Henry Meister of Switzerland, reported that the "greatest difficulty is not always to persuade an English woman to suffer you to carry her off, but to find a convenient opportunity for telling her you wish to do it." He suggested that the chastity of the Englishwoman was preserved not by her natural reserve but by the "interior oeconomy of their houses, and the duties assigned their several domestics," which are "continual checks on their actions." He noted in wonder that the lady's bedchamber was a "sanctuary which no stranger [was] permitted to enter." Meister decided that "there is less art and good fortune required to bring the love adventure to a successful conclusion than there is to open it."[9]

Foreign slurs, perhaps. However, Lady Mary Wortley Montagu, a commentator closer to home, complained about the slipping morals of "our Young Ladys." "To speak plainly, I am very sorry for the forlorn state of Matrimony, which is as much ridicul'd by our Young Ladys as it us'd to be by young fellows; in short, both Sexes have found the Inconveniencys of it, and the Apellation of Rake is as genteel in a Woman as a Man of Quality. 'Tis no Scandal to say, Miss—the Maid of Honnour looks very well now she's up again, and poor Biddy Noel has never been quite well since her last Flux."[10] Matrons, as well as single women, were known to take liberties. Cesar de Saussure wrote that "a wife is not generally unhappy when she discovers her husband has a mistress; on the contrary, it sometimes happens that if her husband so desires it she will be polite towards her rival, but at the same time she will probably console herself with a friend, and thus both husband and wife are happy."[11]

Reports of such liberties alarmed Richardson. In the *Rambler*, he warned the rising generation of young women that they were in danger of making themselves cheap by thronging to public resorts.[12] Always a lover of home and hearth, Richardson believed that when a woman spurned her needle to set out for public amusements, she was heading for trouble. Public resorts and masquerades presented frightening possibilities for disguise, role-playing, and sexual freedom. When Harriet Byron attends a masquerade, she suffers disastrous consequences, barely escaping rape.[13] In his collection of anecdotes of "Manners and Customs" of the eighteenth century, J. P. Malcom describes the dangerous leveling effect of the masquerade:

> This practice afforded opportunities of gratifying very improper curiosity, and of visiting places at unseasonable hours; an instance of this description occurred in May 1724. The White-lion, in Wych-street, had long been famed for riotous assemblies under the pretence of Concerts; and the neighbouring moralists waited with impatience for the hour when they should effectually

transgress the Law: that hour at length arrived, and a posse of Constables, executing a warrant obtained for the purpose, discovered females even of some distinction, tradesmen's wives, their daughters, and many common prostitutes, a collection that really surprised each other; the vicious hardly crediting that they were in so much good company, and the noviciates frightened at the features of unmasked depravity. The latter received wholesome admonition, and were sent home; the former visited Bridewell.[14]

With only a mask, a whore might pass for a lady and a lady might act like a whore. The only difference would lie in the punisher: the whore would be sent to Bridewell, where she would be beaten by her jailers, while the lady would be sent home, where she would be disciplined by her outraged husband.

The fate of the "unmasked" lady is instructive, suggesting that the dangerous freedoms supposedly enjoyed by the eighteenth-century woman may have been more illusory than real. Did the eighteenth-century woman actually enjoy the liberty that Richardson and his contemporaries so greatly feared? E. N. Williams argues that great equality between the sexes existed in Georgian England, reporting that women "read the same books as the men, talked politics with them on an equal footing, and dressed with a similar finery. Even the ladies' magazines, which were then coming in, had nothing specially feminine about them. *The Ladies' Magazine, or Universal Entertainer* which began to appear in 1749, included no recipes, no fashion notes, and no household hints. It did contain ribaldry, however, as did masculine magazines."[15] An absence of household hints and the presence of ribaldry does not, however, insure sexual equality. *The Ladies' Magazine* provided sensational accounts of executions at Tyburn, "The History of England" in questions and answers, and entertaining observations on "that surprizing Insect, called the May-Fly." It also included epistolary fiction of a Richardsonian nature: a letter sent by a tradesman's daughter "of good Repute" to a "Gentleman of great Estate, after She found he coveted her only for a Mistress."[16] It offered, as Alison Adburgham notes, an "astonishing twopence worth,"[17] but inadequately substituted entertaining observations for the formal education the eighteenth-century woman so sorely lacked.

Lady Mary Wortley Montagu complained that "there is no part of the World where our Sex is treated with so much contempt as in England. . . . We are educated in the grossest ignorance, and no art omitted to stiffle our natural reason." She argued that until women were admitted into the polite society and conversation of men, they would not be truly educated: "The knowledge of mankind (the most usefull of all knowledge) can only be acquir'd by conversing with them. Books are so far from giving that Instruction, they fill the Head with a set of wrong Notions from whence spring the Tribes of Clarissas, Harriets etc."[18] Richardson would doubtless have taken offense at this criticism, especially after he took such pains to display his heroines' learning. Harriet takes part in a spirited debate concerning the Ancients and the Moderns, Clarissa's knowledge is celebrated throughout the neighborhood, and even humble Pamela makes reference to the rape of Lucrece and refers to Virgil, as translated by Mr. Dryden. Yet it must be admitted that Clarissa's knowledge of "the world" is largely theoretical, of the *Spectator* nature, more aphoristic than analytic. As Lovelace slyly suggests, she could even cap sentences with the sententious Lord M. (V, 213) [III, 127]

Even when women were allowed educational opportunities, they seemed uneasy about the actual priority of their learning. Clarissa is always pointing out the greater importance of housewifery over learning, and even the bluestocking Elizabeth Carter, admired translator of Epictetus, boasted that her "special good sweet cake," which she made for family christenings, was so highly prized that "several grave notable gentlewomen of unquestionable good housewifery have applied to me for the receipt."[19] Richardson's approval of Miss Carter's domestic expertise can be seen in his remark to Lady Bradshaigh that Miss Carter "is an example, that women may be trusted with Latin and even Greek, and yet not think themselves above their domestic duties." (*Letters*, pp. 177-78) And Johnson characteristically valued Mrs. Carter because she could "make a pudding, as well as translate Epictetus."[20]

With all their "freedom," women of the eighteenth century seemed to accept an inferior position quite matter of factly. In a learned letter to Bishop Burnet, Lady Mary Wortley Montagu complained that women were not allowed books, "but such as tend to the weakening and Effeminateing of the mind." But, she hastened to add, she was not arguing for sexual equality: "I do not doubt God and Nature has thrown us into an Inferior Rank. We are a lower part of the Creation; we owe Obedience and Submission to the Superior Sex, and any Woman who suffers her Vanity and folly to deny this, Rebells against the Law of the Creator and indisputable Order of Nature."[21] William Whately, Vicar of Banbury and author of the popular tract *A Bride-Bush*, a "direction for married persons," would applaud Lady Mary's sentiments. His ideal wife must "firstly . . . acknowledge her inferioritie" and "secondly she must carrie herself as an inferior." He warns that "where the woman stands upon termes of equalitie with her husband (much more if she account herselfe his better) the very roote of all good carriage is quite withered, and the fountain thereof utterly dried up: out of place, out of peace; and woe to those miserable and aspiring shoulders, which will not content themselves to take their roome below the head." Whately does not approve of casual wife-beating, but allows that if a man should have an "intollerable" wife, "he may launce his own arm where it swelleth."[22]

Derek Jarrett suggests that the eighteenth-century "over-

anxious masculine authoritarianism," which we can see in
A Bride-Bush, was a legacy of seventeenth-century Puritan-
ism, with its terror of feminine domination, "which it
seemed to link with sins of the flesh. It was no accident
that the book of Revelation, with its lurid image of an
enthroned woman as the ultimate evil, made such an
impression on the Puritans." The henpecked husband was
the most derided figure of fun in English life and literature. Jarrett reminds us that Dr. Arbuthnot's original John
Bull was such a ridiculous figure, constantly nagged by his
choleric wife for loitering in alehouses and billiard rooms.
"She had to be exorcized, along with John Bull's bovine
tendency to be led by the nose, before the sturdy archetype
of English freedom could emerge at the end of the century."[23] Another popular figure of fun more successful than
John Bull in managing his shrewish wife is clever Mr.
Punch, the anarchic lord of misrule who triumphs over
Judy, the baby, the policeman, the hangman, and, finally,
the devil. Punch, who was first seen on the terrace of Clarissa's own church, St. Paul's of Covent Garden, in 1662,
celebrates the triumph of the individual man over the demands of family and state, satisfying the most heartfelt
longings the Englishman may have had for liberty *and*
superiority.

The many conflicting attitudes towards sexual equality
indicate an uneasiness about the proper role of women.
One sociologist tells us that by 1750 "women were at the
lowest point of degradation. . . . they were useless, they
were uneducated, they were unnatural, their morality was
false, their modesty was false."[24] We are also told that
England in 1750 was a paradise for women. According to
Richardson, women were angels. "You must see," he wrote
to Lady Bradshaigh, "that the Tendency of all I have written is to Exalt the sex." (*Letters*, p. 112) "Exalt" is a happy
choice of words, for in the act of exalting, the worshipper
of the sentimental woman also degrades her. Perhaps historians and commentators debating the role of women were

frequently describing the same situation in different terms: the plight of the sentimental woman, both exalted and lowered at the same time.

In his history of women, written with the "utmost plainness and simplicity of language" for the less-educated women readers, Dr. Alexander remarks that "there is in the fate of women something Singular; they have at all periods, and almost in all countries, been, by our sex, constantly oppressed and adored. And what renders their case still more extraordinary, is, that we have not oppressed, because we hated, but because we loved them."[25] The extent of this oppressive adoration can be seen in an eighteenth-century appraisal of the high regard women enjoyed. England was "the place in the world where the fair sex is the most regarded, and perhaps, deserves to be so. . . . Nor is it easy to comprehend how it is possible to raise them higher with any show of reason, considering their natural incapacity for everything above the sphere they actually move in."[26] Sir Charles, placidly separating the cows from the bulls, could put it no better. In fact, after Sir Charles's speech about male superiority, Lady G., wise girl, immediately understands the importance of his attitude: "O my Sister, said I, taking Harriet's hand, we women are mere Nothings—We are nothing at all! How, my Charlotte! Make you no difference between being Everything and Nothing?" (III, 248) [VI, LV] Alas, there are not many differences between the two conditions. As long as she remained in her exalted sphere of influence in domestic and social life, a woman could be "everything." But if she was foolish enough to leave that sphere, she became "nothing." As Fulke Greville said, if women excell outside their sphere, they disgust rather than please.[27]

It was a commonplace of the time that women achieved their "power" and position of superiority, limited as that might have been, through submission. Dr. Alexander insisted that women could only rule through their "softness and good nature; they must ever be such as throw a veil over the pride of our supposed superiority, and make us believe, that we are exerting that sovereign power, which we consider as our right, when in reality we are yielding it up."[28] The French traveler Monsieur Grosley agreed that the Englishwoman's compliance actually created her power: "In fact, the English ladies and wives, with the most mild and gentle tone, and with an air of indifference, coldness, and languor, exercise a power equally despotic over both husbands and lovers; a power so much the more permanent, as it is established and supported by a complaisance and submissiveness from which they rarely depart."[29] Grosley's emphasis on the coldness and languor of the Englishwoman was not unusual in the eighteenth century. As we saw in the previous chapter, foreign visitors expected to find the English morose, melancholy, and suicidal. Grosley reported that "the gayest and most noisy of all the coteries" he had attended in London was a tea party in Bedlam, where he conversed with several "very neat and clean" madwomen, including the daughter of a French refugee."[30]

Women learned their "complaisance and submissiveness" at an early age. The Marquis of Halifax wrote an immensely popular book for the edification of young girls. His manual, *The Lady's New Year Gift: or Advice to a Daughter*, exerted a strong influence throughout the eighteenth century: by 1774, it had run through twenty-five editions. The marquis examines the nature of feminine power, a severely limited power, through submission, claiming that women "have more strength in [their] *Looks*, than we have in our *Laws*; And more power by [their] *Tears*, than we have by our *Arguments*." Nevertheless, the laws stand firm. One must "make best of what is setled by *Law* and Custom, and not vainly imagine, that it will be *changed* for your Sake." So much for the power of looks and tears. The wife, regardless of her personal feelings, must accept whatever she is given: there is nothing to do "but to endeavour to make that easie which falleth to their

Lot, and by a wise use of every thing they may dislike in a *Husband*, turn that by degrees to be very supportable, which, if neglected, might in time beget an *Aversion*."[31] Even a drunkard husband (and "it will be no new thing if you have a Drunkard for your Husband," Halifax warns) can be considered an advantage: "His *Wine* shall be of your side; it will throw a *Veil* over your Mistakes, it will set out and improve everything you do, that he is pleased with. Others will like him less, and by that means he may perhaps like you the more."[32] Halifax ignores the possibility that the drunkard husband may perhaps like his wife the less, not the more, and beat her bloody to demonstrate his dislike. It is worth noting here that we have now encountered the expressions "draw" or "throw the veil" three times: apprentices must draw the veil over their masters' faults; women must throw the veil over man's pride as they achieve power by submitting; and wine will throw a veil over the submissive wife's mistakes. Hypocrisy, it would seem, is an essential characteristic of the submissive inferior, the proper apprentice and the proper wife.

In his early work, Richardson expresses his own faith in the benefits of submission. A woman must accept her lot, he advises in the *Familiar Letters*. A mother "giving advice to her high spirited daughter" warns that "either *you* or *he* must give way; one of your tempers must be subdued and over aw'd by the other." Naturally, the daughter's temper must give way, since "meekness, condescension, forbearance, are so far from being despicable qualities in our sex, that they are the *glory* of it. And what is *meekness*, my dear, if you are not to be try'd by provocations?" To be "subdued and over aw'd" is the daughter's Christian as well as wifely duty, "the part of a tender *wife* to an *husband* . . . the part of a *Christian* to a Christian. . . . For are we not commanded to return *good for evil*, and to *pray for them that despitefully use us*?" (*Familiar Letters*, pp. 184-85) We must remember here the later Richardson, who presented the tragically ineffectual Mama Harlowe, a chilling model of wifely submission, "subdued and over aw'd" by her husband and son. Subdued and sunk, completely unable to aid her own daughter, she is the logical result of the "meekness" Richardson ostensibly endorses. As he does so often, Richardson manages to have it both ways, recommending submission while he explodes the notion of wifely obedience.

Halifax wrote *The Lady's New Year Gift* for his fifteen-year-old daughter. Three years later, she married the third Earl of Chesterfield, of whom his son's biographer said, "little more need be told than that he was a man of morose disposition and violent passions."[33] Lady Chesterfield could thank her father for teaching her the meekness necessary to bear such a trying marriage. She also bore four sons. The eldest, the fourth Earl of Chesterfield, carried on his grandfather's tradition in his letters to his natural son, Philip Stanhope, in which he observes that women are "only children of a larger growth; they have an entertaining tattle and sometimes wit; but for solid, reasoning good-sense, I never in my life knew one that had it, or who reasoned or acted consequentially for four-and-twenty hours together."[34] Or, as Grandfather Halifax would have said, men are made for reason, women for compliance.

Well might a young bride cherish her drunkard husband. Marriage offered the only means of independence for the eighteenth-century woman. Pat Rogers argues for the importance of marriage, explaining that all women "enjoyed minimal legal rights with regard to property and the like. They had few civic opportunities, no professional openings. But if they married, they could exercise a respectable and indeed honoured function in the community." Pope, Rogers notes, celebrates the power of the submissive woman in his "Epistle to a Lady." The ideal woman is complaisant and submissive:

Or if she rules him, never shows she rules;
Charms by accepting, by submitting sways,
Yet has her humour most, when she obeys.[35]

Pope could be describing Pamela, a heroine he greatly
admired, for no one submits more gracefully than Pamela.
That Mr. B. needed to descend into the servant class to
find such a jewel reveals much about the subservient nature
of the ideal wife. The upper classes in *Pamela* are self-
willed, arrogant, and ill bred. Pamela's greatest challenge
is to reform her bad-tempered sister-in-law, Lady Davers,
who represents the spoiled, proud "quality" Richardson
found so objectionable. When Pamela is presented to the
neighboring gentry, the "ladies" snigger and sneer. The
Countess "of some hard Name, I forget what," stares "full"
in Pamela's face; Lady Brooks regards her "with such a
malicious sneering Countenance, I cannot abide her," and
Lady Towers, "with her usual free air," mocks her beauty:

> Well, Mrs. *Pamela*. . . . I should never care, if I had
> a Husband, and you were *my* servant, to have *you* and
> your *Master* in the same house together. Then they all
> set up a great laugh. I know what I could have said, if
> I durst. But they are Ladies—and Ladies may say any-
> thing.
> Says Lady *Towers*, Can the pretty Image *speak*, Mrs.
> *Jervis?* I vow she has *speaking* Eyes! O you little Rogue,
> said she, and tapp'd me on the Cheek, you seem born to
> undo, or to be undone! . . . I beg, said I, to withdraw;
> for the Sense I have of my Unworthiness renders me
> unfit for such a Presence. (I, 59-64) [I, 39-40]

We know who is unworthy in this scene.

Mr. B. explains the rudeness of the upper classes to
Pamela: they have been brought up improperly. "We are
usually so headstrong, so violent in our Wills, that we very
little bear controul." Indulged at home and in school, the
quality attempt marriage unprepared for the conflict: "The

Gentleman has never been controuled: the Lady has never been contradicted." The result: separate beds, "perhaps Elopements; if not, an unconquerable Indifference, possibly Aversion." (II, 283-85) [I, 401-3] To avoid such a fate, Mr. B. solves the problem neatly by marrying his servant, who eagerly undertakes the tasks B. sets before her. For Pamela, compliance is a way of life.

Pamela's zeal for housewifery expresses Richardson's most conservative ideas about the role of women. She is a throwback, gladly filling those humble tasks that the Georgian lady of the manor would have scorned. In their study of the English countrywoman, the Fussels found that the Georgian lady was becoming "less the housewife and more the lady of leisure. The duties of housekeeping, which she had shared so pleasantly, were beginning to be regarded as beneath the dignity of the female head of the house, and she was content to supervise in a rather more reserved way, possibly through the medium of her gentlewoman or housekeeper."[36] Pamela not only performs housekeeping duties but agrees to devote herself to the study of B.'s every need. He outlines his expectations, issuing forty-eight rules of behavior, one of which is "that I must bear with him, even when I find him in the wrong, *This is a little hard, as the Case may be!*" *He* must be "morally sure" that Pamela prefers him to all men; *she* must bear with his imperfections, watch and study his temper, "and if ever she had any Points to carry, any Desire of overcoming it must have been by Sweetness and Complaisance." By now the formula is familiar enough: women can overcome by sweetness and complaisance, can charm by accepting, "by submitting sway." It is no surprise to find that Mr. B. expects his wife, just as Richardson expects his good apprentice, to "draw a kind of Veil over [his] Faults; that such as she could not hide, she would extenuate." (II, 283-85) [I, 401-403] To his credit, Richardson later revised his notions of complaisance, as we can see in his letter to Solomon Lowe. Defending his refusal to marry Clarissa to a reformed Lovelace, Richardson suggests that Pamela's own marriage to her rake was far from perfect: "Nothing but such an implicit Obedience and slavish Submission, as Pamela shewed to all his Injunctions and Dictates, could have made her *tolerably* happy, even with a *Reformed* Rake." (*Letters*, p. 124)

However circumscribed married life might have been for a woman, it was considered necessary. Life was too dangerous for the woman alone in the world. As Sir Charles Grandison points out, men are responsible for women's welfare: "Were it not . . . for male protectors, to what insults, to what outrages, would not your Sex be subject? . . . I, for my part, would only contend, that we men should have power and right given us to protect and serve your Sex." (III, 248) [VI, LV] Protection from what? The man protected the weaker sex from its own frailty, the evil that lies in the bone, the female sexual nature. Ironically, the very man designed to protect the woman was also ready to despoil her when her guard was down. Unless carefully checked by parents and guardians, the young woman would surely succumb to her own nature. In a "familiar letter" to a "Young Lady, advising her not to change her Guardians, nor to encourage any clandestine Address," Richardson characteristically warns that "I have known several young ladies of your age impatient of the least controul, and think hardly of every little contradiction; but when, by any unadvised step they have released themselves, as they call it, from their try'd friends, how often have they had cause to repent their rashness." (*Familiar Letters*, p. 59)

Women needed protection from their own sexuality, and what better protection than the blessing of a "persuading husband." "How unaccountable are young ladies," Richardson mused to Mrs. Dewes, "who have not the blessing of a *controlling*, or perhaps it would be better said, of a *persuading* husband." (*Correspondence*, vol. IV, p. 111)

Marriage offered the only acceptable way of life: the single life invited either temptation or ridicule and scorn. "Hard fate! poor girls," Richardson recognized, "to be punished with opprobrium if they slide (the tempter and the temptation ever at hand), and with contempt, if they escape sliding; and if some lordly man look not down in pity upon them!" (*Correspondence*, vol. IV, p. 254) In his correspondence, Richardson manages to combine complacency and sympathy, pitying his "poor girls," but never showing any real interest in altering the social realities of his world. In his fiction, however, he appears more subversive. His characters struggle against their "hard fate," exposing the social hypocrisy central to their conflicts. Even a peripheral character like Miss Sally Godfrey, the mother of Mr. B.'s illegitimate child, serves to point out the hypocrisy implicit in Mr. B.'s world. "*I wonder whether poor Miss* Sally Godfrey *be living or dead*," (II, 290) [I, 406] Pamela wonders as Mr. B. issues his forty-eight rules of proper behavior. Richardson clearly perceives the discrepancy between B.'s rules and B.'s own behavior.

One problem the eighteenth-century woman encountered was the choice of her "controlling" husband. The Marquis of Halifax flatly stated that the young girl had no choice at all: "It is one of the Disadvantages of belonging to your *Sex*, that young Women are seldom permitted to make their own *Choice*; their Friends care and Experience are thought Safer Guides to them, than their own *Fancies*."[37] In his letters and novels, Richardson seemed to challenge such an intransigent point of view, but never absolutely. As his biographers suggest, "in spite of his numerous lectures" on the question of parental authority in marriage, Richardson "never managed to be altogether clear" on the rights a woman held in choosing her marriage partner.[38] In a typical exchange with Susanna Highmore he argued, "Is indulgence the measure of obedience? Is the girl to be the judge; and is she to dispense with the word and thing called *duty*, should her parents be less indulgent (if not quite unreasonable; if not absolute Harlowes) than she would have them be?" (*Letters*, p. 131) Could the girl dispense with the "thing called *duty*" or not? The crucial phrase "absolute Harlowes" obscures the issue of filial obedience entirely. For how could the young girl judge whether or not her parents were Harlowes? Richardson himself created a world of absolute Harlowes, driving Clarissa out of her house into Lovelace's waiting carriage while he chastised her for her "faulty" behavior.

Fortunately for the eighteenth-century woman, Clarissa's plight was uncommon. G. E. Mingay found it "unusual" for girls to be married "against their will to displeasing suitors, no matter how appropriate the family connexions. There were some unsuitable marriages, of course, particularly those entered into for political reasons (as when Lord Lansdowne secured the support of a Cornish landowner of sixty by marrying him to his niece of seventeen), but they were rare, except perhaps among the limited number of very influential families."[39] Yet the image of the unwilling bride, however rare in actual instances, possessed great power in the imagination. Fanny Burney, visiting Longleat, the former seat of Lord Lansdowne, thrilled to think of the forced marriage of the sixty-year-old Pendarves to her noble friend, Mrs. Delany. "Here," she wrote in her diary, "at this seat, that heartless uncle, to promote some political views, sacrificed his incomparable niece, at the age of seventeen, marrying her to an unwieldy, uncultivated country esquire, near sixty years of age, and scarce ever sober—his name Pendarves. With how sad an awe, in recollecting her submissive unhappiness, did I enter these doors!—and with what indignant hatred did I look at the portrait of the unfeeling Earl, to whom her gentle repugnance, shown by almost incessant tears, was thrown away, as if she, her person, and her existence were nothing in the scale, were the disposition of a few boroughs opposed them!" Entering the chapel where Mrs. Delany had been "sacrificed," Fanny Burney, "horror-struck," studied the altar as she recalled, "what an offering for ambition! what a sacrifice to tyranny."[40]

In her own memoirs, Mrs. Delany, a friend of Richardson as well as a friend of Miss Burney, recalled her sacrifice with more wit and humor than her indignant friend could manage. Her first meeting with Pendarves was inauspicious: "I expected to have seen somebody with the appearance of a gentleman, when the poor, old, dripping almost drowned Gromio was brought into the room, like Hob out of the Well, his wig, his coat, his dirty boots, his large unwieldy person, and his crimson countenance were all subjects of great mirth and observation to me." The mirth ceased, however, soon enough when she "formed an invincible aversion towards him . . . thought him ugly and disagreeable; he was fat, much afflicted with gout, and often sat in a sullen mood." When she refused to marry Pendarves, Lord Lansdowne frightened his niece into submission, threatening to have a former suitor dragged through the horse pond. The threat was effective: "Such an expression from a man of my uncle's politeness, made me tremble, for it plainly showed me how resolute and determined he was, and how vain it would be for me to urge any reasons against his resolution." All of her "friends" urged the match for its financial advantages: "no one considered the sentiments of my heart."[41] Nor, it appears, did anyone consider the financial settlement too carefully. After seven years of wretched married life, Mrs. Delany found herself a widow without even the small fortune she had expected and certainly earned. Understandably, Mrs. Delany, upon reading of Clarissa's own plight, wrote to Richardson that "I never had so great a Mixture of Pain and Pleasure in the Reading of any Book in my Life. . . . it is impossible to think it a Fiction."[42]

Like Clarissa, Mrs. Delany suffered an uncommon fate, but her sacrifice elicits a common compassion.[43] Her miserable marriage to "Gromio" was the logical extension of the advice given in Halifax's *The Lady's New Year Gift.*

When one submitted, one could become the bride of Pendarves. Fanny Burney, "horror-struck" by such an unequal marriage, never herself accepted a forced union. Her own marriage to the French refugee d'Arblay did not exactly please her family, but she remained beloved Fanny through it all. Nevertheless, she made her own sacrifices in other ways, serving as lady in waiting to the queen, at the expense of her own health and much against her own inclination, to bring honor to her family. She so admired her father that she even burned the manuscript of a play she was writing in deference to his wishes, assuring him that "I shall wipe it all from my memory, and endeavour never to recollect that I ever wrote it."[44] It was an age for sacrifice.

The eighteenth-century woman needed to attend to the wishes of her more "reasonable" friends because her own judgment was feared to be defective. Richardson suspected that women were inferior, tainted in some mysterious way with an original sin even more deeply rooted than the evil in man. As Miss Grandison says, *"There is no wickedness like the wickedness of a woman."* (II, 28) [III, V] Richardson claimed that "man, at the time woman was formed out of his rib, was in a state of innocence. He had not fallen. The devil had need of a helper: he soon found one in Eve. But, if I may be forgiven for a kind of pun, you seem to think, madam, that the faults of men lie in the flesh; the faults of women are deeper—they lie in the bone." (*Correspondence*, vol. VI, p. 165) If a woman's faults were to lie "in the bone," she needed to exercise restraint and reserve to check her "sliding" tendency. The result of this careful process of artificial repression was the sentimental woman, genteelly channeling her sexuality into acceptable outlets of benevolence and tearful sensibility.

Children, as well as parents, guardians, and husbands, saved the "natural woman" from herself. In a "familiar letter" to a "Gentleman of Fortune, who has Children, dissuading him from a Second Marriage with a Lady much younger than himself," Richardson points to the horrors of a childless marriage. Without children of her own to occupy her, the idle wife will "for want of so *necessary* an employment, look *abroad* for amusements and diversions, which however innocent in her first intentions, may not *always* end so." Temptation was ever at hand to lure the giddy woman to look for amusement "out of herself and out of her house." "Out of herself," yet paradoxically *in* her true self, for the true woman was the devil's first helper. Fortunately, children would domesticate the roving woman and keep her prudently occupied: "Childbed *matronizes* the giddiest Spirits, and brings them to reflection sooner than any other event." (*Familiar Letters*, p. 170)

Charlotte Grandison is a most edifying example of the matronized hoyden. Defiantly in need of being saved from herself, she easily confesses that "I believe we women are all rogues in our hearts." (I, 191) [I, XXXVII] Although she realizes that "childbed" will end her roguery, she is helpless to resist the "natural" conspiracy against giddy spirits. Ironically inviting Aunt Selby to visit her "baby-things," she outlines the matron's progress. "What wretched simpletons are we women! Daughters of gewgaw, folly, ostentation, trifle!" she complains. First we show our "sorry fellow" to friends and relations for their approval and praise. Then we show our presents, "our jewels, our laces . . . a sparkle gladdens the eye of every maiden that hangs admiring over them. Ah silly maidens! If you could look three yards from your noses, you would pity, instead of envying, the milk-white heifer dressed in ribbands, and just ready to be led to sacrifice." After a few proud months, the "poor soul" begins "to find apprehension take place of security. . . . And the poor fools, wrapping up their jewels in cotton, with sighs that perhaps they have worn them for the last time, and doubtful whom they may next adorn, cover the decked-out milk-white bed with their baby-things. And to this is your Charlotte reduced." (III, 358) [VII, XXXI] Reduced and exalted, nothing and everything.

After the birth of her child, Charlotte confesses her matronization; she stands forth, "an example of true conjugal felicity" at last. She reports that Lord G. has surprised her in the "natural" act of nursing her baby. Lord G. is "transported" at the sight of Charlotte in "an act that confessed the mother, the *whole* mother." Holding her "Marmouset . . . the little Leech," to her breast, Charlotte has turned into Sir Charles's beneficent cow, giving milk on her milk-white bed. The happy couple forget their "differences" for "the infant is the cement between us." Lord G., showing all of the generosity of the victor, vows that he will never take Charlotte's criticism seriously again: "Never, never more shall it be in your *power* to make me so forget myself, as to be angry!" Charlotte is trapped, matronized at last, for what good is roguery "if it lose its wonted power over you?" The scene closes with mother and child together: "Nurse, said I, bring me again our precious charge. I will be all the mother. I clasped it in my bosom. What shall I do, my little Harriet! Thy father, sweet one! has run away with my Roguery—." (III, 402-404) [VII, XLIII] Besides, children are such a "necessary employment" that a mother hardly has the time to be roguish. Charlotte ends her letter with a postscript: "My women are so impertinent, and my Marmouset is so voracious, that I have been forced to take two days for what once I could have performed in little more than two hours." (III, 409) [VII, XLIII]

When Charlotte Grandison excuses her "whimsical behaviour to Lord G." to her disapproving friend Harriet, she begs, "don't blame my *heart*: my *head* only is wrong." (II, 442) [IV, XXXVIII] Her conscious division of heart and head reveals Charlotte to be, under all of her bold posturing, a sentimental woman with a proper respect for the feeling heart. Reason was the province of the male, the feeling heart the province of the female. This sentimental faith in the heart, the feminine primacy of feeling over thought, excluded women from the cerebral world of men. Reason, in fact, was not to be encouraged, as we see in the case of Charlotte. Charlotte's head prevents her from respecting Lord G., and quite rightly, for he is clearly not her intellectual equal. Her "wrong" head prevents her from feeling "properly," submissively. To make it "right," she must sink her reason and give way to her feelings, becoming the "whole" wife and mother. As Charlotte ruefully recognizes, "I believe I think too much . . . and consideration is no friend to wedlock." (II, 320) [IV, XI]

The sentimental woman could display the feelings of her heart, but only proper feelings. To indicate her properly refined passions, she could shed tears plentifully. Fanny Burney observed with wonder the sentimental Miss Streatfield, who prettily cried on demand. At a house party, Mrs. Thrale claimed that "Sophy Streatfield is never happier than when the tears trickle from her fine eyes in company." To prove her point, she provoked "at breakfast, a scene, of its sort, the most curious I ever saw." "In a wheedling voice," Mrs. Thrale persuaded "the S. S." to cry for the company. While the rest of the company "in laughter, joined in the request—two crystal tears came into the soft eyes of the S. S., and rolled gently down her cheeks! . . . She offered not to conceal or dissipate them: on the contrary, she really contrived to have them seen by everybody. She looked, indeed, uncommonly handsome; for her pretty face was not, like Chloe's, blubbered; it was smooth and elegant, and neither her features nor complexion were at all ruffled; nay, indeed, she was smiling all the time." Such performances were not for Miss Burney: Mrs. Thrale imagined that "she'd be more likely to walk out of my house than to cry because I bid her." The others agreed that Miss Burney was "gentle enough" and could cry "on any proper occasion." "But I must know," Fanny warned, "what for."[45]

Richardson relished the delicacy of his women readers, who were made of softer stuff than Miss Burney. Toying with Lady Bradshaigh's emotional involvement with Sir Charles, Richardson teased her with hints of killing off his hero, making the outraged Lady Bradshaigh wail, "You love to make one weep, you *love* to *kill* people." (*Letters*, p. 295 n.) Richardson's own success suggests that a large number of readers loved to be *made* to weep. Tears of sentiment revealed delicate sensibility; only a brute like the insensible rake Mowbry could withstand the pathos of Clarissa's circumstances. And Lady Bradshaigh was anything but brutal. She tearfully told Richardson of the agony she suffered while reading the last volumes of Clarissa:

> It was purely out of gratitude, and to oblige you, I read the three last volumes. I expected to suffer, but not to that degree I have suffered. Had you known me, Sir, your good-nature could not have pressed me to a mortification so great as that I have experienced. But you do not know what a fool I am. What is such a warm constitution good for but to torment me?
>
> Had you seen me, I surely should have moved your pity. When alone, in agonies would I lay down the book, take it up again, walk about the room, let fall a flood of tears, wipe my eyes, read again, perhaps not three lines, throw away the book, crying out, excuse me, good Mr. Richardson, I cannot go on; it is your fault—you have done more than I can bear; threw myself upon my couch.

Her "dear man" begged her to read no more, "kindly threatened to take the book from me, but upon my pleading my promise, suffered me to go on." Having completed her task, she reported that she was still feeling the "effects" of her suffering: "My spirits are strangely seized, my sleep is disturbed; waking in the night, I burst into a passion of crying; so I did at breakfast this morning, and just now again. God be merciful to me—what can it mean?" (*Correspondence*, vol. IV, pp. 240-42)

What can it mean? Simply that Lady Bradshaigh is a sentimental woman of the first rank. She may wonder about the correct definition of the word "sentimental," as she demonstrates in her well-known question to Mr. Richardson: "Pray, Sir, give me leave to ask you (I forgot it before) what, in your opinion, is the meaning of the word *sentimental*." (*Correspondence*, vol. IV, p. 282) But she instinctively personifies the sentimental in her rarified posturing, her style, and her teasingly incognito romance with Richardson. The lengthy, repetitious description of her anguish perfectly exemplifies the sentimental style, which depends upon repeated assaults on the feelings:[46] "I lay down the book, take it up again . . . read again . . . again I read, again I acted the same part." Lady Bradshaigh consciously played her part to her audience, her "dear man" who suffered her to go on. Without an audience, the sentimental loses its force. Lady Bradshaigh acted out her lachrymose part for another audience as well: "Had you seen me, I surely should have moved your pity." Physically absent (indeed, at this point the two correspondents had never seen each other), Richardson was ever present in his admirer's imagination. His compelling, obsessive book "pressed [her] to a mortification" greater than she *expected* to suffer. For the sentimental woman expected to suffer: "What is such a warm constitution good for but to torment me?" Or, as Clarissa herself complains, *"Delicacy* (may I presume to call it?) *Thinking, Weighing, Reflection,* are not blessings (I have not found them such) in the degree I have them. . . . Oh! my dear! the finer Sensibilities, if I may suppose mine to be such, make not happy!" (III, 278) [II, 167] Yet delicacy was highly valued by its sufferers. Lady Bradshaigh obviously delighted in telling Richardson that she "burst into a passion of crying" in the night, "at breakfast this morning, and just now again." Writing to the moment, in the true Richardsonian manner, Lady Bradshaigh demonstrated her well-oiled emotions for her mentor's inspection.

The sentimental woman, as Lady Bradshaigh so thoroughly revealed, was free with her emotions, but the feelings she displayed were to be sublime, pure, unsullied by sexual passion. Armed with her punctilio, she could "burst into a passion of crying," but she could never take her "passion" any further. In his *Legacy* of patriarchal advice to his daughter, a manual of feminine behavior that overtook Halifax's *The Lady's New Year Gift* in popularity, Dr. Gregory warned against the impropriety of revealing the feelings. If a daughter should, happily, love her suitor (a qualification that says much about the age) he advises her "never to discover to him the full extent of your love, no not although you marry him."[47]

Clarissa's own delicacy and manners keep her "nature" in check. Lovelace complains of the problems of penetrating her punctilio: "Dear Creature!—Did she never romp? Did she never from girlhood to now, hoyden? . . . Sacrilege but to touch the hem of her garment!—Excess of delicacy!—O the consecrated Beauty! how can she think to be a wife! (IV, 216-17) [II, 383] How could the modest woman respond sexually? Her refined sensibilities carefully checked her sexual emotions. In preserving her chastity, she also froze her soul. "A modest woman must be naturally *cold*, *reserved*, and *shy*," explains Lovelace in one breath, while lamenting Clarissa's "natural" indifference in the next. He considers the way to break through his goddess's natural reserve: by intimidation, by love ("the amorous *Seesaw*, as I have called it"); and finally, by surprise. (IV, 377) [II, 492]

"Natural" reserve and coldness preserved the sensible woman's chastity but perverted her "natural" sexuality. The only way a modest woman could respond emotionally was as a victim. The love relationship between the "encroaching" male and the delicate female became sado-masochistic[48] out of necessity. The male, intent upon provoking a response from his victim, assaulted her sensibilities; the woman responded to his assault with a tearful display of emotion. "Indeed, my dear," Clarissa tells Anna Howe, "*I have*

thought more than once, that he had rather see me in tears,
than give me reason to be pleased with him." (IV, 337) [II,
465] Exactly. Tearful scenes provide greater freedom for
Lovelace's advances: "Then she spoke; but with vexation—
I am—I am—*very* unhappy—Tears trickling down her
crimson cheeks; and her sweet face, as my arms still encir-
cled the finest waist in the world, sinking upon my shoulder; the dear creature so absent that she knew not the honour she permitted me." (III, 240) [II, 141]

Mentally "absent," Clarissa is most physically present in
this scene. Lovelace delights in his lover's tears and ridicules the more tender-hearted rakes who retreat from emotional displays. Tears open a new realm of sensible pleasure for the connoisseur in sensation. "Silly fellows" spare
their lady's confusion and rob themselves of "prodigious
pleasure," and "at the same time deprive her of displaying
a world of charms, which only can be manifested on these
occasions." (IV, 114-15) [II, 314] Through her tears, the
modest woman released her sexual frustrations and aggres-
sions; in his cruelty, the immodest man found an outlet
for his sexual aggression.

Tears signal proper feelings. The rakish cousin Jackey
reports with wonder that in the B. household, under Pamela's benevolent influence, "here's strange Doings, as ever
I knew—For here Day after Day, one's ready to cry, without knowing whether it be for Joy or Sorrow!" (III, 320)
[II, 166] In the same vein, Aaron Hill boasted to Richardson of the refined sensibility of one of his youngest admirers, a boy about seven years old who was living with
the Hill family. Listening to Pamela's "Reflections at the
Pond," the child let loose a "succession of heart-heaving
Sobs; which, while he strove to conceal from our Notice,
his little Sides swell'd, as if they wou'd burst, with the
throbbing Restraint of his Sorrow . . his Eyes were quite
lost in his *Tears*: which running down from his Cheeks in
free Currents, had form'd two sincere little Fountains, on
that Part of the Carpet he hung over. All the Ladies in

Company were ready to devour him with Kisses."[49] The formula—tears and devouring kisses—taken to its extreme, results in the sado-masochistic relationship of the sentimental lovers.

Tears come easily in Richardson's world, a world of pain, where people are always hurting each other and getting hurt in the process. "What a world is this," Clarissa laments. "What is there in it desirable? The good we hope for, so strangely mixed, that one knows not what to wish for! And one half of mankind tormenting the other, and being tormented themselves in tormenting!" (II, 38) [I, 265] In Richardson's world, men and women torment each other automatically. As Sir Charles warns his sister, "Men and Women are Devils to one another. They need no other tempter." (I, 439) [II, XXXII] "For, are we not devils to each other," Lovelace asks Belford. "They tempt us; we tempt them." (III, 305) [II, 185] The outcome of the struggle is either marriage or seduction, both perilous states for women. Anna Howe quickly recognizes the trap of courtship: "to be cajoled, wire-drawn, and ensnared, like silly birds, into a state of bondage or vile subordination: to be courted as Princesses for a few weeks, in order to be treated as Slaves for the rest of our lives." (I, 191) [I, 131]

Richardson repeatedly employs the image of the tamed bird to describe the feminine condition. In vain, the subdued bird breaks her wings against her cage: eventually, she will submit. As Lovelace puts it, "We begin, when Boys, with Birds; and when grown up, go on to Women; and both, perhaps, in turn, experience our sportive cruelty." (IV, 12) [II, 245] Lovelace speaks for his age here. Using the same metaphor, the author of *The Art of Governing a Wife* warns: "O how miserable is the Man that marries a high-spirited Woman!" The wise husband trains his wife to submit: "A young Lion is easily tamed. A Bird grows fond of the very Wires of the Cage that confines him"; and so will the young bride grow fond of her cage.

"Since we see a Bear, being a Beast so unwieldy, that it seems not to know how to go upon the Ground, dance upon a Rope, who can despair of infusing all the good Customs and Qualities into a young woman that her Husband Shall propose."[50] Within such a social context, Miss Howe's aversion to the marital "state of bondage" can be more easily understood.

In the following passage, lengthy but too important to abridge, we can clearly see Lovelace's view of the conflict between men and women, illustrated in the "simile of a Bird new-caught":

> Hast thou not observed the charming gradations by which the ensnared Volatile has been brought to bear with its new condition? How, at first, refusing all sustenance, it beats and bruises itself against its wires, till it makes its gay plumage fly about, and overspread its well-secured cage. Now it gets out its head; sticking only at its Beautiful shoulders: Then, with difficulty, drawing back its head, it gasps for breath, and, erectedly perched, with meditating eyes, first surveys, and then attempts, its wired canopy. As it gets breath, with renewed rage it beats and bruises again its pretty head and sides, bites the wires, and pecks at the fingers of its delighted tamer. Till at last, finding its efforts ineffectual, quite tired and breathless, it lays itself down, and pants at the bottom of the cage, seeming to bemoan its cruel fate and forfeited liberty. And after a few days, its struggles to escape still diminishing as it finds it to no purpose to attempt it, its new habitation becomes familiar; and it hops about from perch to perch, resumes its wonted chearfulness, and every day sings a song to amuse itself, and reward its keeper.

> Now let me tell thee, that I have known a Bird actually starve itself, and die with grief, at its being caught and caged. But never did I meet with a Woman who was so silly—Yet have I heard the dear souls most ve-

hemently threaten their own lives on such an occasion. But it is saying nothing in a Woman's favour, if we do not allow her to have *more sense than a Bird*. And yet we must all own, that it is more difficult to catch a *Bird* than a *Lady*.

To pursue the comparison. If the disappointment of the captivated Lady be very great, she will threaten, indeed, as I said: she will even refuse her sustenance for some time, especially if you entreat her much, and she thinks she gives you concern by her refusal. But then the Stomach of the dear sullen one will soon return. 'Tis pretty to see how she comes to by degrees: Pressed by appetite, she will first steal, perhaps, a weeping morsel by herself; then be brought to piddle and sigh, and sigh and piddle, before you; now-and-then, if her viands be unsavoury, swallowing with them a relishing tear or two: Then she comes to eat and drink, to oblige you: then resolves to live for your sake: her exclamations will, in the next place, be turned into blandishments; her vehement upbraidings into gentle murmurings—How *dare* you, Traitor!—into How *could* you, dearest? She will draw you to her, instead of pushing you from her: No longer, with unsheathed claws, will she resist you; but, like a pretty, playful, wanton Kitten, with gentle paws, and concealed talons, tap your cheek, and with intermingled smiles, and tears, and caresses, implore your consideration for her, and your *constancy*: all the favour she then has to ask of you!—And this is the time, were it given to man to confine himself to one object, to be happier every day than other. (IV, 12-14) [II, 245-47]

In his description of the "new-caught" bird, Lovelace mixes remote Augustan abstractions with terrible physical detail. At first, all is safe and removed: he observes the "charming gradations" of the "ensnared Volatile" refusing "sustenance" in its "new condition." But suddenly, the physical detail of the struggle threatens the sense of complacency. The bird "beats and bruises" itself. Now Lovelace returns to the safer literary world of abstractions, making a pun out of the bird's agony as he describes the "gay plumage" that "flies" about the cage. But we are not allowed to forget the very concrete bird, who manages to push its head through the wires, "sticking only at its Beautiful shoulders." We are in the hands of a connoisseur here, who can appreciate the beauty of such pathetically trapped shoulders. Lovelace demonstrates a similarly detached sense of enjoyment when he describes the sufferings of his own caged bird, Clarissa, who gives him "prodigious pleasure . . . displaying a world of charms, which can only be manifested on these [painful] occasions." (IV, 114-15) [II, 314]

In the descriptions of Clarissa's struggles, we find a similar tension between objectivity and subjectivity. Richardson allows his heroine full scope for her passionate rantings, giving her the room to beat and bruise herself against the wires of her cage, but occasionally, at crucial moments, he withdraws his support, leaving her in slightly ridiculous and undignified positions. For instance, after her rape, "in a perfect phrensy," Clarissa begs Lovelace for "the highest act of mercy . . . to kill [her] outright upon this spot—this happy spot." In the ensuing struggle, Clarissa, on her knees, "clasping a chair with her face laid upon the bottom of it," snatches up her head from the chair, "and as hastily popping it down again in terror, hit her nose, I suppose, against the edge of the chair; and it gushed out with blood, running in a stream down her bosom; she herself too much affrighted to heed it!" Lovelace, fearful that she has stabbed herself with "some concealed instrument," prepares to "dispatch" himself with his sword when he discovers that "all [he] apprehended was but a bloody nose, which, as far as I know (for it could not be stopped in a quarter of an hour) may have saved her head, and her intellects." (V, 375-78) [III, 238-40] Bloody noses are not very dignified; indeed, noses altogether, as Sterne delightedly pointed out in the "Slawkenbergius's Tale," are rather ridiculous. Certainly Clarissa's own dramatic descent, from suicide to a bloody nose that "could not be stopped in a quarter of an hour," is both sudden and undignified. Even the internal rhyme is suspect: "hit her nose, I suppose."

To return to the bird, gasping for breath, we find it "surveys, and then attempts, its wired canopy." Again Lovelace plays with the tension between his objectively appreciative eye and the bird's agony: the bird beats and bruises its "pretty" head and pecks the fingers of its "delighted" tamer, whose obvious enjoyment degrades the physical suffering of his victim. But still, the bird ("I have known a Bird actually starve itself, and die with grief, at its being caught and caged") is allowed more dignity than the "captivated Lady," who foolishly is brought to "piddle and sigh, and sigh and piddle." A bird may starve, but a lady always answers the call of her stomach, and "comes to by degrees." The bird beats and bruises itself, but the lady only weeps, threatens, and finally submits, "like a pretty, playful, wanton Kitten." Lovelace complacently depends upon the "sense" of the sentimental woman: "It is saying nothing in a Woman's favour, if we do not allow her to have *more sense than a Bird*." For "sense," read "feeling," possibly even "the faculties of corporeal sensation considered as channels for gratifying the desire for pleasure and the lusts of the flesh," one of the several meanings of "sense" current at the time, according to the *Oxford English Dictionary*. For the feelings and the desire for "pleasure" eventually trap Lovelace's sentimental woman.

Lovelace the artist believes in the truth of symbols. Like a "bird new-caught," his Clarissa will come to "by degrees" in the end. But he is wrong. Clarissa lives in her own metaphoric world. As a saint on the rack, the example of purity for her sex, she would rather suffer the death of a martyr, as she methodically purges herself of her treacherous "feelings," than implore her seducer's "consideration." In his "simile," Lovelace displays ingenuity, egotism, and a tragic misunderstanding of his captured Clarissa. While insisting that Clarissa is an angel, sublime and untouchable, he still depends upon her appetite, her "stomach," to assist him in his seduction. But despite her stomach—for nineteen-year-old Clarissa Harlowe, in excellent health, does have a stomach—and even despite her own confused feelings for her rake, Clarissa can never surrender. In her own metaphoric world, the spiritual arena of the martyr, surrender is unthinkable.

Lovelace's metaphor of sexual conflict expresses Richardson's own recognition of the battle between the sexes, a battle he teasingly waged in his own provocative correspondence. He coyly confessed to Lady Bradshaigh that "I own that I really have so much cruelty in my nature, that I should wish to provoke you now and then, if I knew what would do it, consistent with respect and decency." (*Correspondence*, vol. IV, pp. 232-33) Baiting Miss Highmore, one of his more spirited young ladies, Richardson compared women to spiders, perfectly capable of catching flies but helpless under the finger of "giant man": "But shall I not affront you, if I compare you girls to spiders? Here Arachne (we will call the weaver) draws its web, spreads its snares; hangs up an entangled fly here; another there; a third, and a fourth, if she can get the buzzing insect into her purlieus; and then goes and turns one round, pats another, and enjoys her depredations as she pleases. But how miserably runs the recreant into her hole, when a powerful finger of some giant man brushes down or demolishes her cobweb! This may not exactly quadrate to any particular case; but it came into my head, and down it went." (*Correspondence*, vol. II, p. 220) Who has a more "powerful finger" than the man Richardson, author of the longest book in the English language? Later he confessed to Miss Highmore that "Mr. Edwards accuses me of loving to *tarantalise*; a soft word with him, for tyrannise.

. . . But I subscribe not to the censure." (*Correspondence*, vol. II, pp. 247-48)

In Richardson's conflict-ridden world, men are not always the aggressors, women the caged birds. The roles can be reversed. Lovelace insists that the savagery of women provokes his own sadistic behavior. Women, as well as men, "without the least remorse . . . ensnare . . . cage . . . torment, and even with burning knitting-needles . . . put out the eyes of the poor feather'd songster [Thou seest I have not yet done with birds]; which however, in proportion to its bulk, has more life than themselves (for a bird is all soul)." The bird has more "soul," the woman more "sense" and more sensual cruelty. Lovelace boasts that he once made a "charming little savage" repent her delight in "seeing her tabby favourite make cruel sport with a pretty [as usual, Lovelace's victims are attractive] sleek bead-eyed mouse, before she devoured it." He then tells of the "daughter of an old Epicure," an anecdote notably lacking in the Augustan abstractions we found in his caged-bird metaphor. Here Lovelace uses simple, forceful verbs and naked nouns: "Nor had I at another time any mercy upon the daughter of an old Epicure, who had taught the girl, without the least remorse, to roast Lobsters alive; to cause a poor Pig to be whipt to death; to scrape Carp the contrary way of the scales, making them leap in the stew-pan, and dressing them in their own blood for sawce." (IV, 15-16) [II, 247-48] The ferocity of the appetite in such a woman indicated a sensual nature frightening to the male. In *The Accomplished Fine Rake* (1727), Mrs. Mary Davys describes a dinner scene between her young rake and a whore who flays the skin off twelve roasted fowl. She confesses that "I have a great while longed to fill my stomach with the skins and rumps of fat roasted fowls, and that is all I shall eat." Her rake complains as she seizes the eleventh fowl, flaying it "like a rook." "The next time we dine together," he predicts, "you shall flay me. Sure the whole race of whores are the offspring of Epicurus."[51]

It is worth noting that the tortures the old epicure's daughter inflicted upon animals were not unknown in the eighteenth century. To tempt the jaded palate, "all manner of dreadful tortures were devised for the living animals . . . turkeys were bled to death by hanging them upside down with a small incision in the vein of the mouth; geese were nailed to the floor; salmon and carp were hacked into collops while living to make their flesh firmer; eels were skinned alive, coiled round skewers and fixed through the eyes so they could not move. . . . Calves and pigs were whipped to death with knotted ropes to make the meat more tender." "Take a red cock that is not too old and beat him to death," begins one of Doctor William· Kitchiner's recipes.[52] Clarissa's horror (and Lovelace's anger) towards a world "so strangely mixed" where one half of its creatures torment the remaining half is understandable within such a social context.

Richardson uses Anna Howe to present the woman's view of the sexual conflict. Her cold, unblinking recognition of the war between the sexes dominates her letters. She derides her docile suitor, the colorless Hickman, to keep him at bay: "If I do not make Hickman quake now-and-then, he will endeavour to make me fear." Nature is in a constant state of siege: "All the animals in the creation are more or less in a state of hostility with each other." Once, enraged at a "game-chicken, that was continually pecking at another (a poor humble one, as I thought him)," Miss Howe had him caught and "wrung his neck off" in a *"Pet of Humanity."* After *"his* insulter was gone," the remaining bird grew insolent, "and was continually pecking at one or two under *him.* Peck and be hanged, said I—I might as well have preserved the first; for I see it is the *nature of the beast."* (III, 230) [II, 134] The pecking order is maintained at a terrible cost. Miss Howe must persecute her suitor, lest he triumph over her. If Clarissa lets down her punctilio, she will be overcome. Most marriages in Richardson's world continue the sexual battle on another level, as a state of siege or subjugation. Mr. Harlowe tyrannizes his wife, provoking even Clarissa to criticize her mother's slavery. Mrs. Howe is now a widow, but her former marriage had been a battleground for supremacy. In fact, the portraits of marriage Richardson presents, of slavery or struggle, contradict his explicitly moral stance. While recommending marriage highly, he explodes the myth of marital bliss.

In the battle between the sexes, fear provides a formidable weapon. Solmes relishes Clarissa's aversion, which gives him the chance to terrorize her into submission. He smugly claims that *"Fear* was a better security than *Love,* for a woman's good behaviour to her Husband." (I, 302) [I, 206] Of course, Solmes is odious: his brutal sadism is not endorsed by the author. Or is it? Solmes may guard an extreme flank of the war between the sexes, but he expresses, for Richardson, truisms. As Richardson admitted in one of his letters, "I am sorry to say it, but I have too often observed that fear, as well as love, is necessary, on the lady's part, to make wedlock happy; and it will generally do it, if the man sets out with asserting his power and her dependence." (*Correspondence,* vol. VI, p. 130) Solmes looks forward to asserting his power; Clarissa's submission, were it to come too early, would spoil the fun. Anna Howe reports his theories of marital harmony to Clarissa: "Fear and Terror, the wretch, the horrid wretch!, said, looked pretty in a Bride as well as a Wife: And laughing [Yes, my dear, the hideous fellow laughed immoderately, as Sir Harry told us, when he said it] It should be his care to perpetrate the occasion for that *Fear,* if he could not think he had the *Love."* (II, 66) [I, 284] Solmes would have applauded Judge Buller's ruling in 1782 that "it was perfectly legal for a man to beat his wife as long as he used a stick which was not thicker than his thumb."[53]

One of the reasons for Richardson's insistence upon the physical and mental conflict implicit in sexual relationships is that, on the whole, life without conflict did not interest him. He rejected a happy ending for *Clarissa* because it would have opposed his own view of reality. As he admonished Lady Bradshaigh, a fervent supporter of "Clarissa Rewarded," a writer "who follows Nature and pretends to keep the Christian System in his Eye, cannot make a Heaven in this World for his Favourites; or represent this Life otherwise than as a State of Probation." (*Letters*, p. 108) Happy endings alone make life not only unrealistic but stagnant and dull. "Indeed," he tells Lady Bradshaigh, "the best of our Happiness here is but Happiness by Composition, or Comparison. A becalmed life, is like a becalmed Ship." Cloying happiness does not satisfy: "The very Happiness to which we are long accustomed, becomes like stagnated Water, rather infectious than salutary. *The full Stomach loaths the Honeycomb*. There are sighs that proceed from fullness as well as from Emptiness." (*Letters*, p. 107) We are back in the world of Lovelacian metaphor, but here Richardson opposes his character's libertine faith in "the stomach." Clarissa would rather starve than answer the call of her appetite.

For Clarissa is a sensible woman. And how would one exercise refined sensibility if one were happy? The contented and quiescent person soon loses her sensitivity. Delicacy and sensibility never fatten and grossly prosper. The fallen world forces the feeling person to pit herself (for the feeling person is usually a woman) against circumstances and enter the conflict. Richardson cautioned Miss Highmore that simple content is impossible: " 'Quiet content, you aim at, and not at heroism.' Know you not, my dear, that in such a world as this, and with a feeling heart, content is heroism." To feel, one must suffer. Richardson warned Miss Highmore not to "call those best friends, who give you most pain; yet Lovelace says that women love those best, whether husband, lover, or children, who give them the most uneasiness. Indeed, they must love, or it would not be in the power of the ingrateful to make them uneasy; but, this is more than I intended to say on this subject." (*Letters*, pp. 162-63) "Yet Lovelace says." Richardson often looked to his character's pronouncements on the more delicate points of sexual warfare. Although he qualified his suggestion ("but, this is more than I intended to say on this subject"), the point is clear: pain can be attractive.

Anna Howe discusses the attractive nature of pain in several of her letters. Lovelace, she predicts, would keep a woman's passions alive. No stagnated waters in his wake! He arouses a woman. Comparing him to Hickman, she decides that insolence is essential to a successful courtship: "I very much doubt whether a little intermingled insolence is not requisite from them, to keep up that interest when once it has got footing. Men must not let us see, that we can make fools of them. And I think that *smooth* Love; that is to say, a passion without rubs; in other words, a passion without passion; is like a sleepy stream that is hardly seen to give motion to a straw. So that sometimes to make us fear, and even for a short space, to *hate* the wretch, is productive of the *contrary* extreme." (III, 185) [II, 103]

Clarissa is more ambivalent. On the one hand, she longs for a suitable "protestant" nunnery to hide her from the encroaching world of "man." On the other hand, she prefers the liveliness of a Lovelace to the serenity of a Hickman. Anna Howe coyly compares the two lovers: "Your man, as I have lately said, will always keep up attention; you will always be alive with him, tho' perhaps more from fears than hopes; While Mr. Hickman will neither say anything to keep one awake, nor yet, by shocking adventures, make one's slumbers uneasy." (III, 294) [II, 177-78] Preferring uneasy slumbers to sound sleep, Miss Howe bequeaths Hickman to Clarissa. Insight, as well as vanity, later prompts Lovelace to predict that "had I attacked Miss Howe first, her passions (inflamed and guided, as I could have managed them) would have brought her to my lure in a fortnight." (V, 274) [III, 168] Clarissa politely refuses an exchange of suitors, leaving Hickman—serene, calm, accountable—to Anna Howe in order to set out for rougher waters.

Richardson's heroines always seek aggressive men who will keep their passions alive. Pamela's Mr. B., popping in and out of corners, may be inept, but he is never boring (until his reformation). Lovelace plays a perilous game with Clarissa, provoking her into feeling through love, fear, and surprise. His foreplay is more mental than physical: he predicts that the sensible woman first responds to provocation with her tears; her physical surrender will follow. Finally, Harriet Byron's love for the good man, Sir Charles, causes her as much pain as happiness. The torture Sir Charles inflicts upon faithful Harriet is more mental than physical—minutely detailed descriptions of his protracted and uncertain courtship of the mad Clementina— but certainly effective. Sir Charles's letters from Italy cause Harriet to suffer those "uneasy slumbers" Miss Howe values. In a world of conflict and pain, Richardson's heroines learn not merely to endure their suffering, but to appreciate it.

An analysis of the sexual conflict implicit in *Clarissa* cannot be completed without looking at Richardson's presentation of the Harlowe family's part in that conflict. Until her defection, Clarissa, prudently rejecting improper suitors and modestly yearning for a nunnery, has been a "good child." But, to the horror of her family, Lovelace provokes a sexual response from the good child. Not that her family expects her to remain a virgin. For financial reasons alone, she must marry—but on their terms. Mrs. Harlowe, passively overseeing her daughter's sale to Solmes, serves as the wifely (and motherly) model. "Little did the good old Viscount think," muses Anna Howe, "when he married his darling, his only daughter to so well-appearing a gentleman, and to her own liking too, that she would have been so much kept down. Another would call your

Father a Tyrant, if I must not." (I, 90) [I, 130] Even the meek mother complains of her lot: her husband is "needlessly jealous, I will venture to say, of the prerogatives of his Sex, as to me, and still ten times more jealous of the authority of a Father." (I, 117) [I, 80]

Incestuous fantasies haunt the gloom of Harlowe Place. The dear uncles, cracked brother, and gouty father channel their unsatisfied desires into a violent struggle for control over Clarissa. Since the unacceptable marriage to Lovelace would gratify Clarissa's own desires, her family insists that she marry another, the more odious the better. The Harlowes repeatedly savor the future horrors of the wedding night between Clarissa and Solmes. What better way to satisfy their own desires than by mentally raping their victim? The rapist cannot be attractive, or their victim might enjoy the assault. He must be Solmes, a true sadist, who salivates at the thought of bringing his mistress to heel.

The Harlowe family members eagerly remind Clarissa of Solmes's sexual power over her. As her husband, he will be able to exact payment for her aversion. Betty, Clarissa's "saucy gaoleress" warns her that she "*must* have Mr. Solmes: That therefore I had not best carry my jest too far; for that Mr. Solmes was a man of spirit, and had told HER that as I should surely be his, I acted very *unpolitely*; since, if he had not more *mercy* [that was *her* word; I know not if it were *his*] than I had, I might have cause to repent the usage I gave him to the last day of my life." (II, 71) [I, 288] Solmes's cruelty becomes even more terrible when it is endorsed by the Harlowe family. Brother James especially expresses an intensely sexual energy and a terrible desire to see his sister at the "mercy" of Solmes. Clarissa reports one of the many instances of his violence:

He bolted upon me so unexpectedly, that I was surprised. He took my hand, and grasped it with violence. Return, pretty Miss, said he; return, if you please. You shall not yet be *bricked up*.—Your *instigating* Brother shall

save you from That!—O thou fallen angel, said he,
peering up to my downcast face—such a sweetness *here*!—
and such an obstinacy *there*: tapping my neck.—O thou
true woman—tho' so young!—But you shall not have
your Rake: Remember that; in a loud whisper, as if he
would be decently indecent before the man. You shall be
redeemed, and this worthy gentleman, raising his voice,
will be so good as to redeem you from ruin—and hereafter you will bless him, or have reason to bless him for
his *condescension*; that was the brutal Brother's word! (II,
208-209) [I, 381]

James's fascinated horror at his sister's sexuality pervades
the passage. She will *not yet* be "*bricked up*," a punitive
check on her sexual energy. A "true woman," a fallen angel, Clarissa will be saved from her true self, from her
offensively sexual nature, as the victim of her redeemer
Solmes's sexual appetite.

James's "decently indecent" proposal of Solmes as savior
neatly solves the problem of the fallen angel: her redemption will nullify her fall, for her sexuality will only be
abused, not indulged, in such a relationship. While Clarissa as a sexually independent woman horrifies James, Clarissa as a true victim, blessing her rapist for his "condescension," gratifies him. Anticipating the sacrifice of Clarissa
on her wedding night, James whips himself into a frenzy
of revenge as he goads Solmes to carry out his own fantasies of sexual assault on his sister. His "eyes flaming with
anger," he urges Solmes to persevere: "After she is yours
. . . make her as sensible of your power as she now makes
you of her insolence." (II, 230) [I, 396]

Solmes's power is manifestly sexual: The "fell wretch
. . . his hollow eyes flashing fire . . . biting his underlip,
to show he could be manly," boasts that he will soon have
it in his power to show—Clarissa breaks in, "You have it
in your power, sir." Solmes hedges: "To shew you more
generosity, than, noble as you are said to be to others, you

shew to me. The man's face became his anger: it seems formed to express the passion." Brother James enters: "Sister, Sister, Sister, said he, with his teeth set, act on the termagant part you have so newly assumed—most wonderfully well does it become you. It is but a short one, however. Tyranness in your turn, accuse others of your own guilt—But leave her, leave her, Mr. Solmes; her time is short. You'll find her humble and mortified enough very quickly—Then, how like a little tame fool will she look, with her conscience upbraiding her, and begging of you [with a whining voice the barbarous Brother spoke] to forgive and forget!" (II, 235-36) [I, 399-400]

"Sister, Sister, Sister, said he, with his teeth set." Clarissa, fallen angel, has progressed from an obedient, asexual child to become an independent, sexual woman of eighteen. James's anticipatory delight in her punishment strangely resembles Lovelace's own sexual fantasies of a humbled, mortified Clarissa, "a little tame fool," whining and begging forgiveness for her resistance.

Lovelace, Solmes, and James Harlowe all seek to control Clarissa. Ironically, Solmes exploits the Harlowe family's fear of Lovelace to secure his position as favorite just as Lovelace exploits Clarissa's aversion to Solmes to lure his victim into his waiting carriage. The relationship between brother James and Lovelace becomes even more complicated. Richardson draws intriguing parallels between the two men. Clarissa describes her brother as "a Plotter without a head, and a Brother without a heart." (I, 55) [I, 38] Lovelace fares better as a plotter *with* a head, but Clarissa still decides that "he wants a *heart*: And if he does, he wants everything." (I, 296) [I, 202] Both men treat their victim like a game bird, setting elaborate snares to trap her. Clarissa reports, "Thus, my dear Miss Howe, has my Brother got me into his snares; and I, like a poor silly bird, the more I struggle, am the more entangled." (I, 163) [I, 112] We have already seen Lovelace's elaborate use of the hunt and the "bird new-caught," reluctantly accepting its imprisonment.

Lovelace likes to think that he is the master manipulator of the Harlowe family, predicting that he will make brother James "dance" upon his "own wires." (I, 215) [I, 147] Belford disagrees that James Harlowe is merely Lovelace's puppet and suggests that the rake, not the brother, is being manipulated: "what art thou more, or better, than the instrument even of her implacable Brother, and envious Sister, to perpetuate the disgrace of the most excellent of Sisters, which they are moved to by vilely low and sordid motives?" (IV, 123) [II, 320] In their unrelenting obsession to mortify Clarissa, both James Harlowe and Lovelace become mechanical, "machines," exploiting themselves as well as each other to achieve their goal. When Lovelace arrives with Clarissa at St. Albans, he impersonates a dear brother safeguarding his wanton "sister" from her sexual desires for a "confounded rake": "I topt the Brother's part on Monday night before the Landlady at St. Albans; asking my Sister's pardon for carrying her off so unprepared for a journey; prated of the joy my Father and Mother, and all of our friends, would have on receiving her; and this with so many circumstances, that I perceived, by a look she gave me, that went thro' my very reins, that I had gone too far." (III, 56) [II, 16] And, of course, Lovelace does go too far, acting out the sexual fantasies brother James can only express in his rigidly authoritarian attempt to rule his sister through Solmes.

Like the Harlowes, Lovelace ultimately wants to degrade Clarissa, to abuse her sexuality. If she is ever to be awakened sexually, she must be a slave to *his* desires, not a sensual being in control of herself. The delicate woman, sublimely repressed, is truly more sister than lover, more victim than partner to man. In such a world of repression and sadism, sexual desire for the sublime woman becomes distorted and incestuous. In *Clarissa*, Richardson examines this distortion as a part of the struggle for mastery that dominates sexual relationships. As a daughter, sister, and lover, Clarissa struggles to establish her own sexual identity, but in the face of such opposition she is forced to sublimate her sexual nature and turn herself into an angel not of this world, safe in death from violation.

In *Sir Charles Grandison*, the conflict between the sexes persists underground. All the power of *Clarissa* has been domesticated. Richardson still toys with the idea of incest: Sir Charles's admiring sisters, his oddly platonic relationship with Clementina, and his peculiar habit of adding passionate admirers like little Emily to his "family" seem vaguely incestuous. But the incest implication, like Hargrave's attempted rape, never actually threatens; it only teases the reader.

In *Grandison*, Richardson makes some of his strongest statements about the war between the sexes, but he allows the war to be waged only in theory. Harriet Byron recognizes the enemy and warns that "men, many men, are to be look'd upon as savages, as wild beasts of the desart; and a single and independent woman they hunt after as prey." (I, 64) [I, XIV] Like Miss Howe, Harriet Byron uses animal imagery to emphasize the savagery of the struggle: "The hyaena, my dear, was a *male* devourer. The men in malice, and to extenuate their own guilt, made the creature a *female*. And yet there may be male and female of this species of monsters. But as women have more to lose with regard to reputation than men, the male hyaena must be infinitely the more dangerous creature of the two; since he will come to us, even into our very houses, fawning, cringing, weeping, licking our hands; while the den of the female is by the highway-side, and wretched youths must enter into it, to put in her power to devour them." (I, 24) [I, VI]

At first, *Grandison* seems to promise action. Miss Byron appears to be "proper prey" for Greville, a rakish type who comes into her "very house . . . fawning, cringing, weeping, licking" and biting her hands. In one encounter, "the strange wretch pressed [her hand] so hard to his mouth, that he made prints upon it with his teeth." When Harriet withdraws her hand, he snatches the other, "and patting it, speaking thro' his closed teeth, You may be glad you have an hand left. By my soul, I could eat you." (I, 101) [I, XX] But all the cannibalistic threats are mere posturing. Greville never does more than snarl and gnash his teeth. The more serious threat, Sir Hargrave Pollexfen, miserably fails to seduce Harriet, losing three front teeth in the fray. "Men and Women are Devils to one another," but not in Sir Charles's drawing room. The conflict persists on the periphery of the novel, but at the center punctilio reigns.

Sir Charles, Harriet reports, "is used to do only what he ought. Dr. Bartlett once said, that the life of a good man was a continual warfare with his passions." (II, 157) [III, XXII] Vowing never to be seen "by those I love," in "passion," (III, 49) [VI, XVIII] Sir Charles proves victorious. Harriet Byron brilliantly captures his unrelenting nobility when she wonders, "Do you think, my dear, that had he been the first man, he would have been so complaisant to his Eve as *Milton makes Adam*. . . . No; it is my opinion, that your brother would have had gallantry enough to his fallen spouse, to have made him extremely regret her lapse; but that he would have done *his own duty*, were it but for the sake of posterity, and left it to the Almighty, if such had been his pleasure, to have annihilated his first Eve, and given him a second—But, my dear, do I not write strangely?" (II, 609) [V, XXXI]

In Sir Charles's well-regulated world, annihilation is no more than Eve deserves. By allowing Miss Byron to mock her lover's rigid sense of morality, Richardson allows her to voice his reader's own annoyance with the saintly paragon. But Sir Charles still remains the good man, the moral model, and there is no room for troublesome Eves in the Grandisonian paradise. Mark Kinkead-Weekes suggests that

Grandison expresses Richardson's most heartfelt wishes for a communal society of good men and women, "to overcome human isolation and to lay hold of an image of people bound together by stronger ties than blood."[54] Certainly Richardson's last novel seems to attempt to palliate the tragic isolation of *Clarissa*. Clarissa had yearned for the world to be one large family; Sir Charles creates such a world by virtue of his goodness.

His goodness, however, is a masculine goodness, and his vision of the ideal community expresses Richardson's most conservative sexual attitudes. For Sir Charles, there is no wickedness like the wickedness of a woman. As the good man, he must protect and curb the weaker sex from its own frailty as well as from the encroaching hyaenas of the male sex—for neither his sister Charlotte, who lacks the sense, nor his lover Harriet, who lacks the strength, can stand alone. While Richardson expressed his faith in the strength and self-sufficiency of women through Pamela and Clarissa, both heroines who could not only stand alone but triumph alone, he expressed his greatest pessimism through Sir Charles. His paragon advocates a family of man, but one severely patriarchal. Rebellious Clarissa would not have enjoyed being part of it. We must look back to *Clarissa* for Richardson's celebration of the actions of a woman who answers only to herself.

THREE • Down from the Pedestal: The Fallen Woman in Richardson's World

> There is no wickedness like the wickedness of a woman.
> CHARLOTTE GRANDISON (II, 28) [III, V]

> A fallen woman is a worse devil than even a profligate man.
> LOVELACE (III, 338) [II, 208]

> A woman without delicacy is a beast; a woman without the *appearance* of delicacy is a *monster.*
> The Lady's Magazine[1]

ALTHOUGH Sir Charles Grandison would have annihilated Eve for her transgressions, Richardson was not so doctrinaire in his own life. He befriended "fallen" women, contributed to the Magdalen House, and even gave financial and emotional support to the dubious Laetitia Pilkington.[2] Yet in spite of his acts of charity, Richardson revealed a strong dislike for the fallen woman, fearing always the "true woman" that lurked beneath every modest young girl's facade. Both feminine figures—the sublime, pure maiden and the fallen woman—animated the imagination of the eighteenth century. While the sentimental "angel" was honored for her sexually sublimated nature, her fallen counterpart often absorbed the sexual aggression withheld from the angel. However chaste the angel might be, she was always in danger of falling: no one was ever safe from ruin. Richardson's world was filled with pitfalls for the modest woman: seducers and rapists lurked in every shadow. Even while he regarded the whore with disgust, Richardson seemed compelled to dwell upon the sexual nature of the fallen woman and the potentially fallen nature of her angelic counterpart.

To understand Richardson's fictional treatment of the fallen woman, we should first look at the sexual stereotypes of the eighteenth century in history and literature. Letters, memoirs, diaries, court records of rape trials, whores' biographies, and, of course, the novels, help to recreate, at least in part, the historical "reality" the fallen women of Richardson's time would have experienced. The records themselves, however, reflect the prejudices of their age, making an absolute historical truth impossible to recover. When we look at the sentimental novels and plays, the stereotypes tell us one important thing: virtue had to be tested, proven under fire. Only after undergoing her trial could the sentimental object of adoration be elevated to her proper sphere. And even at the pinnacle, she was still at risk, liable to fall. The elevated woman, preserver of morality, won her exalted place because she had been lowered, literally or figuratively. Fallen women serve as a warning, in part, to keep their respectable counterparts in place.

On the surface, Richardson follows the degradation/elevation formula. As we have seen, "virtue in distress" energizes his best work. For one concerned with the preservation of feminine chastity, Richardson certainly placed his own modest heroines in compromising situations, threatening rape and ruin to them all, degrading and elevating them at the same time. Treating them as accessibly "low," he established their nature: they were women, not angels. Their sufferings, however, would purify them, exalting them again to their angelic heights. Mr. B. treats Pamela like a common slut, pinching and prodding her, threatening to strip her, and calling her vulgar names, before he raises her to his lofty heights. Once she has become Mrs. B., she is sublimely untouchable. Harriet Byron must be mortified both physically (when she is almost raped by Sir Hargrave) and emotionally (when she suffers the humiliation and suspense of waiting the outcome of Sir

Charles's courtship of Clementina) before she receives her reward. Clarissa, imprisoned in a brothel, raped, and thrown into a sponging house, suffers the greatest humiliation but also receives the greatest reward: she literally as well as figuratively becomes an angel too good for this world.

Yet in spite of his adoption of the sentimental formula, Richardson transcends its limitations. His heroines become characters of integrity and independence, women who support themselves and forge their own fates. As we shall see in comparing traditional sentimental heroines with Pamela and Clarissa, Richardson's heroines elevate themselves, depending ultimately upon themselves for their salvation.

As we have already seen, Richardson's imagination subverted and transcended his moral intentions. His didacticism freed him to write, to take up issues and problems that he could not have investigated without a moral license. Then, released from his moral censor, he could create fictions of sensation and power that often threaten to burst their moral framework. Behind his circumstantially realistic facade, a fantastic, lurid sensibility is always at work in his fiction. Ostensibly, he described his fallen whores in loving detail to frighten his reader into virtue, just as he allowed his Lovelace to rape Clarissa in order to keep other young misses from a fate worse than death. In theory, his reader swallows the gilded pill of morality for his (or more likely her) own good. But in practice, in the real world that Richardson longed to redeem through his fiction, the virginal reader is just as likely to sigh for a Lovelace to undo her and to entertain fantasies of leaving her father's house on the next coach loitering outside the garden wall. And why not? If Clarissa, paragon among maidens, cannot escape her fate, who else can? Yet Mr. Richardson continues to warn, wagging his finger in his reader's face, underlining his moral with his intrusive footnotes blackening Lovelace's character, always careful to illustrate the pit yawning beneath the foolish young reader.

When I began this study and looked into the pit Richardson offers his reader, I assumed that the author's obsession with virgins and their fallen counterparts was not only lurid and sensational but highly unrealistic. Richardson's fantasies of abduction and rape, brothels and rakes, read like a hothouse variety of daydream. But as I began to investigate the social and historical reality of the eighteenth century, I discovered that when he seems most lurid Richardson may in truth be the most realistic. Or, more precisely, he writes realistically of a world that his readers believed to be true, using their own assumptions to authenticate his fictions. Writing to his reader, tucked safely away in the country—or, if she lived in the city, snug in her closet, the urban equivalent of paradise—Richardson warned against the monstrous evils of London, where Harriets could be kidnapped and Clarissas raped, where whores passed for ladies and rakes ruled the day. He was endorsing the communal fears and beliefs of his readers. His treatment of this material remains subversive, but the sexual stereotyping Richardson exploits in his fictions, the fallen reality he presents to be true, reflects a "reality" his readers recognized. Richardson the artist transcends the limitations of the sentimental formula while Richardson the realistic moralist exploits and develops the cultural biases and beliefs of his readers.

Here is one such belief, a commonplace of Richardson's time: whores were everywhere in London, clogging the streets and crowding the corners with their soiled wares. And most contemporary observers of the eighteenth century would support this "fact." Fifty thousand whores (the most frequently quoted number) roamed the streets, every one of them somebody's fallen sister, daughter, or wife. Archenholtz, one of the historians offering this high figure, added that he appreciated the profession of prostitution: like Mandeville, he applauded a system of private vices and public virtue. Without whores, he predicted that London would fall. Outlawing prostitution would be "very pernicious to the trade and commerce of a country like

England. If it was resolved to establish at London, as there was at Vienna, a tribunal of Chastity, the great city would soon be depopulated; the natural melancholy of the English would exceed all bounds; the fine arts, in terror, would fly from the country; numberless methods of subsisting which give bread to one half of the inhabitants would be annihilated, and that superb metropolis be changed into a wild and weary desert."[3] Misson, another foreign visitor, reported that whores could be found everywhere, "distributed all the Town over."[4] They mainly concentrated in Covent Garden or Drury Lane, but, as Grosley reported, the whores, with "more liberty and effrontery than at Rome itself," ranged themselves at night "in a file in the footpaths of all the great streets in companies of five or six, most of them dressed very genteely."[5]

The great number of prostitutes may have been exaggerated. The figure of 50,000 was issued by a London magistrate, Patrick Colquhoun, in his *Treatise* on the indigent and criminal population.[6] His statistical methods, casual at best, were challenged in 1839. Leon Radzinowicz cites a report drafted by Chadwick, which noted that "the whole male population of London, Westminster and the parishes within the Bills of Mortality was, according to the census of 1801, only about 400,000. On this basis, after deducting the number of children and aged, there would be left not more than 150,000-200,000 who might be considered as supporting the vice of prostitution. 'Allowing that all were licentious in their habits, the learned Magistrate's estimate gave one prostitute for every three or four males, and alleged that every third or fourth female was a professed prostitute.' " Radzinowicz finds Colquhoun's estimate unlikely, but adds that "even assuming them to be grossly inaccurate, they were significant because they were accepted at the time as statistical measurement of the crime and immorality then prevailing."[7] Richardson's own abhorrence of prostitutes is more easily understood when we realize that whether or not there actually were thousands of whores lining the footpaths, people of the time believed this to be the case. In London, women lived over a precipice. For Richardson, the threat of the great numbers of whores served as his moral imperative: women needed to be saved from themselves and their seducers.

The power of *Clarissa* comes partly from the power of Richardson's own beliefs, however warranted: London was a wilderness of vice; seducers and rapists were everywhere; once fallen, always fallen. Richardson's triumph lies in his unorthodox and personal use of such conventional wisdom. That London was a "wilderness" of vice was an eighteenth-century commonplace. A collection of three vade mecums for country gentlemen, warning them what to expect in London, offers a remarkable similarity in both content and language. The first manual, *Tricks of the Town laid open: or a Companion for Country Gentlemen*, a 1747 reprint of a vade mecum originally published in 1699, warned that London was "*a kind of large Forest of wild Beasts, where most of us range about at a Venture, and are equally Savage, and mutually destructive one of another.*"[8] The second vade mecum, *A Trip Through the Town*, in its fourth edition in 1735, says the same thing: London is "a Kind of large Forest of *Wild Beasts*, where most of us range about at a venture, and are equally savage, and mutually destructive one of another."[9] The warning in *A Trip from St. James's to the Exchange* should come as no surprise: again London is "a Kind of large Forest of wild Creatures, ranging about at a venture, equally savage, and mutually destructive of each other."[10] Books like these three vade mecums and King's *Frauds of London*, also warning the country gentry of the tricks of the town, reinforced a belief in the evils of London. Whether or not "wild creatures" ranged about the London wilderness, ready to debauch the naive visitor, the country gentleman, armed with his manual, expected and no doubt even hoped for the worst.

In his own *Familiar Letters*, Richardson did his best to warn off the unwary visitor to London. He included the letter of a young lady who managed to elude the snare of a procuress. Fresh from the country and looking for employment, the young girl is "overtaken by an elderly gentlewoman of a sober and creditable appearance," who sends her to "Mrs. C in J——n's Court, Fleet Street." The neighborhood, she reports, "looked genteel." (As it should. Richardson himself lived close by in Salisbury Court, Fleet Street. Richardson emphasizes the imprudence of letting down one's guard anywhere, no matter how genteel the surroundings may appear. Procuresses were everywhere, even in one's own respectable courtyard.) Mrs. C, dressed in "a splendid manner," leads the unsuspecting lady to her parlor, "elegantly furnished," where she offers her negus, a punch of wine, warm water, and orange. The country girl recalls that Mrs. C "ply'd me very close with the liquor, which she again said was innocent and weak; but I believe it was far otherwise; for my head began to turn round, and my stomach felt a little disordered." Barely minutes before the "disordered" girl would have been forced into prostitution, she is providentially warned of her fate by a young gentlewoman, "dress'd in white sattin, and every way genteel," who tearfully tells her that she is "now in as notorious a brothel, as in London." The lady in white satin explains that she too was lured into the evil house, detained by force, and robbed of her virtue. "Thus, in a shameful round of guilt and horror, have I lingered out ten months; subject to more miseries than tongue can express." With the lady's help, the country girl escapes, "in so much hurry and confusion, as to leave [her] hood, fan, and gloves behind [her]," but not her virtue. Richardson adds: "N.B. This shocking story is taken from the mouth of the young woman herself, who so narrowly escaped the snare of the vile procuress; and is fact in every circumstance." (*Familiar Letters*, pp. 72-76) All of the elements of the collective seduction fantasy are here in Richardson's "true" warning: the victim in white, the drugged wine, the seemingly benevolent procuress. Only the miraculous escape is different.

Richardson's warning expressed a common fear of the time—that Mother Midnights lurked on every corner and frequented every coach stop to carry off unsuspecting young ladies. Archenholtz reported the scandalous practice of the procuresses meeting the daily coaches. Poor, innocent country girls, coming to town for employment, would happily accept "the friendliest advances" of the seemingly respectable "mothers." He warned that "bawds and false officers of justice are ever on the watch, the most infernal stratagems are practiced, and the most abominable snares are laid for [the country girl], till yielding to necessity, the poor abandoned creature consents to her irretrievable undoing."[11]

To prevent such practices, Sir John Fielding, a chief magistrate deeply concerned with moral reform, issued a special warning to "young ladies new to London":

> Any one of these, who happens to have a fresh look and a tolerable share of beauty, will have also very good fortune, if she escapes the delusive snares, which are laid daily by the agents of hell for the ruin of innocence.
> . . . Immediately on their arrival in town, and sometimes sooner, even upon the road to it, there are miscreants of both sexes on the watch to seduce the fresh country maiden, with infinite protestations of friendship, service, love and pity, to prostitution, shame and misery. For this purpose the very carriages which convey them are hunted and examined; the inns, where they are to alight, are beset by these infernal hirelings, who, as the Devil is said sometimes to appear like an angel of light, put on the demure shew of modesty and sanctity for their deception.

Even if the country girl did manage to escape the procuresses meeting her stage (she may have been warned by Hogarth's first engraving of *A Harlot's Progress*), she still faced danger: snares were everywhere. If she went to the registry office to seek employment, warned Sir John Fielding, she risked further involvement in prostitution, for "most of these have close connections with the pimping tribe."[12] Registry offices were notorious haunts, "the markets of pimps and procuresses" and "warehouses of iniquity."[13] In his tract, *Virtue in Humble Life*, Jonas Hanway warned that "no country lass can suspect half the wicked arts which are played off to seduce young females in that sink of iniquity, *London*. . . . great caution is necessary in going to what they call *public registry offices*."[14] Dorothy Marshall reports that these offices "were mere frauds, run by sharks, having only too often an uncomfortably close connection with the trade of prostitution."[15] John Moir sternly warned in his manual *Female Tuition* that "you had better turn your daughter into the street at once, then place her out to service. For ten to one her master shall seduce her, or she shall be made the *confidante* of her mistress's intrigues."[16] The servant girl evidently could never relax. Even if she could find a genuine position and managed to escape the snares of her master, she was still warned to beware of public places. In his study of prostitution, Michael Ryan warned that "another fertile source of vice is the practice of sending nurse maids and female servants with children into the royal parks, and squares, where there are always seducers, procurers, or procuresses."[17] And there were *always* seducers, procurers, or procuresses out there in Richardson's world. The threat of seduction animated the imagination of the eighteenth century.

Rape is the central action of *Clarissa*, but it also enters into Richardson's other novels. Harriet Byron narrowly escapes being raped and forced into marriage to the villainous Sir Hargrave; Pamela is threatened with rape several times. Curiously, all the rapes would seem to be communal affairs. Lovelace employs Mother Sinclair and her nymphs to overcome Clarissa. Sir Hargrave uses his servant, a "horrible-looking clergyman," and one Mrs. Awberry, accompanied by her two good daughters. While B. first attempts to seduce Pamela on his own, he quickly resorts to the aid of massive Mrs. Jewkes, who delights in holding down her victim. Later on, B. even considers sending in the repulsive Colbrand to subdue rebellious Pamela, reversing the tradition of *droit de seigneur*.

The threat of rape (what could one weak girl do to protect herself from so many attackers?) served to keep the young girl at home, out of harm's way. *Clarissa* was Richardson's most chilling warning: if his saint could not escape her fate, what chance would a common girl out and abroad ever have? And any young girl out on her own was clearly asking for it. Richardson suggests that on some level Clarissa and Harriet provoked their punishment: Clarissa should never have left Harlowe Place; Harriet should not have succumbed to the temptations of the masquerade. The young girl, to protect herself against the encroaching male, was to stay at home under the protection of—the encroaching male, now acting in a more domesticated role as husband, father, or brother. For one woman's brother could be another woman's seducer.

Nice problems of moral behavior become murky here. Clarissa, under Richardson's code, should never have left the protection of her home. Yet her alternative to flight was the odious Solmes. A rape upon her person committed by her legal husband, no matter how unwanted, would in society's eyes be no rape at all. Faced with the prospect of enduring Solmes's "love," a prospect eagerly awaited by James and Bella, Clarissa can only flee her home. Lady Mary Wortley Montagu archly noted that any girl "that runs away with a young Fellow without intending to marry him should be carry'd to Bridewell or Bedlam the next day."[18] But if Solmes had been forced on an unwilling Clarissa, the violence of his "love," and the force of her aversion would probably have also driven her into Bedlam.

To rape is to attempt to master, to assert one's will upon another. Solmes's desire for mastery is fairly straightforward: he wants to subdue Clarissa, to punish her for her obvious contempt for him. Lovelace's reasons for raping Clarissa become more complicated: he wants to know her, to penetrate her most inner part and, by knowing her, master her. But his rape fails miserably. As R. F. Brissenden points out, the rape is a "failure on all counts, a completely hollow victory. In the first place, he has to drug her into insensibility, so that it can be regarded as a token rape only; in the second, the result of the assault is not to make Clarissa love him but to confirm her hatred and contempt for him."[19] Clarissa continues to battle Lovelace even in her death, vowing she "forgives" the "wretch" his sins. After her death, Lovelace commands Belford to give him Clarissa's heart, "to which I have such unquestionable pretensions, in which once I had so large a share, and which I will prize above my own." He plans to "keep it in spirits. It shall never be out of my sight." (VIII, 48) [IV, 376] Unable to capture her soul, Lovelace will content himself with the pickled heart torn from the corpse of his beloved.[20]

It is appropriate for Lovelace to seek the ownership of Clarissa's preserved heart, for rape is not only an act of mastery but an act of possession. Under English law in the eighteenth century, victims of rape were considered in two categories, as victims of sexual molestation and as victims of property theft. Bride capture or "heiress stealing" was a well-known way of obtaining both a woman and a fortune. Heiress stealing was made a nonclergyable offense[21] punishable by death under Henry VII in 1486. The statute 3 Henry VII c.2 refers to any person who "against her will, took away any woman, whether maid, widow, or wife, who had substance either in goods or lands, or was an heir apparent, and afterwards married her or consented to her marriage to another, or defiled her." By 1597, the benefit of clergy was also taken away from procurers or accessories before the fact. As Radzinowicz points out, heiress stealing "was not a purely sexual offence—the predominant motive

being economic—and therefore it could perhaps be included in the class of offences against property."²² In 1615,
the twelve-year-old daughter of Mr. Bruton was carried
off into another county, where she was forced to marry one
Morris. Since Bruton already had a son for his heir, his
daughter, neither an heiress nor an owner of property in
her own right, had no legal recourse. Her case was judged
not within the statute, "for men will not commonly steal
women that are nothing worth." The statute against heiress
stealing came up for repeal in the Parliamentary Commit-
tee of 1770, but was retained. Edmund Burke defended
the statute, arguing that "no crime could be more atrocious
than a rape of this sort, its consequences being even worse
than those of murder, since they insuperably connected the
aggrieved woman with the person she abhorred."²³ In his
history of women, Dr. Alexander praised English rape
laws for affording "to the public all the security which the
law can give for the chastity of their wives and the legiti-
macy of their children."²⁴ Patrilineal descent and chastity
of the "wife" rather than the "woman" may have been
safeguarded, but the rights of the unpropertied, unmarried
woman were often in question.

In the eighteenth century, prosecution for rape was difficult. The charge of rape could only be sustained, stated
Blackstone, when the offense had been committed "against
the woman's will." If the consent were obtained by fraud,
it was no rape.²⁵ Since only the victim and the rapist could
know the truth, rape was difficult to prove. Unfortunately
for the victim, many jurors refused to believe that a woman
could truly be raped. As Swift ironically suggested in his
ballad celebrating the case of Dean Sawbridge of Fernes,
sentenced to hanging for rape:

> If Maidens are ravish't, it is their own Choice,
> Why are they so willful to struggle with Men?
> If they would but lye quiet, and stifle their Voice,
> No Devil nor D———n could Ravish 'em then.²⁶

Clarissa would have found it difficult to prove her own rape in a court of law. Wisely, she refuses to prosecute Lovelace, arguing that "little advantage *in a Court* (perhaps bandied about, and jested profligately with) would some of those pleas in my favour have been, which *out of Court*, and to a *private* and *serious* audience, would have carried the greatest weight against him—such, particularly, as the infamous methods to which he had recourse." (VII, 230) [IV, 184] Her assumptions are correct, for Lovelace has carefully established his innocence publicly. Under law, the rape victim was required to report the crime as early as possible. According to Blackstone, early English law required that after the rape, the woman was to "go to the next town, and there make discovery to some credible persons of the injury she has suffered: and afterwards should acquaint the high constable of the hundred, the coroners, and the sheriff with the outrage." In the reign of Edward I, the victim had forty days to make the complaint. By the eighteenth century, when Blackstone wrote his commentaries, the time limit had officially disappeared, but he warned that "the jury will rarely give credit to a stale complaint." Clarissa's own complaint would surely have been considered stale. She was raped the night of 12 June, escaped from Lovelace on 28 June, and was still explaining her reasons for *not* prosecuting on 19 August.

Since the rape victim was frequently her only witness, her word was to be unimpeachable. Blackstone cites Matthew Hale's judgment that if she "be of evil fame, and stand unsupported by others; if she concealed the injury for any considerable time after she had the opportunity to complain; if the place, where the act was alleged to be committed was where it was possible she might have been heard, and she made no outcry, these and the like circumstances carry a strong, but not conclusive presumption that her testimony is false or feigned."[27] Runaway Clarissa stands unsupported, cast off by her family and friends. From the start, Lovelace carefully implicates her in her own seduction, introducing her to his friends as "his wife," and exposing her publicly at the theater, at church, and at Hampstead. Clarissa never contradicts his claims about their marriage: her sense of discretion and her faith in the power of her own integrity inhibit her instinct for survival. In a court of law, "bandied about, and jested profligately with," Clarissa would have had little chance of winning her case.

The problems Clarissa would have encountered in court can be seen in the case of Sarah Woodcock v. Lord Baltimore. Miss Woodcock, a twenty-nine-year-old milliner, claimed that Lord Baltimore entrapped her, held her captive, and raped her. Although she accused him of raping her on 21 December, she did not make a formal complaint against him until 29 December, a delay that helped Baltimore's defense. After the rape, Baltimore, like Lovelace, introduced Miss Woodcock to his friends socially. Lord B. examined her on this point: "During the time these people were there, did you betray by your manner or countenance that anything extraordinary had happened to you?" Sarah answered, "No I did not; I supported myself as well as I could." Lord Baltimore, on the other hand, was able to parade forth numerous witnesses supporting his version of the case: the laundry maid, the cook, the postilion, the footman, the butler, the land steward, the housemaid, a friend of eight years' standing, the housekeeper, a carpenter in his employ, the music master, and finally another butler. Not surprisingly, all witnesses (most of whom were in Baltimore's employ) supported the defense argument that Sarah Woodcock had been a strumpet willingly for His Lordship. Their testimony apparently overwhelmed the medical evidence that the body of Miss Woodcock had suffered a good deal of violence. Miss Woodcock's story failed to convince the court. The judge explained his caution in the matter, pointing out that rape is a crime "which in its nature can only be proved by the woman on whom it is committed: for she only can tell whether she consented or no; it is . . . very easy to be made and hard to be disproved."[28] Lord Baltimore was acquitted, but he still left England forever, accompanied by his modest harem of eight houris, two black attendants (whom he called his Corregidores, because they policed his women), and a personal physician.[29]

We have Richardson's own opinions on another famous case of seduction. In 1748, Mrs. Muilman published *An Apology for the Conduct of Mrs. Teresia Constantia Phillips.* She claimed that in 1721, when Constantia was thirteen years old, she met Lord Chesterfield, a man whom, we remember, considered women only "children of larger growth." "On such adventures [he] went by the name of Thomas Grimes."[30] After several declarations of love, Chesterfield *"press'd her extremely to drink a Glass or two of Wine, and when she consented, he deceiv'd her, by giving her Barbadoes Water."* When Constantia asked to go home (the Barbadoes Water "was not sufficient to lull her into a great Submission"), Chesterfield detained her by force. "Tears and Prayers were all in vain." Then, according to Mrs. Muilman, Chesterfield ripped open the lacing of Constantia's coat with a penknife, "which he perform'd with such a Precipitation, as even to cut her," and raped her. After two months of dalliance, he deserted her.[31] Bonamy Dobrée discounts the scandalous story, arguing that Chesterfield merely "had a perfectly ordinary low amour with Miss Phillips, even then by no means so intact as she pretended." (Mr. Dobrée does not give us more definite information about her shady adolescent past.) Despite the popularity of the *Apology*, which went into a second printing, Dobrée claims that "nobody who mattered seemed to take any notice" of the scandal.[32]

However, Richardson noticed, and at first appeared sympathetic to Mrs. Muilman's story. In 1748, he wrote Lady Bradshaigh, "What think you has not Mr. Grimes to answer for, in the ruin of Constantia Phillips when but Eleven Years of Age, and abandoning her to the Town in two Months, if the Story she tells be true?—What Ruins,

the Consequences of *her* Ruin, may not be laid at his Door."
(*Letters*, p. 115) But in 1750 he appeared to have withdrawn his sympathy, for he published Mrs. Chapone's defense of Lord Chesterfield, *Remarks on Mrs. Muilman's
Letter to the Right Honourable the Earl of Chesterfield.* He
also wrote to Mrs. Chapone that Mrs. Muilman, Mrs.
Pilkington, and Lady Vane were "a Set of Wretches, wishing to perpetuate their Infamy." (*Letters*, p. 173) A political sense of discretion or perhaps a more personal disgust
at the many memoirs depicting sexual outrages changed
Richardson's mind. We must remember, however, that
Clarissa arranges to have the epistolary record of her own
outrage published—a memoir that in "real life" would have
created an infamous stir.

In spite of the difficulties of proving rape, man still
could not rape with impunity. Colonel Francis Charteris,
a notorious adventurer, was found guilty of the rape of
Anne Bond in 1730, a conviction long overdue. Even his
generous biographer, E. B. Chancellor, who generally admires rakes as "rather . . . decorative, even delightful
fellow[s]" who awaken a "fellow feeling," finds Charteris
disgusting, the "complete negation of everything which
mankind has been taught to honour and respect."[33] We can
see a picture of Charteris in the first plate of Hogarth's *A
Harlot's Progress*: he stands in the doorway with his pander
Gourley, watching Mother Needham procure Moll Hack-
about.[34] The dubious *Authentick Memoirs* of Charteris reveal that the colonel's usual method of seduction resembled
Mr. B.'s plans for Pamela. Aided by a bawd with the
improbable name of Mary Clapham, a veritable Mrs.
Jewkes, he entrapped and raped young women. Mrs.
Clapham would hold the victim "fast by her Shift," ignoring the girl's cries, knowing her business too well "to
be diverted from it by Tears and Intreaties."[35] Before his
1730 trial, Charteris had already been prosecuted for one
rape in Scotland: a miller accused him of raping his wife
at gunpoint. Since Charteris fled Scotland to escape pros-

ecution, he was automatically found guilty, but he received a pardon for the crime in 1722. In 1728, Fog's *Weekly Journal* reported his growing reputation: "We hear a certain Scotch Colonel is charged with a Rape, a misfortune that he has been very liable to, but for which he has sometimes attained a *Nolle Prosequi*. It is reported now that he brags that he will solicit for a Patent for ravishing whomever he pleases, in order to put a stop to all vexatious suits which may interrupt him in his pleasures hereafter." It is not surprising that in 1730, at the age of seventy, in spite of the usual testimony of the usual servants and employees (this time a valet, a servant, the housekeeper, the master of a ship, and an upholsterer) claiming their employer's innocence, Charteris was found guilty of rape.[36]

Just as Charteris's reputation as a whoremonger helped to convict him of rape, Lord Baltimore's own reputation helped to save him. Baltimore was, above all, a peer. The indignity of coming to trial at all, he insisted, should serve as ample punishment for any crime: "Libertine as I am represented, I am sure I have sufficiently atoned for every indiscretion, which a weak attachment to this unworthy woman may have led me into, by having suffered the disgrace of being exposed as a criminal at the bar."[37] Simply, he was an aristocrat, while his victim, that "unworthy woman," was merely a common milliner. When a woman dared to step out of her class (or when she was involuntarily pulled out of it, as in the case of rape), she exposed herself to great risk.

All women were at risk when they were out and abroad, especially when the quality mingled with the servant class. Women, it was feared, were becoming too bold; they needed to learn their place. A fluid social system threatened any proper sense of order: no longer could one distinguish between mistress and servant; they acted alike, dressed alike, and frequented the same public resorts.[38] Daniel Defoe complained that it "is a hard Matter now to know the

Mistress from the Maid by their Dress, nay very often the maid shall be much the finer of the two." The maid from the country quickly became a "town lady" who could "drink Tea, take Snuff, and carry her self as high as the best."[39] Monsieur Grosley noticed that servant maids "attend their ladies in the streets and in the public walks, in such a dress that if the mistress be not known, it is no easy matter to distinguish her from her maid."[40] The author of *A Trip from St. James's* reported his own difficulty in telling mistress from maid: he observed a lady who was "moving with such awful State and Majesty, that her graceful Deportment bespoke her nothing less than a Person of the first Rank. . . . *A Countess*, who I thought was going to give her an Invitation to the Opera, or to make a party at Quadrille, gave her a gentle Reprimand for loading her fine *Brussels* Head and Ruffles with such a Quantity of Starch."[41]

The servant maid might have looked like a lady, but it was frequently suspected that she acted like a whore. Mr. B. makes a logical mistake when he assails Pamela's virtue; she is, after all, a lady's maid. Defoe described the "amphibious life" of domestic servants who "rove from Place to Place, from Bawdy-House to Service, and from Service to Bawdy-House again, ever unsettled, and never easy." Their roving way of life disrupted society: "this Amphibious Life makes 'em fit for neither, for if the Bawd uses them ill, away they trip to Service, and if their Mistress gives 'em a wry Word, whip they're at a Bawdy-House again, so that in Effect they neither make good Whores or good Servants."[42] In his satirical *Directions to Servants*, Swift addressed the servant girl as if she were Shamela herself, exploding any pretense of virtue: "If you are in a great Family, and my lady's Woman, my Lord may probably like you, although you are not half so handsome as his own Lady. In this Case, take Care to get as much out of him as you can; and never allow him the smallest Liberty, not the squeezing of your Hand, unless he puts a

Guinea into it." He advises her to make her master pay
for every new attempt, "threatening to cry out, or tell your
Lady, although you receive his Money: Five Guineas for
handling your Breast is a cheap Pennyworth, although you
seem to resist with all your Might; but never allow him
the last Favour under a hundred Guineas, or a Settlement
of twenty Pounds a Year for Life."[43]

In Richardson's world, where servants may look like
ladies and act like whores, there is a terrible fear of appearances. Lovelace can establish Clarissa in a brothel, sur-
round her with whores masquerading as ladies, and pass
off his valet for a gentleman friend of Uncle John's. A
"correspondent" to Richard Steele's magazine *The Theatre*
described a similarly treacherous world of appearances. Be-
lieving that she was visiting people of quality, genteel
"Leucippe of Oxford" was in fact lured to a brothel: "It
is the manner of those houses to give each other the names
and titles of such women of beauty and quality as they
resemble in air, shape, and stature; and upon novices and
foreigners they impose them as the real persons: but I remember there was my Lady Dutchess of such a place, a
charming hussey; then the Countess of elsewhere; then my
Lady Dowager of a third town; then a superannuated Vol-
unteer, an old bully, who was called Sir John, and his
tawdry consort, one after another, deigned to salute me."
In such a complicated world of disguise, the innocent have
no defenses. Leucippe succumbed in the end.[44] Goodness
and purity were never enough to combat such artifice.
Wrapped in her mantle of integrity, Clarissa still finds
herself raped, thrown into prison, and finally dying in a
questionable area of Covent Garden, that "great square of
Venus," where enough lewd women strolled "in sufficient
numbers to populate a mighty colony."[45] Her own church,
St. Paul's of Covent Garden, was notorious as a trysting
place. But then Richardson always managed to place his
spotless heroine in unsavory situations. Hampstead, once
fashionable, had by the early half of the eighteenth century

become a low resort descended upon daily by coaches filled with "crowds of disreputable characters, male and female, attracted by the gambling and other low diversions."[46] Yet Clarissa, instinctively pure, ends up there twice, once accompanied by Lovelace, once pursued by him. Clarissa repeatedly compromises herself by simply being in the wrong place at the wrong time.

Eighteenth-century London held snares for the unwary man as well as the innocent woman. The monstrous fallen woman (who was, we must remember, initially seduced by the monstrous male) was always abroad. Magically, the innocent victim, ravished and betrayed, had become overnight a hardened whore who delighted in ruining men. A strumpet, warned Captain Alexander Smith in his history of cuckolds, "is the Highway to the Devil: and he that looks on her with Desire, begins his Voyage: He that stays to talk with her mends his pace; and whosoever enjoys her, is at his Journey's end."[47] In *The Secret History of Clubs*, Ned Ward described a particularly disgusting meeting of whores, the Bawd's Initiating Club. "Airy *Phillis*" bolts in, her "taudry Silks half torn off her Back;" a Miss Daphne rattles in "with torn Pinners, a black Eye, and her beautiful Phiz full of revengeful Scrathes [*sic*]." All the while Madam Bibbington sits, "Drunk as the Devil, with her Garments so disoblig'd by Second-hand Claret, that she stinks as bad as a Country Sheriffs Breath at the latter-end of the Sises." The whores "swear like *Scotch* officers; talk Bawdy like so many Midwives; boast of their Bed-Adventures like Bullies of their Duels, and open all their loose Intrigues with as much Pleasure, as they do their Arms to a vig'rous Gallant." The women so far "excell the lewdest of Men in all Manner of Obscenity, that it would make a Rake blush, and the worst of Libertines abjure the Conversation of all Mercenary Harlots to be Witnesses of their Impudence."[48]

Ward sounded as morally outraged as Belford in his warning against the lewdness of whores. Yet whores could and did pass for genteel, neat ladies. They fooled Leucippe of Oxford, and they even fooled the scrupulous Miss Harlowe. Henry Meister reported that the "Priestesses of Venus" in London had "more reserve and timidity, with a degree of decorum and even prudery, beyond anything to be found among bacchants of our country."[49]

The more respectable whore was at least genteel enough to be admitted to church, where she continued to ply her trade. Richard King warned that old bawds frequented church services with their "young nun (as they themselves call her) on their arm who, whilst the old creature, with eyes cast upwards, simulates piety and utters hypocritical prayers, tries to lead astray some man suitable for her purpose. When the service is over, the old woman on going out stumbles suddenly, falls down or faints as suits her purpose."[50] The young man would naturally escort the mother and daughter home to "stay on." Unknowingly, he had been procured. Prostitutes also used newspaper advertisements to procure their business. Archenholtz reported that advertisements frequently represented whores "as young, well-educated and of considerable means," looking for a husband. In return they would only ask for "small capital" or "decent business." The inexperienced often "fell—and woke to find himself—but too late, betrayed."[51]

Even a virgin was not always what she seemed. To meet the great demand for virgins to satisfy what Ivan Block calls the "English Defloration Mania," prostitutes took elaborate measures to restore their virginity. Charlotte Hayes boasted to George Selwyn that "a woman could lose her virginity five hundred times and yet continue to pass as a virgin. Dr. O'Patrick had restored her own thousand times lost virginity." With the aid of astringent plants, pieces of broken glass, leeches, sponges, or fish bladders soaked in blood, any woman could be a virgin.[52] In 1770, an act was passed to protect the unwary male from female predators who were not what they seemed: "That all women of whatever age, rank, profession, or degree, whether vir-

gins, maids, or widows, that shall from and after such act
impose upon, seduce, or betray into matrimony, any of his
Majesty's male subjects by the scents, paints, cosmetic
washes, artificial teeth, false hair, Spanish wool, iron stays,
hoops, high-heeled shoes, etc., shall incur the penalty of
the law now in force against witchcraft and like misde-
meanours, and that the marriage upon conviction shall stand
null and void."[53] Outraged Richardson, revealing his whores
bereft of their paint and plumpers, and Swift, slyly enu-
merating the artifices in his lady's dressing room, could be
no more devastating than such a soberly worded list of
outlawed artifices.

Determining the eighteenth-century attitude towards the
fallen woman becomes complicated when we encounter so
many versions of the truth. Whores were portrayed as
triumphantly debauched, like Charlotte Hayes boasting of
her ever-renewed virginity, or as wretches like Richardson's Sally Martin and Polly Horton, both of whom suffer
miserable ends. One popular tradition of whore biography
celebrated the prostitute as "the entrepreneur who exploits
her fallen condition to rise in the world of men, who deliberately makes her spiritual ruin her material enrich-
ment. She achieves power, pleasure (she takes great personal pleasure in her work; there are no suffering whores
with hearts of gold and tender sensibilities), and independence impossible to eighteenth-century un-emancipated
woman."[54] Histories like those of the "Celebrated Sally
Salisbury" and the "Posture Mistress, Elizabeth Mann"
presented bold, witty whores, admirably suited for their
jobs. The whore's main failing frequently seemed to be an
intelligence not suited to her station. Had Sally Salisbury
*"apply'd herself to Learning, she would have been the Prodigy
of her Age."*[55] Elizabeth Mann was educated above her station: her father "bestow'd such an Education on her, I will
not say above what his Circumstances might allow of, but
what was then generally thought, much above his Rank

and Condition of Life."[56] Here, once more, we find the repeated emphasis on proper station: one could never leave one's place without suffering radical consequences. Richardson used this same convention in his own sketches of Polly and Sally. Sally Martin, the daughter of a "substantial mercer," apes the quality: "At Fifteen or Sixteen, she affected, both in dress and manners, to ape such of the quality as were most Apish." (VIII, 285-86) [IV, 537] Polly Horton, indulged by her flighty mother, is educated "under the influences of . . . books so light and frothy, with the inflaming additions of Music, Concerts, Operas, Plays, Assemblies, Balls, and the rest of the rabble of amusements of the modern life." (VIII, 295) [IV, 544]

In Richardson's world, the fallen woman is a wretched creature doomed to a bad end. Yet his own Clarissa transcends the conventions he employs. She avoids the traditional paths awaiting her: she does not take to the streets, does not marry her seducer, and does not become pregnant. Contrast her fortune with the fates of two other seduced maidens, Nancy Friendly, the heroine of *The Accomplished Fine Rake* (1727), and Louisa Mildmay, the penitent of *Memoirs of a Magdalen*. Both seduced maidens willingly accept the offer of marriage from their seducers. Lacking Clarissa's sense of dignity, they eagerly allow themselves to be "elevated" by the very men who lowered them.

After drugging the eminently respectable Nancy Friendly with an opiate hidden in a macaroon, her favorite sweet, the "accomplished fine rake" basely rapes her. When she becomes pregnant, Nancy retires to her family home to raise her child, without any idea of the father's identity. After several years of debauchery, the rake returns to the long-suffering Miss Friendly to confess his crime and win her love. Although at first the "poor lady trembled with resentment" over her seducer's "barbarous usage," she "recalls" her temper and her child, and in "pity" to the little macaroon, she agrees to marry her rake on the condition that he make her son his heir.[57] Marriage, as Lovelace ardently believes, heals the greatest wounds.

The *Memoirs of a Magdalen* (1767) consciously imitates *Clarissa*, but its heroine glaringly lacks Clarissa's integrity. Louisa Mildmay eagerly accepts marriage from the man who seduced and then rejected her. Virtuous but sensual, she foolishly allows her betrothed lover to seduce her before marriage. Appalled by her lack of virtue, he self-righteously casts her off *after* the seduction. If she has fallen once, he wonders, will she not fall again with someone else? Although he sounds suspiciously like Lovelace, Sir Robert Harold denies that he is behaving like the "contemptible blockhead . . . who did not imagine there was a modest woman existing." Lovelace delayed marrying Clarissa for a "pleasant" reason: he feared that she was actually virtuous. But, Sir Robert insists, "how opposite is the motive of my conduct; but hush, recollection! down busy devil, down—I have waked a scorpion in that retrospect, which stings one to distraction."[58]

Hugh Kelly, the ghost writer of the *Memoirs*, imitated Richardson's content as well as his style ("but hush, recollection!"). In one scene, we find Louisa in the back parlor of a pretended gentlewoman (actually a procuress). Reading *Clarissa*, she has "just got into that passage where the vile Lovelace attempts the sanctity of her chamber at midnight, in the house of that detestable monster Sinclair,"[59] when her own detestable landlady betrays her. A rake, procured by the "gentlewoman," abducts Louisa from the parlor to keep her prisoner until she succumbs to him. After seven months, still untouched (she defended herself with a penknife), she escapes, seeking refuge at the Magdalen House. Her punctilious seducer eventually discovers her, realizes her true virtue, and offers marriage, which she hastily accepts. Once again, marriage makes up for a great deal of suffering.

Nancy and Louisa are typical literary figures of the

eighteenth century, perhaps more broadly drawn than some, but still drawn along conventional lines. Both heroines were at first worshipped for their sublime nature, attempted, and discovered to be not angels but women. At this, they were thrown off for their base sexual nature, only to be finally elevated once again as respectable and angelic wives. The sensual saint, or angelic whore, can be found, in differing degrees, throughout the eighteenth century in the works of Fielding, Sterne, Burney, Goldsmith, and Sheridan, and in numerous sentimental comedies. The angelic nature of the sensual saint complemented the active, unsteady, and exciting nature of her rake or demirake husband. But the delicate woman was, at the same time, degraded in the eyes of society before reaching her reward of marriage. Often she was debased by the same lover who viewed her as sublime. Sublimity and accessibility reinforced each other.

One of the more attractive examples of the sensual saint is Sophia Western. At first she appears remarkably active and independent; she has our respect for her adventurous inn-frequenting that Richardson judged to be low and shocking. But Sophia is both elevated and degraded at the avuncular whim of her narrator. Her mock-heroic introduction to the reader demonstrates Fielding's skillful and humorous undercutting of the image he is deifying: "Reader, perhaps thou hast seen the statue of the *Venus de Medicis*. Perhaps, too, thou hast seen the Gallery of Beauties at *Hampton-Court*. Thou mayest remember *each bright* Churchill *of the Gallaxy*, and all the toasts of the *Kit-Cat*."[60] Sophia's descent from goddess to toast of the Kit-Cat is remarkably sudden, but the life of a goddess is filled with its ups and downs. The sublime Sophia gets more than her share of prodding and pulling and poking. She is almost raped by Lord Fellamar; lives with Lady Bellaston, a lady of questionable morals; travels with her cousin Mrs. Fitzpatrick, who is being kept by an interested admirer; is mistaken for the Pretender's mistress, Jenny Cameron; and is toasted as the easiest lay in Bath by an entire regiment of soldiers. All this and sublimity too. Sophia emerges from her trials triumphantly untouched. Soothed by Fielding's benevolent narrator, we overlook his sadism and enjoy the comedy. We never fear Sophia's fate: her violation is one of image, not person. At the end of both novels, Sophia and Clarissa are immaculate. But Richardson allows his heroine to be raped, purifies her through her suffering, and permits her to transcend her violation. Fielding's way is not so narrow and difficult. Living in the comic, not the tragic world, his heroine only temporarily loses her reputation. Ready to become the redeemer of Tom Jones, Sophia stands intact, secure in her virginity and her sublimity.

Laurence Sterne is another writer who loves to mix his delicate sentiment with more than a hint of indelicate behavior. And who is *Jenny*—my kept mistress, my child, could she be my friend, Tristram Shandy teases. The nature of Yorick's relationship with his Eliza, tearfully memorialized in his *Journal* and transmuted in his *Sentimental Journey* (1768), is predicated upon the heartfelt hope that both of their spouses will die within the year, thank you. In one labored breath, Yorick rhapsodizes on the purity of Eliza, in another he offers her money from his Freudian purse: don't be squeamish my dear, or would you rather have a large post chaise? And then there is the mystery of Yorick's malady—venereal disease? Could it be? Eliza emerges from the *Journal* impossibly pure, yet mysteriously soiled at the same time.

Fanny Burney treats the sentimental angel more seriously. Sterne's levity disappears, leaving us with Evelina, a painfully naive young lady who is constantly finding herself in embarrassing and questionable circumstances. Instinctively pure and genteel, she is surrounded by vulgar relations and improper protectors. A terrible brutality is at work in *Evelina* (1778), sexual aggression expressed through bad manners, especially in the conflict between the equally unspeakable Captain Mirvan and Madame Duval. Evelina's idealized suitor Lord Orville is always encountering her in painfully improper circumstances. His heroine unwittingly makes gross social errors, even strolling through the Vauxhall Gardens with two prostitutes. Evelina's purity and shame are inseparable.

There are important differences between Richardson's, Fielding's, Sterne's, and Burney's treatment of the sublime angel. Fielding's avuncular narrator may be whimsical, but he never threatens. Trusting his meticulously ordered plot line, we rest assured that however low Sophia sinks, she will be painlessly elevated in the last chapter. Sterne can be artfully quirky, but he also never threatens. He delights in the irony of the human condition, in the absurd fact that a sentimental man *can* have venereal disease, that Eliza is both a sentimental icon, the picture he places on his sentimental desk, and a flesh and blood woman with an all too flesh and blood husband. Fanny Burney, on the other hand, is enraged, but her anger is so unrelieved by art that in its diffuse force it loses its total significance. She lacks the distance and irony we find in Jane Austen, who presents us with similar outrages of brutally and vulgarly bad manners, but subtly and ironically, allowing her reader an essential degree of detachment. Richardson does not allow his reader to enjoy the comic detachment Austen provides. He forces us to become "correspondents" involved with Clarissa's fate. By providing us with four narrators all expressing radically different points of view, he shapes his sense of rage. His understanding of the tragic element implicit in the sexual conflicts that are treated humorously by Fielding and Sterne and angrily by Fanny Burney makes his use of the angel/whore figure complex and disturbing.

An interesting twist to the formula of elevation and degradation occurs in Oliver Goldsmith's *She Stoops to Conquer* (1773). Kate Hardcastle deliberately debases herself to attract her lover, placing herself in the accessible servant class because young Marlowe suffers from what he describes as the Englishman's malady. Modest women hold no attraction for him:

> MARLOW. I don't know that I was ever familiarly acquainted with a single modest woman—except my mother—But among females of another class you know—
> HASTINGS. Ay, among them you are impudent enough of all conscience.
> MARLOW. They are of *us*, you know.[61]

"Mother" and "*us*, you know." (Certainly Freud thought he knew the root of the Englishman's malady.)

Goldsmith returns to a more conventional situation in *The Vicar of Wakefield* (1766), presenting us with the usual sadism and masochism we have come to expect in the sentimental novel. The entire Primrose family is put to the rack before it wins its reward: imprisonment, disappointment and humiliation are its daily lot. After purifying the family through their sufferings, the benevolent Thornhill gives one more turn of the screw before he exalts his heroine, offering her in marriage to a vulgar confidence man, complete with dowry, if the trickster will take her off his hands.

We can also find a remarkable combination of sublimity and sexual aggression in some of the least read plays in English literature, sentimental dramas. In their vulgar execution and exploitation of sentimental conventions they are most revealing. The dilemma of the sensual saint in Steele's *Conscious Lovers* (1722) is glaring enough for the dullest playgoer. Indiana, the chaste pasteboard heroine, is viewed by the world as a kept woman. Her chastity is intact, but her reputation has been endangered by the benevolently careless actions of her lover, Bevil Junior, who is keeping Indiana out of "disinterested" moral charity. He is saving his heroine financially, but he is also destroying her good name. As Paul Parnell says, "Evil minded persons might infer that he is keeping her, but Bevil is so noble that such imputations are of course unfair. . . . he refuses to recognize the imprudence and irresponsibility of his actions."[62] Indiana laments, "For, oh! I can't reproach him, though the same Hand that rais'd me up to this Height now throws me down the Precipice."[63]

Miss Louisa Dudley, the heroine of Cumberland's *West Indian* (1771) also suffers the ups and downs of sentimental life. The hot-blooded Belcour falls violently in love with her at first sight, but he mistakes her for a kept woman and treats her accordingly. Interestingly, Louisa admits her attraction for her West Indian in spite of—perhaps even because of—his impolite advances. "Fie, fie upon it!" she exclaims. "Belcour pursues, insults me; yet such is the fatality of my condition, that what should rouse resentment, only calls up love."[64] When he learns the true nature of Miss Dudley, Belcour asks her to assume her proper role as healer and moral censor, once more raising her to her proper height. He assures her that her moral sense will reform him: "I know I'm tainted with a thousand faults, sick of a thousand follies; but there's a healing virtue in your eyes that makes recovery certain; I cannot be a villain in your arms." Out of her arms, however, he is not so trustworthy, as he penitently anticipates. Just as sentimental women expect to suffer, sentimental men expect to cause their suffering: "I beseech you, amiable Louisa, for the time to come, whenever you perceive me deviating into error or offence, bring only to mind the Providence of this night, and I will turn to reason and obey."[65] An angel's lot is not a happy one.

George Colman and David Garrick combine chastity and debauchery, virginity and pregnancy in the same sentimental heroine, Fanny Sterling, of *The Clandestine Marriage* (1766). Fanny is secretly married to poor but honest Lovewell, but the secret will be revealed soon enough: the "virgin" is four months pregnant. Unaware of his daughter's condition, her father offers her in marriage to the highest bidder, Sir John Melvill—intended to be the husband of Fanny's sister. Mr. Sterling echoes the rhetoric of Harlowe Place as he labors in the market to receive the best price for his girls.[66] At first he appears offended by Sir John Melvill's request to exchange one sister for another: "Mighty fine, truly! Why, what the plague do you make of us, Sir John? Do you come to market for my daughters, like servants at a statue fair? Do you think that I will suffer you, or any man in the world, to come into my house like the Grand Signior, and throw the handkerchief first to one, and then t'other, just as he pleases? Do you think I drive a kind of African slave-trade with them?" But, soothed by the prospect of a bigger settlement, he agrees to Sir John's proposal, reasoning that "since you only transfer from one girl to another, it is no more than transferring so much stock, you know."[67] Fanny suffers throughout the matrimonial bargaining, constantly fearing exposure and assault from her assorted lovers. Even her husband questions her chastity at one point, disliking the way his chaste, pregnant bride is being courted as though she were an accessible virgin. Like the other sentimental heroines, Fanny must be humiliated before she receives her hard-earned elevation.

To return to Richardson's transformation of the conventional stereotypes of his age is first of all to return to the stereotypes themselves, to the rules of the sentimental game rakes and virgins play for the highest stakes of all. Once fallen, always fallen, Lovelace confidently believes, setting his sensual saint directly over the precipice waiting for gravity to take its course. According to a popular eighteenth-century saying, woman was a temple built on a sewer.[68] Swift couldn't have said it better. Early in their virginal careers, women were forced to choose between the roles of saint and whore; there could be no middle ground.

In *Clarissa*, Richardson develops the paradox of the sentimental woman. Could an angel possess a body and, con-

versely, could a flesh and blood woman be an angel? Miss
Howe raises an important issue when she writes to the
runaway Clarissa, "Heaven preserve you in honour and
safety is my prayer. What you do for change of cloaths, I
cannot imagine." (III, 212) [II, 122] Indeed, how could
a delicate woman preserve her "honour" without a clean
change of linen? Belford thinks he has the solution, for to
him Clarissa is all spirit, no body. He cannot even imagine
her "plunged so low as into the vulgar offices of domestic
life." His goddess does not require fresh clothing because
his goddess does not possess a body. Physical intercourse
with such an angel would be sacrilegious: "Were she mine,
I should hardly wish to see her a Mother, unless there
were a kind of moral certainty that Minds like hers could
be propagated. For why, in short, should not the work of
Bodies be left to *mere* Bodies?"[69] (IV, 10) [II, 243] The
"mere bodies" of Mrs. Sinclair's house, according to Belford, belong to another species altogether; they are the fallen
angels, the "true women." Yet paradoxically, James Harlowe can only see the fallen nature of his sister. To him,
Clarissa is all body, an affront to his twisted, incestuous
sensibility. Lovelace sees Clarissa to be both angel and
woman, a naively sublime maiden too good for this world
and a flesh and blood goddess whose "purple lips" and
heaving bosom all too palpably prove her to be a true
woman.

In his exhaustive investigation of women, Richardson
exploits and transforms the conventionally reductive image
of woman. While ostensibly holding the sexless angel as
his standard of purity, he exalts not a virgin but a raped
woman as his saint. He told Miss Mulso that he was "apt
to believe that there is many a contaminated soul, that has
an uncontaminated body to carry it about." (*Letters*, p.
186) And, conversely, there can be an uncontaminated soul
that has a contaminated body to carry it about. Such a soul
is Clarissa, both raped and spotless. While Richardson ostensibly demands punctilio, he is really advocating a spir-

itual purity. His saint transcends her physical and social circumstances: when most violated, she stands most inviolate. This spiritual purity cannot be the product of a course in proper manners; it transcends all rules of decorum.

The subversive implications of Richardson's raped saint can be better appreciated in light of contemporary opinions. *The Lady's Magazine* decreed that "a woman without delicacy is a beast; a woman without the *appearance* of delicacy is a *monster*." *The Gentleman's Magazine* also voiced this preference for appearances, insisting that "Women must not only be but seem decent."[70] In *Clarissa*, Richardson is not on the side of the angels but on the side of the monsters, for while society views Clarissa's actions as monstrous or insane, Richardson presents her as a saint able to transcend the world of mere appearances.

Women presented a problem not only for Richardson but for his age. Once a woman slipped from her pedestal, would she be irretrievably fallen? Could a woman be anything but a saint or a whore?[71] Swift was far from alone in his abhorrence for the appetite and bodily functions of women: no one could forget the dank sewer beneath the temple.

In a world where a woman was always in danger of "falling," her slightest sexual response could hold profound implications. In the sexual warfare discussed in the previous chapter, a woman was doomed to marriage or seduction or, if she was unlucky, spinsterhood.[72] Either married or seduced, a woman would reveal her sexuality. Matronized she would be safer: like Charlotte Grandison, she could channel her sexual energy towards her "Marmouset" nursing at her breast. Seduced, she would be ruined beyond hope, and, ironically, would be safe from falling any lower. The single state was the most perilous, for the chaste virgin would always be in danger of sliding. As Lovelace reveals, chastity presented a constant challenge to the encroaching male: "All that's excellent in her Sex is this Lady! Until by MATRIMONIAL, or EQUAL intimacies,

I have found her *less than angel*, it is impossible to think of any other." (I, 220) [I, 150] Presumably, once she has revealed her sexual nature, Clarissa will lose her attraction. Within such a context, Dr. Gregory's warning that a wife must never tell her husband of her love for him makes more sense.[73] Intimacy, "MATRIMONIAL, or EQUAL," created contempt.

Armed with her punctilio, the sentimental woman needed to resist her own "nature" to preserve her position as angel. Freely acknowledging that women were the "better half" of men, rakes then struggled to penetrate their victims' punctilio, to make them reveal their "true" selves, the darker side of the better half. By exalting the "weaker" but "purer" sex, and by exacting an impossibly high standard of resistance, the encroaching male could determine any degree of sliding as a "fall." Harriet Byron fully recognizes the dilemma of the chaste woman when she complains that "flattery is the vice of men: That they seek to raise us in order to lower us, and in the end to exalt themselves on the ruins of the pride they either hope to find, or inspire." (I, 18) [I, V] Harriet may recognize the problem, but she cannot escape her fate: too many forces are in league against her. Greville, the posturing rake, sadistically imagines her fall: "But lovely as Miss Byron's person is, I defy the greatest Sensualist on earth not to admire her mind more than her person. What a triumph would the devil have, as I have often thought, when I have stood contemplating her perfections, especially at church, were he able to raise up a man that could lower this Angel into Woman?" (I, 9) [I, II] Richardson's old friend, that great "sensualist" Colly Cibber, picked up Greville's challenge, smacking his lips over the heroine's "person": "The delicious meal I made of Miss Byron on Sunday last, has given me an appetite for another slice of her, off from the spit, before she is served up to the public table; if about five o'clock tomorrow afternoon will not be inconvenient, Miss Brown and I will come and piddle upon a bit more of her." (*Corre-*

spondence, vol. II, p. 176) Being "piddled upon" by the
dunce laureate might not be a dignified fate, but Harriet
Byron was designed for humiliation. Richardson explained
to Miss Mulso that he intended to make Harriet shine
after she had been "humbled by her love (suspense in love
is a mortifier)." After a proper amount of mortification,
he intended to "raise her." (*Letters*, p. 190) And Harriet
does suffer, even losing her bloom temporarily: "there is
a languor in her fine eyes, that I never saw in them before
. . . she has more meekness and humility in her countenance, than, methinks, I would *wish* her to have," reports
Thomas Deane. (II, 30) [III, VI]

In Richardson's world, to be exalted, the sublime woman
first had to be degraded. Such a need for the control and
mortification of women suggests an obsessive fear of female
sexuality. Richardson regarded the fallen woman as an obscenity. In the *Familiar Letters*, he claims that an unfaithful woman is far worse than an unfaithful man.[74] Lovelace
echoes this dislike: "A fallen woman is a worse devil than
even a profligate man." Lovelace chafes at the taunts and
insults of Mrs. Sinclair's women as they mock his lack of
success with Clarissa. They tease him with the fears every
man must have about the "naturally cold" woman: "They
thought I knew, if any man living did, that if a man made
a goddess of a woman, she would assume the goddess; that
if power were given her, she would exert that power to the
giver, if to nobody else—and D——r's wife is thrown into
my dish, who, thou knowest, kept her ceremonious husband at haughty distance, and whined in private to her
insulting footman. Oh, how I cursed the blaspheming
wretches!" (III, 338-39) [II, 208] Like Cibber, who relished another slice of Miss Byron, Lovelace regards women
as objects for consumption, to be thrown into his "dish."
The danger is that the objects might have appetites of
their own. Who would risk arousing the sexual desire of
D——r's wife or Pope's "Sin in State," who is "Chaste to
her Husband, frank to all beside, /A teeming Mistress,

but a barren Bride."⁷⁵ In the eighteenth century, a woman's power lay in her womb. By bearing another man's child, she would not only cuckold her husband and cut the property lines but would also exert the power of her own sexual appetite over that of her husband. Lovelace, however, refuses to allow such a terrible prospect. His example of the unfaithful woman, D——r's wife, still must "whine" to her insulting footman. Lovelace can never allow the possibility that a woman might enjoy absolute power, but forces her to whine before some male, the "lower" the better.

Richardson's fear of the fallen woman becomes most obvious in his Swiftian brothel scene at the death of Mrs. Sinclair. The rank stench, the slops, filth, and rotting flesh depict the whore as the ultimate obscenity. Belford reports the scene with energetic horror, revealing his inability to accept the physical nature of women in his obsessive, fascinated description of their bodily functions. He tells Lovelace that if he had ever seen such women "unprepared for being seen," he would hate "a profligate woman as one of Swift's Yahoos or Virgil's obscene Harpyes, squirting their ordure upon the Trojan trenchers; since the persons of such in their retirements are as filthy as their minds." Belford finds it "evident, that as a neat and clean woman must be an angel of a creature, so a sluttish one is the impurest animal in nature." Women are Yahoos, throwing their shit at one another, or Harpies, squirting their ordure. An angel does not excrete, of course, because she possesses no body. But even Belford cannot escape the fact that the angel and the slut, far apart as they may appear, are related creatures. The fear that the angel can descend into the impurest animal in nature paralyzes him.

The transformation from angel to whore seems magical. Like the Spenserian Bower of Bliss, the quasi-respectable Sinclair house, which even deceived a sensitive critic like Clarissa, becomes a stinking, slop-filled pigsty. The neat and elegant daughters, who passed themselves off as modest readers of sermons and sentimental dramas, reveal themselves to be filthy harridans whose touch infects a pure man. The daughters loll about in "shocking dishabille . . . stockenless some; only under-petticoated all . . . half of them (unpadded, shoulder-bent, pallid-lipt, limber-jointed wretches) appearing, from a blooming Nineteen or Twenty perhaps over-night, haggard well-worn strumpets of Thirty-eight or Forty." (VIII, 55-56) [IV, 381] The transformation is magical—and necessary. For Belford, the fallen woman must be vile, never attractive. Blooming nineteen-year-old girls must become, in the course of one sinful night, haggard strumpets twice that age.

More women, younger "but not less obscene in their appearance," join the sordid tangle of bodies, "subordinate sinners" in the Sinclair hell. They are "unpropt by stays, squalid, loose in attire, sluggish-haired, under-petticoated only as the former, eyes half-opened, winking and pinking, mispatched, yawning, stretching, as if from the un-worn-off effects of the midnight revel; all armed in succession with supplies of cordials (of which every one present was either taster or partaker) under the direction of the busier Dorcas, who frequently popp'd in, to see her slops duly given and taken." Belford's, and surely Richardson's, vivid horror consciously echoes Swift's disgust with the impure animal, woman, who takes cordials and gives forth slops. But Richardson judges his own picture to be more "*decent* . . . better justified." In a self-serving footnote, he reminds the reader that "whoever has seen Dean Swift's Lady's Dressing-room will think this description of Mr. Belford not only more *natural*, but more *decent painting*, as well as better justified by the *design*, and by the *use* that may be made of it." (VIII, 56-57) [IV, 381-82] There is a great difference between Swift's picture of Celia and Richardson's brothel scene, most obviously in the degree of detachment of the two writers. Swift's poem is humorous; he distances himself through wit as he enjoys depicting his subject. Celia amuses rather than horrifies him.

Furthermore, Swift does not preserve Belford's dichotomy between the genteel woman and the whore. His *Celia, Celia, Celia* shits. Not Polly or Betty or Sally, but *Celia*, a lady. Swift makes no distinction between Belford's neat and clean angel and the impure animal; they are both women, rising "from stinking Ooze . . . gaudy Tulips rais'd from Dung."[76] Richardson is less rigorous in his analysis and less amused by the animal functions. Presumably Clarissa, without an apparent change of clothing, even bereft of her hoop, still remains neat and elegant. No "unsav'ry Odours fly" from her direction. Clarissa, although she lives in a brothel surrounded by "mere" bodies, never descends into a woman, even in her rape. Her persecution preserves her purity.

Persecution purified, but it served another purpose as well. It would have taken the restraint of a saint *not* to persecute a sentimental woman: her reserve and her masochism invited attack. Somehow a normal amount of aggression must be released; when it was cut off short by the punctilio-armed maiden, it manifested itself in another way. The excessive amount of prodding, poking, pinching, and bumping Clarissa endures seems extreme, but excessive pressure is necessary to provoke some sort of response. And how else could the sentimental woman demonstrate her sensibility?

Although Richardson ostensibly endorsed many of the sexual stereotypes of his age, he differed radically from his contemporaries when he set out to execute his beliefs. Unlike the sentimental dramatists with their pathetic Indianas and Fannys, alternately degraded and elevated by their conscious lovers, Richardson created heroines of integrity who raise themselves up by their own efforts to deal with their own destinies, not one-dimensional representations of sociological problems. His women, from Pamela to Harriet Byron, respond to the demands of their feminine roles, but their characters are not designed solely to point out a moral or to establish a feminine norm. Pamela Andrews may be a consummate player of the sentimental role, but she is also a character in her own right. She cooperates fully as the sublime woman, degraded and then exalted. In fact, she revels in her part, exploiting it to her own advantage. *Pamela* aroused a storm of anti-Pamelas precisely because Pamela so perfectly played her part, emphasizing the "roguery" of the delicate woman so broadly that a public cry of hypocrisy applauded her efforts.

Pamela does what every sentimental woman does, only she does it better. Humorously and deftly, she makes her fortune by exploiting her only marketable resource, her virginity. She plays her role easily because she is not encumbered with an essential self. Educated above her station, Pamela has no fixed position. She has been "brought up wrong, as Matters stand." (I, 97) [I, 62] Playing the part of "humble and teachable" worker, she attempts to scour a pewter plate: "I could do't by degrees: It only blister'd my Hand in two Places." Although Pamela does not officially fit in anywhere, she is willing to make a valiant try at assimilation. She is out of joint with her background: "I shall make a fine Figure with my Singing and my Dancing, when I come home to you! Nay, I shall be unfit even for a *May-day* Holiday-time; for these Minuets, Rigadoons, and *French* Dances, that I have been practising, will make me but ill Company for my Milk-maid Companions that are to be." (I, 99) [I, 63] Her dislocation gives her the freedom to play different roles until she finds a self that fits. Always flexible, she is ever ready to forgive B.'s many insults. Clarissa, on the other hand, never forgives. Until her rape, Clarissa operates from an essentially fixed position: her status and breeding determine her actions. Unlike Pamela, she never learns the importance of living by her wits until, in the last days of allegorical letters, it is too late.

Pamela's talent for assimilation and disguise can be seen early on in her story. Preparing to leave the B. household, she dresses herself elaborately in her new humble garb: "I trick'd myself up as well as I could in my new Garb." "Trick'd" is a curious word for Richardson to use here. It means two things, to dress and to deceive. Its primary meaning, popularly used in the eighteenth century, is "to deceive by a trick, to cheat," and also "to beguile *into*; to induce into by trickery." Even its secondary meaning retains a sense of deceit. According to the *Oxford English Dictionary*, in Richardson's time "trick" also meant "to dress, array, attire, to deck, prank; to adorn (usually with the notion of artifice)." By introducing such an ambiguous word, Richardson suggests that on some level Pamela is preparing to deceive Mr. B. And B.'s outrage at Pamela's trick comes as no surprise: "Come in, said he, you little Villain! for so he call'd me; Good-sirs! what a Name was there! Who is it you put your Tricks upon." (I, 70) [I, 43–44]

When Pamela describes her country costume, she reveals her ambiguous position with her excessive use of conjunctions: she wears a "round-ear'd ordinary Cap; but with a green Knot . . . plain-leather Shoes; but yet they are what they call *Spanish* leather, and my ordinary Hose, ordinary I mean to what I have been used to: tho' I shall think good Yarn may do very well for every day." (I, 67) [I, 41-42] Deceptively simple, her costume disguises a complex character.

When Pamela trots downstairs in her new garb, "descending with Ease, Innocence, and Resignation," Mrs. Jervis, "all in Amaze," notes in admiration, "What! *Pamela* thus metamorphos'd!" Mr. B. enters the game, taking Pamela for her own sister, "so neat, so clean, so pretty." Making her move, Pamela announces, "O Sir, said I, I am *Pamela*, indeed I am: indeed I am *Pamela her own self!*" When B. protests, complaining that since he had resolved never to notice her again, she disguised herself "to attract me, and yet pretend, like an hypocrite," Pamela defends her "own self" ingeniously, explaining that she has "put on no Disguise." In fact, she adds, "I have been in Disguise indeed ever since my good Lady your Mother took me from my poor Parents." (I, 68-71) [I, 43-44] Her rich clothes, disguising her real self, whatever that might be, would disgrace her at home; her "humble suit" will serve as good holiday garb.

Pamela's shifting sense of her social station affects her sense of sexual modesty. Pamela Andrews, maidservant, forgives repeated assaults, pokes, and insults from Mr. B. But Pamela B., keeper of the B. morals, is sublimely unapproachable, too delicate even to consider the vulgar duties of marriage. Showing himself to be a master of circumlocution, B. blushes even to hint at the remote possibility of future little B.'s; his chaste proposal of parenthood is barely intelligible: "And, let me tell you, my *Pamela*, that I can add my Hopes of a still more pleasing Amusement, and what your bashful Modesty would not permit you to hint. . . . I hope to have superadded to all these, such an Employment, as will give me a View of perpetuating my happy Prospects, and my Family at the same time; of which I am almost the only one, in a direct Line." Pamela blushes, but is "not displeased at the decent and charming manner with which he insinuated this distant hope." (II, 32) [I, 236] A "superadded happy prospect" is a far cry from B.'s former expressions like "saucy slut" and "sauce-box." After the wedding, B. allows himself to be more explicit; spanning Pamela's waist with his hands, he tells her that although he would regret her to lose her sweet shape, "I shall think nothing but that Loss wanting, to complete my Happiness." Pamela puts her "bold Hand before his Mouth" and says, "Hush, hush! O fie, Sir!—The freest thing you have ever yet said, since I have been yours!"

Pamela's qualification is appropriate: "since I have been yours." Elevated to the role of sublime female, lifted from her degraded position as accessible slut, she can no longer be treated with "freedom," nor can she respond freely. Her flexibility and pertness disappear. After the scandalous discussion of future B.'s and changing shapes, Pamela blushingly admits that "your Wishes, in everything, shall be mine; but pray, Sir, say no more!—He kindly saluted me, and thank'd me, and chang'd the subject.—I was not too free, I hope!" (II, 186) [I, 336] The flexible girl fossilizes into a rigid matron, guardian of the B. family expectations and prejudices. Pamela can never be "too free" again.

In *Clarissa*, Richardson was determined not to write a second *Pamela*. Resolutely denying his heroine the happy ending her readers demanded, he explored the tragic consequences of the sentimental formula. His refusal to make Clarissa another example of virtue rewarded is dramatically illuminated in his correspondence with Lady Bradshaigh. Calling herself "Belfour," the earnest lady wrote Richardson anonymously "to plead in behalf of your amiable Clarissa." Hearing "that some of your advisers, who delight in horror (detestable wretches!) insisted upon rapes, ruin and destruction," she begged the author to "make your almost despairing readers half mad with joy." She urged him to marry a reformed Lovelace to the purified Clarissa. Her motives, she confessed, were twofold: a deep devotion to the saintly Clarissa and (though she blushed for it) a special fondness for Lovelace. "A sad dog! Why would you make him so wicked, and yet so agreeable." (*Correspondence*, vol. IV, pp. 178-80)

Several letters from "Belfour" followed: "I shall frighten you with another letter so soon after my last. Methinks I hear you say,—'What! every post! No respite! No quiet! No hopes of being relieved from the persecution of this troublesome woman!' " (*Correspondence*, vol. IV, p. 202) But Richardson adamantly refused to make his correspondent happy. Critically, he had already paid the price for rewarding virtue: the many anti-Pamelas deterred him from too visibly rewarding virtue another time: "Had I drawn my Heroine reconciled to Relations unworthy of her, nobly resisting the Attacks of an intrepid Lover, overcoming her

Persecutors, and baffling the wicked Designs formed against her Honour; marrying her Lovelace, and that on her own Terms; educating her own Children—What however usefull, however pleasing the Lesson, had I done more than I had done in Pamela?" (*Letters*, p. 92)

Richardson's reasons fell on deaf ears: Lady Bradshaigh refused to relinquish her desire for the reformed rake's marriage to the divine Clarissa, despite the author's decree that there "cannot be a more pernicious Notion, than that which is commonly received, That a reformed Rake makes the best Husband." (*Letters*, p. 94) In Belfour's rakeproof plans for a happy ending, Clarissa, "assisted by her own divine reflections," would recover her health, but would still refuse to see Lovelace. "Overwhelmed with grief, remorse, and self condemnation" Lovelace would be "thrown into a dangerous fever." Out of charity, Clarissa would visit Lovelace on his sickbed: "What an interesting scene might you there introduce." After much reflection, Clarissa would agree to marry Lovelace on his deathbed to insure his salvation. "Methinks I see her his wife, or wife elect, kindly attending, and administering means for his recovery, (which we will imagine for some time doubtful); he eagerly receiving it, as draughts of life from her hands. . . . What moving tender scenes could you draw upon such an occasion! and with what pleasure could I sob, and dedicate a deluge of tears to those scenes, and to the worthy objects." (*Correspondence*, vol. IV, pp. 203-205) Lady Bradshaigh's sentimental fifth-act redemption, complete with a "deluge of tears," failed to move Richardson, who insisted on the impossibility of uniting Lovelace and Clarissa in anything but their own imagination. "Indeed, Madam," he protested, "I could not think of leaving my Heroine short of Heaven." (*Letters*, p. 104)

Heaven is the only reward befitting a Clarissa. In fact, we can almost accuse Richardson of parodying the sentimental formula. Clarissa consciously prepares to receive her reward as the bride of Christ, on the whole a far more

satisfying lover than the pernicious reformed rake. But
sentimentalists expected their women to be angels in imagination, not in fact. Clarissa carries the sentimental formula to an extreme, enduring ultimate suffering to enjoy
the ultimate reward. Her integrity sets her above the conventional "Conscious Lover" heroine, who after the required amount of degradation is elevated as sublime wife
and moral helpmate. Clarissa's own sense of herself prevents her from accepting the "marriage heals all" happy
ending that society expects of her. She refuses to play the
game.

Anna Howe, the intrepid gamester who knows how to
keep lovers at bay, is immediately aware of Clarissa's role
in the matrimonial game she has unwittingly entered.
Writing to her at St. Albans, Miss Howe admonishes her
friend to be particular in her correspondence because a
"stander-by may see more of the game than one that plays."
(III, 44) [II, 7] Later, when the logical end to the game,
marriage, is not reached, Miss Howe coaches Clarissa: "You
have a very nice part to act: And I will add that you have
a Mind that is much too delicate for your part. But when
the Lover is exalted, the Lady must be humbled. He is
naturally proud and saucy. I doubt, you must engage his
pride, which he calls his honour: And that you must throw
off a little more of the veil." (III, 98) [II, 44]

This worldly wisdom galls Clarissa. "Would to Heaven
I were not to play! For I think, after all, I am held to a
desperate game." (III, 154) [II, 82] Clarissa tries to throw
off the veil, but she cannot stomach the part: while Lovelace "is to be mighty stately, mighty *mannish*, mighty *coy*,
if you please! And then must I be very humble, very submissive, and try to insinuate myself into his good graces:
With downcast eye, if not by speech, beg his forgiveness
for the distance I have so perversely kept him at!—Yes, I
warrant! . . . But I cannot, cannot see him! (IV, 91) [II,
298]

When she finally does see Lovelace, she scorns the submissive role, offering to call off the game entirely: "I have a great and invincible spirit, or my own conceit betrays me—Let us resolve to quit every regard for each other that is more than civil." (IV, 96) [II, 301-302] Clarissa is made of finer stuff than Louisa Dudley. She cannot lower herself in order to be elevated. Even when she has been humbled by force, she remains above Lovelace. In their first interview after the rape, he is struck by her majestic appearance: "She entered with such dignity in her manner, as struck me with great awe, and prepared me for the poor figure I made in the subsequent conversation." (V, 347) [III, 218]

Clarissa's strength of character gives tragic stature to her role as the sentimental woman. She is elevated after the proper amount of suffering, but not by Lovelace. She elevates herself. After her rape, she has nothing left to lose. Her virginity, that jewel that Pamela so deftly preserved, is gone, and with it her reserve. She becomes even more tough-mindedly candid than her doughty friend Miss Howe as she testifies to her rape without shame. Anna Howe, brave as she may appear to be, still betrays a squeamishness about the actual nature of her friend's rape. She expresses outrage that Colonel Morden should have "indelicacy enough to have gone into the nature of the proof of the crime upon which they wanted to have Lovelace arraigned." (VII, 356) [IV, 269] Clarissa is not so nice, although she does express the hope that "my cousin has not taken the liberties which you (by an observation not, in general, unjust) seem to charge him with." (VII, 365) [IV, 275] Clarissa's phrases, "not, in general, unjust" and "seem to charge him with," undercut, by their dry understatement, Miss Howe's righteous indignation. Freed from the conventions of society—for as a raped woman she is no longer *of* proper society—Clarissa controls her own fate, independent of the wishes of her family and friends. She directs her own death consciously and deliberately, posthumously dispensing the property she so carefully denied herself in her lifetime.

Because Clarissa elevates herself and stands independent of society, she gains a moral freedom unavailable to the calcified sentimental woman like the matron Pamela or Louisa Dudley. Clarissa makes her own place: she does not take on the name and position of Lovelace or become the keeper of his sliding morals. The salvation of his soul is his own affair; she will only "forgive" him and leave him to his fate.

Tragically, Clarissa and Lovelace can never come together. Their essential differences make a fifth-act redemption impossible. Pamela, flexibly altering her character to meet her circumstances, is finally able to pick up her third bundle and assume her new social role as Mrs. B. In *her* final days, Clarissa sells her clothing. Social symbols have little to do with her destiny. She prefers to devise her own personal symbols, which she carves on her coffin.

In her death as in her life, Clarissa rebels against social norms. Marriage will not cure all; death will not testify to her shame, but to her triumph. Ironically, her death has been viewed as the first in a long, painful line of seduced maidens dying of grief.[77] Joseph Wood Krutch, who grudgingly admires Richardson for having integrity in spite of himself, makes the commonly accepted observation that Clarissa's death is "brought about by her one violation of the conventional code" and "in no way challenges the assumption that all is fundamentally well both in human society and the universe at large."[78] On the contrary, Clarissa's life and death absolutely challenge the social system. She refuses to "come to by degrees" as Lovelace so smugly expects. In her death she triumphs over the social code that ordains that a woman must not only be decent but seem decent. She also triumphs over Richardson's own "familiar letter" code of proper behavior. Violated, and known to be violated, Clarissa has more virtue than any virgin. Always distrustful of the world of appearances, Richardson celebrates the virtue within.

It was not easy for Richardson to deny a happy ending

to his Clarissa, for his emotional investment in his character was extremely strong. When Lady Bradshaigh angrily asked him, "How can anyone . . . think with Pleasure of parting with what they love, supposing their End ever so glorious," he sadly gives an account of his own losses: one wife, six sons ("all my Sons!"), two daughters, a father, two brothers, and a dear friend—"No less than Eleven concerning Deaths attacked me in two Years." "The Case therefore," he tells his sentimental friend, "is not what we should like to bear, but what (such is the Common Lot) we must bear, like it or not." (*Letters*, pp. 109-11) For Richardson, Clarissa's death was something to be borne, the logical outcome of her character. Much as he loved to play godlike author, frightening his correspondents with absurd threats, he could not bend his plot to accommodate the sentimental formula. Clarissa and Lovelace transcend their tradition, enriching sentimentality with the integrity of the tragic imperatives of their personalities.

FOUR • Horrid Romancing: Richardson's Use of the Fairy Tale

Was ever the like heard? . . . But this, to be sure, is horrid romancing!

Pamela (I, 243-44) [I, 156]

I N THEIR STUDY of fairy tales, Iona and Peter Opie include among their illustrations one of Joseph Highmore's portraits of Pamela.[1] Pamela is telling a nursery tale to a pensive-looking Miss Godwin, five of the B. cherubs, and the nursery maid, "delightedly pursuing some useful Needlework, for the dear Charmers of my Heart." They wait, "all as hush and as still, as Silence itself," for moral allegories about the two good little boys and the two good little girls who married "and made good Papas and Mammas, and were so many Blessings to the Age in which they lived." There were also tales of three naughty little boys and one naughty little girl who break their mother's heart and come to bad ends. One boy drowns at sea, one turns thief, and one begs for bread, while the "naughty girl, having never loved Work, pined away in Sloth and Filthiness, and at last, broke her Arm, and died of a Fever." (IV, 438-41) [II, 462-64] As usual, evil, more than good, stimulates Richardson's imagination. Pamela also tells the rousing tale of "four pretty ladies [who] lived in one genteel neighbourhood," Coquetilla, Prudiana, Profusiana, and Prudentia, "their several Names denoting their respective Qualities." (IV, 442) [II, 465] Not a giant or a fairy in the lot.

Yet in spite of the prosaic quality of Pamela's tales, the

Opies' choice for their frontispiece is still appropriate, for Pamela not only told nursery tales, but acted in them as well, playing in her less matronly days a plucky Cinderella to Mr. B.'s ill-conceived Prince Charming. Richardson's Cinderella won her prince not "once upon a time," but in the here and now, so convincingly that the good citizens of Slough celebrated her fictional wedding in reality.[2] Readers believed in Pamela's fairy tale: an "anonymous gentleman" objected to Pamela's extraordinarily small waist, predicting a craze of tight lacing, and even Henry Fielding feared that Pamela's matrimonial success would inspire other servant girls to throw themselves at their masters, with dire results.[3]

In his best novels, *Pamela* and *Clarissa*, Richardson managed to combine the elements of romance and reality so effectively that he was able to convince his readers to accept the fantastic as commonplace. And if his readers did believe the "truth" of his fiction, Richardson did nothing to disillusion them. Hiding behind the mask of the editor, supplying prefaces, footnotes, and postscripts to manufacture one more level of reality, he encouraged, even insisted upon, maintaining what he called the "Historical Faith" in fiction. When William Warburton unwittingly called attention to the fictional nature of Richardson's work in his preface to *Clarissa*, Richardson politely objected, withdrawing the preface from later editions: "Will you, good Sir, allow me to mention, that I could wish that the *Air* of Genuineness had been kept up, tho' I want not the letters to be *thought* genuine; only so far kept up, I mean, as that they should not prefatically be owned *not* to be genuine: and this for fear of weakening their Influence where any of them are aimed to be exemplary; as well as to avoid hurting that kind of Historical Faith which Fiction itself is generally read with, tho' we know it to be Fiction." (*Letters*, p. 85) Richardson's hedging is painfully apparent here. In spite of his disclaimer, he did want his fiction to be "thought" genuine, depending upon "that kind of Historical Faith" to establish his sphere of exemplary influence.

Richardson always jealously guarded his moral sphere. He wanted, above all, to be taken seriously, to be placed, as he suggested to Lady Echlin, on the proper side of the bookshelf next to the graver moralists, where he could perfect as well as amuse his reader. As we have seen in the previous chapters, Richardson's desire to perfect his reader caused him to invent complex characters of independence and integrity who, in the process of perfecting themselves, create themselves. His perfectionism also led him to create fictional worlds that may appear commonplace but in fact are fantastic—prosaic nightmares. For to perfect his reader, Richardson first had to catch him, and to catch him, he had to lure him in with the promise of a sensationally romantic world, yet a world described realistically enough to pass his moral censor.

Richardson's admirers generally accepted the author's concern for the "Air of Genuineness" as evidence of his realism.[4] Joseph Spence, for instance, praised Richardson's "plain and natural Account of an Affair that happened in a private Family, just in the manner it did happen. He has aimed solely at following Nature; and giving the Sentiments of the Persons concerned, just as they flowed warm from their Hearts." The "Sentiments" of the "natural" Harlowe family flow warm enough in *Clarissa*, a plain and natural account of duels (one on the first page), rape, abduction, and imprisonment—the everyday affairs of a "private" (privately mad) family. Nothing could be more natural. Philip Skelton, another of Richardson's contemporaries, also praised the author's attention to nature. *Clarissa* "comes home to the Heart, and to common Life," unlike those inferior romances filled with "a Croud of mere imaginary Amours, Duels, and such-like Events."[5] Somehow Skelton managed to overlook the fantastic aspects of the "Amours, Duels, and such-like Events" crowding the pages of *Clarissa*.

This is not to Skelton's discredit, however, for Mr. Richardson was loath to allow anyone to focus upon the sensational nature of his fiction. He was, throughout his novels, the severest critic of the romantic inventions he exploited. Listen to Mrs. Pamela on the subject of romance. Apparently forgetting her own melodramatic role-playing, she rebukes romantic Miss Stapylton for filling her commonplace book with the "beautiful Things and good Instructions, to be collected from Novels and Plays, and Romances." There were "very few Novels and Romances that my Lady would permit me to read," Pamela sternly recalls, "and those I did, gave me no great Pleasure; for either they dealt so much in the *Marvellous* and *Improbable*, or were so unnaturally *inflaming* to the *Passions*, and so full of *Love* and *Intrigue*, that hardly any of them but seem'd calculated to *fire* the *Imagination* rather than to *inform* the *Judgment*."

Romantic heroines tend to be especially faulty:

> what principally distinguishes the Character of the *Heroine* is, when she is taught to consider her Father's House as an inchanted Castle, and her Lover as the Hero who is to dissolve the Charm, and to set at Liberty from one Confinement, in order to put her into another, and, too probably, a worse: To instruct her how to climb Walls, drop from Windows, leap Precipices, and do twenty other extravagant Things, in order to shew the mad Strength of a Passion she ought to be asham'd of: to make Parents and Guardians pass for Tyrants, and the Voice of Reason to be drown'd in that of indiscreet Love, which exalts the other Sex, and debases her own. And what is the Instruction that can be gather'd from such Pieces, for the Conduct of common Life? (IV, 425-26) [II, 453-54]

Pamela could well be outlining the plot for *Clarissa*, Richardson's moral primer for "the Conduct of common Life."

In her introduction to Richardson's correspondence, Anna

Laetitia Barbauld discussed the "natural" aspects of Richardson's writing: "That kind of fictitious writing of which he has set the example, disclaims all assistance for giants or genii. The moated castle is changed to a modern parlour; the princess and her pages to a lady and her domestics. . . . we are not called on to wonder at improbable events, but to be moved by natural passions." (*Correspondence*, vol. I, xxi) Mrs. Barbauld at least acknowledged the romantic elements of Richardson's fiction, but it would be more precise to say that "the modern parlour is changed to a moated castle." For Richardson transformed common reality, investing the most ordinary situations with menace and wonder. The Harlowe family's "modern parlour," filled with swelling Arabella, squatting Solmes, ranting James, raging Father, and wraithlike Mama, holds horrors. Richardson was able to abstract the terrors of common life— the envy, jealousy, fear, and lust—make them part of his character's psyche, and then project them back to the reader. James, consumed with a monstrous jealousy, becomes a monster to Clarissa. Since we see and experience what Clarissa does, we also see him as a monster, as terrible as any that ever stalked a fairy tale. By making the horrors and wonders part of his character's psyche, Richardson authenticated his fairy tale, never hesitating to supply a few "real life" horrors of his own: the monstrous Colbrand, Uncle Antony's moated house, and Clarissa's squalid prison. But the most effective horrors remain closest to home: in the cozy parlor conferences that erupt into violence; in those scenes in which Clarissa and Lovelace, sedately sipping tea, suddenly fling each other about the room. Incorporating the elements of fairy tale and romance, Richardson always attended to the menace of the ordinary.

When he laid down the uncompleted volume of the *Familiar Letters* to begin writing *Pamela*, Richardson moved from the familiar to the novel. And moral aphorisms were always "familiar." We have already seen his obvious delight in making moral maxims in *The Apprentice's Vade*

Mecum. In his edition of *Aesop's Fables*, Richardson revised and to some extent moralized L'Estrange's version of the *Fables*, first published in 1692. Highlighting the "useful," and banishing the "trivial or a loose Conceit," he "presumed to alter, and put a stronger Point to several of the Fables themselves, which we thought capable of more forcible Morals."[6] The mammoth *Collection of the Moral and Instructive Sentiments, Maxims, Cautions, and Reflexions*, gleaned from his three novels, reflects his continuing pride in his ability to make a moral with the best of them. We need only look at a few of the maxims Richardson found in *Pamela* to see the great difference between the simple moral aphorisms and the more complex dramatic action of his novel.

In his "Cautions to young Female Servants," he warns that a "handsome Female Servant should not wish to live in the house of a Single man, since she will be likely by it to suffer in her reputation in the world's eye." Sage enough advice, but unheeded by Richardson's own "handsome Female Servant," Pamela Andrews, who gladly reported to her parents that she was staying on to take care of Mr. B.'s linen *after* the death of her mistress. Richardson also warns "young women" to avoid the company of a man "capable of rudeness": "A young Woman whose virtue has been once attempted, yet throws herself into the same person's company, or continues where he is, when she can avoid it, ought to charge herself with the consequences, if she receive new indignities." But in his first novel, Richardson examines the actions of his own "young woman," who ostensibly avoids B. after his first attempts, yet manages to stay in his way. "Trick'd up" to make her farewell, Pamela effectively throws herself into B.'s company and rekindles his waning desire for her. Pamela's mixed feelings, expressed through actions both ambiguous and calculating, complicate Richardson's simple maxims. Richardson can firmly state that "the man who is capable of rudeness to a woman, to whom he professes honourable love, ought to be rejected as an husband, by a woman of virtue and spirit, for his sake, as well as for the sake of her own honour."[7] But at the same time, Richardson created a world of far greater latitude, in which a woman of "virtue and spirit" gratefully and humbly accepts the man "capable of rudeness" as her husband and master.

In his preface to his *Collection*, Richardson explains that since the narrative "was only meant as a vehicle for the *instructive*," he would now separate the maxims "expressing *elevated thoughts, beautiful sentiments*, or *instructive lessons*" from the "engaging incidents" that might divert the reader's attention from the moral.[8] But to separate the maxims from the action is to alter the very meaning of the novel by ignoring the complications provided by such "engaging incidents." Although he never lost sight of the moral in *Pamela*, Richardson's experiments with the epistolary novel indicated his need to make his moral in a wholly different way, replacing aphorisms with characters and transforming the commonplace with the elements of romance, fairy tale, and myth, thereby complicating his simple moral in the process.

In Richardson's novels we find a sense of fantasy made concrete, almost commonplace. Richardson created a literature "having both body and hidden depths," a literature Roland Barthes would describe as "clouded." In an analysis of the difference between the "transparent" literature of the early eighteenth century and the "clouded" literature of the late eighteenth century, Barthes argues that "literary form" in the late eighteenth century "develops a second-order power independent of its economy and euphemistic charm; it fascinates the reader, it strikes him as exotic, it enthralls him, it acquires a weight. Literature is no longer felt as a socially privileged mode of transaction, but as a language having both body and hidden depths, existing both as dream and menace."[9] Richardson's readers "felt" the dream and menace of his novels. Aaron Hill's servant boy sobbing over Pamela; Aaron Hill himself, confessing that he can never escape Mrs. Jewkes, "who often keeps me awake in the Night"; and even Fielding's Parson Tickletext, complaining that "if I lay the book down *it comes after* me"— all testify to the emotional power Richardson enjoyed over his readers.[10] Combining romance and reality, Richardson uncovered the dream and the menace implicit in the ordinary.

The terms romance and fairy tale are often used interchangeably in this chapter, for it is almost impossible to separate them in any sensible way. By the middle of the eighteenth century, the romance and the fairy tale were often considered to be one and the same, nursery links to the "world of fine fabling."[11] By 1740, the middle-class reading public tended to reject the aristocratic French heroic romance, as well as its English imitations by writers like Roger Boyle and Aphra Behn. Even as early as 1691, a spokesman for *The Athenian Mercury* mocked "knight-errantry" for its "Loving, Sighing, Whining, Rambling, Starving, Tilting, Fighting, Dying, Reviving, Waking, Staring, Singing, Crying, Praying, Wishing, Composing, Writing, Serenading, Rhyming, Hoping, Fearing, Despairing, Raving."[12] But while it was judged to be "not at all convenient for the Vulgar, because [it] give[s] 'em extravagant Ideas's of practice," and generally "soften[s] the Mind,"[13] the romance was still preserved in the nursery.

Arthur Johnston traces the gradual descent of the medieval romance to the chapbook, deciding that "few nurseries in the eighteenth century can have been without the chapbook version of the romances, little twenty-four page booklets, badly printed on poor paper with crude illustrations of *Guy of Warwick, Bevis of Southampton, Valentine and Orson, Don Bellianis* and *The Seven Champions of Christendom*."[14] "Authentic" medieval romances as well as imitations, such as *Tom a Lincolne, the Red Rose Knight*, which went into a thirteenth edition in 1704,[15] remained popular throughout the seventeenth and eighteenth centuries. Although severely abridged, romances like *The Seven Champions*, "suited to the meanest Capacity," were still expected by their high-minded prefacers "to enrich the Fancy, as well as to divert the Learned." Thomas Warton found that the chapbook romances, "however monstrous and unnatural" they might appear "to this age of reason and refinement," were the source "from which young readers especially in the age of fiction and fancy, nourished the SUBLIME."[16]

One such young reader was Samuel Johnson, who learned to read from *The Seven Champions*. And Richardson, as we have already seen, "early noted for having Invention," was frequently asked to make up romances to amuse his schoolmates. "One of them, particularly . . . was for putting [him] to write a History, as he called it, on the Model of Tommy Potts . . . of a Servant-Man preferred by a fine young Lady (for his Goodness) to a Lord, who was a Libertine." (*Letters*, pp. 231-32)[17] Certainly Richardson came in contact with chapbooks in the printing house of John Wilde, where he served as an apprentice. Wilde printed "jest books or old-fashioned popular fiction like *The Most Pleasant History of Tom a Lincolne*."[18] Always diffident about his lack of learning, Richardson was not one to brag about his familiarity with low chapbook romances; he preferred to reminisce about his early passion for *Orlando Furioso*.[19] Dictionary Johnson, secure in the public recognition of his erudition, could more carelessly, even gleefully, indulge himself in animated discussions of *Jack the Giant Killer*, but Samuel Richardson, master printer, would remain silent or, if pressed, deny the claims of romance.

For the record, Richardson, along with many other novelists, firmly rejected the "romance" and all it represented. But when Richardson rejected the romance in his various prefaces and letters, he was not necessarily rejecting heroic or even chapbook romance at all, but more likely disassociating himself from the novella, that shortened, more lurid form perfected by Eliza Haywood and Mary Manley. Dieter Schulz suggests that Defoe, Richardson, and Fielding reacted against the romanticized novella, a "shorter and debased variant of the heroic romance," rather than the romance itself.[20] The novella, as John Richetti points out, appealed to a middle-class audience unprepared to "cope with the sheer bulk and complication of the heroic romance, but too 'sophisticated' to be satisfied with chapbooks." Mrs. Manley recognizes in the preface to her *Secret History of Queen Zarah* that "these little Pieces which have banish'd Romances are much more agreeable to the Brisk and Impetuous Humour of the English, who have naturally no Taste for long-winded Performances." The English may have lost their taste for psychological complexity and convoluted idealism, but they had retained their taste for sexual fantasy. Mrs. Manley's secret histories and Mrs. Haywood's novellas exploit the sexual antagonism of the romance, appealing to the communal "myth" of the "destruction of female innocence by a representative of an aristocratic world of male corruption."

This myth, the plight of the helpless, virtuous female pitted against the malign, masculine, aristocratic world, is, Richetti reminds us, a "well-known eighteenth-century preoccupation, from its prominence in the drama to the prose fiction which begins with Richardson and expands all over Europe."[21] This sexual conflict pervades the sentimental drama, where many of the themes and conventions of the heroic romance surfaced. The physical distresses that plagued beleaguered virtue—the archetypal shipwrecks, captures by pirates, and occasional bouts of slavery—all became stock features of the drama as well as the romance. This strange mixture of romance, novella, and drama complicates an analysis of Richardson's work. When Clarissa compares herself to a ship foundering, ready to split on the rocks or strike on the sands, when she wildly begs to be sold into slavery rather than marry Solmes, she could be echoing dramatic, heroic, or popularly romantic conventions—all at the same time.

An attempt to unravel strands of the romance from strands of the fairy tale is further complicated by a critical search for the "true" romance, the medieval romance. The medieval romance can also be traced back to that "phenomenon that the anthropologists call 'the cultural lag,' "—the chapbook. Henry Knight Miller dismisses French heroic romances, not to mention their debased novella followers, for deviating from the true chivalric path of romance as preserved in the chapbook.[22] We are back once again in the nursery, where tales of giants, along with the adventures of Guy of Warwick, nourish a taste for the sublime.

It is equally difficult to trace fairy tale conventions in any definite way. We know they were about, but since so many tales were transmitted orally it proves almost impossible to pin them down. Once the tales were printed, we can at least suggest that they were being read. Johnson is one of the fairy tales' more vigorous champions, insisting that babies need not moral tales but giants and castles to "stretch and stimulate their little minds."[23] *Jack the Giant Killer*, first printed in England in 1711, was a favorite tale. Confessing to Mrs. Thrale that in an idle moment he had been reading of Jack's exploits, Johnson teased her with the notion that "so noble a narrative" could call up in him the soul of enterprise.[24]

Many other tales besides Jack's had been published in the early eighteenth century, and certainly even more were extant orally. Perrault's *Histoires ou contes du temps passé*, translated into English in 1729, introduced Cinderella, Sleeping Beauty, Little Red Riding Hood, Blue Beard, and Puss in Boots. *Jack in the Beanstalk* first appeared in 1734, while *Tom Thumb*, glorified in many chapbooks and celebrated in Fielding's farce, had been in print since 1621. In their study of the fairy tale, the Opies trace an early version of Cinderella, "Rashin Coatie," back to the *Complaynt of Scotland*, first published in 1540.[25] Through tales

both printed and oral, preserved in the nursery and published abroad, the stories of giants and damsels, shipwrecks
and heroic slaves, mingled in the popular imagination.

Although we cannot be certain exactly how various fairy
tales and romances extant in the eighteenth century actually
began, we can be fairly certain how they ended: happily
ever after. The romance, patterned and providential, "is a
way of ordering the world under God in secular times."[26]
Presenting an "ideal type" of romance, Henry Knight Miller
argues that although the genre does not deny "that the 'actual world' is full of mutability and fluctation and chaotic
particulars . . . it normally seeks to transcend this merely
present and mutable physical scene, to find values in a 'real'
order that is unchanging and eternal."[27] The transcendence
can be spiritual or magical, depending upon the degree of
enchantment in the tale, but always a higher order is restored. "The romance structure, like that of comedy, wherein
larger world and smaller world are harmonized at the last,
is almost inevitably that of the completed figure." While
literature that refuses resolution generates a certain pleasing anxiety, "the characteristic pleasure of romance and of
comedy comes, rather, from their natural completion of
the figure, and their inevitable suggestion that a new figure
is thereby generated."[28] We shall see the way Richardson
closed his own circles in *Pamela* and *Clarissa*. Fearful of
losing her accustomed place upon the death of her mistress,
subject to the whims of her master, Pamela, imprisoned,
exiled from her own parents, wins B. and returns to her
true home as mistress of Mr. B.'s domain, enlarging a
circle of moral regeneration through her gently didactic
letters. Driven off by her harsh relations, Clarissa leaves
her father's house, wanders in exile from St. Albans to
London to Hampstead and back again, where once again
in the wilderness of London she becomes initiated into the
ways of the fallen world. After her rape, through her will,
she makes her painful return at last to her true father in
heaven, closing the figure as she closes another circle in

the serpent motif of her coffin. However, her completed figure, unlike Pamela's, excludes her persecutors. As she ascends to her true home, she leaves her family and Lovelace hanging, suspended in guilt and grief that are impossible to resolve.

Ostensibly, Richardson the moralist, reconciled to earthly woe, had little truck with happy endings. " 'Happy, happy.' That is such a word with you chits," he taunted Miss Mulso. (*Letters*, p. 312) When Lady Bradshaigh demanded her happy ending for Clarissa, Richardson severely reminded her that life must be endured, not necessarily enjoyed. Richardson seemed to associate a desire for happiness with the undeveloped aspirations of the young ladies he both advised and chided. "I am not," he told Miss Mulso, "a woman, child. I do not think the world made for me." (*Letters*, p. 321) Yet despite his scorn for happy endings,[29] in his first novel, Richardson celebrated the Cinderella story, significantly assuming the character of a fifteen-year-old chit to make his point. The fairy tale formula freed Richardson from the demands of reality, allowing him to create a world of absolute moral values where virtue is not only desirable but rewarded, and not in heaven but in the here and now.

Richardson's middle-class readers responded to his vision because they needed to believe in the mythic possibilities he offered them. Pamela's progress symbolized their own cultural progress; her tale foretold their own ascendancy.[30] Mircea Eliade finds that myths and fairy tales all celebrate, on some level, the beginnings, the initiation *rites de passage* of a culture. Myth narrates a "sacred history" of a "creation"; it tells how something began to be, the dramatic breakthrough of the sacred into the world.[31] Pamela tells the "sacred history" of her own elevation, her breakthrough into a higher class, as she celebrates the beginning of a new way of thinking about class distinction. "My *Soul*," Pamela boasts, "is of equal Importance with the Soul of a Princess." (I, 213) [I, 137]

Pamela's sacred history tells of the death of her old inadequate self and her rebirth on a higher plane of existence. Her story begins like many fairy tales and myths, with the death of a parental figure. Her mistress, her cultural mother who has instructed her in the genteel graces, has died, leaving the house in an uproar. To establish herself as the true daughter of her aristocratic mistress, Pamela must undergo a series of trials testing her virtue and her worth. Her trials actually increase her strength, as B. notices when he claims credit for half the merit of her wit, "for the innocent Exercises you had had for it from me, have certainly sharpen'd your Invention." (I, 317) [I, 205] Pamela's rebirth is represented symbolically when she contemplates death by drowning, struggling with her most dreadful enemy, "the Weakness and Presumption . . . of her own Mind." (I, 230) [I, 148] She finally rejects suicide, delivered from a "worse enemy," than B.: herself. The significance of the drowning motif becomes more apparent when we learn that Mr. B. has also narrowly escaped drowning "in crossing a Stream, a few days ago, in pursuing his Game." (I, 243) [I, 156] The news of B.'s escape from death forces Pamela to recognize her own ambivalent feelings for him: "What is the Matter, that, with all his ill Usage of me, I cannot hate him? To be sure, I am not like other People!" Freed from her "worse" enemy, a paralyzing self-consciousness, and forced to examine her own feelings, Pamela travels out of her wilderness better prepared to make clear choices, to accept, eventually, a reformed B. Her written account of her trial by the pond as well as her recorded concern for his safety moves B. to offer marriage: her rebirth transforms his own feelings for his "game."

Fairy tales, G. K. Chesterton decided, are all conditional tales: "If you really read the fairy-tales, you will observe that one idea runs from one end of them to the other—the idea that peace and happiness can only exist on some condition. This idea, which is the core of ethics, is the core of the nursery tales."[32] Pamela operates in such a conditional world. Her virtue determines her worth: lost chastity means lost opportunity. In Pamela's world, all characters play by the rules. B. may rant, Jewkes may cuff, but no real harm is done as long as Pamela remains steadfast. In his study of the psychology of fairy tales, Bruno Bettelheim finds this faith in steadfastness in all fairy tales, the belief that "a struggle against severe difficulties in life is unavoidable, is an intrinsic part of human existence—but that if one does not shy away, but steadfastly meets unexpected and often unjust hardships, one masters all obstacles and at the end emerges victorious."[33] Bettelheim's insistence upon the positive virtue of all fairy tales can be qualified, but certainly we can agree that the idea of steadfastness, ostensibly "the core" of Richardson's own ethics, dominates *Pamela*. As long as she accepts the conditions of her trial, chastity and steadfastness, she will "emerge victorious."

But not everybody can be a Pamela. The third condition of Pamela's world, quality, would have kept the most aspiring servant girl, however steadfast, out of her story altogether. The Opies make an important point about Cinderella, suggesting that her story "is not one of rags to riches, or of dreams come true, but of reality made evident."[34] Cinderella was always worthy of the prince; the "wonderful" happens when he recognizes her worth. His perception, not Cinderella's person, has been transformed. In the same way, B. must recognize Pamela's quality. She is clearly superior to anyone else: "Where she had it, I can't tell; but I never met with the Fellow of her in my Life," B. muses. (I, 41) [I, 26] "Thou art as witty as any Lady in the Land," says Mrs. Jervis, "I wonder where thou gottest it." (I, 52) [I, 34] "See that Shape! I never saw such a Face and Shape in my Life; why she must be better descended than you have told me!" (I, 65) [I, 40]

Descent, of course, has nothing to do with it. Richardson is offering a new definition of quality, unrelated to birth and position. The "quality" in the novel are a sad lot—rude, ignorant, and spoiled. Lady Davers, the main offender, outrages Pamela's sense of justice. The pure bloodlines of the rich, she suggests, are polluted; their high position is actually low: "Many of these gentry, who brag of their ancient blood, would be glad to have it as wholesome and as *really* untainted as ours!" She is the "*high-minded* Pamela," scorning the "*lowly*" Lady Davers, "*lowly*" because she has stooped to such vain pride. (II, 23) [I, 229-30]

Richardson refuses to end his novel until every character has paid tribute to Pamela's "quality." Sir Jacob Swynford, a coarse, swinish man "with large irregular Features," whose family goes back to the Norman Conquest, presents the final challenge. Strutting, whistling, swaggering, he refuses to acknowledge his low-born niece, roaring that "her Birth's a Disgrace to our Family." Pamela's supporters trick Sir Jacob by introducing Pamela as a lady of quality. Predictably, "Lady Jenny" enchants him with her beauty, wit, and talent. She makes, it seems, too great a conquest: "I was afraid," Pamela archly notes, "if he sat next to me, he would not keep his Hands off my Hoop." Sir Jacob salutes "Lady Jenny" as the finest Lady in *England*," wishing only that "Mr. *B*. had marry'd so happily as with such a charming Creature; One, he said, that carried Tokens of her high Birth in her Face, and whose every Feature and Look shew'd her to be nobly descended." (III, 304-17) [II, 156-64] When Pamela reveals her true identity, Swynford is converted: "But curse me, that was his strange Word, if I was ever so touch'd before!" Pamela's status is firmly fixed; her reality is made evident to all. As B. remarks, "Now she has made this Conquest, she has completed all her Triumphs." (III, 320) [II, 166]

But Pamela's triumph is unique. No sooner does Richardson redefine quality than he hedges. His heroine may have crossed the boundary separating the serving from the ruling class, but Richardson makes it clear that it would

be easier to be born a countess than to become another
Pamela. Swearing his fealty to Mrs. Pamela, Sir Jacob
still worries over B.'s dangerous example: "I am in Love
with my new Niece, that I am: But still one thing sticks
with me in this Affair; and that is, What will become of
Degree or Distinction, if this Practice of Gentlemen marrying their Mothers' Waiting-maids (excuse me, Madam)
should come into Vogue." (III, 323) [II, 168] B.'s answer
would soothe the most querulous aristocrat. There can be
no other Pamela: no two princes in one age could be "in
danger" of finding another. The position has been filled.
As the Opies remind us, in most fairy tales "noble person-
ages may be brought low by fairy enchantment or by human beastliness, but the lowly are seldom made noble."[35]

For her reality to become evident, Pamela must transform the society that has initially denied her recognition.
B. is the first victim of her "magic." "I believe," he complains, "this little Slut has the Power of Witchcraft, if ever
there was a Witch; for she inchants all that come near her."
(I, 55) [I, 36] Richardson points out the connections between love and magic, connections worked to death by poets,
but new for B.

To transform B.'s way of thinking, Pamela must redefine two words central to his understanding: love and honor.
When B. is first "inchanted" by Pamela, he readily admits
his love. "I must say I love you," he assures her, offering
her an "honourable" settlement in exchange for her virginity. (I, 107) [I, 69] B.'s love, what Richardson would call
the "Paphian stimulus," must be domesticated before he
can value Pamela as an individual rather than a mere body.
His whole manner changes. The Mr. B. who formerly
lunged at Pamela's bosom now modestly and euphemisti-
cally hints of "perpetuating my happy Prospects, and my
Family at the same time." B. declares his new kind of love
to be not guilty but chaste: " 'I do own to you, my *Pamela*,
said he, that I love you with a purer Flame than ever I
knew in my Life. . . . I know more sincere Joy and Sat-

isfaction in this sweet Hour's Conversation with you, than all the guilty Tumults of my former Passion ever did." (II, 32-33) [I, 236] Pamela's evident delight with her wedding night indicates that Richardson did not advocate a marriage without passion, but a marriage of considerate, gentle passion, of domesticated love. B.'s notion of honor must be similarly transformed. He has always assured Pamela of his honor, but the honor of a keeper to his mistress, the worldly honor Pamela recognizes as "Ruin! Shame! Disgrace!" (I, 163) [I, 105] Mrs. Jewkes mocks her overly nice concern with mere words, for she does not understand their implicit magic: "Your Ruin!—Why ne'er a Lady in the Land may live happier than you, if you will, or be more honourably us'd." (I, 183) [I, 118] Pamela makes no objections to being *used*: "O how I love to be generously used," she crows when B. begs her to return to him. (II, 13) [I, 224] But she insists upon her own notion of honor—marriage, not keeping. When B. complies, she accepts him gratefully.

Pamela changes B. from a rake to a husband, a transformation as sudden as any in a fairy tale. Since we never know B.'s inner thoughts, assuming he has any, we cannot tell how the transformation has taken place. The magic seems more remarkable for this reason, but also less convincing. Although Mr. B. denies that he was ever a libertine, his early involvement with Sally Godfrey, his "Italian duel," and his outrageous abduction of Pamela suggest a history of rakish behavior. But after he decides to marry Pamela, he suddenly becomes a sober, sententious young man, wisely expostulating on the importance of early dining hours (II, 178-79) [I, 331] and piously visiting sick friends. (II, 189-90) [I, 339] His temporary relapse with the countess comes as a welcome change.

Pamela works her magic on the other characters as well. Mrs. Jewkes becomes a pious housekeeper; Colbrand is transformed into a lovable mastiff guarding the family hearth from intruders like Lady Davers. Lady Davers herself becomes Pamela's most ardent follower, begging her guidance in letters of fulsome compliments. Only Jackey, the would-be rake, fails to improve. His punishment is a poor marriage to a cast-off whore of "quality."

As Mr. B. initially suspected, Pamela, the little slut, "has the Power of Witchcraft." Sir Jacob Swynford thinks the same thing when he encounters an entire household singing the low-born girl's praises: "You talk in the language of Romance; and from the Housekeeper to the Head of the House, you're all stark-staring mad. . . . I'm in an inchanted castle, that's certain. What a plague has this little Witch done to you all?" (III, 310) [II, 160] Pamela controls her physical surroundings as well. When she shows B. her gypsy letter, smuggled to her in the loose grass, he marvels that the man "who thinks a Thousand Dragons sufficient to watch a Woman, when her Inclination takes a contrary Bent, will find all too little, and she will engage the Stones in the Street, or the Grass in the Field, to act for her." Such magic, B. suspects, is of the mind, spiritual more than physical. "If the Mind, said he, be not engaged, I see there is hardly any Confinement sufficient for the Body." (II, 36) [I, 239]

To Pamela's way of thinking, B.'s entire estate is transformed. As the newly married Mrs. B., taking a turn in the garden, she notices "what a different Aspect every thing in and about this House bears now, to my thinking, to what it once had! The Garden, the Pond, the Alcove, the Elm-walk. But, O! my Prison is become my Palace; and no wonder every thing wears another Face!" (II, 151) [I, 313] No wonder at all; the change has taken place in Pamela's mind, the wonders become part of her psyche. But once part of her mind, they possess the power to transform reality. Not a stone on the Lincolnshire estate has been turned, but the essence of the place has completely changed, from prison to palace. By changing everyone's way of thinking about her, Pamela has transformed reality.

Pamela's imagination can imprison as well as free her.

Projecting her own fears of Mr. B. onto her surroundings, she transforms two harmless cows into threatening
bulls. At first, planning her escape, Pamela is frightened
by a "horrid Bull" staring her "full in the Face, with fiery
saucer Eyes." No ordinary bull, he must be in league with
her captors. "Do you think there are such things as Witches
and Spirits? If there be, I believe in my Heart, Mrs.
Jewkes has got this Bull of her side." Lucifer has "got into
the Shape of that nasty grim Bull to watch me!" Venturing
out to escape once again, Pamela is frightened back into
the house by not one but two bulls: "Well, thought I, here
is double Witchcraft to be sure! Here is the spirit of my
master in one bull, and Mrs. *Jewkes*'s in the other: now I
am gone, to be sure!" (I, 204-205) [I, 131-33]

Even when she discovers that the two "supposed Bulls"
were only "two poor Cows . . . that my fears had made
all this rout about," she is not "fit" to escape. Pamela remains enchanted by her own fears. In a letter to Aaron
Hill, Richardson explained that he had dismissed the "improbable and marvellous" in *Pamela* to "promote the cause
of religion and virtue." (*Letters*, p. 41) But Richardson
never did actually dismiss the "improbable and marvellous," but instead transmuted them, making them part of
his character's mind.

Transforming B.'s estate, projecting her own fears onto
the landscape, Pamela always reminds the reader of her
symbolic importance. Her careful attention to her dress
reflects her awareness of the role she plays.[36] Costume has
special importance in fairy tales. We may not know the
proper names or genealogy of a fairy tale character, but
we often know what he or she is wearing: red-colored cloaks,
leather boots, diamond-covered gowns. Cinderella's transformation from rags to finery, clogs to glass slippers, reflects her internal condition, making her reality evident to
the prince. No one is more sensitive to the importance of
the proper costume than Pamela. When she first plans to

leave the B. household, she immediately considers the inappropriateness of her fine dress: "Being pretty well dress'd, I might come to some Harm, almost as bad as what I would run away from. . . . O how I wish'd for my grey Russet again, and my poor honest Dress, with which you fitted me out; (and hard enough too it was for you to do it!) for going to this Place, when I was not Twelve Years old." (I, 21) [I, 13] She has, of course, outgrown her grey Russet both literally and figuratively. Dressed above her station, she symbolizes her displacement.

Since fine clothes would be ridiculed back home, Pamela decides to get " 'quipp'd in the Dress that will become my Condition." (I, 50) [I, 32] The word "become" works in three different ways here. Its most obvious meaning is "suit" or "befit": Pamela needs humble clothes to suit her lowly condition. But "become" also means "to come to be," suggesting that lowly dress, symbolizing a lowly state, will "come to be" Pamela's condition: her choice of dress will actually determine her position in life. "Become" has another meaning as well: "to grace, to adorn, to look well." The simplicity of Pamela's humble costume actually attracts B., becoming her so well that he claims she has surpassed her former self. (I, 70) [I, 43] By rekindling B.'s interest, Pamela's becoming costume aids her to become Mrs. B.

Pamela also emphasizes the symbolic importance of her costume when she makes up her well-known three bundles. (The number three has great power in fairy tales.) Wearing only the clothes from "poor Pamela's bundle," she sets aside the "clothes and linen my lady had given me" and my "ever-worthy master's presents" until B. recognizes her worth. Even after she has become elevated, she hesitates before dressing in her finery. Her simple dress has gained her fame in the neighborhood, inspiring visitors to beg her to appear in the humble garb. Always happy to narrate her "sacred history," Pamela eagerly complies, explaining that "there will be the less Reason to fear I should forget the high Obligations I shall have to the kindest of Gentlemen, when I can delight to show the humble Degree from which his Goodness has raised me." (II, 61) [I, 255] After illustrating her lowly origins, however, Pamela willingly reclaims her two fine bundles, "and taking my Fan in my Hand, I, like a little proud Hussy, look'd in the Glass, and thought myself a Gentlewoman once more)." (II, 85) [I, 270-71] Never one for the finer points of symbolism, Mrs. Jewkes is simply relieved to find Pamela looking like "her Lady indeed."

Like all good fairy tales, *Pamela* ends happily ever after—when it does end. Unfortunately, for about five hundred pages it seems unlikely to end at all. Richardson finally concludes his continuation of *Pamela* on an apologetic note: "The Editor thinks proper to conclude in this Place, that he may not be thought to deserve a Suspicion, that the Extent of the Work was to be measured by the Patience of its Readers." (IV, 453) [II, 472] Some readers possessed infinite patience. The tireless Aaron Hill greatly admired *Pamela II*, wondering "Where will your wonders end?"[37] Other readers were asking the same question more critically. Stephen Duck, the "Thresher Poet," confessed that he did not "feel [his] mind Affected and Interested so much for Pamela" in the third volume. "*Instruction*," Richardson loftily explained to Duck, "is my main End, and if I can *Entertain* at the same time my View will be complete." He sent an outline of the book's "events" to Duck. It was, sadly, a fairly accurate plan of the novel, including Pamela's Sunday behavior, "the Pregnant Circumstances to a Mind so Apprehensive as Pamela's, a Debate about Mothers being Nurses to their Children . . . her Observations on a Tragedy, a Comedy, an Italian Opera, and a Masquerade; from the last of which will arise a Distress, that possibly will answer your kind Objection; in a strong Jealous Scene—Then her Opinion and Practice on the Subject of a first Education &c." (*Letters*, pp. 52-53)

Rather than end at all, the novel fades into a blurred

vision of domestic bliss. Richardson's reluctance to end his story reveals a sense of dissatisfaction with his "happy ending." Burying his reader in countless examples of Pamela's goodness, he protests too much. Richardson was so determined to prove his heroine's worth that it would seem, on some level, that he did not believe Pamela, or indeed any "chit," was worthy of a happy ending. Remember his admonition to Miss Mulso: " 'Happy, happy,' it is such a word with you chits." Pamela must never stop proving her right to happiness: she is always on trial. When B. dallies with a countess, leaving a pregnant Pamela to wonder at his behavior, he is not on trial. Pamela is. She must shine, proving herself once more to be noble and pure, the exalted creature worthy of her happy ending.

For all his adoration of sublime women, deep down Richardson seems to have had reservations about their true worth. He solved the problem of worthiness in *Clarissa*: a dead heroine is a safe heroine, freed from trials and temptations. Richardson's refusal to end *Pamela* decisively may have come from his distrust of human happiness: life was to be endured, not enjoyed. Although he believed in the theory of "Virtue Rewarded," and could happily write conduct manuals promoting the cause of such virtue, he could not, it seems, present a happy ending convincingly in dramatic terms. In *Clarissa*, he confronted this problem by showing the impossibility of earthly happiness in a world where one half of mankind torments the other. Clarissa must look to heaven for her reward, for she shall receive none on earth as long as she lives. Dead she is glorified, but alive she is an embarrassment.

In *Clarissa* Richardson rejected the happy ending of the fairy tale. Even though Clarissa faces her trials as every fairy tale heroine must, with steadfast faith and courage, the "sacred history" of her "spiritual breakthrough" ends tragically and pessimistically. For although the world of Clarissa is "conditional," all of its conditions are tragic.

Resistance and steadfast faith cannot alter Clarissa's fate: she is raped, regardless of her actions. Wherever she turns, one more accomplice magically appears to aid her persecutors. Lovelace notes with surprise that the good ladies of Hampstead serve him as effectively as "Mother" Sinclair. And why not? All the world would seem to be in league against Clarissa.

In his greatest novel, Richardson retains the elements of magic and the threat of violence central to the fairy tale, but he reverses his reader's expectations. He exploits the reader's need for a happy ending by introducing conventional fairy tale characters—the wicked stepmother, the slimy frog prince, the ugly stepsister, a Prince Charming ready to rescue the princess from her castle. But in the end, he inverts the formula: Prince Charming rescues the captive princess only to imprison and rape her. The Opies tell us that the hero of the typical fairy tale is "almost invariably a young person, usually the youngest member of the family, and if not deformed or already an orphan, is probably in the process of being disowned or abandoned."[38] Clarissa, the youngest member of her family, fits this description perfectly: she is about to be abandoned; her household is in "tumults," her suitor has just wounded her brother in a duel, and her family is preparing to force her to marry the odious Solmes. The conditions of her grandfather's will have set Clarissa apart from her family, exposing her to the jealousy of James and Arabella. Richardson is very careful to present reasonable explanations for their hatred, for he is ostensibly constructing a world of cause and effect, a "realistic" world circumstantially described. But no amount of rationalizing can explain the violence and intensity of their hatred; it is basic to their personalities. James and Arabella are the evil brother and sister of a fairy tale. As Anna Howe points out, it is in their nature for them to persecute Clarissa: "You can no more change *your* nature, than your persecutors can *theirs*. Your distress is owing to the vast disparity between you and them. . . . Do

they not act in character?—And to whom? To an Alien.
You are not one of them." (II, 64) [I, 282-83] As mar-
velous a child as any changeling in fairy tale or romance,
Clarissa is clearly set apart from her relations from the
start. How did she get it? Lovelace wonders in his first
letter to Belford. There are folks who even remember her
being born, but he sometimes doubts her mortality. Even
Clarissa questions her brother's and sister's vile natures.
Isn't the world supposed to be one great family?

The isolation Clarissa suffers is both physical and psychological. Family members have the ominous habit of
withdrawing, silently "dropping away," to cut Clarissa off
from normal family intimacy. The Harlowe formula is
simple: intimidation followed by withdrawal. In a typical
encounter: "My Father sat half-aside in his elbow-chair,
that his head might be turned from me; his hands clasped,
and waving, as it were, up and down; his fingers, poor
dear gentleman! in motion, as if angry to the very ends of
them. My Sister sat swelling. My Brother looked at me
with scorn, having measured me, as I may say, with his
eyes as I entered, from head to foot." Surely, so far, a
"natural" family scene. Circumstantially and realistically,
Richardson is describing a nightmare taking place not at
night, but at that most innocent hour, tea time. How can
the "poor dear gentleman," head turned, hands "clasped
and waving," fingers in motion, and Bella, "swelling" like
a creature in a nightmare, be viewed as anything but unnatural?

Duly intimidated, Clarissa watches the family members
"drop away": "My Brother bid the Footman who attended,
leave the room. I, said he, will pour out the water. My
heart was up at my mouth. I did not know what to do with
myself. What is to follow? thought I. Just after the second
dish, out stept my Mother.—A word with you, Sister
Hervey! Taking her in her hand. Presently my Sister dropt
away. Then my Brother. So I was left alone with my
Father." After a stern scene, her father leaves Clarissa

completely alone, on her knees: "He was pleased to withdraw, leaving me on the floor; saying, That he would not
hear me thus." (I, 51-54) [I, 35-37] Another time, as
Clarissa enters one door to the parlor, her "friends" scurry
out at the other: "I saw just the gown of my Sister, the last
who slid away." (II, 202) [I, 377] Richardson's verbs
"slide" and "drop" dehumanize the Harlowes, making them
seem mechanical and oddly sinister.

On one occasion, Clarissa attempts to control her isolation. Left with Solmes, who presses his "ugly weight" against
her hoop, she watches her friends drop away in their accustomed way: "Before the usual breakfast-time was over
my Father withdrew with my Mother, telling her he wanted
to speak to her. Then my Sister and next my Aunt (who
was with us) dropt away. My Brother gave himself some
airs of insult, which I understood well enough; but which
Mr. Solmes could make nothing of: and at last he arose
from *his* seat. Sister, said he, I have a curiosity to show
you. I will fetch it. And away he went, shutting the door
close after him." This time Clarissa takes the initiative,
withdrawing as well, leaving "the man hemming up for a
speech." (I, 101) [I, 69] But her withdrawal is merely
negative; she must retreat to her chambers in disgrace.
Her closet becomes a prison as well as a refuge. Soon the
keys "of every-thing" are taken from her, and Betty becomes her jailer, guarding her isolation.

Clarissa's isolation distorts her view of reality. Cut off
from her family and friends, she is allowed to overhear
hints of her fate, frightening and often deceptive in their
cryptic nature. Even her own servant, Hannah, is ostra-
cized: "Late as it is, they are all shut up together. Not a
door opens; not a soul stirs. Hannah, as she moves up and
down, is shunned as a person infected." (I, 158) [I, 108]
Clarissa may not even tarry on her way "up and down the
back-stairs, that the sight of so perverse a young creature
may not add to the pain you have given every-body." (I,
167) [I, 114] Although she dominates the family confer-

ences and conversations, she is at the same time kept apart
from the family members, who laugh and triumph over
her fate: "Going down to my Poultry-yard just now, I
heard my Brother and Sister and that Solmes laughing and
triumphing together. The high Yew Hedge between us,
which divides the Yard from the Garden, hindered them
from seeing me." (II, 40) [I, 266] The yew hedge separates her from her family another time when, forbidden to
show herself to her father, she hides behind the shrubbery
until he passes by: "You cannot imagine what my emotions
were behind the yew-hedge, on seeing my Father so near
me. I was glad to look at him thro' the hedge, as he passed
by: But I trembled in every joint when I heard him utter
these words: Son James, to You, and to Bella, and to You,
Brother, do I wholly commit this matter." (II, 252) [I,
411]

While yew hedges,[39] insolent servants, and back stair-
cases cut off Clarissa from "normal" reality, her internal-
ized fears exaggerate her trials. Listening for the sounds
of the carriage wheels of her "judges," she imagines Solmes's
presence, "altho' it happened that he was not there." Her
heart "flutter[s]" to hear "the chariot of the one, and then
of the other, rattle thro' the courtyard, and the hollow-
sounding footstep giving notice of each person's stepping
out, to take his place on the awful bench, which my fancy
had formed for them and my other judges! That, thought
I, is my Aunt Hervey's! That my Uncle Harlowe's! Now
comes my Uncle Antony! And my imagination made a
fourth chariot for the odious Solmes, altho' it happened
that he was not there." (I, 327) [I, 223] Like Pamela's
"supposed bulls," Solmes's imaginary chariot, the product
of Clarissa's "fancy," helps to imprison her.

Clarissa's fears are not always unjustified. On the other
side of the yew hedge, reality ever threatens. Clarissa lives
in a remarkably violent world of duels, abduction, rape,
and suicide. Most fairy tales are violent; some, like the
tales of the Brothers Grimm and Charles Perrault, exces-

sively so. Heels are cut off, stomachs slit open, eyes put out. Fairy-tale heroes and heroines seem to expect to encounter such atrocities: they come with the territory. Bruno Bettelheim finds "the element of *threat* crucial to the fairy tale—a threat to the hero's physical existence or to his moral existence," noting that "as soon as the story begins, the hero is projected into severe dangers."[40] By presenting his scrupulously exact correspondents, who record the most minute circumstances of everyday life, Richardson authenticates the terror. We begin to take for granted the violence always present, threatening to burst the framework of his novel.

In Clarissa's world, the most innocent circumstance can suddenly become dangerous. For instance, a trivial scene with Mama quickly turns violent, almost without warning. At first all is calm: "Sit down, Clary Harlowe; I shall talk to you by-and-by: And continued looking into a drawer among Laces and Linen, in a way neither busy nor unbusy." One page later, Clary and her mother are wrestling with each other: "Yet tear not yourself from me! [wrapping my arms about her as I kneeled; she struggling to get from me; my face lifted up to hers, with eyes running over, that spoke not my heart if they were not all humility and reverence]. . . . I arose trembling, and hardly knowing what I did, or how I stood or walked, withdrew to my chamber." (I, 129-32) [I, 89-91] Recognizing the inherent kinetic energy in the most aimless actions "neither busy nor unbusy," Richardson exploits the latent violence of the commonplace.

In a later scene, Lovelace and Clarissa take breakfast together, civilly and politely, until violence erupts. Lovelace asks Clarissa to take a dish of tea with him:

> She a dish—I a dish. Sip, her eyes her own, she; like a haughty and imperious sovereign, conscious of dignity, every look a favour. Sip, like her vassal, I; lips and hands trembling, and not knowing that I sip'd or tasted.

I was—I was—Issp'd—(drawing in my breath and the liquor together, tho' I scalded my mouth with it) I was in hopes, Madam—

Dorcas came in just then.—Dorcas, said she, is a chair gone for? Damn'd impertinence, thought I, thus to put me out in my speech! And I was forced to wait for the servant's answer to the insolent mistress's question. William is gone for one madam. This cost me a minute's silence before I could begin again. And then it was with my hopes, and my hopes, and my hopes, and my hopes, that I should have been early admitted to—What weather is it, Dorcas? said she, as regardless of me as if I had not been present. A little lowering, madam.—The Sun is gone in.—It was very fine half an hour ago. I had no patience. Up I rose. Down went the Tea-cup, Saucer and all.—Confound the Weather, the Sunshine, and the Wench! (IV, 213-14) [II, 381]

Outwardly all is polite and decorous: she a dish, I a dish; sip, sip; what is the weather? Inwardly all is violent: scalded mouth, insolent mistress. Since Lovelace, always the ironic artist, is speaking, the agony is humorous: "And then it was with my hopes, and my hopes, and my hopes, and my hopes." And finally the violence erupts. "Down went the Tea-cup," ending the charade of civilized intercourse. One page later, the carefully controlled Clarissa throws herself into a chair, "her sweet face all crimsoned over with passion." Richardson's characters are violent, almost mad in their passion as they fling their crockery and their bodies about their well-appointed rooms.

There is, of course, a "reason" for the violence. Richardson always gives "natural" explanations for his nightmare visions. Clarissa must be pushed out of Harlowe Place into Lovelace's waiting carriage. "Nothing," she vows, "but the *last* extremity shall make me abandon my Father's house." (II, 76) [I, 291] Richardson must bring his heroine to this "last extremity" while making his readers be-

lieve in her dilemma. Incorporating the elements of romance, Richardson presents a hostile world always
threatening Clarissa. He even includes the threat of "A
Chapel! A moated house!" The very stuff of romance.

The final interview with Solmes, a living embodiment
of the "last extremity," is a nightmare. James runs amuck,
storming through the parlor calling his sister vile names.
Isolated once again, Clarissa can barely distinguish the distant voices babbling her fate: "Nobody was there. I sat
down, and had leisure to weep; reflecting upon what my
Cousin Dolly had told me. They were all in my Sister's
parlour, adjoining: For I heard a confused mixture of voices,
some louder than others, which drowned the more com-
passionating accents. *Female* accents I could distinguish the
drowned ones to be." (II, 216) [I, 386] Clarissa appears
mad at this point, hearing voices, reflecting, dreading, while
"nobody was there." Later in the interview, Clarissa hears
her sentence thundered down from her invisible father. In
her attempt to confront her accusers, she flings herself against
the parlor door to fall flat on her face in an ominously
empty room. "But every-body was gone." As usual, her
persecutors have withdrawn, leaving her to face only herself and her fears. Unable to withstand such an atmosphere
of hostility and persecution, she leaves home with Lovelace, convinced of the hopelessness of her dilemma. In his
"plain and natural account," Richardson brings Clarissa
and his reader to the "last extremity."

Psychologically Clarissa has been brought to the last extremity, but in "reality" her situation is not so desperate.
As we have seen, Clarissa, mentally adding Solmes's carriage to the family procession, "altho' it happened that he
was not there," can exaggerate her plight. Wildly she begs
her aunt: "Let me but be single—Cannot I live single? Let
me be sent, as I have proposed, to Scotland, to Florence;
any-whither: Let me be sent a slave to the Indies; any-
whither—Any of these I will consent to." (I, 343) [I,
234] Or even more macabre: "If there were no other way,

I would most willingly be buried alive." (I, 211) [I, 143]
When Clarissa histrionically considers slavery in the Indies
and live burial, she acts in a "romance" world of ogres,
monsters, and murder that dominates her way of thinking
in the "real" world. Her fears, both real and imagined,
imprison her more effectively than Uncle Antony's moated
house could ever do. The tension between what Clarissa
experiences in "reality," and what she experiences emotionally gives the novel great psychological power.

At times, Clarissa can recognize the limits of her persecution. She demands of her insolent servant, "What will
they do, Betty? They won't kill me? What *will* they do?"
(II, 121) [I, 322] The Harlowes are united against Clarissa, but their unity is based on fear as well as hostility.
Their power can always be punctured. As Uncle John confesses, all the family members are afraid to see Clarissa,
because they fear being "made as so many fools." (II, 96)
[I, 305]

Clarissa's persecutors can be found out to be fools, but
they also retain their authority. Her world is filled with
monsters of her own mind, creatures of nightmare. The
Harlowe family, "larger than life," can be more evil, more
violent, more willful than possible. Yet, at the same time,
its members seem "realistic," substantial characters of weight.
The gouty father, walking twice around the room; fat-
faced Bella taunting Clarissa with her rich, new wedding
patterns; brother James taking a turn in the garden with
Solmes; and ineffectual Mama, looking through Clarissa's
drawers, "neither busy nor unbusy," appear solid, but they
are also fantastic. Father, mysteriously out of sight, thun-
ders down his curses like an Old Testament god; James
hisses his threats of violence, an incestuous monster poi-
soned by jealousy; spiteful Bella swells in anger, the evil,
ugly stepsister puffed up like a toad. Only Mama, a wraith
with the blood sucked from her, does nothing, and her
passivity is the most fantastic of all.

The odious Solmes, "the wretch," is the frog prince who

disgusts the princess with his ugliness, but a frog prince who can never be transformed; he will always be the loathesome creature of nightmare. Splay-footed, bent and broad-shouldered, he squats on chairs with his ugly weight; "he is a very bold, staring man." (I, 100) [I, 68] We can almost hear him croak. Like the princess in the fairy tale, Clarissa can barely look upon him without showing her disgust. Anna Howe supports Clarissa's aversion to Solmes, poking fun at the horrid wretch, the hideous fellow. "What odd heads some people have!—Miss Clarissa Harlowe to be sacrificed in marriage to Mr. Roger Solmes!—Astonishing!" (I, 58) [I, 40] The true horror of Solmes lies in his sexuality,[41] the threat of such an odious frog making love to the divine Clarissa. While James and Arabella eagerly anticipate the prospect, Anna Howe warns what "a dreadful thing must even the *Love* of such a Husband be!" (I, 184) [I, 126] Love from such an "insolent, overbearing," yet "insinuating, creeping mortal" would be an outrage.

Lovelace's cohorts, Mrs. Sinclair and her "daughters," are both realistically and fantastically described. Mrs. Sinclair, the good widow of an officer in the guards, seems plausible enough at first. Clarissa reports that although she has "an odd winking eye; and her respectfulness seems too much studied, methinks, for the London ease and freedom," Mrs. Sinclair is "extremely civil and obliging." (III, 316-17) [II, 193] However, on the night of the rape, when she reveals her true nature, Mrs. Sinclair becomes a dragon, terrorizing Clarissa into submission. Lovelace reports that "the old dragon straddled up to [Clarissa], with her arms kemboed again,—Her eyebrows erect, like the bristles upon a hog's back, and scouling over her shortened nose, more than half-hid her ferret eyes. Her mouth was distorted. She pouted out her blubber-lips, as if to bellows up wind and sputter into her horse-nostrils; and her chin was curdled, and more than usually prominent with passion." (V, 313) [III, 195-96] Dragon, hog,

ferret, and horse, Mrs. Sinclair is a monster in a nightmare, a fairy tale opponent who can never be defeated
because, for once, Prince Charming is in league with her
to ravish, not release, the princess. When Clarissa manages
to escape Sinclair's house, Belford describes her keeper's
rage. She has become a witch: "The Mother, foaming at
the mouth, bellowed out her orders. . . . See that guilty
pyeball devil, was her word. . . . But I'll punish her.
. . . Put on the great gridiron this moment [an oath or a
curse at every word]: Make up a roaring fire—The cleaver
bring me this instant—I'll cut her into quarters with my
own hands; and carbonade and broil the traitress for a feast
to all the dogs and cats in the neighbourhood; and eat the
first slice of the toad myself, without salt or pepper." (VI,
103-104) [III, 312-13]

Sinclair's daughters are also transformed from genteel
young women into the slatterns Belford describes with such
horror. Without the paint and padding necessary to prop
up their sagging foundations, the young ladies change into
monsters overnight: "And half of them (unpadded, shoulder-bent, pallid-lipt, limber-jointed wretches) appearing,
from a blooming Nineteen or Twenty perhaps over-night,
haggard well-worn strumpets of Thirty-eight or Forty."
(VIII, 56) [IV, 381] Corruption and decay lie under their
paint and stays, just as a nightmare of corruption and violence underlies the "natural" facade of *Clarissa*.

Clarissa is a fairy story about reality, narrating the ways
"reality becomes evident." In spite of the oppression of her
family and the stratagems of Lovelace, Clarissa must reveal her own nature to herself as well as to others. Before
she is elevated to sainthood, she must recognize her pride,
her attraction to Lovelace, her fatal innocence. She must
come to terms with her personality as it is stripped down,
her mad self raving in the cryptic poems and letters she
writes after her rape.[42] Only then can she recreate herself
and reveal her true reality.

Lovelace presents the greatest threat as the Prince Charming who betrays her expectations. Her family's plan to force her into marriage with Solmes is straightforward enough, what Chesterton would call "conditional." As long as Clarissa resists, she remains safe. But Lovelace, a sorcerer of great invention, works a more subtle magic: he alters the world of appearances, turning a brothel into a boarding house and a whore into a lady. Yet although Lovelace feverishly alters the conditions of Clarissa's life, changing the rules cavalierly as he transforms her reality, he can never transform the condition of his own life. Clarissa herself becomes the central condition of his own reality, mocking his lack of soul with her own transformed sense of self. As she transcends her fate, stripping off her old self to rebuild a pure soul untouched by Lovelace's artifice, Lovelace sinks further into himself, unable to break out of his self-limiting inventions. Without a Clarissa to give his life meaning, existence becomes void. Death at the hands of Morden becomes preferable to such empty reality.

Clarissa begins her story naively confident in the power of her own goodness. She has been the favorite child for eighteen years, cossetted and nurtured by her family. Even when her family turns on her, forcing her to flee with Lovelace, she still has faith in her judgment, rejoicing in her sturdy will. Miss Howe echoes her optimistic faith in the world of appearances when she complacently advises her to watch her companions at Mrs. Sinclair's carefully. If they are not "right" people, she shall find them out in "one breakfasting." (III, 327) [II, 200] This, Clarissa sadly learns, is nonsense.

By the time of her death, Clarissa completely revises her view of the world: it is an unfriendly place that must be fooled. Understanding by now Lovelace's game of deception and disguise, she tricks him with her allegorical letter, promising to meet him "in time" at her father's house, forgetting to add that her "father" is in heaven. She is, she tells Miss Howe, afraid "that it is a step that is not strictly right, if Allegory or Metaphor be not allowable to one in her circumstances." (VII, 253) [IV, 200] In a fallen world of false appearances, one must look to allegory as the only way to express truth and to deceive deceivers.

Richardson places great importance upon symbol and allegory. Clarissa must look past the literal to the underlying meaning of life, to the life beyond death. As she approaches death, her behavior and announcements become more oblique, less candid. Clarissa has learned to protect herself. Only after her death, freed from the threat of Lovelace, can she reveal her final reality, her sainthood, to all. The last volume of *Clarissa* bears witness to the revealed truth: everyone must acknowledge her sainthood before her story can end. Lovelace's dying vision of Clarissa, his plea to "let this expiate," is the final confirmation of her reality made evident to all.

Clarissa's world is metaphoric to an extraordinary degree. Circular in structure, her novel begins and ends with a duel. Its actions, beginning in the legal complications of Clarissa's grandfather's will and ending in the legal simplicity of Clarissa's own will, run out the course of one year. Clarissa ends the novel where she began, home at Harlowe Place, once again the chaste paragon of virtue and the cynosure of all eyes. Dead, to be sure, but back in the bosom of her family. The entire book centers on Clarissa, who magically controls the fates and opinions of all who come into contact with her. Lovelace may construct his magnificent plots to move the action, but his victim dominates all at the center. Toying with a complicated spider/fly metaphor, Lovelace muses that "whatever our hearts are in, our heads will follow. Begin with *Spiders*, with *Flies*, with what we will, Girl is the centre of gravity, and we all naturally tend to it." (III, 67) [II, 23] Lovelace, the Harlowes, Belford, and the reader all tend to the center of gravity, Clarissa, crowding into "the silent slow procession" at last to gaze at her symbolic, "eye-attracting" coffin.

When Clarissa resorts to allegory, setting up her carved coffin for a writing table, selling her clothes to dramatize her detachment from the real world, she is turning herself into a symbol. Both Clarissa and Lovelace are highly aware of the significance of their own symbolic natures. Other characters in the book also respond to their metaphoric value. As Mrs. Hervey writes to Clarissa: "But you want to clear up things—*What* can you clear up? Are you not gone off?—With a Lovelace too? . . . what power will he be thought to have over you!—He!—Who? *Lovelace*—the vilest of libertines! Over whom?—A *Clarissa*." (III, 271) [II, 162] Lovelace is not only the vilest of libertines, he is "a Lovelace"; Clarissa is "a Clarissa." The two literally become symbols for themselves.

Like the dual world of their novel, Clarissa and Lovelace are at once mundane and fantastic. The epic, heroic aspects of their characters are expressed in their inner lives. What is at work is what Ortega y Gasset discusses in "A Short Treatise on the Novel." Speaking of Don Quixote, he speculates that "although the realistic novel was born in opposition to the so-called novel of fantasy, it carries adventure enclosed within its body."[43] The fantastic adventures related in the books of chivalry possess a powerful underground reality in the imagination of Don Quixote. Both Don Quixote and Clarissa break through the mundane boundaries of their everyday worlds. Don Quixote makes literal the metaphors of chivalry, acting out society's unenforceable code in an unprepared world. The world resists Don Quixote because he takes seriously what the world can only pretend to believe in. In the same way, Clarissa personifies the metaphor of her society: tragically, she believes in chastity and acts on her belief in spite of the compromises urged upon her by a worldly society that values appearances more. What makes Don Quixote and Clarissa unique is not their inner lives, but the dramatic way they manifest their inner lives, acting out their fantasies in the real world. And what makes Richardson unique is the way he uses his exemplary characters to act out fantasies of fairy tale and romance he ostensibly rejects in his moral novel.

To maintain the moralistic facade, he does present us with a middle-class paragon: witness Anna Howe's postmortem account of her friend's daily round of good deeds. (VIII, 217-47) [IV, 490-510] In her account book, Clarissa is a prig; in her closet, an impassioned saint. Depending upon the point of view, her life, culminating in her rape, can be seen as monumental or commonplace. Lovelace, for one, complains about her "notions" after the rape: "But peoples extravagant notions of things alter not facts, Belford: And, when all's done, Miss Clarissa Harlowe has but run the fate of a thousand others of her Sex— only that they did not set such a romantic value upon what they call their Honour; that's all." (V, 318) [III, 199] But that's not all. Clarissa's notion alters Lovelace's reality. By treating the moral code with extravagant seriousness, she forces society to evaluate its own moral position. She is working a powerful magic here, transforming not only Lovelace but society.

As in *Pamela*, Richardson pays careful attention to the importance of costume in his creation of the Clarissa symbol. The Harlowe family's concern with dress is materialistic, nouveau riche. The patterns "of the richest silks" her father has ordered from London to tempt Clarissa into marrying Solmes reflect the showy grandeur of Harlowe Place, which Lovelace insists "sprung up from a dunghil, within every elderly person's remembrance." (I, 249) [I, 170] Mrs. Harlowe proudly tells Clarissa that the patterns are "the newest, as well as richest, that we could procure; answerable to our station in the world; answerable to the fortune, additional to your Grandfather's Estate, designed you; and to the noble Settlements agreed upon." (I, 304) [I, 207] Richardson's irony is strong here: Solmes's settlements are hardly noble, but the patterns, new and rich, like the Harlowes, are certainly answerable to the Harlowe family's station.

As Clarissa transforms herself from girl into saint, she also transforms her appearance, becoming less individualized. In the early part of the novel, as often noted, Clarissa is a pert, fashionable young woman, stylishly dressed. When she flees with Lovelace, he describes her costume in great detail. (III, 28) [I, 512] But once under his control, she is no longer individuated Clary Harlowe but a more abstract symbol of supplication and violation. In the fire scene, we see her eyes streaming, her hair disheveled, her bosom heaving. Lovelace replaces the minute detail of the curiously embroidered morning gown with emotionally charged words of a vague, sensory nature. (IV, 392) [II, 503]

The night of the rape, Clarissa, even more stylized, appears to be pure victim: "her shining tresses flowing about her neck; her ruffles torn, and hanging in tatters about her snowy hands. . . . And down on her bosom, like a half-broken-stalked Lily, top-heavy with the overcharging dews of the morning, sunk her head, with a sigh that went to my heart." (V, 308-310) [III, 192-93] After the rape, Clarissa sells her clothing, explaining that she will need only a shroud in death. Her needs have diminished greatly as her separation from the material world becomes more pronounced. Later, dying in her rented room, Clarissa adopts the broken lily emblem as her own symbol, covering her coffin with emblems of her fate, "the head of a white Lily snapt short off, and just falling from the stalk." (VII, 338) [IV, 257] By making the lily symbol her own, she transforms it. As Mark Kinkead-Weekes suggests, "the lily is no longer a lachrymose symbol of desecrated innocence untimely cut off." The lily "is the psalmist's emblem of the transitoriness of *all* human life. 'The days of man are but as grass,' the inscription reads, 'he flourisheth as a flower of the field: For, as soon as the wind goeth over it, it is gone; and the place thereof shall know it no more.' "⁴⁴ Free at last of the demands of her family and of the symbol-making magic of Lovelace, in her final days Clarissa deliberately and consciously controls her own self-image.

Lovelace also sees himself as a symbol, more powerful and fantastic in his imagination than in his life. At times his romantic self-image approaches the ridiculous, as in his plaintive letter sent from the "Ivy-Cavern, in the Coppice—Day but just breaking." "*Good God!* What is *now* to become of me!—How shall I support this disappointment!—No new cause!—On one knee, kneeling with the other, I write!—My feet benumbed with midnight wanderings thro' the heaviest dews, that ever fell: My wig and my linen dripping with the hoar-frost dissolving on them!—Day but just breaking—Sun not risen to exhale—May it never rise again!—Unless it bring healing and comfort to a benighted soul." (II, 129-30) [I, 327] The style here is more bombastic than usual, but the complaint is familiar: Lovelace is being undervalued. In his imagination he is a romantic hero, a knight fighting for his lady. Thinking of Don Quixote, he describes his suffering for Clarissa: "Purchased by a painful servitude of many months; fighting thro' the Wild-beasts of her family for her, and combating with a Wind-mill Virtue, which hath cost me millions of perjuries only to attempt; and which now, with its damn'd Air-fans, has tossed me a mile and a half beyond hope!" (V, 17) [II, 518] Out of joint with his time, Lovelace quixotically battles conventional windmills, carrying romance within his realistic body.

Lovelace represents himself as a symbol of greatness wasted on an undeserving world of mediocrity. He is certain that his greatness lies in his "active soul," forced in its pedestrian, middle-class culture to channel its energy into rakish schemes of seduction. But in another culture, "had I been a Prince! To be sure I should have made a most *noble* Prince! I should have led up a military dance equal to that of the great Macedonian. I should have added kingdom to kingdom, and despoiled all my neighbour-sovereigns, in order to have obtained the name of *Robert the Great*. And I would have gone to war with the great Turk, and the Persian, and the Mogholl, for their Seraglios; for not one of those Eastern Monarchs should have had a pretty woman to bless himself with, till I had done with her." (V, 67) [III, 26-27] Instead, he goes to war with the Great Harlowe and the brother and the Solmes for their one girl: Clarissa. His way of reaping glory in an inglorious world. One must make do in these diminished times.

Always changing, Lovelace does not stick to one consistent symbol. He can battle windmills and play knight-errant, but he can also reverse his role, playing the ogre in the castle who imprisons the princess. He taunts Belford for his failure to prevent Clarissa's rape. You knew my plans, he reminds him, "thou shouldest, like a true knight-errant, have sought to set the Lady free from the inchanted castle." (VIII, 165-66) [IV, 456] Indeed, a true knight would have killed the ogre if necessary. In all things, Lovelace manages to have it both ways: he is both rapist and savior, villain and hero, ogre and knight.

At Hampstead, Lovelace suddenly sees himself as another figure both heroic and villainous, Satan, the perfect foil to Clarissa's Christ figure. When he confronts her, he exults in his resemblance to Satan, significantly to Milton's Satan: "I unbuttoned therefore my cape, I pulled off my flapt slouched hat; I threw open my great coat, and, like the devil in Milton [an odd comparison tho'!] *I started up in my own form divine./ Touch'd by the beam of her celestial eye./ More potent than Ithuriel's spear!*" Grandiosely reversing romantic expectations, Lovelace seems at first the archetypal hero of romance who, returning from his quest in disguise, "flings off his beggar's rags" to stand forth in the "resplendent" garb of the prince.[45] But at the exact moment he seems most splendid he is in fact plotting to rape Clarissa. His metamorphosis startles the company, suggesting to at least one incredulous soul that the comparison to the devil is most appropriate. The serving maid "would have it, that I was neither more nor less than the devil, and could not keep her eye from my foot; expecting, no doubt, every minute to see it discover itself to be cloven." (V, 88-89) [III, 41-42]

Like Milton's Satan, who cannot fly that hell within himself, Lovelace lives in a hell of his own making; "already is there a hell begun in my own mind." (VII, 408) [IV, 304] Clarissa calls her seducer a serpent, another "form divine" of Lovelace and Satan: "Yet am I glad this violent spirit *can* thus creep; that like a poisonous serpent, he *can* thus coil himself, and hide his head in his own narrow circlets." (VII, 367) [IV, 276] We have encountered the serpent before, the principal device of Clarissa's coffin: "Neatly etched on a plate of white metal, is a crowned Serpent, with its tail in its mouth, forming a ring, the emblem of Eternity; And in the circle made by it is this inscription: CLARISSA HARLOWE/ April X/ [Then the year]/ AETAT XIX." (VII, 338) [IV, 257] When Milton's Satan, after creeping around the walls of Paradise (as Lovelace creeps around the walls of Harlowe Place), first spies Adam and Eve, he excuses his plans to destroy their happiness with an argument both specious and tragic. He seeks "League" with his victims, "And mutual amity so strait, so close,/ That I with you must dwell, or you with me,/ Henceforth."[46] Like Satan, Lovelace seeks this same league with Clarissa, compelled by necessity to have her with him in "mutual amity so strait, so close," even if he needs to destroy her and himself in the struggle to achieve such a union. On her coffin, Clarissa places her name within the coils of the serpent. For damnation or redemption, she and Lovelace are fated to come together finally in death, in the motif of her coffin. The serpent symbolizes eternity; it may also, as Ian Watt suggests, represent "an endlessly self-consuming sexual desire."[47] And surely, in the end, it symbolizes the eternal union, the "completed figure," of the infernal and divine, Lovelace and Clarissa.

Symbolism is conspicuously absent from *Sir Charles Grandison*. Instead Richardson gives us models: the good man, his good wife, the saucy miss who has been domesticated into the good wife. The only character remotely symbolic is Clementina, who fancifully draws angels and saints, and meditates on a map of the British Dominions hour after hour—but we all know that she is mad. (II, 254) [III, XXXII] While *Clarissa* tragically disappoints fairy tale expectations, *Grandison* never lets them develop. There is very little room for the imagination in Richardson's last novel, a prosaic domestication of the world of fantasy: moral overwhelms myth. The core of romance so vital to *Pamela* and *Clarissa* is curiously transformed. Jocelyn Harris finds that "the spirit of romance is diffused throughout the novel."[48] This spirit, however, is so very diffuse, so thinly spread out, that it almost disappears altogether. The romantic elements in *Grandison* are cut down to a prosaic, manageable size, sanitized, and relegated to the "Italian" segments of the novel.

The rakish father of Sir Charles was a poet, suggesting that on some level Richardson regards "art" to be illicit, or at least dangerous. Miss Grandison prudently suggests that "to be a poet, requires an heated imagination, which often runs away with the judgment." (I, 311) [II, XI] There is no fear of Sir Charles's "heated imagination" running away with his judgment. No rake, he is also no artist, but a purely social animal. When Mrs. Beaumont cautions Clementina about the suitability of Sir Charles, she asks, "Are you sure, madam, that the Chevalier has not art?— He has great abilities. Men of great abilities are not always to be trusted. They don't strike till they are sure." Speaking more truth than she knows, Clementina answers, "He has *no* art, madam. He is *above* art. He *wants* it not." (II, 167) [III, XXIV] Precisely the problem in *Grandison*. Richardson elevates the heart and sinks the art, forgetting that artifice is necessary to convince his reader of the authenticity of the heart.

In *Grandison*, Richardson sanitizes any elements of fantasy that have managed to stray into his novel. Harriet attends a masquerade dressed as an Arcadian shepherdess, but is abducted for her sins. She blames her woes on her inappropriate costume; shepherdesses do not belong in Sir Charles's world. A typically admiring transcription of Sir Charles's "wit" reveals the way Richardson sinks the fantasy material that he powerfully exploited in *Clarissa*. Recalling Lovelace's frustrated desires to be a knight-errant, a Quixote battling windmills for Clarissa, and also recalling his more chilling recognition of his role as the giant who has imprisoned Clarissa in his castle, let us look at Sir Charles's use of these same images. When the vanquished Hargrave insists upon seeing Harriet Byron, Sir Charles demurs:

SIR HAR.   What, Sir! You would not turn *Quixote* again?
SIR CH.   No need, Sir Hargrave. You would not again
          be the *giant* who should run away with the
          lady.
          The gentlemen laughed. (I, 254) [II, IV]

Quixotes and giants are domesticated as the threat of a duel develops into an opportunity for a bloodless celebration of Sir Charles's gentility.[49]

In *Grandison*, Richardson banishes the romance to Italy, where it flourishes in that warm, exotic climate. Italy is "in the same uncultivated state, as the minds of their women. The garden of the world, as Italy is called, is over-run with weeds: And, for want of cultivation, the very richness of its soil becomes its disease." (III, 361) [VI, XXXI] Madness, violence, and passion—what Harriet would call "weeds"—thrive on foreign ground; sanity and gentility are reserved for England.

The only "romantic" character in the novel takes her part uneasily. Clementina would be more comfortable in a melodrama than in Sir Charles's drawing-room comedy. Richardson had mixed genres before, contrasting Clarissa's She-Tragedy speeches with Lovelace's rakish wit. But in *Clarissa*, the mixture worked because Richardson's characters conflicted so finely with each other, testing the assumptions implicit in their contradictory personalities. Clementina's pathetic agony, however, seems curiously unconnected to the rest of the novel. Were she to struggle against the dominating wit of a rakish Sir Charles, surely a contradiction in terms, or at least against a villain of worth, we might take her more seriously. But since any pressure brought to bear upon her finely tuned soul cannot come from Sir Charles, the good man, her persecution remains outside the novel, taking place in exotic Italy, hermetically sealed from the rest of the story. When she finally does arrive in England after Sir Charles is safely married and immune to her pathos, Clementina seems more like a ghost than a flesh and blood character, a subplot heroine of little consequence.

In fact, none of the Italian characters matter very much. It is appropriate that in his list of characters Richardson gives us three categories: men, women, and Italians. His Italians are a different breed altogether, romantic but insubstantial. As ambassadors of passion, they seem absurdly melodramatic. Lady Olivia plans to kidnap Sir Charles. "What she would have done with me, had the attempt succeeded, I cannot imagine," Sir Charles wonders. "I should not have wished to have been the subject of so romantic an adventure—A prisoner to a Lady in her Castle!" (II, 651) [V, XL] Her enterprising plan transforms Sir Charles into a sentimental "heroine" threatened by abduction, suggesting that the "good man" of Richardson's imagination possesses feminine rather than masculine virtues. In England, transplanted to a less luxurious soil, Lady Olivia attempts to murder Sir Charles: "She pulled out of her stays, in a fury, a poinard, and vowed to plunge it into his heart." (II, 380) [IV, XXIV] But her action belongs in an Italian opera, not an English drawing room. Sir Charles prudently reminds her of her place: "Unhappy violent woman! I return not this instrument of mischief! You will have no use for it in England." Chastened, Olivia returns to Italy, and gentility returns to England.

Why do we believe in Richardson's violent fairy tales? How does he authenticate his nightmares and convince us that we are reading "plain and natural" accounts of real life? He gives us a clue in the "hints" of prefaces for *Clarissa*: "Attentive Readers have found, and will find, that the Probability of all Stories told, or of Narrations given, depends upon small Circumstances; as may be observed, that in all Tryals for Life and Property, the // Merits of the Cause are more determinable by such, than by the greater Facts; which usually are so laid, and taken care of, as to seem to authenticate themselves." To the objection that "*the History is too minute*," Richardson answers that "its Minuteness [is] one of its Excellencies."[50] In his postscript to the fourth edition of *Clarissa*, Richardson defends the epistolary method as a way to document reality. "The minute particulars of events, the sentiments and conversation of the parties, are, upon this plan, exhibited with all the warmth and spirit, that the passion supposed to be predominant at the very time, could produce, and with all the distinguishing characteristics which memory can supply in a History of recent transactions." (VIII, 326) [IV, 562] The components of the Richardsonian formula are all here: minute particularities, sentiments, and passions. "The probability of all Stories told, or of Narrations given, depends upon small Circumstances." These in turn render probable improbable passions and sentiments.

No one follows Richardson's attention to "minute particulars" more closely than Lovelace, who boasts to Belford that "I love always to go as near the truth as I can." (III, 52) [II, 13] As Morris Golden has pointed out,[51] to achieve a convincing union of truth and fiction, Lovelace pays strict attention to "small Circumstances." It is no coincidence that Lovelace, impresario and artist, sounds much like Richardson, impresario and artist, in his admiration for the minutiae: "I never forget the *Minutiae* in my contrivances. In all matters that admit of doubt, the *minutiae* closely attended to, and provided for, are of more service than a thousand oaths, vows, and protestations made to supply the neglect of them, especially when jealousy has made its way into the working mind. (III, 201-202) [II, 115] In Richardson's world, the "working mind" creates its own reality. Clarissa is susceptible to Lovelace's use of the minutiae because her working mind is in the process of creating her personal reality. Reality lies within—within the mind, within the writing closet where Clarissa retires to make sense of her experience.

As he tutors his gang of rakes in the proper way to behave in front of the divine Clarissa, Lovelace warns them that "deep, like golden ore, frequently lies my meaning, and richly worth digging for." Attend to the minutest circumstance, he advises, parodying the desired end of his own use of minutiae—seduction and fatherhood. "The hint of *least* moment, as *you* may imagine it, is often pregnant with events of the *greatest*." (III, 353) [II, 218] Be implicit, he tells his rakes. And Richardson advises his reader to do the same. "The hint of *least* moment, as *you* may imagine it," may completely alter our sense of what we are reading. The Tomlinson fraud is perhaps Lovelace's greatest triumph of minutiae. He passes off one of his own itinerant servants as the respectable neighbor of Uncle John Harlowe. Along with Clarissa, the reader accepts the reality of Tomlinson's identity without reservation.[52]

Lovelace's strategic attention to detail can be seen in Tomlinson's explanation of his recent friendship with Uncle John: "But through an acquaintance of no longer standing, and that commencing on the bowling-green [*Uncle John is a great Bowler, Belford*]." (IV, 313) [II, 449] "Uncle John is a great Bowler." This authentic circumstance lends credibility to the fiction of Tomlinson. Lovelace's (and Richardson's) talent for making the incredible credible can also be clearly seen at Hampstead. The suspicious Miss Rawlinson, wary of Lovelace's good intentions, protests that his affair with Clarissa "bore the face of Novelty, Mystery, and Surprise." True, admits Lovelace, "Ours was a very particular case: That were I to acquaint them with it, some part of it would hardly appear credible." Since they all "seem" to be "persons of discretion," he agrees to give them "a brief account of the whole; and this in so plain and sincere a manner, that it should clear up to their satisfaction every-thing that had passed, or might hereafter pass between us." (V, 101) [III, 50] In just such a "plain and sincere . . . manner," Richardson authenticated his fictional world of "Novelty, Mystery, and Surprise," careful to make the incredible credible to the severest critic. Like Lovelace, he created fantastic contrivances, building up his fantasy with solid facts, pieces of commonplace reality.

We can find many examples of the way Richardson authenticated fantasy in *Pamela* as well as in *Clarissa*. Colbrand becomes a creature of nightmare proportions in Pamela's letters: "He is a Giant of a Man, for Stature; taller, by a good deal, than *Harry Mawlidge*, in your Neighbourhood, and large-bon'd, and scraggy; and has a Hand!—I never saw such an one in my Life. He has great staring Eyes, like the Bull's that fright'd me so." (I, 225) [I, 145] Here Richardson authenticates Pamela's nightmare of the "great staring Eyes, like the Bull's that fright'd me so" with homely detail: "taller, by a good deal, than *Harry Mawlidge*," in the neighborhood. Colbrand's hideous masculinity threatens Pamela sexually: like the bull, he represents the animalistic forces of sexuality, nature out of control.

In his attempt to present Mr. B. as a redeemable rake, Richardson introduced threatening foils like Colbrand and Mrs. Jewkes. While Mr. B. plots the seduction, his un-

derlings actually act out his desires: B. gets the girl while
Colbrand and Jewkes get the blame. Pamela can eventually
love Mr. B., in spite of his repeated outrages, because her
fears are deflected towards Colbrand, who is the scapegoat,
like the bull, for his master's lust. Pamela even connects
the two men in her mind: "When I went to bed I could
think of nothing but [Colbrand's] hideous Person, and my
Master's more hideous Actions; and judg'd them too well
pair'd, and when I dropp'd asleep, I dream'd they were
both coming to my Bed-side, with the worst Designs." (I,
226) [I, 145]

Richardson goes even further, suggesting that Colbrand
will soon be the author of "more hideous actions" to accommodate his master. Mrs. Jewkes has told Pamela that
"she has Reason to think [Mr. B.] has found a way to
satisfy my Scruples: It is, by marrying me to this dreadful
Colbrand, and buying me of him on the Wedding-day, for
a Sum of Money! Was ever the like heard?—She says it
will be my Duty to obey my Husband; and that Mr. *Williams* will be forced as a Punishment, to marry us; and
that, when my Master has paid for me, and I am surrender'd up, the *Swiss* is to go home again, with the Money,
to his former Wife and Children; for, she says it is the
Custom of these People to have a Wife in every Nation."
"Was ever the like heard?" "But this," Pamela adds, "to
be sure, is horrid romancing!" (I, 243-44) [I, 156] Horrid romancing to be sure. Pamela's qualifications under-
state the highly unlikely nature of B.'s marriage plot. The
reader of eighteenth-century fiction is accustomed to an occasional Fleet marriage, but Mr. Williams, "forced as a
Punishment," to perform the marriage of an unwilling
Pamela, strains the most generous reader's belief. But we
still believe in the romantic possibility of the sham marriage because Pamela invests the plot with realistic detail.
She evaluates its legal possibility, takes it seriously, and
convinces the reader to do the same: "Yet, abominable as
it is, it may possibly serve to introduce some Plot now

hatching! . . . But can a Husband sell his Wife, against her own Consent?—And will such a Bargain stand good in Law?" (I, 244) [I, 156][53] The moment Pamela entertains the legal possibility of such a marriage, the reader believes in the legal (and actual) dilemma. Pamela's fears, fed by her most "horrid romancing," become reality.

Richardson's careful attention to the minutiae convinces us that his fairy tales, filled with violence and passion, are plain and natural accounts of real life. As Hazlitt pointed out, Richardson's novels have "the romantic air of a pure fiction, with the literal minuteness of a common diary. The author had the strongest matter-of-fact imagination that ever existed, and wrote the oddest mixture of poetry and prose."[54] It is in the union of the nightmare and the diary, romance and reality, that Richardson demonstrates his genius.

It only remains for us to wonder about Richardson's reasons for using fairy tale elements in his novels. Richardson always cared deeply about the truth of his fiction. He wanted to be believed, and to be heeded. Let us reexamine his letter to Warburton, in which he insisted upon retaining the *"Air* of Genuiness." He feared that if his "letters" were "owned not to be genuine," their influence would be weakened. From the beginning of his literary career, Richardson jealously guarded his influence. He wanted to direct his reader's behavior, tell him how to become a proper apprentice, how to dun a debtor politely, how to propose marriage, how to reject such a proposal— in short, how to live and, finally, how to die. Richardson was always fascinated with the process of becoming, with social transformations. The flexible nature of the "young girl," as yet undeveloped, about to "become" a wife, mother, saint, strongly attracted him, as we can see in his selection of both heroines, friends, and correspondents. Fairy tales suited Richardson's interest in transformations, in Eliade's "sacred history" of "creation," allowing him to focus on the "natural" development of his characters.

In *Pamela*, Richardson sought a dramatic form to convey his moral: virtue will be rewarded. Significantly, he chose the fairy-tale formula, for Pamela's progress could only be found in fantasy, not in "real" life. But, as always, Richardson wanted to be believed. His realism, his attention to the minutiae, authenticated his fairy tale. The fairy tale was necessary in order to make the moral work, and the realism was necessary in order to make the fairy tale believable.

In *Clarissa*, Richardson left the optimistic world of *Pamela*, moving beyond his moral altogether. *Clarissa* expresses Richardson's dreams of social and spiritual integration, but even more strongly it reveals his fears of the menace of the ordinary, the threat of the separated self, the inevitable clash of cultures implicit in the battle between Clarissa and Lovelace. While *Pamela* celebrates the morals of the always rising middle class, *Clarissa* examines these morals more closely, and finds them wanting. Clarissa achieves spiritual elevation at the expense of the society that condemned her. After he introduced fairy-tale elements into his novel, Richardson reversed his reader's expectations, leaving us with a bleak world of triumphant giants, false Prince Charmings, and raped princesses. The happy ending we long for takes place not on earth but in heaven.

We must feel the strain of such a solution. Melvyn New suggests that Richardson's providential scheme, at odds with his method of characterization and the radical individualism it entails, reflects "that moment in Western thought when the antithetical ideas of man as God's creature and man as the radical product of his own autonomous will came together in uneasy and temporary alliance." Richardson is able to project both views simultaneously. "Clarissa can respond to the world as God's creation and yet open to us her whole subconscious mind, in which God himself is merely one more creation."[55] This synthesis was, at its best, a tenuous one, a strange mixture Richardson was to reject altogether in his final novel, where the moral consumes the individual. Clarissa's happy ending leads into death.

In his essay on the fairy tale, J.R.R. Tolkien suggests that the element of "escape" can be found in all fairy tales— escape from the fallen world, from our sense of separation, and from harsh reality. The "oldest and deepest desire, the Great Escape," is "the Escape from Death."[56] In *Clarissa*, Richardson forced the harshest reality upon his reader: Clarissa disowned, Clarissa raped, Clarissa imprisoned, Clarissa dead. There are no happy endings here, only a sense of shame and waste. Yet he also offered an escape from the nightmare, "the Great Escape" from death through the myth of eternal life. Clarissa, untouched, sublime, escapes the sordid reality of the Harlowes and Solmeses of the world. The shame and waste remain for mere mortals, but for Clarissa, at least, annihilation offers the final escape into joy.

Richardson needed to write fairy tales to convince his readers and himself of the truth of his moral—for his moral alone, sadly inoperable in a reality his artistic imagination forced him to confront, was never enough.

FIVE • A Lovelace in Every Corner: The Rake Figure in Richardson's Novels

The heart of man is said to be inscrutable: but this can scarce be truly said of any writing man. The heart of such still shews and needs must shew itself beyond all power of concealment; and without the writer's purpose, or even knowledge, will a thousand times and in a thousand places, start up in its own true native colour, let the subject it is displayed upon bend never so remotely from the un-intended manifestation.—How many have I heard declare (and people, too, who loved truth dearly, and believed they spoke it), that they charmed themselves in reading Pamela; when all the while, It was Mr. Richardson they had been reading.

AARON HILL to RICHARDSON
(*Correspondence*, vol. I, p. 105)

I write, I do anything I am able to do, on purpose to carry myself out of myself; and am not quite so happy, when, tired with my peregrinations, I am obliged to return home.

RICHARDSON to MISS MULSO
(*Correspondence*, vol. III, pp. 190-91)

We shall certainly cook the book if we believe that Richardson is to be identified with Lovelace, and that Lovelace's "Freudian" theory about the hypocrisy of the eighteenth-century sex-code (the product of custom and education, disguising the true sexual nature of women) is the right one.[1]

MARK KINKEAD-WEEKES

WE HAVE SEEN the way Richardson transformed the commonplaces of life into art, assimilating and subverting sexual stereotypes as he invested reality with elements of fantasy and romance. At its best, Richardson's art is peculiarly transformational. His finest creation, Clarissa, pushes the commonplace clichés of self-improvement to their limits, turning herself into an impassioned martyr at odds with the society whose morality her creator is ostensibly buttressing. Richardson set out to uphold the cultural and sexual stereotypes of his time, but as he explored the rules of decorum and punctilio, he subverted them, celebrating the independence, both spiritual and moral, of a woman who challenges the social code. Altering our ideas about the common reality he claims to imitate, Richardson employs elements of romance and fairy tale to create a nightmare world both subversive and disturbing. And in this fantastic world, no one is more disturbing than Lovelace, along with Clarissa the most complex of Richardson's characters. Aesthetically most like his creator, Lovelace the artist works to transform Clarissa's reality, transforming his author's reality in the process, freeing him to expand and complete himself. In these final three chapters, we shall look at the ways the author, working from a position essentially fluid, developed and refined an idea of the created character and the created self. Setting out to discover truth in his fiction, Richardson ended up discovering himself transformed in his letters and novels.

One of the commonplaces of literary criticism is the danger of confusing the artist's life with his work, in effect confusing life with art. Well and good in theory, but, as with most commonplaces, not always applicable in practice. When we explore the "life" of Richardson in his correspondence and his slight attempt at autobiography in his letter to Stinstra, we are faced with a most intriguing problem—the author's conscious and deliberate assumption of his literary characters. To ignore Richardson's delight in exploiting the fantasy material of his own characters, to deny his own interest in creating a self-image less diffident and more successful through his literary creations, is to fail to come to terms with Richardson's completed self, the self he invented. We cannot arbitrarily separate the man's life from his art if he himself deliberately forged them together.

Aaron Hill confidently believed that the Richardsonian heart could not be concealed. But the Mr. Richardson he thought he knew, the respectable printer of Salisbury Court who seriously discussed sentimental aesthetics and the perfidy of Mr. Pope, showed a far different heart than the Mr. Richardson who teased and cajoled Sophia Westcomb in his letters, acting as a mock-severe Papa chucking the dimpled chin of a juvenile devotee. Hill seemed to suggest that all of *Pamela*—and, accordingly, all of *Clarissa*—were the "true" Mr. Richardson. This is too simple, of course, and would leave us with a severely fragmented personality: part Solmes, part B., part Jewkes, part Pamela; everything and nothing. Yet certainly, on some basic level, Richardson expressed himself through his characters, especially those favorite characters he refers to again and again in his letters, inventing their characters to invent himself. Mr. Richardson, a conventional and diffident man, lived as much as he could in his imagination, where he could be confident and free. When Richardson wrote, he "carried himself out of himself" to become a free person of his imagination, transcending his commonplace personality.

Freed to create his fictions to redeem his reader, Richardson was also freed to explore sensational, dramatic channels of experience normally closed to him. Lovelace, dramatic, energetic, witty, and bold, all that Mr. Richardson could only be in his imagination, offered his creator a way out of his diffident self into the world of imaginative free play and artifice. And just as Lovelace offered Richardson a way out, the rake offers us a way into the author, a way, as Aaron Hill would put it, of reading Mr. Richardson himself.

This chapter deals with only one aspect of the Richardsonian personality, his profoundly significant imaginative connection to his character Lovelace. There surely is a great deal of Clarissa and Pamela in Richardson as well. We must not reduce Richardson by identifying him solely with his rake. But because Lovelace spoke so often for his creator, at the risk of "cooking the book," we need to look at the relationship between the artistic rake and the rakish artist.[2] The approach of this chapter will be at first historical, for in looking at the rake as Richardson and his contemporaries viewed him, we can then see the way Richardson both absorbed and transformed the rake for his own purposes. Certainly the rake is central to Richardson's novels, controlling the plot as he designs *his* plots to catch his prey. His effectiveness is directly proportionate to the power of the novel: by setting up the conflict, he forces the other characters to respond to his machinations. Mr. B. begins his career unimpressively, grabbing, pinching, and popping out of closets. Energy without art. By comparison, Lovelace is the master artist, devising complex schemes to control Clarissa and, through her, to control life itself. For him, seduction yields self-expression, freeing Lovelace from mundane reality. As much as Lovelace represents the triumphant freedom of Richardson's imagination, the world of *Grandison* signals a paralysis of Richardson's power. There are no effective rakes in the novel, merely impotent parodies. Sir Charles lives out Lovelace's fantasies of power and seduction in a morally and socially acceptable way. But when schemes of power become socially realizable, they also become flat and uninteresting.

The real rakes in Richardson's world were seldom so banal, although they were never as exciting in person as Richardson made his own rake in imagination. As always, Richardson assimilated and transformed cultural stereotypes for his own ends. In truth, the rakes were a mixed lot: scoundrels like Francis Charteris; aged voluptuaries like Lord Baltimore; sadists like George Selwyn, who particularly enjoyed public executions; political activists like John Wilkes; and dilettantes like Francis Dashwood.[3] If they had anything in common at all, it was a need to go beyond the norm, to break the rules either morally, sexually, socially, or intellectually. The word "libertine" originally described one manumitted from slavery, a freedman. The libertines of the eighteenth century were determined to deliver themselves from the slavery of everyday life, from the rules restricting everyone else's behavior.

With his active interest in history, travel, and writing, Lovelace would have been classified as a rather superior type of rake, a Francis Dashwood rather than a Colonel Charteris. (It must be admitted, however, that Richardson places his rake in poor company, with doltish Mowbray and pathetic Belton; only Belford seems worthy of Lovelace's friendship.) While Colonel Charteris appears to have been motivated by a mean lust, the Dashwood Dilettanti rakes were more intellectually inspired.

Dashwood was the leading member of the Society of Dilettanti, established in 1732 to promote scholarly and artistic interest in Italy and later in Greece. At the monthly meetings held at the Bedford Head Tavern, Covent Garden, the members sported the usual ritualistic paraphernalia: togas, long crimson robes, lighted tapers, and serpent staffs. But the society also sponsored serious work, backing an expedition to Greece in 1750. Two of its members, Nicholas Revett and James Stuart, investigated and categorized many antiquities that were in danger of completely disappearing; they published their findings in 1762 in a distinguished study, *The Antiquities of Athens, Measured and Delineated*.[4] Dashwood's later involvement with the Medmenham Brothers in his neogothic abbey is again cluttered with the trappings of dressing up and pornographic ritual.[5] But inversions of religious ritual and dabblings in the occult can indicate a desire to know, to stretch the mind. The Lovelacian rake is driven by the need to penetrate experience, to gain power over the physical and metaphysical. That penetration can be used in a sexual as well as an intellectual metaphor is not surprising.

In his later years, Dashwood became the great friend of

Benjamin Franklin, another famous rake (as well as self-improver) pursuing knowledge both physical and metaphysical. In 1773, Dashwood and Franklin collaborated on a revised Book of Common Prayer, which was widely used thereafter in American churches.[6] Their pious effort calls up Lovelace's own mocking suggestion that he and Belford should end their days "turned Hermits" in "the two old Caves at Hornsey." Naturally, Lovelace impiously turns the image upside down: "What figures would a couple of brocaded or laced-waistcoated toupets make with their sour screw'd-up half-cock'd faces, and more than half-shut eyes, in a kneeling attitude, recapitulating their respective rogueries? This scheme, were we only to make trial of it and return afterwards to our old ways, might serve to better purpose by far, than Horner's in the Country Wife, to bring the pretty wenches to us."[7] (VII, 18-19) [IV, 42]

When Lovelace places his penitent rakes in their "old Caves," he dresses them in brocaded or laced-up waistcoats, costumes appropriate to their status. For the rake is not merely any man of loose character, but a man of fashion. The true rake, fashionably bored, is more likely to be a man of the town than a man of the city. In his comedy *The Scowrers*, Thomas Shadwell plays with the exclusive status of his rakes. His chief "scowrer," Sir William Rant, delights in breaking windows, attacking the night watch, whoring, and drinking. Yet however crude his behavior might seem, he is *Sir* William, a man of quality. Whachum, a mere city wit who aspires to become a "scowrer," can never achieve Sir William's heights. "Tis a hard thing to scowrer naturally and handsomely," Whachum learns. He vainly tries to imitate his hero, but Sir William sends him back to the city where he belongs: "Why look you, Gentlemen, you City-Puppies, you impertinent conceited Rascals! Go and swagger at *Puddle-Dock*; but do you think we will suffer such awkward sneaking coxcombs, to wench, drink and scowrer to usurp the Sins of Gentlemen."[8]

And the "Sins of Gentlemen" were many. "Did I tell

you of a race of Rakes call'd the Mohacks," Swift asked
Stella, "that play the devil about this Town every Night,
slitt peoples noses, & beat them &c." As we know from
The Spectator as well as other contemporary accounts, "&c."
included eye-gouging, overturning coaches, and nailing up
women in tubs and rolling them down hills. The notorious
exploits of the Mohocks may seem more fictional than real,
but they were widely believed at the time. They certainly
impressed the usually thrifty Swift, who reported to Stella
that "I came home in a Chair for fear of the Mohocks,"
complaining that "they have put me to the Charge of some
Shillings already."

The Mohocks were, Swift decided, Whigs with "malicious Intentions agst the Ministers & their Friends."[9]
Generally, the rake was out of joint with his time and out
of power with his establishment. If Tories were in power,
he would be, as Swift feared, a Whig; if Walpole were in
control, the rake would be a Jacobite, like the Duke of
Wharton opposing the Hanoverian succession, or a liber-
tarian like John Wilkes, or part of the Prince of Wales's
shadow court playing at Dilettanti games with Francis
Dashwood. Disaffected, the rake sought power, but power
on a personal level: on a crude Mohock level, physical
prowess, gouging out a few eyes and breaking a few windows to prove it; on a "higher" physical level, seductive
prowess, ravishing a few maidens to prove it; and on a
more esoteric level, intellectual prowess demonstrated in
"blasphemous" experiments with the occult.

Lovelace's sententious uncle, Lord M., might urge his
nephew to go into politics, but recognition in the political
world of the Walpolian Robinocracy, a world ruled by
Harlowes, would be difficult indeed for Lovelace. As the
Harlowes' own investigation of his "character" shows, he
would never be trusted. From the start, his aristocratic
behavior was found to be "very faulty."[10] All of Richardson's heroes avoid participating in public life: even the
relentlessly middle-class aristocrat Sir Charles establishes

his benevolent rule privately, not publicly. Significantly, in his famous autobiographical letter to Stinstra, Richardson connected his own family's fortunes to the Duke of Monmouth's, placing himself in a powerless aristocratic tradition of disaffected bastards. His father, he claimed, was "personally beloved by several Persons of Rank, among whom were the Duke of Monmouth & the first Earl of Shaftesbury; both so noted in our English History." Such noble favor "subjected him to be looked upon with a jealous Eye," and forced him to retire to Derbyshire, "tho' to his great Detriment."[11] A noble reason for Richardson's humble beginnings, but more likely fiction than fact. No biographer has been able to verify Richardson's assertion; in fact, Eaves and Kimpel point out that although the Duke of Monmouth had been beheaded on 15 July 1685, Richardson's father had still not left London over two years later. They suggest that business difficulties rather than political pressure may have made it necessary for Richardson's father to get out of London, but they caution that the reason is still uncertain.[12] Although we cannot learn the truth about Richardson's romantic version of his background, we can still appreciate his conscious identification with "Persons of Rank" and, more important, with rebels.

Distortions of the truth can often reveal as much as truth itself. As Roy Pascal notes in his study of autobiographical truth and design, the invented situation can reveal a potential reality perhaps more significant than what actually took place.[13] Through his rakes, the transformed products of his own disaffected imagination, Richardson found a way to rebel against the system that had excluded his father, "beloved" of Monmouth. At the same time, however, Richardson could remain a man of the City, master printer of Salisbury Court, Fleet Street, working in the society that upheld the Walpole regime. His strength came from the solidity of such a foundation, his freedom came from the bastard child of his imagination—Lovelace.

Richardson's next attempt to link up with the aristocracy

appears to be even more fantastic. As a humble apprentice, he was "engaged in a Correspondence with a Gentleman greatly my Superior in Degree, and / of ample / Fortunes, who, had he lived, intended high things for me." Another "fact" that cannot be established. This "Master of the Epistolary Style" gave young Samuel an "Account of his Proceedings, and what befell him in the different Nations thro' which he travelled." Such adventures would have provided "great Helps" for Richardson's own fictional accounts, but alas, "many Years ago, all the Letters that passed between us, by a particular Desire of his (lest they should ever be published) were committed to the Flames."[14] Would Richardson, Epistolaire Extraordinaire, ever have burned a letter without making two or three copies?

Richardson became involved with another superior gentleman in 1723 when he worked for the mercurial, romantic Duke of Wharton. *The True Briton*, ostensibly published and printed by "T. Payne," an apprentice printer who was imprisoned for his treason, was actually printed by Richardson. Eaves and Kimpel caution against connecting Richardson too closely with Wharton: "Whether the Duke of Wharton served, as he well could have, as one of the models for Richardson's later rakes is uncertain—his printer need not have known him intimately."[15] Nevertheless, the similarities between Wharton and Lovelace are interesting. Wharton, "the scorn and wonder" of his age, in his bold and audacious *The True Briton*, attacked the Walpole regime, the world of men of property risen from dunghills that Lovelace himself combats in his own personal war on the Harlowe family. Like Lovelace, Wharton displayed an erratic genius and misdirected energy. The author of his supposed *Memoirs* states that "there never appeared in any Gentleman so much good Wit with so little true Discretion." Like Lovelace, with his "surprising memory; and a very lively imagination," (I, 74) [I, 50] Wharton frequently turned to history to justify his rebellion. For both rakes, the times were clearly debased, over-run with men of property like the Harlowes. They looked to the golden age of military conquest and glory for inspiration. Wharton could "run over the most remarkable Facts in the *Grecian, Roman* and *English* History, with the Lives and Actions of the celebrated Men in the different Ages of the World, in an amazing manner."[16] In *The True Briton*, Wharton takes a Lovelacian view of history when he tells the anecdote of a meeting between Alexander the Great (one of Lovelace's heroes) and a corsair. When Alexander asks the pirate how he dares to scour the seas at such an "insolent Rate," the pirate answers, *"Why, truly . . . I scour the seas for my Profit and my Pleasure, just as you Scour the World; Only I am to be a Rogue for doing it with one Galley, and you must be a mighty Prince, forsooth, for doing the same Thing with an Army."*[17] Lovelace frequently justifies his own "scouring" in the same manner: "But had I been a Prince! To be sure I should have made a most *noble* Prince!" (V, 67) [III, 26] His rape of Clarissa, he protests, is no worse than the actions of the *"pius* Aeneas": "Dost thou not think that I am as much entitled to forgiveness on Miss Harlowe's account, as Virgil's hero was on Queen Dido's? . . . Why then should it not be the *pius* Lovelace, as well as the *pius* Aeneas?" (VII, 2) [IV, 30-31] Whether or not Richardson knew Wharton intimately, his own portrayal of Lovelace's disaffected idealism reflects a profound understanding of the kind of rebel Wharton was.

Apart from his personal involvement with Wharton, it is in his correspondence rather than in his life that Richardson appears most Lovelacian. While the public Richardson was diffident and socially uneasy, in his private letters, free to play, Mr. Richardson delightedly tyrannized over his readers. Teasing his impressionable young ladies, he hinted of the dire fates awaiting their "exalted lovers." What to do with Sir Charles, he mused, kill him off in a duel?

But shall we first marry him?—Shall we shew Harriet,
after a departure glorious to the hero, in her vidual
glory?—Mother of a posthumous—son or daughter?—
Which—. . . . Or shall we remove him by a violent
fever—or by the treacherous sword of Greville, pretending friendship and reconciliation; and make the assassin
a vagabond, a Cain?—. . . . But there would be no end
of the complicated woe!—You think I have a talent at
such scenes.—Who would not pursue, who can resist his
talents? (*Letters*, pp. 216-17)

He toyed with the idea of a "glorious Exit" for Harriet,
boasting, "I can draw, I fancy, a charming Child-bed Death,
a glorious Trial for Sir Charles!" (*Letters*, pp. 276-77)
How they squealed their protests, the Misses Highmore,
Mulso, and Westcomb (Lady Bradshaigh the loudest), en-
treating "Papa" to spare their favorites. Miss Highmore
suggested to Miss Mulso a reason for the "shocking" dream
of Miss Byron's:

I verily believe Mr. Richardson has been spiteful enough
to send these shocking aerial visions, which discompose
the gentle slumbers of the most amiable of her sex, only
to revenge himself on you and I, two saucy girls that
pretend to be so sure that happiness must reward the
virtue and heroic sufferings of the exalted lovers, for
whom we interest ourselves so strenuously; let us remember he can cut their thread of life at pleasure; their
destiny is in his hands, and I am not certain that our
security may not provoke him to destroy them, for he
has set his imagination on the glow. (*Correspondence*, vol.
II, p. 317)

Dear Mr. Richardson sounds Lovelacian: "he can cut their
thread of life at pleasure; their destiny is in his hands." As
Lovelace says, "What signifies power, if we do not exert
it?" (IV, 135) [II, 328] Both the artist and his creation
revel in the creative prerogative. Lovelace, after revealing

the true identity of "Captain Mennell," his own invention, exults in his authority: "I have changed his name by virtue of my own single authority. Knowest thou not, that I am a great Name-father? Preferments I bestow, both military and civil. I give Estates, and take them away at my pleasure. Quality too I create. And by a still more valuable prerogative, I *degrade* by virtue of my own imperial will, without any other act of forfeiture than for my own convenience. What a poor thing is a monarch to me!" (IV, 44) [II, 267] Like Richardson, his own "name-father," Lovelace values his creative prerogative, the authority of his imperial will to create or degrade. The two are involved in the same enterprise, to persuade their audience to accept the reality of their created worlds.

At times the worlds intersect. The Bradshaigh letters offer a fascinating record of life imitating art. Richardson and his coy lady, "Belfour," as Lady Bradshaigh disguised herself, took on the roles of their favorite "exalted lovers." Richardson did a better job as Lovelace than Lady Bradshaigh as Clarissa, for she confused punctilio with coquetry, coyly promising and then refusing to meet the author in St. James's Park, the site of so many more successful clandestine appointments. Her whimsical behavior frustrated the gallant Richardson, who compared himself to Don Quixote, battling windmills of custom with his lance (*Correspondence*, vol. IV, p. 320), just as Lovelace compared himself to the unfortunate knight. (V, 17) [II, 518]

In his letters to "Belfour," Richardson deliberately imitated the dialogue of his own characters. When the skittish lady confessed that she had visited his doorstep without revealing herself, he lamented, " 'But a brick wall perhaps,' says Clarissa, 'between Mr. Lovelace and me.' " (*Correspondence*, vol. IV, p. 342) Richardson finally detected the identity of his romantic correspondent, employing methods of intrigue worthy of his Lovelace. Lady Bradshaigh revealed herself when she visited the home of Mr. Joseph Highmore, Richardson's illustrator, to gaze worshipfully at Highmore's portrait of Richardson. "Belfour" was wise to withhold her real identity for so long, for once revealed, she "dwindle[d] into a woman in fact," a plump matron living in the country. The games went on, the letters continued, but without the same degree of anxious interest. Richardson needed to provoke Lady Bradshaigh with threats of killing off Sir Charles or with hints of his interest in polygamy to elicit the same emotional engagement he formerly enjoyed.

For the games always require new inventions to progress. Life without play palls. Nobody knows that better than Lovelace, whose desire for control and love of play express important aspects of the Richardsonian personality. Just as Lovelace fashions a middle-class boarding house out of a brothel to seduce Clarissa, Richardson created a "realistic" middle-class world filled with fantastic schemes of invention, dominated by a painful struggle for control— all to seduce his reader into goodness. Lovelace embodies the tension between Richardson's moral and aesthetic commitments, allowing his creator the freedom to travel through forbidden channels of experience he had long been interested in exploring.

There can be no doubt that Richardson was conscious of his identification with Lovelace. He even used his character as a source of material for his own letters, frequently quoting his rake: "What a rogue, as Lovelace says, is human nature." (*Letters*, p. 159) The most significant link between Richardson and his character is in their absolute need for art as a way out of the common limitations of experience. Art makes order out of the chaotic stuff of life, a life in which eleven close relations and friends can die unexpectedly in two years. "I cannot tell why," confessed Richardson, "but my nervous disorders will permit me to write with more impunity than to read." (*Correspondence*, vol. I, p. cxci) "Fresh cause of aggravation!—But for this scribbling vein, or I should still run mad," (V, 28) [II, 525] rants Lovelace. Richardson and Lovelace both suffer from nervous disorders. Lovelace's affliction is at first less obvious, for he acts out so many of his fantasies that his neurotic melancholy rarely has the opportunity to assert itself. But after Clarissa's death, Lovelace does go mad; for him "the whole world is but one great Bedlam." (VIII, 49) [IV, 377] His medical treatment resembles the barbarically thorough cures for melancholy prescribed to Richardson by Dr. Cheyne: fasts, vomits, tar-water tonics; perfectionism through bodily purges.[18]

To be mad is to be outside society, an appropriate position for Lovelace's attack on societal norms. Max Byrd points out that this antisocial element in madness threatened the eighteenth century's established sense of order: "Hostility to ordinary middle-class values [was] associated instantly, automatically, with insanity; and insanity with confinement." For the Augustan, madness was especially threatening because it was feared to be self-generated, caused not by devils or gods but by the self alone: "In the Augustan Age fear of the insane springs from the inescapable conclusion that it is *ourselves* who cause madness, that human beings possess an unpredictable self-altering, self-destructive potential. . . . The alternative external explanations of human madness that had served earlier cultures held their ground poorly in the face of an advancing skeptical science and a weary, often defensive religious establishment."[19] In Lovelace, Richardson dramatically demonstrated that the self-created man could also become the self-created madman. We can make our own fates with terrible precision, becoming a saint like Clarissa or a madman like Lovelace. One of the strongest arguments Richardson could make for his insistence upon moral certainties was Lovelace's terrible isolation and madness without those certainties. Without a moral imperative, Lovelace creates such a convoluted world of fantasy that he eventually loses himself in it. Once he manages to convince Clarissa of the authenticity of his invented world, he can never return her or himself to reality without exposing his own lies and thereby destroying himself, the self that exists in that fictive world. Fulfilled only when he controls his world through art, Lovelace finally becomes trapped in his own creation.

Comic invention, dramatic impersonation, and disguise all impose order on Lovelace's world. I cannot live without my plots, he cries: "I am confoundedly out of conceit with myself. If I give up my contrivances, my joy in stratagem, and plot, and invention, I shall be but a common man: Such another dull heavy creature as thyself." (V, 362-63) [III, 229] Only art, ironically the same art that leads him out of a sane, "normal" reality, can bring him back from impending madness. For without Clarissa, Lovelace's "Whole Soul is a blank: the whole Creation round me, the Elements above, beneath, and every thing I *behold* (for nothing can I *enjoy*) are a blank without her!" (VI, 215) [III, 388] "Life is a burden to me," he tells Belford. "I would not bear it upon these terms for one week more, let what would be my lot; for already is there a hell begun in my own mind." (VII, 408) [IV, 304] Only scribbling and invention can stave off the madness, the invention that paradoxically distorts his sense of reality even further, forcing him deeper into his obsession.

And the madness is always impending. When Belford chastises his friend's levity while Clarissa lies dying, he justifies his "foolery": "Indeed it is to this *deep Concern* that my *Levity* is owing: for I struggle and struggle, and try to buffet down my cruel reflections as they rise; and when I cannot, I am forced, as I have often said, to try to make myself laugh, that I may not cry; for one or other I must do." Life cannot be borne without "lucid intervals" of mad invention:

> There is something owing to Constitution, I own; and that this is the laughing-time of my life. For what a woe must that be, which for an hour together can mortify a man of Six or Seven-and-twenty, in high blood and spirits, of a naturally gay disposition, who can sing, dance,

and scribble, and take and give delight in them all?—
But then my grief, as my joy, is sharper-pointed than
most other mens; and, like what Dolly Welby once told
me, describing the parturient throes, if there were not
lucid intervals, if they did not come and go, there would
be no bearing them.[20] (VII, 346-47) [IV, 262-63]

The "parturient throes" of Dolly Welby brought forth a
child, no doubt a bastard. The "parturient throes" of Richardson, made bearable by intervals of invention, brought
forth his own bastard child, mad and fantastic Lovelace.
Clarissa was, of course, legitimate.

Invention carries Richardson out of himself into the world
of appearance and play, a world of disguise that had long
attracted him. He once asked Elizabeth Carter an intriguing question: "Did you never madam, wish for Angelica's
Invisible Ring, in Ariosto's Orlando?—I remember when
I first read of it, having then more faith in romance than
I had afterwards, I laboured under a real uneasiness for a
whole week, from the strong desire I had to be master of
such a one. I was a very sheepish boy, and thought I should
make a very happy use of it in a multitude of occasions."
(*Letters*, pp. 235-36) By the time Richardson confessed his
childhood desire to Miss Carter, he was, alas, still "very
sheepish," frequently lamenting his diffidence in his letters
and conversations. But he had found a way out of his
sheepish exterior—his art. Invisible rings were no longer
necessary: instead of making himself invisible to observe
the actions of others, he could go even further, by creating
characters out of his own head and controlling their actions. And he could still remain invisible, the "editor" of
his fictional letters, always present but never observed, except in the result of his manipulations. Disguised as editor,
Richardson could control his characters, and indirectly
control the response of his reader. Occasionally the commonplace Mr. Richardson of Salisbury Court may seem to

appear before us, the wheezing moralist pressing his footnotes and warnings upon the reader. But the black-frocked preacher was also in disguise; perhaps the "real" Richardson was most invisible when he appeared to be most blatantly visible.

Less obviously sheepish (although Lovelace insists that he was always a bashful man), Lovelace takes on fantastic, elaborate roles to deliver himself from the world of experience. Preparing to visit Clarissa on her deathbed, he dresses "in a never-worn suit, which I had intended for one of my wedding-suits; and I liked myself so well that I began to think with thee, that my outside was the best of me." (VII, 141-42) [IV, 124] When he becomes Caesar, Robert the Great, Don Quixote, "*pius* Aeneas," Lovelace fills the void of his own soul. Yet paradoxically, in his role-playing and invention, Lovelace reveals himself the most profoundly, perhaps as Richardson revealed himself in his writing. According to Geoffery Ashe, "dressing up" had "for the eighteenth-century minds, a link with the idea of emancipation. The ritual masquerader was getting outside the established order by becoming exotically 'other,' like an actor wearing a mask." The costumes of the Divan Club, for instance, were elaborately Turkish: "Members were expected to wear blue turbans and colourful robes, and to carry daggers" as they made their standing toast to The Harem.[21]

Disguised, the Richardsonian character can discover, literally uncover, his own self. Lovelace uses disguise not only to liberate himself, but also to inspire self-discovery in others. Dosing himself with a "few grains of Ipecacuanha," vomiting the blood of pigeons and chickens, Lovelace feigns illness to try the affections of Clarissa. The disguise works well: "Every one now is sure that she loves me. Tears were in her eyes more than once for me. She suffered me to take her hand, and kiss it as often as I pleased." (IV, 294) [II, 436] The illness may be feigned, but it provokes an authentic response in Clarissa, a discovery of her own feelings: "I am really very uneasy. For I have, I doubt, exposed myself to him, and to the women below . . . if he be but not generous, I shall have cause to regret this surprize; which (as I had reason to think myself unaccountably treated by him) has taught me more than I knew of myself." (IV, 297) [II, 438] In his own correspondence, Richardson played various roles to provoke his correspondents into revealing themselves: paternalistic father figure, would-be polygamist, supporter of women's rights, chauvinistic moralist, diffident suitor, and arrogant "celebrated" author. Discussing the reticence of a mutual friend, Mrs. Sheridan urged Richardson to play the role of father confessor: "Get Penny to your Confessional. . . . Nobody, like you, has the art to penetrate into the secrets, and unwind the mazes of a female heart." (*Correspondence*, vol. IV, pp. 162-63) "I love, thou knowest," confesses Lovelace, "to trace human nature, and more particularly female nature, thro' its most secret recesses." (V, 230) [III, 139] His method of "penetration" into the secrets of female nature is more physical than Richardson's: he thinks that if he can "know" a woman physically, he will know her nature. But as he sadly learns, by raping Clarissa he can only know her physically; he never penetrates the secret recesses of her soul. Richardson's way was more subtle: he wanted to penetrate the hearts of his correspondents, to know personal details of their everyday lives in order to better understand them, and to "banish" the diffidence and reserve that could prevent him from "knowing" them.[22]

The best way to penetrate the secrets of the female nature would be to become a woman. Lovelace considers this possibility when he entertains the notion of separate churches for men and women to promote public piety. (For how can a well-intentioned rake keep his mind on God when his female prey is present?) He decides that segregation could never stop a Lovelace from pursuing his plans for seduction: "Were . . . life to be the forfeiture of being found at the female churches, I believe that I, like a second

Clodius, should change my dress, to come at my Portia or Pompeia, though one the Daughter of a Cato, the other the Wife of a Caesar." (III, 68-69) [II, 24] Like Tiresias, Lovelace thinks that he has a "good deal" of the soul of a woman within him. He was "*originally*" a "bashful mortal." "Indeed I am bashful still with regard to this Lady—Bashful, yet know the Sex so well!—But that indeed is the *reason* I know it so well:—For Jack, I have had abundant cause, when I have looked into *myself*, by way of comparison with the *other* Sex, to conclude that a bashful man has a good deal of the soul of a woman; and so, like Tiresias, can tell what they think, and what they drive at, as well as themselves." (III, 114-15) [II, 55]

Like Lovelace, Richardson, a most bashful mortal, possessed a "good deal of the soul of a woman." He was never happier than when he was tracing "female nature, through its most secret recesses," in his correspondence, in his paternal meetings with his young misses, and in his novels. Perhaps too much has been made of Richardson's feminine coteries, so admiring of dear "Papa." Eaves and Kimpel rightly point out that Richardson also enjoyed the company of men like Edward Young, Edward Moore, and Aaron Hill.[23] But clearly, Richardson did encourage a certain feminine sensibility, an appetite for domestic detail, and a sympathy for the problems of women.[24]

By seeking to penetrate the "female heart," Richardson and Lovelace endeavor to master experience, penetrating themselves as well. Seeking Tiresian secrets of the female heart, Lovelace looks also for the secret of himself. Tragically, he destroys himself in the search, losing the soul he tries to fix.

A master plotter on the grand scale, Lovelace is driven to exert his control over his world. But, returning to the rake figure in all of Richardson's novels, we can see that his first rake was not so well developed. Mr. B. is more Mohock than dilettante: his rakery is simple, uncomplicated, and ineptly lustful. For him, seduction is a case of tickle and rub, not a quixotic attempt to conquer the world. He is a clumsy advocate of surprise, lurching out of corners to grab, pinch, and fondle the ubiquitous and provocatively kerchiefed Pamelian bosom. As Pamela reports, "What poor Stuff was all this, my dear Mother, from a Man of his Sense! But see how a bad Cause and bad Actions, confound the greatest Wits!" (I, 36) [I, 23] The Restoration comedy's duel of wits gives way to random insults: "foolish Slut," "Hussy," "Pretty Fool," "Saucy Slut," and "Saucebox" punctuated (predictably) by B.'s putting "his hand in my Bosom." Fielding's transformation of Mr. B. from Squire to Booby is not startlingly original, for the raw material is already present in Richardson's character.

The struggle between Mr. B. and Pamela manages to be funny and serious at the same time. Piety and buffoonery mix to create a comic romance. Notice the combination of prayer and prurience in the following tiff: "O how my Heart throbb'd! and I began (for I did not know what I did) to say the Lord's Prayer. None of your Beads to me Pamela! said he; thou art a perfect Nun, I think. But I said aloud, with my Eyes lifted up to Heaven, *Lead me not into Temptation, but deliver me from Evil*, O my good God! He hugg'd me in his Arms, and said, Well, my dear girl, then you stay this Fortnight, and you shall see what I will do for you." (I, 109-110) [I, 70] Throbbing hearts, uplifted eyes, prayers, and suggestive promises ("you shall see what I will do for you") provide the novel with a comic energy that lasts as long as the seduction plot. When Mr. B. succumbs to Pamela's charms, the book's vitality vanishes. All energy is channeled into an apotheosis of Pamela's virtue. But in the first half of his novel, Richardson brilliantly balances comedy and melodrama. Pamela may "not know what [she] did," but her author knew what he was very deliberately doing—developing a pattern of provocation, prodding, and piety.

We can know B.'s actions, clumsily executed; we can watch him grope for Pamela's person; but we can never

know him. Since Pamela narrates her own story, we can
never enter into B.'s mind to discover any but the most
basic, lustful motivations. His intrigue, clumsy and ill-
constructed, seems to serve a simple purpose—seduction
for seduction's sake.

When B. disguises himself as Nan, the drunken serving
maid, he plays a role for the simple end of getting into
Pamela's bed. Sitting in a corner, "in a Gown and Petticoat
of hers, and her Apron over his Face and Shoulders," he
begins a performance remarkable for its lack of original-
ity. There is no dialogue:

> How do you do? [asks Pamela.] She answer'd not one
> Word. . . . I tremble to relate it! the pretended She
> came into Bed, but trembled like an Aspen-leaf; and I,
> poor Fool that I was! pitied her much. . . . the guilty
> Wretch took my Left Arm, and laid it under his Neck,
> as the vile Procuress held my Right; and then he clasp'd
> me round the Waist! Said I, Is the Wench mad! Why,
> how now, Confidence? thinking still it had been *Nan*.
> But he kissed me with frightful Vehemence; and then
> his Voice broke upon me like a Clap of Thunder, Now,
> *Pamela*, said he, is the dreadful Time of Reckoning come,
> that I have threaten'd. (I, 276-78) [I, 178]

Imagine what Lovelace would do in the same situation: he
would *become* Nan, comically drunken, relishing her slurred
dialogue and unsteady gait. Mr. B.'s disguise is in costume
only.

We cannot fault B. entirely for such a shabby performance. Once again, we have not been allowed access to his
thoughts and fears; we are not allowed to see beneath the
costume he wears. The few times that the "editor" instead
of Pamela reports B.'s actions, and, better still, when he
is allowed to write a letter of his own, B. assumes more
definition. In his letter to Goodman Andrews, Mr. B. displays more invention than ever before. He blames Pamela's scandalous letters, "so injurious to my Honour," on

her romantic turn of mind, and suggests that she is in love with a young destitute clergyman. (I, 120-21) [I, 77] His letter to Farmer Norton, the tenant who keeps Pamela overnight on her journey to Lincolnshire, reveals an even greater ability to plot and invent: he is sending him a young gentlewoman, "much against her Will, who has deeply embark'd in a Love-affair, which will be her Ruin, as well as the Person's to whom she wants to betroth herself." To oblige her father, the benevolent Squire B. is sending her to one of his houses, "where she will be well us'd, to try, if by Absence, and Expostulation with both, they can be brought to know their own Interest: And I am sure you will use her kindly for my sake; For, excepting this Matter, *which she will not own*, she does not want Prudence and Discretion." (I, 139) [I, 89] Mixing fact, filial piety, and fiction, Mr. B. manages a convincing piece of plotting. Not Lovelacian, but not the work of a Booby either. In the brief time B. has to establish his own identity, he does quite well for himself. For once, he is a mind thinking as well as a body lunging. In *Pamela*, Richardson learned the importance of giving his main characters their own voices. When Lovelace writes his own letters, he is given the opportunity to carve out his own identity.

The rake figure barely exists in the second half of *Pamela*. Reformed Mr. B.'s relapse with the countess is designed more to magnify Pamela's virtues than to create a convincing portrait of a rake. We do find, however, a would-be rake in Jackey, the foppish nephew of Lady Davers, who foolishly attempts to seduce Polly Barlow, a would-be Pamela in the B. household. The affair, a mediocre parody of the Pamela/Mr. B. romance, never develops, due to Pamela's watchful eye. She has contempt for both parties. Polly is "poor, poor *Polly Barlow!* . . . sunk indeed! Too low for Excuse, and almost beneath Pity." (III, 376) [II, 195] Jackey "*cuts*, to use his own Word, a considerable Figure in a Country Town.—But see—Yet I will not say what I might—He is Lord *Davers*'s Nephew;

218 • Chapter Five

and if he makes his *Observations*, and *forbears* his *Speeches*,
(I mean, can be silent, and only laugh when he sees somebody of more Sense laugh, and never *approve* or *condemn*
but in *Leading-strings*), he may possibly, pass in a croud of
Gentlemen." Jackey is a debased rake, the first of many in
Richardson's novels. He cannot even write correctly: "I
hope you can read my Letter. I knowe I write a *clumsy*
hand, and *spelle moste lamentabelly*; for I never had a Tal-
lent for these thinges. I was readier by halfe to admire the
Orcherd-robbing Picture in *Lillie's* Grammar, then any other
parte of the Book." (III, 393-96) [II, 204-205] There
can be no greater criticism in Richardson's world.

Lovelace, on the other hand, one of the "readiest and
quickest of writers," immediately invites suspicion. What
on earth can be his subject, Miss Howe wonders: "That
you and I, my dear, should love to write, is no wonder.
We have always, from the time each could hold a pen,
delighted in epistolary correspondencies. Our employments are domestic and sedentary; and we can scribble upon
twenty innocent subjects, and take delight in them because
they *are* innocent, though were they to be seen, they might
not much profit or please others. . . . [a Richardsonian
judgment on the purpose of correspondence well worth
noting] But that such a gay, lively young fellow as this,
who rides, hunts, travels, frequents the public entertainments, and has *means* to pursue his pleasures, should be
able to set himself down for hours together, as you and I
have heard him say he frequently does, that is a strange
thing." (I, 72-74) [I, 49-50] But Lovelace delights in his
scribblings because they are not innocent. Women, says
Miss Howe, need correspondence as an escape from their
limited existence. So does Lovelace. As a man of rank and
property, he may have the means to pursue pleasure, but
merely the pleasure of a common man. Correspondence
provides him an escape from common, stifling existence
and, even more important, a means to the discovery of a

more vital, imaginative self, the true self within and without.

Lovelace's imagination defines his self. Like Faustus, he seeks a dominion that "stretcheth as farre as doth the minde of man."[25] On the surface, his plots are designed to entrap his victims of seduction. But seduction merely focuses his invention and free play. In his first letter to Belford, Lovelace explains his motivation in crude terms: "It was in my early manhood—with that Quality-jilt, whose infidelity I have vowed to revenge upon as many of the Sex as shall come into my power." (I, 212-13) [I, 145-46] In his "Recapitulation" of the letter's contents, Richardson attributes "Pride, Revenge, Love, Ambition, or a Desire of Conquest, his *avowedly* predominant passions." (I, 355) [I, 519] But even in this first casting of the Lovelace personality, revenge cannot adequately account for his actions; his restless imagination drives him onward: "Those confounded Poets, with their terrenely-celestial descriptions, did as much with me as the Lady: They fired my imagination, and set me upon a desire to become a goddess-maker." Always seeking novelty, Lovelace must "create beauty, and place it where nobody else could find it." (I, 212-13) [I, 145-46] What more successful creation than Clarissa Harlowe, purified through her sufferings, hidden in her "nunnery"?

Not content merely to create the Clarissa goddess, Lovelace writes the scenario of his own romance as well. Half comically, half melodramatically, he describes his wretched vigil before the shrine of his saint. Like Satan prowling outside Eden, he creeps basely about the proud Harlowe paddock and garden walls, strolling at midnight "thro' unfrequented paths, and over briery inclosures," catching his death of cold for a "few cold lines" from his goddess. "But was ever hero in Romance (fighting with giants and dragons excepted) called upon to harder trials?" (I, 218) [I, 149]

B.'s desires are simple: he wants Pamela's body. More

ambitiously, Lovelace strives for Clarissa's soul as well. The heart of his "charming frost piece" fascinates him because of its very impenetrability. He endeavors to know Clarissa, to reduce her sublime nature to a sexual one. His drive for power over her and over himself is tempered by only one thing, his mocking sense of humor. Lovelace's sense of irony undercuts his pretensions of power and mastery: "I am taller by half a yard in my imagination than I was," he boasts after taking Clarissa away from her home. "I look *down* upon every-body now. . . . I took off my hat, as I walked, to see if the Lace were not scorched, supposing it had brushed down a star; and before I put it on again, in mere wantonness, and heart's-ease, I was for buffeting the moon." (III, 33) [I, 515] As seducer, Lovelace moves the plot; as actor, he provides the suspense; and as satirist, he provides comic relief by ridiculing his own pretensions.

When Lovelace is most bombastic, he is, of course, most comic: his fantasies of seduction, both ridiculous and grandiose, undercut the seriousness of his villainy. As the novel progresses, his plans for sexual conquest grow to epic (and sometimes mock-epic) proportions. The harem fantasy particularly interests him. While he sits "supinely cross-kneed," reclining on his sofa, he sees Clarissa, "the sweet rogue, late such a proud rogue, wholly in my power, moving up slowly to me, at my beck, with heaving sighs, half-pronounced upbraidings from murmuring lips, her finger in her eye, and quickening her pace at my *Come hither, Dearest.*"

Harem fantasies flourished in the eighteenth century. In her "Turkish Letters," Lady Mary Wortley Montagu developed the paradox that the "enslaved" Turkish women enjoyed more freedom than their "free" English counterparts. When she first visited a Turkish bath, "she painted a ravishing picture of the beautiful bathers, who when they saw her corset believed she had been locked in it by her jealous husband."[26] Even Dr. Johnson entertained a few unexpected notions about harem life. "I have often thought," he told Boswell, "that if I kept a seraglio, the ladies should all wear linen gowns—or cotton; I mean stuffs made of vegetable substances. I would have no silk; you cannot tell when it is clean. It will be very nasty before it is perceived to be so. Linen detects its own dirtiness." Boswell confessed that to hear "the grave Dr. Samuel Johnson, 'that majestick teacher of moral and religious wisdom,' while sitting solemn in an arm-chair in the Isle of Skye, talk, *ex cathedra*, of his keeping a seraglio, and acknowledge that the supposition had *often* been in his thoughts, struck me so forcibly with ludicrous contrast, that I could not but laugh immoderately."[27]

The more affluent and more adventurous acted out Dr. Johnson's "suppositions." Archenholtz described an Indian nabob's harem near Soho: "He had a legal wife, but six odalisks besides, who all slept near her in separate beds. These beds stand in a circle, in order to facilitate the nightly round . . . made with his wife's consent."[28] Lord Baltimore kept a harem in Kensington. In her memoirs, one of his sultanas reported that Baltimore ran his harem in an orderly manner, requiring regular bathing and small-pox inoculation. His girls were not allowed to read in bed, and were allowed "no more than four glasses of wine" after dinner, "and the same after supper; except for the sultana chosen for the evening, to whom the bashaw allows eight, at night." The memoirs suggest that Baltimore had difficulty satisfying the sexual needs of one woman, "making a violent fit of the cholic his apology,"[29] let alone the needs of a harem. Certainly on some level the harem fantasy (or reality) must be connected to a sense of sexual inadequacy. Absolute control over a woman's body becomes especially important to a man who cannot attract a woman with his sexual prowess.

To return to the heaving, sighing Clarissa moving slowly up to Lovelace "at [his] beck," we can see that his own harem fantasy is remarkably passive. While he reclines,

Clarissa moves towards him. (For all of his threats, Lovelace is never an active lover. Even in the rape, he resorts to drugs and the assistance of whores before he manages to complete the act.) Lovelace imagines that after a reasonable amount of time, the heaving Clarissa, tendering "her purple mouth [Her coral lips will be purple then, Jack!]," demonstrating her obligation to him, will convince Lovelace to make her his wife: "Then, Jack, the rapture! then the darted sunbeams from her gladdened eye, drinking up, at one sip, the precious distillation from the pearl-dropt cheek! Then hands ardently folded, eyes seeming to pronounce, God bless my Lovelace! to supply the joy-locked tongue: her transports too strong, and expression too weak, to give utterance to her grateful meanings!—All—All the studies—All the studies of her future life vowed and devoted (when she can speak) to acknowledge and return the perpetuated obligation!" (IV, 21-22) [II, 251-52] This is all very funny, especially Clarissa's lifelong study of perpetuated obligation "when she can speak." Lovelace enjoys the idea of perpetuated obligation. Women, he and the "gentle Waller" say, are born to be controlled: "A tyrant-husband makes a dutiful wife." (IV, 265) [II, 416] (It is remarkable how Lovelace, Solmes, and Richardson all sound alike on this matter.) His "ideal" wife would think of no one but her Lovelace: "I would be the subject of her dreams, as well as of her waking thoughts. I would have her think every moment lost, that is not passed with me: Sing to me, read to me, play to me when I pleased; no joy so great as in obeying me." (IV, 264) [II, 416]

Lovelace must come first. "Either I am a principal in this cause," he tells Belford, "or I am nothing." (VII, 262) [IV, 205] He pursues his sexual targets for the delight of coursing more than for the delight of intercourse: the chase and the first shot attract him, not the pleasures of the sensual life. "I have always been aiming at the merit of a first discoverer," he tells Belford. "*Once any other man's*, and *I* know it, and *never more mine*." (IV, 283) [II, 428][30]

Lovelace boasts to "honest" Joseph Leman that "I have ever had more pleasure in my contrivances, than in the End of them. I am no sensual man; but a man of spirit— One woman is like another. . . . In Coursing all the sport is made by the winding Hare. A barn door Chick is better eating." (III, 249) [II, 147]

Just as Clarissa is more angel than woman, Lovelace is more spirit, demonic rather than angelic, than man. Both Clarissa and Lovelace are engaged in a terrible struggle over the body of Clarissa, yet on a very basic level they have no concern with bodies at all. Even as Lovelace enumerates his lady's charms, her heaving bosom and purple lips, he is plotting to conquer her soul.

Lovelace prizes the well-laid plot, not the well-laid girl: "What, as I have often contemplated, is the enjoyment of the finest woman in the world, to the contrivance, the bustle, the surprizes, and at last the happy conclusion, of a well-laid plot?—The charming *roundabouts*, to come to the *nearest way home*;—the doubts; the apprehensions; the heartakings; the meditated triumphs—These are the joys that make the blessing dear.—For all the rest, what is it? What but to find an Angel in imagination dwindled down to a Woman in fact?" (VI, 8) [III, 248] Lovelace would have appreciated Dr. Gregory's warning that girls should never reveal their charms, lest they "reduce" the young "angel to a very ordinary girl." The ordinary commonness of life, the angel dwindled into a woman "in fact" drives Lovelace to create his fictions of seduction to break out of the limitations of everyday life. Clarissa provides him with a suitable opponent, for she refuses, even after being raped, to dwindle down into a woman "in fact." Instead, she turns herself into an angel "in fact," untouched by his violation.

Lovelace's fantasies assume a frantic energy, becoming more and more elaborate as the novel progresses. Not content with one conquered beauty, he envisions Anna Howe and Clarissa in twin bondage: "How sweetly pretty to see the two lovely friends, when humbled and tame, both sitting in the darkest corner of a room, arm in arm, weeping and sobbing for each other!—And I their Emperor, their then *acknowledged* Emperor, reclined at my ease in the same room, uncertain to which I should first, Grand Signor like, throw out my handkerchief." (IV, 195) [II, 369] Some day, Lovelace fantasizes, the two "lovely friends" will proudly compare notes on their relationships with him: "A charming Girl, by the same father, to her friend's charming Boy; who, as they grow up, in order to consolidate their mamas friendships (for neither have Dreams regard to *consanguinity*), intermarry; change names by Act of Parliament, to enjoy my estate—and I know not what of the like incongruous stuff." (VI, 12-13) [III, 251]

Number counts for Lovelace, who in a more heroic time would "have gone to war with the Great Turk, and the Persian, and Mogholl, for their Seraglios." (V, 67) [III, 26] Quality is of the first concern (he plans to seduce a Clarissa, not any common trull), but quantity makes the enterprise even more satisfying. When he imagines Clarissa as a mother, two little Lovelaces, not one, nestle at her alabaster breast. (IV, 355) [II, 477] The desire to return to the breast is a common enough fantasy, but Lovelace will become *two* little Lovelaces, getting twice as much "mother" as anyone else. For Lovelace, twice is still not enough. His Isle of Wight fantasy is even more elaborate: Lovelace will ravish Anna Howe, her mother, and her maidservant, efficiently crossing class lines and satisfying his desire for both mother and daughter.

In the Isle of Wight daydream, the imagination reigns supreme: whatever Lovelace wills must happen. " 'Tis plaguey hard, if we cannot *find* or make a *storm*," (IV, 270) [II, 420] he confidently predicts. After the mass rape, he plans to free the women, hoping that they will prosecute him in a public court, public in its admiration for Lovelace. Crowds press close, admiring his form and beauty:

Then, let us look down, look up, look round, which

way we will, we shall see all the doors, the shops, the windows, the sign-irons, and balconies (garrets, gutters, and chimney-tops included) all white-capt, black-hooded, and periwigg'd, or crop-ear'd by the *Immobile Vulgus*; while the floating *street-swarmers*, who have seen us pass by at one place, run with stretched-out necks, and strained eye-balls, a round-about way, and elbow and shoulder themselves into places by which we have not passed, in order to obtain another sight of us; every street continuing to pour out its swarms of late-comers, to add to the gathering snowball.

A "dozen or two of young maidens" will go to court to beg for Lovelace's life. "And what a pretty show they will make, with their white hoods, white gowns, white petticoats, white scarves, white gloves, kneeling for me, with their white handkerchiefs at their eyes, in two pretty rows, as his Majesty walks through them, and nods my pardon for their sakes!" (IV, 275-77) [II, 424] In an exhaustively comic spectacle,[31] wild and grandiose, Lovelace bombards the reader with gratuitous detail presented for the delight in the very sound of the words themselves: "garrets, gutters, and chimney-tops included," "white-capt, black-hooded, and periwigg'd, or crop-ear'd," and his newly coined word, "*street-swarmers*." Outrageously repetitive,[32] he defies the limits of proper prose: "white hoods, white gowns, white petticoats, white scarves, white gloves, kneeling for me." When the reader, dazzled by the whiteness of the vision, reaches the maidens "kneeling for me," he feels relief that Lovelace has finally released him. But Lovelace pushes even further: "with their white handkerchiefs at their eyes." The spectacle, not the action, concerns the artist here: the pattern of two pretty rows of young white maidens extends the scope of his own life. Lovelace defines himself by the outrageous fantasies of his imagination. By creating an entire world of "street-swarmers" and kneeling maidens, he overcomes the limitations of common life. And as long as his imagination controls his reality, he cannot descend into a "common man" any more than Clarissa can dwindle into a "woman in fact."

Defining his own existence is not enough for Lovelace, who must create reality for the other characters in his world as well. From the moment Lovelace gains Clarissa's trust, he manipulates her sense of reality. By transforming the isolated summer house on the Harlowe estate into a bedlam of noise and by changing Joseph Leman into a threatening mob of Harlowes, he manages to drive Clarissa from her own house. Lovelace even transforms Clarissa herself, beginning his metamorphosis at the inn at St. Albans: "Ovid was not a greater master of metamorphoses than thy friend. To the mistress of the house I instantly changed her into a Sister, brought off by surprize from a near Relation's (where she had wintered) to prevent her marrying a confounded Rake [I love always to go as near the truth as I can] whom her Father and Mother, her elder Sister, and all her loving Uncles, Aunts, and Cousins abhorred." (III, 52) [II, 13] Ironically, Clarissa's new prison, St. Albans, is guarded jealously by a "brother" even more dangerous than James Harlowe.

Going as near to the truth as he can at the Widow Sinclair's, Lovelace creates an entire world, peopling it with a respectable widow, her two honest nieces, Captain Mennel, and Tomlinson, perhaps his most convincing fraud. When Tomlinson acts as Lovelace's emissary at Hampstead, Lovelace takes the opportunity to flaunt his theatrical talents. Affected by Clarissa's innocence, Patrick McDonald begins to balk at playing Tomlinson. Undaunted, Lovelace manages to overcome his scruples and directs him to let "unconcern and heart's-ease once more take possession of thy solemn features. Thou hast hitherto performed extremely well. Shame not thy *past* by thy *future* behaviour; and a rich reward awaits thee. If thou *art* dough, *be* dough; and I slapt him on the shoulder—Resume but thy former shape—And I'll be answerable for the event." (V, 221) [III, 132]

Hampstead serves as another theater for Lovelace's imagination. In a "narrative of the dramatic kind," he plays one of his more elaborate roles, that of the gouty old gentleman. Powdering his hair, slouching his hat, Lovelace transforms himself, borrowing a pair of "coarse, but clean stirrup-stockens" to cover up his aristocratic "clocked stockens." But Lovelace's pains to create his "good gouty appearance" are largely gratuitous. Clarissa has been in his power all along, ever since the moment of detection. "Not a bad mimic," Lovelace "stump[s] away cross to the Bowling-green" on borrowed cane "to practise a little the hobbling gait of a gouty man" to fill his own need for invention, free play, and escape from the self. He delights in mastering the details of his costume. "Well observ'd," he applauds the kind gentlewoman who calls attention to his clocked stockings; she has become a fellow player in his imaginary world. A pair of "coarse, but clean, stirrup-stockens" are indeed "the best in the world for the purpose," (V, 76-77) [III, 32-33] valued for their exact and appropriate nature.

Attend to the "minutiae," the coarse but clean stockings, say Lovelace and Richardson, for it is through the minutiae that the artist can seduce his audience. But Lovelace and Richardson also appreciate the minute particulars for their own sake. When Lovelace instructs Tomlinson on the proper riding dress to wear before his suspicious Clarissa, he fills his letter with his own delight in detail. Do not "let your Boots be over clean," he warns; have your "Linen rumpled and soily. . . . Remember . . . to loll, to throw out your Legs, to stroke and grasp down your Ruffles, as if of significance enough to be careless." Lovelace is creating a character of significance, lovingly adding the detail, "the *minutiae*, where art (or *imposture*, as the ill-mannered would call it) is designed," to create a world he can control.

In his instructions to Tomlinson, Lovelace ruefully adds
that "being afraid of controul," he has often "brought controul upon" himself. (VI, 90-91) [III, 304] His complicated creations force him to produce more and more lim-
iting inventions. Reality is always out there, resisting total
control both comically and tragically. Lovelace becomes
entangled in his plotting, always fearing that one messenger from the "real world" of Anna Howe will enlighten
his captive. Forgeries and disguises keep up the pretense
for a while, but by the time of Clarissa's death, Lovelace's
inventions possess a manic quality. In his attempt to visit
the dying Clarissa, Lovelace, disguised as a tradesman,
savagely reveals his aggression and frustration. Pretending
to make a sale, he pushes the awkward fingers of a footman
through a pair of gloves: "The fellow said, the gloves were
too little. Thrust, and be d——nd to thee, said I: Why
fellow, thou hast not the strength of a cat. Sir, sir, said
he, laughing, I shall hurt your Honour's side. D——n
thee, thrust, I say. He did; and burst out the sides of the
glove. Will said I, where's thy pruning knife? By my Soul,
friend, I had a good mind to pare thy cursed paws." (VII,
152-53) [IV, 132] The occasion, more than the game,
makes Lovelace's invention seem inappropriate. Pruning
knives and pared fingers are no more threatening than mass
rape off the Isle of Wight, but now we are not allowed to
forget the dying Clarissa juxtaposed to the merry Lovelace.
To clear the stage for Lovelace's tradesman game, Clarissa
left her room early in the morning to be dragged around
London in a hired chair. As Mrs. Lovick informs Lovelace, "she rested not two hours, for fear of you." (VII,
162) [IV, 138]

In Clarissa's final days, comedy and tragedy cannot mix:
the struggle is seen solely in Clarissa's tragic terms. Even
Lovelace rejects the comic world of disguise and play. When
Sally Martin "plays" Clarissa, whining and praying,
Lovelace is "*Belforded* all over" and "cursed her most de-
voutly for taking my Beloved's name in her mouth in such

a way." But "the little devil was not to be balked; but fell a crying, sobbing, praying, begging, exclaiming, fainting, that I never saw my lovely girl so well aped." (VII, 156-57) [IV, 134-35] Sally's "virtuous" imitation horrifies him, for "one sees that art will generally so well supply the place of nature that you shall not easily know the difference." Lovelace, "a perfect Proteus,"[33] (III, 153-54) [II, 82] usually appreciates the possibilities of artifice, but not when *he* is being deceived. For art is slippery, especially loose in the hands of a Sally Martin.

We can see Richardson's ambivalence towards Lovelace and his art in his correspondence. He told Aaron Hill that he intended that Lovelace's character would be unamiable: "I once read to a young Lady Part of his Character, and then his End; and upon her pitying him, and wishing he had been rather made a Penitent, than to be killed, I made him still more and more odious." (*Letters*, p. 73) To Lady Bradshaigh he wrote that, fearing he had made Lovelace too wicked to obtain any sympathy, he first "try'd his Character, as it was first drawn, and his last Exit, on a young Lady of Seventeen." When she showed by her tears that "he was not very odious to her for his Vagaries and Inventions," he "threw into his Character some deeper Shades. And as he now stands, I verily think that had I made him a worse Man, he must have been a Devil." (*Letters*, p. 113) Had Lovelace remained the character first outlined in his opening letters, vowing revenge in every sentence, his villainy might have been better believed. But once Richardson began to develop his character, investing him with wit, grace, and imagination, his "last Exit" became even more difficult to accept. Richardson had as much trouble degrading Lovelace as Milton had degrading Lucifer.

Richardson might have advised his correspondents to look for the unamiable qualities in his rake's character, but whenever an unwary reader seriously criticized his creation, Richardson's own attachment to Lovelace asserted itself. Edward Moore unluckily complimented the author by attacking the "Mischiefs" of his creation: "That to have a Heart to conceive the Mischiefs of a Lovelace, and to have the *smallest Spark* of Goodness in that Heart, is of more Merit than the whole Catalogue of Virtues." "How Sir!" answered Richardson indignantly: "Have you read Lovelace's Bad, and not his Good? . . . Is he not generous! Is he not, with Respect to *Meum* and *Tuum* Matters, just? Is he not ingenuous? Does he not on all Occasions exalt the Lady at his own Expence?" He admits that "with regard to the Sex" his rake "sticks at nothing," but "are there not many Lovelace's in this Particular?—Men, who, if they do not so much Mischief as Lovelace did, do, nevertheless all that is in their Power to do? Ah! my dear Mr. Moore!—But I will only Repeat, that there are more Lovelaces in the World, than the World imagines there are." (*Letters*, pp. 88-89) Or, as Lovelace boasts, "*Lovelace's in every corner, Jack!*" (V, 74) [III, 31] At once justifying and vilifying, Richardson played a dangerous game with Lovelace's character. "Is he not ingenuous?" He? Lovelace or Richardson?

By damning his character with monitory footnotes and authorial intrusions, Richardson was free to develop in his fiction his villain's fantasy world. Schemes of mass rape would be legitimate as long as Richardson emphasized the negative aspects of his character at the same time. In denying the creative genius of Lovelace, he gained the freedom to express parts of his own personality he could not reveal any other way. Richardson's artistic strategies are similar to Swift's, as Gardner Stout has defined them: "Swift's vivid parodies and personations [in the *Tale of a Tub*] are often projective embodiments of repressed aspects of his own personality as the *Tale*'s author. His parodies allow his buried self to speak through him, while enabling him to maintain that the voice he is parodying is antithetic to himself as satiric speaker." Satisfying the demands of conscience through satiric negation, Swift was free to "create satiric fictions representing and gratifying his repressed impulses and fantasies, while simultaneously denying them."[34] A similar principle of denial is at work in *Clarissa*. Without the moral license supplied by his condemnation of his creation, Richardson could not have invested Lovelace with such energy and power. Lovelace's "excursions" into the world of repressed fantasy originate in the deepest recesses of Richardson's own sensibility: "But how I *excurse*," crows Lovelace after spinning his fantasy of segregated churches for men and women. (III, 69) [II, 24] Richardson understood Lovelace's need for excursions; he had taken a few himself to "carry [himself] out of [himself]," and was "not quite so happy when, tired with [his] peregrinations," he was "obliged to return home."

In *Sir Charles Grandison*, Richardson took no chances that his audience could overlook the unamiable character of the rake. In his attempt to legitimize the fantastic excursions of Lovelace, Richardson emasculated the rake figure, losing his artistic potency in the process. Sir Charles is able to realize Lovelace's fantasies in the public world, but his triumph seems stale and respectable. As mover of the novel's plot, Sir Hargrave, the main "rake," fails miserably. In *Grandison*, Richardson appears to have been compelled to degrade his rakes, to show those mischievous young admirers of Lovelace once and for all that the rake should be avoided. Hargrave blusters, snarls, and fails to abduct Harriet Byron, losing three front teeth in the abortive attempt: "Lord bless me, my dear! . . . A man so vain of his person! O how must he be exasperated." (I, 200) [I, XXXIX] Hargrave's misfortunes continue: beaten by robbers outside of Paris, he completely collapses, "so miserably sunk in his spirits . . . so miserable in himself, that he could hardly thank [Grandison] for saving a life so wretched." (II, 665) [V, XLV]

Mr. Everard Grandison, cousin to Sir Charles, shabbily parodies Lovelace, skulking around resorts in mean dis-

guise to entrap silly women. Lady G. reports that he has
been seen at Cuper's Gardens, "dressed like a Sea-officer,
and skulking, like a thief into the privatest walks of the
place." (II, 441) [IV, XXXVII] "The *first* formerly in
the fashion," Cousin Grandison has sunk "in so few months,
gaunt sides; his half-worn tarnish'd-laced coat, big enough
to lap over him; hollow cheeks, puling voice, sighing heart,
creeping feet." (II, 653) [V, XL] In his description of
the degraded rake, Richardson exploited his own humorous fantasy material, the image of himself as a "sly sinner,
creeping along the very edges of the walks" of Tunbridge
Wells. (*Letters*, p. 88) Richardson, stealing in and out of
bookstores, becomes Jackey, with his "creeping feet,"
"skulking, like a thief into the privatest walks of the place."
Richardson was killing off the rake figure in himself,
transforming him into an inept clown.

On the surface—and Sir Charles exists primarily on the
surface—the good man bears little resemblance to the
Lovelacian rake. For A. D. McKillop, Sir Charles's
"ideals are within reach for his time and place, so that he
can never go to war with his world or be involved in the
quixotic clash of ideal and real."[35] Lovelace, as we have
seen, is always battling windmills in his struggle to impose
his ideals upon the resisting world. Yet, in the final analysis, Grandison is a more successful Quixote than Lovelace, genteelly living out the wildest Lovelacian fantasies.

Lovelace can only be an emperor in his imagination: in
another time he would be Caesar, Robert the Great, "*pius*
Aeneas." But the time is right for Sir Charles, a man of
feeling rather than action. Sir Charles receives public acclaim for his superiority. Even his enemies praise him:
Mr. Merceda would "rather have Sir Charles Grandison
for [his] friend than the greatest prince on earth," while
Mr. Bagenhall would "rather be Sir Charles Grandison in
this past hour, than the Great Mogul all [his] life." (I,
252) [II, IV] Harriet thinks that the Indies should be his:
"What a king would he make. Power could not corrupt

such a mind as his." And "Caesar, said Dr. Bartlett, speaking of him before Mr. Deane and all of us, was not quicker to destroy, than Sir Charles Grandison is to relieve." (I, 446) [II, XXXIII] Harriet prefers him to "a King, in all his glory," (II, 34) [III, VII] and later confesses that "he appeared to me in a much more shining light than a hero would have done, returning in a triumphal car covered with laurels, and dragging captive princes at its wheels. How much more glorious a character is that of *The Friend of Mankind* than that of *The Conqueror of Nations*." (II, 70) [III, XIV] Lovelace can almost be heard in the wings, gnashing his teeth in frustration. Grandison is winning his glory! Am I not an emperor, a Caesar, a hero, Jack? Lovelace repeatedly demands and never receives public recognition of his greatness. He reigns over his fantasy world, but in the drawing room he is only the rakish Bobby Lovelace. Grandison wins his drooping laurels.

Sir Charles realizes Lovelace's sexual fantasies as well as his dreams of conquest. Lovelace may dream of the day he will "drop the handkerchief" before the tamed Miss Howe and Clarissa, but Sir Charles enjoys a harem in his own drawing room. "I was told," reports Lord W., "within this month past, that no fewer than Five Ladies, out of one circle, declared, that they would stand out by consent, and let you pick and choose a wife from among them." (II, 43) [III, IX] Sir Charles approaches polygamy in his triangular friendship with Harriet and Clementina. Lady G. provocatively suggests that her brother, if anyone, deserves both women: "Betwixt her excellencies and yours, how must my brother's soul be divided!—I wonder he thinks of either of you. Ass and two bundles of hay, Harriet. But my brother is a nobler animal. He won't starve. But I think, in my conscience, that he should have you both. There might be a law made, that the case should not be brought into precedent till two such women be found, and such a man, and all three in the like situation." (III,

195) [VI, XLV] In their pledge of triple friendship, Sir
Charles, Harriet, and Clementina literally enact a marriage ritual, consecrating a "little temple" to their eternal
friendship. Polygamy evidently intrigued Richardson.[36] He
teased Lady Bradshaigh that it would serve as a moral cor-
rective for loose women, "taming" and "domesticating"
spirits "that are not a credit to the sex, and who are inca-
pable of acting upon principle . . . who would wish that
such creatures as those were not slaves?" (*Correspondence*,
vol. VI, p. 219) Neatly, Richardson's ideal polygamy would
control those "creatures" who dared to live "in defiance of
duty," making them subservient to the male common-
wealth. Lovelace also proposes a form of polygamy in his
plan for yearly marriages, changed every St. Valentine's
Day, an excellent "means of annihilating, absolutely annihilating, four or five very atrocious and capital sins": rape,
murder, duelling, jealousy, and barrenness. (V, 292-93)
[III, 181] But in spite of Lovelace's plots and Richardson's teasing speculations, it is Sir Charles who wins the
day, playing the "Grand Signor" to all the neighborhood.
The rake is dead; long live the good man.

Unfortunately, most readers would prefer to spare
Lovelace and kill off Sir Charles. As we have seen, even
Richardson was fascinated with the notion of getting rid of
his hero: "Shall we remove him by a violent fever—or by
the treacherous sword of Greville. . . . What horrors attending the murder might be painted!" Lovelace energized
Richardson, freeing him to explore the hidden and forbidden aspects of experience. Sir Charles, on the other hand,
living out Lovelace's fantasies of sexual and social conquest, retarded the imagination and free play so central to
the vision of *Clarissa*. The failure of *Grandison* raises an
important question: can fantasy be realized yet retain its
force? Lovelace attracts the reader because he expresses deeply
felt needs we all share for freedom, self-expression, dominance, and free play. To succeed, fantasy must express
desires impossible to realize, equally impossible to quell.

SIX • Created Selves: Richardson's Development of His Characters

And therefore the particulars of my Story, and the base Arts of this vile man, will, I think, be best collected from those very Letters of his (if Mr. Belford can be prevailed upon to communicate them); to which I dare appeal with the same truth and fervor as he did, who says,—*O that one would hear me! and that mine adversary had written a book!—Surely I would take it upon my shoulders, and bind it to me as a crown!*
                              CLARISSA (VII, 48) [IV, 61]

I will write a Comedy, I think. I have a Title ready; and that's half the work. *The Quarrelsome Lovers.* 'Twill do. There's something new and striking in it.
                              LOVELACE to BELFORD (IV, 50) [II, 271]

As Clarissa depends even upon her seducer's correspondence for vindication, Richardson demonstrates throughout his career an unwavering faith in the world of letters. In the act of creating characters engaged in perfecting themselves, he investigated the possibility of not only perfecting but inventing the self—through the word. In the telling of their stories, his characters try on new personalities, analyze past actions, adapt themselves to literary models, stripping away what offends while piecing together what fits. They literally create themselves from the fragments of their fictional reality. The word defines their world.[1]

We come to know Richardson's characters by their vocabulary; personal style becomes as important as personal action. Richardson's choice of the epistolary method was a happy one, granting him the tools, the space, and the freedom to develop distinctly different characters speaking directly to the reader. Pamela lives, warts and all, because she speaks to the reader, grabbing us by the sleeve and drawing us into her plight. In *Clarissa*, we listen to four different speakers trying to make sense of their world, acting, reacting, evaluating, even altering their experience as they describe it. In *Grandison*, Richardson uses the epistolary method in a more celebratory, less dramatic way. No villains are granted the pen in Richardson's last novel, no Lovelaces intercept and alter the letters, the very fabric of existence, between Miss Howe and Clarissa. Admiring characters report the glories of Sir Charles in chorus. The sense of development and discovery that animates the first part of *Pamela* and all of *Clarissa* disappears. For Richardson's best work, we must return to *Clarissa*, where his characters record their reality in their letters as they test, develop, and utterly change their ideas about themselves and their world, transforming themselves with their words.

The transformation can be unsettling for characters and readers alike. Self-discovery can painfully contradict the moral absolutes Richardson intended to promote in his novels. All the while Richardson worked in his fiction to restore order to a fragmented world, he was in truth creating a fictional world of ambiguous and relative values. The moralist ends up creating a world in which moral maxims no longer apply. To a great extent the ambiguity implicit in his fictional world reflects his own shifting sense of self. Setting out to perfect his reader, Richardson ended up completing himself as a character in his own letters, a creature certainly as opaque and complex as his characters in fiction. When Johnson noted of Clarissa that there was always "something which she prefers to truth," he spoke of the creator as well as the character. Truth alone, expressed in the alienation of Clarissa's despair, must be transcended to be borne. When Richardson takes his Clarissa to the limits of her personality, when he forces her (and us) to confront the diminished fragments of herself in need of transformation, Richardson breaks through the limits of his own fiction, dramatically replacing his moral with more complex meaning.

In the far simpler world of the *Familiar Letters*, words were tools, letters neatly finished edifices, models to be followed. Confidence in the world of form fills his letter manual. Richardson outlines, and thereby predicts, the progress of the courtship between a lover and his coquettish mistress in four letters. In the first, the gentleman "resents" her "supposed Coquetry"; the second letter gives us her "Answer"; this is followed by "The Gentleman's submissive Reply"; and finally by the "Lady's forgiving Return." (*Familiar Letters*, pp. 108-111) Presumably this pattern will not vary in real life. Such a naive attitude towards the predictability of experience is central to a faith in the efficacy of epistolary models.

In *Pamela*, however, Richardson begins to explore the complexity of experience. The early Pamela, pert young girl rather than moldy moral matron, acts in an individual rather than an exemplary way. She uses her letters to examine and develop her own evolving ideas about herself. Both Pamela and Mr. B. share a highly developed sense of the literary expectations of their roles. Pamela's letters help her to refine and define the significance of her actions, a significance duly noted by B., who reads Pamela's letters as if they were a guidebook for his behavior, recording the past and forecasting the future.

The literary self-consciousness Pamela and Mr. B. share can be seen early on in the novel. B. often justifies his actions with fictional precedent. Why shouldn't he rape Pamela, he asks: "Whoever blamed *Lucretia*? All the shame lay on the ravisher only; and I am content to take all the blame upon me, as I have already borne too great a share for what I have not deserved." Pamela's warning to justify herself "*Lucretia* like" with her death delights B. She knows the plot: "O, my good girl! said he, tauntingly, you are well read, I see; and we shall make out between us, before we have done, a pretty Story in Romance, I warrant ye."

(I, 31) [I, 20] While B. acts like a character in search of his story, Pamela, quick to oblige, tells her own "pretty Story" in her letters, where she turns herself into a symbol of virtue in distress, so powerful a symbol that "a Pamela" becomes as significant a literary metaphor as "a Lucretia." B. quickly appreciates the literary quality of their affair, the opportunity "for a Tale every Day to good Mother *Jervis*, and what Subjects for Letter-writing to your Father and Mother, and what pretty Preachments you may hold forth to the young Gentlemen!" (I, 88) [I, 56] Her "pretty Preachments" literally compel B. to make Pamela his wife: her letters give him "a very high Opinion of [her] Wit and Innocence," (I, 312) [I, 202] while her "mournful Relation" of her thoughts of suicide with their "sweet Reflections" upon her escape touch him "sensibly." (I, 329) [I, 213] In recording her trials, Pamela creates an image of herself and her captor. As B. warns her, "Since you take me for the Devil, how can you expect any Good from me?—How, rather, can you expect any thing but the worst Treatment from me—You have given me a Character, *Pamela*; and blame me not, that I act up to it." (I, 287) [I, 185]

B. dotes on Pamela's records of his actions almost more than he dotes on the girl. How he longs "to see the Particulars of [her] Plot," for "there is such a pretty Air of Romance, as you relate them, in *your* Plots and *my* Plots, that I shall be better directed in what manner to wind up the Catastrophe of the pretty Novel." (I, 316-27) [I, 205] When Pamela returns to B. after she had been sent away, his first question concerns her letters rather than her person; indeed by now they are one and the same. "He begg'd me to sit down by his Bed-side, and ask'd me, If I had obliged him with sending for my former Pacquet?" (II, 19) [I, 227] B. needs his script to go on with the romance.

The play goes on after marriage. In spite of her matronly disapproval of melodrama, Mrs. Pamela never misses an opportunity to cast herself in purely melodramatic roles. Quaking before an unfaithful Mr. B., who has begun to dally with a dangerously loose countess, Pamela timidly taps on his closet door and breaks into a tragedy speech: "Thus poor *Hester*, to her Royal Husband, ventur'd her Life, to break in upon him unbidden. But that *Eastern* Monarch, great as he was, extended to the fainting Suppliant the golden Sceptre." Always one to pick up a cue, B. extends his hand. "I hope, my Dear, by this Tragedy Speech, we are not to expect any sad Catastrophe to our present Misunderstanding." (IV, 172) [II, 299]

Barely ten pages later, Pamela slips easily into another role as she stands before her errant husband "as *Paul* did before *Felix*" to recall him to his duty. (IV, 185) [II, 307] When the B.'s reconcile their difference, they make up in the by now traditional way, reading and rereading Pamela's letters on the subject of B.'s infidelity. B. promises to forgive any harsh words Pamela might have written in "the Bitterness of [her] Heart," as Pamela graciously complies with his request for her epistolary record of her trials, begging only that B. will "take care [his] Health suffers not by . . . sitting up; for the Nights are cold and damp." (IV, 199-200) [II, 316-17]

Richardson's first novel was an experiment in form and subject, brilliantly uneven, yet in this first attempt we can watch the author develop his ideas about character. Throughout the first half of her novel, until she freezes into matronage, Pamela's personality grows, awkwardly perhaps, but definitely, as she records her impressions "to the moment." Her words not only record but create her experience. Although his moral exemplar serves first as a model designed to perfect the reader, she develops into a character of independence and strength. On the surface, Pamela is the self-made heroine, triumphantly becoming the paragon Mrs. B. for her trials. But Pamela's own personality, ambiguous, self-conscious, and calculated, transcends her rather limited moral pattern. When Pamela saucily smiles at her image in the mirror, complacently noting that she has never liked herself better (I, 67) [I, 42] she is a person of complexity, not a one-dimensional moral model. Yet although Pamela is a complex character, she presents herself to the reader so simply that she exposes herself to charges of hypocrisy. When Pamela records her experiences "to the moment," she is using an epistolary style that comes from Richardson's own notion of the "working mind":[2] the mind is always in the process of creating its own sense of reality. Richardson's faith in the working mind reflects a Lockean empiricism, a confidence that the senses will enable us to perceive and make sense of reality. Once, however, it is recognized that we perceive "reality" through our senses, it follows that we can also be deceived and betrayed through these same senses. Although Richardson ostensibly expressed a belief in the world of absolute truths, the black and white *Vade Mecum* world of filial piety and obedience, in his novels he created a world of flux, where his characters employ their senses to perceive conditions that may change at any moment, where monstrous fathers and bad masters exert their control.

Pamela defends the "absolute" virtue of chastity, but she demonstrates her faith in her static virtue in a flexible and unfixed way. To attract Mr. B. even while she is fending him off, Pamela must be as adaptable as she is steadfast. She records her movements as they occur, without time or opportunity for evaluation. When we read her letters, we are looking directly into her working mind, seeing her make sense of her experience. Her naive reactions, which may appear complacent and self-serving, reveal her motivations too honestly for comfort. A penchant to tell all, even when she exposes her own shrewd awareness of her best interests, makes Pamela a vivid and substantial character who may, at times, embarrass our sense of propriety. In examining her open, unstructured style, we can come to view her revelations as more honest than hypocritical.

Even in the first letter, Pamela reports everything, refusing to subordinate her various subjects. She has "GREAT Trouble, and some Comfort" to report. Her mistress's death, the trouble, deserves a paragraph blotted with tears: "O how my Eyes run!" she explains. Pamela fears that the death will end her position and send her packing, but in paragraph two she allays her parents' fears: "so comes the Comfort." She will not be sent off after all, but remains to take care of Mr. B.'s linen. B. has taken her hand before all of the servants to give her four golden guineas. The focus of the letter now shifts to the palpable guineas, which clever Pamela has hidden in her late mistress's pill box, "wrapp'd close in Paper, that they mayn't chink," before sending them to her parents "by *John* our Footman, who goes your Way." Finally Pamela asks her parents to pray for her, and begins to close the letter. But suddenly she records another incident, unexpected, outside of the boundaries of her letter. Mr. B. has broken in on her to read the very letter she is now composing. As he holds her by the hand and compliments her on her spelling, Pamela "did nothing but curt'sy and cry, and was all in Confusion at his Goodness. Indeed he is the best of Gentlemen, I think." (I, 1-4) [I, 1-2] In one letter, the reader progresses from trouble to comfort to confusion, and a qualified faith in B.'s goodness. We learn in the second letter that Pamela's parents are even less sanguine. They warn Pamela that "when he has given you so much Money, and speaks so kindly to you, and praises your coming on; and Oh! that frightful Word, that he would be kind to you, if you would do *as you should do*, almost kills us with Fears." (I, 3) [I, 5] This second interpretation (perhaps Mr. B. is not the "best of Gentlemen") complicates Pamela's situation: we are now given two ways of thinking about one event. If the reader has already suspected B.'s actions in the first letter, speculating about the reasons for Pamela's "confusion," he has helped to create the novel, giving shape to the loosely structured information Pamela allows him to have.

In her second letter, Pamela reveals a change in her own state of mind. Her parents' letter has made her heart, "which was overflowing with Gratitude for my master's Goodness, suspicious and fearful." She resents her parents' fears for her honesty, insisting that she will be dutiful "*till Death*," and would willingly "embrace" poverty, rags, bread and water, rather than "forfeit my good Name." "I will die a thousand Deaths rather than be dishonest any way," she vows. After her histrionic pledges, however, she qualifies the entire tone of her letter with her observations on the affability of B. and the civility of Mrs. Jervis: "Sure they can't *all* have Designs against me because they are civil!" she muses, offering just the sort of juxtaposition anti-Pamelists relish—idealistic resolve to be dutiful undercut by her practical, prosaic faith in good manners. This juxtaposition, however, can come from a mind working, as well as from a mind rationalizing. (I, 6-7) [I, 4-5] Throughout her story, Pamela tries to understand her circumstances, often offering several interpretations of the same event. When we share in her evaluations, we closely identify with her character.

Richardson's exhaustive writing "to the moment" does not always succeed. He puts too much emphasis upon the wavering sensibilities of one naive girl, whose reflections sometimes sound merely silly. "Tortured with twenty different doubts in a minute," Pamela tortures her reader as well, offering far too many reflections for one straining paragraph. Should I stay a week, a fortnight? Will I relent at his kindness? Should I accept his offer of riches? He means honor—dishonor. And on and on. (I, 110-11) [I, 70-71] Insisting upon the validity of the most minute circumstance, Pamela "writes on," promising her parents to continue writing "as long as I stay, tho' I shall have nothing but silliness to write; for I know you divert yourselves on Nights with what I write, because it is mine." (I, 66-

67) [I, 41] If everything Pamela reports has value because it is "hers," all elements of her tale, details of her new "plain muslin tucker" and complacent reflections on the pleasures of innocence take on equal significance. We can see this in the famous description of her homespun dress, in which she mingles piety and pride, innocence and calculation. Donning her humble straw hat "with its two blue strings," Pamela looks in her glass, "as proud as anything." Indeed, pride fills her letter—pride in her finery, which she is wise enough to lay aside; pride in her new garb, both charming and appropriate; and pride in her "Ease, Innocence, and Resignation." After preening on her appearance ("To say the truth, I never liked myself so well in my life"), Pamela congratulates herself on her "humble Mind" and, paradoxically, on her ability to meet with a shocking disappointment even while she exactly and shrewdly takes inventory of her own homespun finery. Pamela candidly exposes her material concerns, giving the reader the opportunity to cry hypocrisy as she juxtaposes familiar, material details like green knots and Spanish leather to her pious aphorisms. Yet Richardson's rather awkward rendering of Pamela's experiences exactly as they take place, a rendering particularly easy to parody, comes from his desire to create a mind in the process of establishing its peculiar sense of reality. We come to know Pamela precisely because she does let us learn how concretely her mind works. (I, 67-68) [I, 41-42]

In his second novel, Richardson demonstrates a more assured and complicated style in his composite picture of reality. In *Clarissa*, four different correspondents "writing to the moment" encourage each other to investigate and develop their ideas about their experience. Pamela never enjoyed such encouragement. For instance, when she wonders about her inability to hate Mr. B. in spite of his repeated outrages, she does not enjoy the freedom Anna Howe offers Clarissa to examine her changing and contradictory feelings. Pamela can only record her bewilderment in her journal, which at the moment nobody is reading: "I look'd after him out of the Window, and he was charmingly dress'd. He is a handsome, fine Gentleman;—What Pity his Heart is not as good as his Appearance! Why can't I hate him?—But don't be uneasy if you should see this; for it is impossible I should love him; for his Vices all *ugly him over*, as I may say." (I, 268-69) [I, 172] How Miss Anna Howe would seize on such an admission. Indeed my dear, why can't you hate him! If his vices ugly him all over, pray, why should you find him so handsome? With no one to test and refine her feelings, Pamela must later show surprise at her unexpectedly "treacherous heart." Her confusion may strike us as false, even hypocritical, but it comes from her lack of opportunity to investigate growing feelings, not from deliberate emotional suppression. Clarissa's feelings for Lovelace, on the other hand, are given the time to develop. Anna Howe encourages, indeed demands, continuous examination and reexamination of the heart, insuring that nothing will awkwardly surprise the reader.

When she becomes Mrs. B., Pamela never surprises us again. The flexibility and adaptability of her personality vanish with her marriage. As Mrs. B., Pamela is more paragon than personality, truly a morally exemplary model to satisfy Richardson's most rigid intentions. Following B.'s endless rules of behavior, excelling all of her neighbors at carving, singing, mothering, and praying, Pamela cannot be surpassed.

In the second part of *Pamela*, Richardson introduced several correspondents, but underemployed them, giving them little more to do than testify in chorus to Pamela's goodness. The style of Pamela's chronicle of married life loses the immediacy of her earlier letters.[3] Freed from conflict, she no longer has the need to write "to the moment." Instead, she sends long thoughtful treatises on educational theories adopted from Mr. Locke, examples of her moral fairy tales, and demonstrations of her dramatic criticism—

works of great judgment but little interest to any but the most sycophantic audience. Significantly, although Richardson shows great interest in self-improvement and self-creation, he loses interest in his characters once they perfect themselves. A perfected, self-created character either becomes a boring paragon like Pamela or a Christian martyr like Clarissa. The creative process, not the result, is what engages both author and reader.

It would be difficult to find a heroine more literary than Clarissa, who judges her surroundings by the quality of second-hand books she finds in her closet and asks for salvation not from heaven but from the edited collection of her seducer's letters. When she threatens suicide, she brandishes, appropriately, a penknife. The pen and penknife are, after all, her most trusted and familiar weapons. Binding her adversary's book of letters to her as her "crown," Clarissa demonstrates complete faith in the world of letters, a faith that Richardson both supported and undercut. Leo Braudy sees an optimism in *Clarissa*, a belief that "language can work: letters can be ways to communicate and justify."[4] But letters can also deceive. Clarissa's record of her seduction reveals a world of deceit, forgery, and masquerade. The very letters she values might easily be counterfeit, forged by the artist Lovelace. In her attempt to understand the "truth" of her experience, she and her editor Belford must painstakingly unravel Lovelace's riddle. The term "correspondence," which holds both social and sexual connotations, suggests a coming together of hearts and minds. But in their long, merciless history of correspondence, in their struggle to know one another, Clarissa and Lovelace never come together except in rape, the greatest violation of intimacy.

Clarissa and Lovelace correspond to define themselves; by recording their experiences they establish their reality. But tragically, their versions of reality conflict too greatly to coexist—except in Richardson's book, the artist's world of letters where art unifies the disparate stuff of experience.

The lovers write in essentially two different genres. Clarissa, the Christian martyr, pushes the limitations of sentimental she-tragedy into the purer tragic form, while Lovelace becomes increasingly isolated in his role as comic rake: "I will write a Comedy, I think. I have a Title ready; and that's half the work. *The Quarrelsome Lovers*. 'Twill do." 'Twill not do at all, and even while Lovelace later laments that Clarissa is dying for a "mere jest," (VII, 344) [IV, 261] he cannot give up his version of comic reality unless he turns to the exaggerated rodomontade of heroic tragedy. Alternately ranting his demand for Clarissa's heart and teasing Belford about his marriageable cousin Charlotte, Lovelace self-consciously plays both parts until death. Without his role-playing he is nothing at all.

There is nothing private about the epistolary world of Lovelace and Clarissa. They use their letters to record their own image for the reading public. Anna Howe reminds Clarissa to "write in so full a manner" to convince the widest audience, for if "any-thing unhappy should fall out from the violence of such spirits as you have to deal with, your account of all things *previous* to it will be your best justification." (I, 3-4) [I, 2] Later Miss Howe suggests that letters can both make and judge experience: "If any-thing occur that you would tell me of if I were Present, fail not to put it down in writing. . . . Great consequences, like great folks, generally owe their greatness to small causes, and little incidents." (III, 44) [II, 7]

By recording their experience, correspondents can learn their motives: often style reveals nuances of feeling to the writer as to the reader. Anna Howe teases Clarissa for her change of style in letters to her brother and sister. Clarissa has already rationalized her altered manner to Miss Howe, anticipating her criticism: "In short, you will have more cause than ever to declare me one far gone in Love, if my *reasons* for the change of my style in these Letters, with regard to Mr. Lovelace, do not engage your more favourable opinion." (I, 198) [I, 135-36] But the acute Miss

Howe suspects that style may disclose more than Clarissa's carefully stated reasons. She chides her friend: "If then, there be not a reason for this change of style, which you have not thought fit to give me, be so good as to watch, as I once before advised you, how the cause for it will come on—Why should it be permitted to steal upon you, and you know nothing of the matter?" (I, 273) [I, 187] Attention to one's style leads to self-realization. As Clarissa grows increasingly aware of the "reasons" for her change in style, her fatal "conditional liking" for her rake, the reader and Anna Howe share in her discovery.

The fatal attempt of Clarissa and Lovelace to know each other dominates their relationship, generating a highly charged tension between the sexual and spiritual connotations of their quest. In *Pamela*, as Ian Watt points out, the barriers between Pamela and Mr. B., which are "internal and real," are broken down. Watt suggests that the dialogue between the lovers is "an exploration of the forces that have made them what they are."[5] The total harmony established between them in their marriage and its blissful aftermath, boring as it may be to the readers, establishes a true "correspondence," embodying an essential optimism that, with luck and pluck and God, differences can be dissolved. But, as Richardson suggested to Solomon Lowe, the correspondence between Pamela and B. also depended upon the "implicit Obedience, and slavish Submission . . . Pamela shewed to all [B.'s] Injunctions and Dictates." (*Letters*, p. 124) And Clarissa could never submit. Her story ends not in marriage and correspondence but in death and tragic isolation.

In the fortressed and restricted world of *Clarissa*, correspondence offers a way to break down the isolation.[6] Even after death, Clarissa can define as well as defend herself in her letters. But the freedom the pen allows can also imprison, for outside the sanctity of the closet, Clarissa is powerless.

Although the letters of Clarissa and Lovelace are central to the novel, we never see the correspondence that took place between them. Extracts of Lovelace's letters to Clarissa are often included in Clarissa's packets to Miss Howe, but Clarissa's letters to Lovelace remain a mystery. Rightly so, for letters between Clarissa and Lovelace would show a "correspondence" that could never take place. The lovers cannot "correspond" because they are impenetrable, exploring the "forces that have made them what they are," but never able to make any conclusions. "We are both great watchers of each other's eyes; and indeed seem to be more than half afraid of each other," Clarissa reports. (III, 169) [II, 93] On another occasion: "He looked at me with great confidence; as if (notwithstanding his contradictory bashfulness) he could look me through; while my eye but now-and-then could glance at him." (III, 75) [II, 29] "Sometimes," Clarissa considers, "we have thought him one of the most undesigning *merely* witty men we ever knew; at other times one of the deepest creatures we ever conversed with. So that when in one visit we have imagined we fathomed him, in the next, he has made us ready to give him up as impenetrable." (I, 295) [I, 201] Lovelace fares no better: "All my fear arises from the little hold I have in the heart of this charming Frost-piece . . . to have a heart so impenetrable: and *I*, the hitherto successful Lovelace, the addresser—How can it be?" (I, 216) [I, 148]

While Clarissa and Lovelace push each other into polarities, playing angel to devil, victim to rapist, light to darkness, tragedy to comedy, heaven to hell, Richardson explores the notion of self. Can we know what we are, what makes us, and can we alter ourselves? His idea of personality is complicated. Both Clarissa and Lovelace, remorselessly probing each other's secret selves, reveal themselves to be absolute and essential, yet at the same time relative and fluid, adapting to an ever-shifting world. In a stylistic analysis of *Clarissa*, Irwin Gopnik discusses Richardson's "network-like system of verbal ironies" that maintain the tension in the novel between "rhapsody and sentiment, archness and anxiety, pertness and piety," preventing the different roles of the principal characters from "being separated and polarized in the action."[7] Even as they force each other into their polarized roles, Clarissa and Lovelace are connected to each other by the strongest bonds. Both generous, both proud, clearly superior intellectually to every other character, they show a strong affinity for each other all the while their "essential" differences drive them apart.

Throughout the novel a debate rages over other important differences, not in characters but in the meaning of words: generosity, honor, virtue, purity, piety, obedience. Richardson is conducting a "search for the right word and the right meaning,"[8] a search complicated when the meanings keep changing and contradicting themselves. "What names will perverseness call things by!" Uncle Antony snorts. "A prudent man, who intends to be just to everybody is a covetous man!—While a vile, profligate Rake is christened with the appellation of a gallant man; and a polite man, I'll warrant you!" (I, 234-35) [I, 160] Although the good uncle is championing Solmes, whom we all know is odious, his argument stands. For in Clarissa's world, a world of Harlowes as well as Howes and Lovelaces, the meaning of "Solmes" is relative. He is a "generous" man to the Harlowes. "Such terms, such sentiments," they cry. And he is a monster to Clarissa. When Uncle Antony complains, "What names will perverseness call things by," he is calling particular attention to his own perverseness, but also to the relativity of meaning in his world.

At a crucial point in the family negotiations, Uncle John admits to Clarissa that her mother fears seeing her, even going as far as "lock[ing] herself in, because she knew she must not see you upon *your* terms, and you are resolved you will not see her upon *hers*." (II, 96) [I, 305] In Richardson's world, experience is presented in "your terms" and "her terms," "our terms" and "their terms." Such experience is so fragile that one dissenting voice, one misdirected letter revealing deception, can shatter reality in "one's terms." The epistolary method gave Richardson a way into the separate experiences of four characters: Clarissa, Lovelace, Anna Howe, and Belford. Life experienced on their individual, often radically different, terms complicates the reader's expectations of a simple "reality." The result is complex, rich, and satisfying, an extraordinarily early attempt to solve the problem of point of view.

James Harlowe, for instance, is presented alternately as monster and bugbear. Clarissa describes her brother's ungovernable tyranny, his passionate obsession with her sexuality. The "brutal Brother" bolts upon her, grasps her hand with violence, taps her neck, and whispers "as if he would be decently indecent" as he terrorizes her. (II, 208-209) [I, 381] But to Anna Howe, James Harlowe is an ass, an "indoor insolent" who turns himself into a bugbear. (II, 13) [I, 248] Miss Howe deflates the emotionally charged image of the brutal brother—but then Miss Howe is also insulated from his indoor insolence. She may threaten to send James a challenge, to call him to account for his actions, but her bravado has little meaning in a society where a woman's challenge would only be subject to ridicule. Her satirical judgment of James is as biased and ineffectual as Clarissa's is hysterical and overblown. Mixing hyperbole with ironic understatement, Richardson creates a character both monstrous and ludicrous, allowing his reader to hold two radically different views at once. But then, Richardson always liked to have it both ways.

If the meaning of character proves relative in Clarissa's world, then from the start she is the most difficult to fix. You are "so steady, so uniform in your conduct," Miss Howe tells her friend in her first letter, "so desirous, as you always said, of sliding through life to the end of it unnoted . . . *Rather useful than glaring*, your deserved motto."

(I, 2) [I, 2-3] Yet, as Miss Howe can already see, Clarissa is being "pushed into blaze," more glaring than useful. She may seek to slide through life "to the end," unnoted, but in her death, as in her life, Clarissa blazes away, illuminating the novel. Arabella, one of Clarissa's severest critics, mocks her sister's glaring fame. "*I hid not my light under a bushel*, she would say that for me," Clarissa reports, "But was it not a little hard upon me, to be kept from blazing on a Sunday?" (I, 319) [I, 218] The spite and jealousy implicit in Bella's criticism does not necessarily make it untrue. As he frequently does, Richardson uses negative characters to get at the truth. For, in truth, Clarissa's virtue is notorious, glaring, "blazing": she is the "celebrated, the blazing Clarissa." (III, 283) [II, 170] When Lovelace tracks her down at Hampstead, he describes her "blazing" on him "in a flood of light, like what one might imagine would strike a man, who, born blind, had by some propitious power been blessed with his sight, all at once, in a meridian Sun." (V, 88) [III, 40] Later Lovelace tries to rationalize Clarissa's nature, taking partial credit for her splendor: "It is owing to the uncommon occasions she has met with that she blazes out upon us with such a meridian lustre." (VII, 345) [IV, 261] The glare she sought to avoid has become part of herself. Always famous for what Bella calls her "charitable ostentation," Clarissa, refined through her "uncommon" sufferings, internalizes the public glare: she blazes from within. By the time Lovelace reports his dream in which an "angelic form . . . all clad in transparent white" takes Clarissa to heaven, we are prepared for her transfiguration. Lovelace can only clutch at her robe, "all stuck thick with stars of embossed silver," as he sinks into a dark hole, separated forever from her blazing light. (VII, 158-60) [IV, 136]

Just as she is more glaring than useful, Clarissa is often more various than uniform. "O she is all variety," (IV, 387) [II, 499] Lovelace tells Belford. Leo Braudy suggests that Clarissa is a "totally interior being" in conflict with the "totally exterior" character Lovelace.[9] But Clarissa is a various, ambiguous character who may claim that she is "purging the external world," but nevertheless remains, even in her death, very much concerned with it. As we saw in the first chapter, Clarissa controls the material world posthumously, urging Miss Howe to marry Hickman, setting up Mama Norton at "her" dairy farm, and making sure that Miss Dolly Hervey, not Arabella, inherits her library. If, as Braudy suggests, Clarissa holds a message of self-sufficiency, self-creation, and self-containment,[10] we must question the nature of the self Richardson has created. Clarissa the saint, blazing away in her usual modest fashion, has as ambiguous a self as Clarissa the modest, punctilious young lady who elopes with Lovelace, the notorious woman-eater.

Clarissa, for one, has no doubts about the nature of herself. She has been cheated, tricked, betrayed "out of" herself. "Cheated out of myself from the first," she complains to Tomlinson (V, 225) [III, 135] remembering an essential Clarissa, untouched by Lovelace, beloved of her family, free from outside pressure. But we can never see this Clarissa, except in the priggish post-mortem portrait Anna Howe sends to Belford. The Clarissa we see "from the first" is always reacting to the demands of her family and to the strategies of Lovelace; she is never free to be "herself." The Harlowe demands are great: "The heart, Clary, is what I want," (I, 131) [I, 90] says Mama, ominously foreshadowing Lovelace's later demand for Clarissa's pickled heart. In her struggle with her family, Clarissa must lose her compliancy, surprising the Harlowes, who expect their Clary to act like "herself," meek and accommodating. "My temper, I know, is depended upon," Clarissa admits, but she refuses to play the part her family expects of her, to be *"worthy of the name of Daughter."* (I, 132-35) [I, 91-93] The Clarissa who is "above disguise, above art," (III, 34) [II, 1] confesses that she is "grieved to be driven to have recourse to the following artifices. . . ." (II, 330)

[I, 465] Frankness and honesty can only work in a frank and honest world; the Harlowe family's intransigence creates the need for secrecy and artifice.

Lovelace applies even greater pressure to Clarissa, tampering with her perception of reality. She must always be on guard, never "herself" in Lovelace's world, where whores become ladies and pimps become gentlemen. The man, she complains, is a "perfect Proteus." His shape of the moment forces her to alter her own: "Don't think *me* the changeable person, I beseech you, if in one Letter I contradict what I wrote in another; nay, if I seem to contradict what I said in the same Letter; for he is a perfect chameleon; or rather more variable than the chameleon." (III, 154) [II, 82] Lovelace's protean nature forces Clarissa to assume a coldness unnatural to herself. "Must I not, *with such a man*, be wanting *to myself*, if I were *not* jealous and vigilant?—Yet what a life to live for a spirit *so open*, and naturally *so unsuspicious*, as mine." (III, 49) [II, 11] We receive a great sense of loss here. Clarissa can never be herself again.

After the rape, Clarissa becomes obsessed with her violated sense of self. "*O my dearest Miss* HOWE! Once more have I escaped," she writes, "but alas! I, my *best self*, have *not* escaped! . . . But still upon *Self*, this vile, this hated *Self!*—I will shake it off, if possible." (VI, 115) [III, 321] Her pathetic "papers," written in her madness following the rape reveal a severe sense of dislocation: "My name is—I don't know what my name is!" No longer Harlowe, she can never be Lovelace: she is nothing. "I am no longer what I was in any one thing," she writes Anna Howe. "In any one thing did I say? Yes, but I am; for I am still, and I ever will be, Your true ———." (V, 327-28) [III, 205-206] Your true ———, for at this point Clarissa has no identity. "I shall never be what I was," she tells Lovelace. "My head is gone. I have wept away all my brain, I believe." (V, 334) [III, 210] Clarissa must "shake off" her body to create a new spiritual self free from Lovelace's penetration.

In his sensitive analysis of Clarissa's fragments, Mark Kinkead-Weekes discusses Clarissa's overwhelming sense of violation. Once inside her, Lovelace is always part of her: "O Lovelace! if you could be sorry for yourself, I would be sorry too—But when all my doors are fast, and nothing but the key-hole open, and the key of late put into that, to be where you are, in a manner without opening any of them—O wretched, wretched Clarissa Harlowe! For I never will be Lovelace—let my Uncle take it as he pleases." (V, 335) [III, 210-11] Clarissa experiences "the agony of knowing that the opening in her body, in spite of the fact that her senses and her intellect have been wholly unmoved, has enabled Lovelace to 'be where you *are*'— not 'were'—to be always part of her inner consciousness, having touched her most private being."[11] To drive Lovelace out of herself, Clarissa must reject her body altogether.

Just as Clarissa's fragments and her first letter to Anna Howe reveal her great sense of disorientation, her following letters indicate a new sense of purpose. To create a new self, she must first break out of Lovelace's artificial reality and establish the truth of the past. She writes to Lovelace's relatives, Uncle John's housekeeper, Mama Norton, and Hannah Burton for evidence, "with a view to detect Lovelace" and to learn the truth. Letters here serve to build a "true" reality to replace the false reality Lovelace constructed out of his forgeries and disguises. As Anthony Kearney points out, Clarissa's "epistolary recovery" parallels her spiritual recovery.[12] In her letters, Clarissa is creating a new self, without shame and without violation.

Lovelace also creates himself in a world filled with the raw materials for his inventions, "dough" like Tomlinson and Captain Mennel, ready to be shaped by the master artist. But underneath the inventions lies a blankness. Clarissa has provided definition for Lovelace: her goodness has provoked his strategies and villainy. But when she is gone, there remains nothing but the more and more frantic inventions. Lovelace seeks death from Morden because he finds no joy in living: the inventions have failed to please. In *Clarissa*, Richardson explores a disturbing notion of the self: Clarissa can recreate herself, but at the great expense of self-annihilation. Lovelace vainly tries to disguise the blankness of himself, but is left with nothing, a terrible void. The answer lies in heaven, offering cold comfort to the common reader in the real world.

Great differences separate Clarissa from Lovelace, yet their characters are so closely connected in Richardson's imagination that at times they appear to imitate each other. Both set themselves apart from society to follow their ideals. In her strict adherence to society's moral code, Clarissa destroys herself and her family. Ironically, as she embodies the social metaphors of filial piety and chastity, she drastically alters the code. By assuming the role of violated virgin, Clarissa insures that society will not view sexual violation in the same way again. Lovelace flagrantly attacks the social code, but depends upon its power to bring Clarissa to him. He cannot imagine that she could refuse to marry him, for in his worldly code marriage heals all. By conforming to social values, Clarissa rebels: by rebelling, Lovelace ultimately conforms.

Both find themselves isolated from their families. Clarissa is shunned by all members of her family, imprisoned in her room and forced to use the back stairs to spare her relatives from suffering her presence. After the rape, Lovelace's relatives also attempt to isolate him. Their methods, however, are less effective. Lovelace boasts that he has "the best" half of the house to himself, "while the two pursy Sisters, the old gouty Brother, and the two musty Nieces, are stived up in the other half, and dare not stir for fear of meeting me: Whom (that's the jest of it) they have forbidden coming into their apartments." (VII, 86) [IV, 87] Like Clarissa, Lovelace is put on trial by his family "for all my sins to my beloved Fugitive." His trial parodies Clarissa's countless conferences with her "august tribunal," the stern-faced Harlowes. "With horrible grave faces was I received. The two Antiques only bowed their tabby heads; making longer faces than ordinary; and all the old lines appearing strong in their furrowed foreheads and fallen cheeks." (VI, 221) [III, 393] The trial ends triumphantly for Lovelace: "Did ever Comedy end more happily than this long tryal?" (VI, 249) [III, 411] As usual, Lovelace mistakenly believes that he is operating in a comic world, while all the while he has been taking part in Clarissa's tragedy.

Both Clarissa and Lovelace go mad. After the rape, drugged and degraded, Clarissa mourns her loss, her certainty that she will never be what she was. Lovelace experiences a similar sense of loss: "I am still, I am still, most miserably absent from myself. Shall never, never more be what I was!" (VIII, 140) [IV, 439] In his madness, Lovelace remembers being worked upon by shadowy, whispering creatures, "tiptoe slaves . . . armed with gallipots, bolus's, and cephalic draughts; delivering their orders to me in hated whispers; and answering other curtain-holding impertinents, enquiring how I was, and how I took their execrable potions, whisperingly too! What a cursed Still-life was this. Nothing active in me, or about me, but the worm that never dies." (VIII, 147) [IV, 443] Lovelace's memory of the flitting creatures of his madness, "delivering their orders to me in hated whispers," resembles Clarissa's drugged memory of her rape. She has "some visionary remembrances . . . of female figures, flitting, as I may say, before my sight." (VI, 191) [III, 372] Both images represent a fearful, almost mechanical Other, a force robbing Clarissa and Lovelace of their identities.

Each suffers isolation in death, as in life. Clarissa, separated from her family and friends, dies with words of forgiveness, severely qualified forgiveness, to make expiation for her rape. Lovelace parodies Clarissa once more in death. Mortally wounded by Morden, he is taken to the "nearest cottage" to die with only his French valet for company. His last words, "LET THIS EXPIATE" record his vain attempt to join his "Sweet Excellence! Divine Creature! Fair Sufferer!" (VIII, 276-77) [IV, 530] Lovelace and Clarissa, so different in essentials, yet so similar, can only come together symbolically in the serpent motif of Clarissa's coffin.

Lovelace may cry out to Clarissa on his deathbed, but his abortive atonement is uttered impotently in an empty universe. We cannot see Clarissa reaching down to pull him into heaven, for no one in *Clarissa* can save anyone else. Isolated and alienated, Clarissa has had to work out her salvation independently. And although she can plan to "redeem" her family through her will, she only succeeds in condemning them to perpetual despair. As Gillian Beer notes, "Clarissa becomes a saint, but she is not a redemptress." She "saves her own soul," but she can never "save mankind."[13] To save herself, Clarissa must recreate herself, stripping away what offends, purging herself of her sinful self-loathing, to reconstruct a new, pure, inviolate Clarissa able to transcend the role of raped victim. Her deliberate steps towards death, the carved coffin, the purchased shroud, the black-bordered post-mortem letters ready to be delivered, help her to control her fate.

By the time of her carefully arranged funeral, Clarissa has become a saint. The weeping throngs of "her poor" crowd around her coffin "with respectful *whisperings*," attracted by the cryptic plates and emblems, admiring it "the more, when they were told, that all was of her own ordering." (VIII, 76-77) [IV, 395-96] Control is ever sweet, even after death. In her death, as in her life, Clarissa serves once more as an exemplary model of vindicated purity. She does not, however, leave a saint's *Vade Mecum* for others to follow. Although he began his career to perfect his reader, confidently supplying moral exempla in the service of God and society, in the work he most loved, *Clarissa*, Richardson explores the complex actions of an individual who rejects both her family and society to discover herself. *Clarissa* expresses most clearly Richardson's faith in the possibility that the self can renew and recreate itself, yet it also reveals his awareness of the limitations of that created self. Clarissa pays a high price to exert her will—her life. By rewarding Clarissa in heaven, Richardson is not, as Brian Downs suggests, substituting a heavenly audit for an earthly one,[14] but is questioning the possibility of any earthly rewards. If Clarissa cannot be rewarded on earth, whoever can? What profits moral instruction? Richardson managed to resolve, or more likely to avoid, these issues in his next novel, in which Sir Charles Grandison, prosperously reaping the rewards of his virtue, blandly erases any questions *Clarissa* may have raised. Sir Charles, Richardson's good man, lives firmly and forthrightly in the real world, surrounded by admiring family and friends, creating his paradise here on earth. He complacently wears the "mask" of the sentimental Christian, never happier than when he is generously forgiving a wrongdoer of his sins. The questions Richardson raised in *Clarissa* remain, long after interest in Sir Charles wanes. But Richardson was never so brave again.

In *Sir Charles Grandison*, letters serve a more public than private purpose, to maintain and celebrate relationships as well as explore them. As A. D. McKillop notes, the "lending and forwarding of long files of letters, so that one group may be informed about the other, is part of the pattern of the book." Correspondents frequently act as a chorus, praising the goodness of Sir Charles, the merit of Harriet, or the pathetic sensibility of Clementina. Although the *Grandison* letters lose their analytical significance, they still retain their power. Letters confirm reality; for an experience to have importance, it must be written down. For instance, even after the Misses Grandison have personally learned the intimate details of Harriet's abduction firsthand, they still request that she supply them with the written record of her experiences, for in letters lies the truth. Harriet promises she will "cheerfully communicate" her relation of the "shocking affair." (I, 392) [II, XXVII] When the Grandison sisters describe the tyranny of their father, they are evidently referring to their notes of their mistreatment as well as their memories. "But what say my minutes," interrupts Charlotte at one point. The Richardsonian correspondent must scrupulously take minutes of his experience, for memory alone is never reliable enough. When Sir Charles breakfasts with the blustering Sir Hargrave, he prudently brings along a stenographer to record their conversation, inspiring McKillop to suggest that the "natural inclination of Richardson's busy bodies in our own enlightened times would be to tap telephones and plant dictaphones."[15]

The letter allows the Richardsonian correspondent to define and declare his affections, for all to see and appreciate. Love declared on paper means far more than love declared orally. When Emily asks Harriet to reassure her of her love—"tell me, that you love me as well as you did in the chariot"—Harriet explains that now she loves her better because "I have been putting part of our conversation upon paper, and so have fastened your merits on my memory." (II, 28) [III, V] "Better," because the pen expresses more truth than the person can. Sir Charles demonstrates his faith in letters when he begins to court Miss Byron. He mysteriously arrives at her home, like a "courteous Ghost," with a bulging "pacquet" of letters to explain his circumstances and his relationship to Clementina. After leaving the packet with Grandmother Shirley, he withdraws, without even seeing the bewildered Miss Byron. Presumably, his letters will be more persuasive than his person. (III, 15-18) [V, VIII]

In spite of Richardson's epistolary sophistication, he does not use the letter in *Grandison* to develop his characters. Instead, letters confirm an ordered reality already established before the novel even begins. The dynamic sense of play so integral to both *Pamela* and *Clarissa* almost entirely disappears from Richardson's last novel. Mr. B. and Pamela, playing against each other's conventional type as they worked out their own domesticated romance, Clarissa and Lovelace playing tragedy queen to rake, and saint to Satan, created each other's sense of self as they tried to fix each other's personality. But Sir Charles, already fixed, has nowhere to go. He is inalterably a good man. Harriet may perhaps be refined through her suffering, as she loses weight and self-confidence waiting for Clementina to hand over Sir Charles, but the essential Harriet, gently acidic, intelligently poised, is with us from the start. Only Charlotte Grandison is given the opportunity to "develop," but in a completely controlled experiment directed by brother Charles, who with the aid of Harriet and his sister, oversees Charlotte's progress through the mazes of marriage and motherhood. There can be only one ending to the playful warfare between Lord G. and Charlotte—matronly surrender cemented by the loving "Marmouset" nestled on Charlotte's milk-flowing breast. We never feel threatened by the outcome of the battle, for it has been preordained by Sir Charles, one of heaven's more efficient saints.

It is puzzling why Sir Charles's goodness should be so repellent. We are fairly comfortable with Clarissa's saintliness, awed rather than irritated by her spiritual excesses. But Sir Charles's goodness does not attract. As Richardson's virtuous heroine, Clarissa is active, never passive, always judging herself, stripping away what offends, refining what satisfies. She never stops changing herself and her ideas about her world until her deliberate end, when she begins the painful course of negation leading to her death. And few would ever bother with a record that dealt only with Clarissa's final days, when she finally becomes fixed into her saintly position of grace. We read *Clarissa* for its densely complex account of her personality under fire. Although she mouths doctrines celebrating passive renunciation, Clarissa is always active and direct, especially in her preparations for death, when she takes upon herself all of the duties usually left to survivors.

Sir Charles, on the other hand, is dramatically passive. From birth he has followed the dictates of higher authority—his sainted mother, the Reverend Dr. Bartlett, even his debauched father. He obeys his father automatically, out of filial piety, even when he is wrong, agreeing, for instance, to respect his wishes and stay away from his two sisters when they sorely need his support. Sir Charles always does what he ought and, even more often, does not do what he ought not do. He does not duel, does not gamble, does not masquerade, does not give in to his passions. Yet he never seems to suffer in his self-denial; it comes to him naturally.

We are faced here with a problem of point of view. We cannot know Sir Charles's nature—the extent, for instance, of those terrible passions he keeps in check—without knowing his letters. For in Richardson's world, to know the letter is to know the man. Sir Charles's letters are public documents, to be shared, passed around Grandison Hall, and discussed. He writes most of them to Dr. Bartlett, a man of great piety and little humor. Letters to such a saint must by their very nature be self-consciously moral. Had Sir Charles a Belford, even a reformed Belford, to write to, his letters may have relaxed to the point of self-disclosure. But in the pompous, self-congratulatory epistles Sir Charles sends to Dr. Bartlett and family we can find no evidence of human personality. For Clarissa, the letter was a tool of self-analysis, a weapon against creeping complacency or self-pity, but in Sir Charles's hands the letter becomes a tool of self-advertisement.

Of the three principal characters in *Grandison*—Sir Charles, Harriet Byron, and Clementina—only Harriet is granted full epistolary privileges. Her letters—witty, impressionistic, occasionally introspective—give us an insight into her character. We can share in her anguish as she chafes under the yoke of patience that sits so harshly upon her. Clementina does not fare so well. We depend on her anxious relatives and Sir Charles to provide news about her condition. Their letters inform us that she sits drawing maps of England and pictures of angels, that she tears her clothing and runs shrieking from the room, but since we have little insight into her behavior, and little connection to her personality, her madness remains merely pathetic. Richardson portrayed Clarissa's madness from the inside out in her fragments of letters, her meditations, her painful attempt to piece her personality back together. But we observe Clementina solely from without, as an interesting example of virtue in distress, but never as a character who threatens our sense of self.

Richardson allowed Clarissa a great deal of latitude emotionally and psychologically. The power of the novel comes from its unflinching exposure of its heroine's capacity for self-delusion as well as her triumphant self-creation. Flexible enough to blacken deliberately the spotless facade of his saint, Richardson could not bend at all in his depiction of Sir Charles, forced to bear the burden of perfection throughout the novel. He insisted on Sir Charles's humanity in his letters, confessing to Miss Mulso that he is "sprinkling" a "few unpremeditated faults" into his good man's character, "lest I should draw a *faultless monster*." (*Letters*, p. 185) But Richardson only speaks of Sir Charles's faults; he never shows them. Stiff-necked, filled with pride as well as piety, Clarissa is allowed to be human, but Sir Charles, granted only the privileges of a plaster saint, remains a model of self-possession rather than self-creation. Letters embalm his goodness, preserving his exemplary behavior for posterity.

SEVEN • A Man of Letters: The Private Letter in Life & Art

I verily believe Mr. Richardson has been spiteful enough to send these shocking aerial visions, which discompose the gentle slumbers of the most amiable of her sex, only to revenge himself on you and I. . . . I am not certain that our security may not provoke him to destroy them, for he has set his imagination on the glow.

MISS HIGHMORE to MISS MULSO
(*Correspondence*, vol. II, p. 317)

That you and I, my dear, should love to write is no wonder. . . . Our employments are domestic and sedentary; and we can scribble upon twenty innocent subjects, and take delight in them because they *are* innocent. . . . But that such a gay, lively young fellow as this, who rides, hunts, travels, frequents the public entertainments, and has *means* to pursue his pleasures, should be able to set himself down to write for hours together, as you and I have heard him say he frequently does, that is the strange thing.

ANNA HOWE to CLARISSA (I, 74) [I, 50]

BUT not so strange at all. Why would a lively young fellow like Lovelace turn to the letter when he has ample means to "pursue his pleasures"? Richardson understands his rake's motive completely. Lovelace writes to go beyond the limits of the commonplace, to express those hidden parts of himself that could not be released legitimately in any other way. Young ladies, domestic and sedentary in their habits, are not the only scribblers in Richardson's world. Anybody who needs to get out of himself can do so, disguised and released in letters.

In this final chapter, I will discuss Richardson's own use

of the personal letter. In the previous chapter, we looked at the ways Richardson's characters invent themselves as they correspond, exploring, developing, and altering their ideas about reality. In much the same way, Richardson invented his own reality in his novels and letters, working to create a self that is bolder, freer, and more adventurous than he could ever hope to be in "real life." In his novels, an intricate network of letters confirming, denying, and reaffirming the existence of a comprehensive world unified through the word testifies to his own faith in the creative possibilities open to him as an artist. Art could provide the control over experience he so needed.

Almost without realizing it, we, his readers, come under that control. Carefully manipulating his "forged" and "authentic" documents, Richardson draws us into his fictional world just as Lovelace, through his artifices and disguises, draws Clarissa to her fate. Richardson's private letters, in which he acts alternately paternal, coquettish, moralistic, tyrannical, sententious, rakish, and pious, also bear witness to his personal need to expand and control his life through his art.

In his letters, Mr. Richardson could be spiteful, playful, and shocking as he set his imagination on the glow. And, disguised behind one of his many masks, he could pursue forbidden interests with impunity, something he had been doing since adolescence, when he wrote love letters for fervid but unlettered girls in the neighborhood. The letter liberated Richardson from the commonplace, expanding himself and his world. In the same way, the epistolary method in his novels allowed him to create a more satisfying reality peopled with characters of his own making, confronting circumstances of his own invention.

We have come full circle. Richardson the moralist set out to perfect his readers and ended up, through his fiction and letters, if not perfecting, then certainly completing himself. In transforming the stuff of everyday life in his work, he freed himself to enter, for transient moments at the least, a headier, more satisfying fictional world that he could control.

Of course, as always, the most subversive interests had to be moralized and accounted for in the most didactic self-improving terms. Familiar letters, he argued, offered "rules to live by as well as forms to live by." The most sensational of Pamela's collected letters were "exemplary," models of Christian behavior under stress, to be studied, not relished. Clarissa's anguished record of madness and self-disintegration was to be read for its "moral," as a sermon on virtue, while even Lovelace's disturbing attacks on society were accounted exemplary, models of behavior not to be imitated. Richardson was always adept at explaining away the most "shocking aerial visions" in the name of morality, but nonetheless his letters remain behind, his own testimony to his obsessive need for invention and play.

We can see the contradictory stances the author could take in the following quotations. The first is Richardson trying to bolster up a shrinking Miss Westcomb, working at banishing her diffidence: "Be pleased yourself, my dear Selena, to know, that the Pen is almost the *only Means* a very modest and diffident Lady (who in Company will not attempt to glare) has to shew herself, and that she has a *Mind*." (*Letters*, pp. 67-68) The second quotation comes from Lovelace, preening himself on his expert forgeries as he prepares to intercept and alter Miss Howe's letters to Clarissa: "I am always careful to open Covers cautiously and to preserve Seals entire. I will draw out from this cursed Letter an alphabet. Nor was Nick Rowe ever half so diligent to learn Spanish, at the Quixote recommendation of a certain Peer, as I will be to gain a mastery of this vixen's hand." (V, 51) [III, 16]

Letters can both justify and deceive. The "dear Anna," confident in the sanctity of her writing closet, can "shew herself" through her letters and prove "that she has a *Mind*." The pen offers her the means to justify herself to others, who might otherwise see her only as a diffident young creature shrinking at the tea table. Lovelace, on the other hand, delights in the possibilities letters offer for deception, for clever and careful forgeries. We can examine Richardson's double view of correspondence in a typical exchange between Clarissa and Lovelace. Returning from "an Airing with my Charmer," Lovelace suggests an exchange of letters between them to promote trust. Since Clarissa, wise girl, is reluctant, Lovelace, to convince her of his "sincerity," elaborates upon his own reasons for letter-writing: "It was writing from the heart (without the fetters prescribed by method or study) as the word *Cor-respondence* implied. Not the heart only; the soul was in it. Nothing of body, when friend writes to friend; the mind impelling sovereignly the vassal-fingers. It was, in short, friendship recorded; friendship given under hand and seal; demonstrating that the parties were under no apprehension of changing from time or accident, when they so liberally gave testimonies which would always be ready, on failure, or infidelity, to be turned against them." (IV, 286) [II, 431]

Lovelace reveals an extraordinary notion of correspondence here, one Richardson both shares and distrusts. Familiar letters record sentiments of friendship that are apparently valid even when the friendship itself fails. The testimony stands, to be "turned against" the unfaithful friend. Letters can express what life fails to offer: the printed word takes on more significance than the experience itself. Richardson believed in the pen's ability to transcend social circumstances. His modest woman, "never glaring" at a social gathering, could shine in her closet, showing her wit in well-turned phrases.

Richardson's faith in correspondence gave him the confidence to use the familiar letter as a way into the minds of his characters. But in his exploration of the role of the letter in the struggle between Clarissa and Lovelace, he subverts the authenticity of the letter. The letter itself is only an empty tool of communication. Yet its very neutrality gives it the power to alter circumstances. When

Lovelace intercepts and forges Anna Howe's letters, he controls and irrevocably changes her friend's fate. And he reminds us of the relative, transient nature of Clarissa's, and our, reality, a reality too fragile to withstand the outside pressure of a hostile force.

The letter, that vessel of pure, ardent friendship, becomes in Lovelace's hands an instrument of deception. Ironically, Richardson entrusts Lovelace with the speech about the "truth" of correspondence at the very time that the rake is planning to deceive Clarissa through her letters. The trusted familiar letter becomes the forged letter, penned with the "*crow-quills worn to the stumps*" of Lovelace's invention. (V, 172) [III, 98]

When Richardson manipulates our sense of the truth in fiction, we become uneasy with the epistolary form. Yet paradoxically, we believe more than ever in the reality of the fiction the author creates.[1] For the forged letter suggests that letters not forged are "real." The "true" correspondence between Anna Howe and Clarissa (as opposed to Lovelace's forged letters) becomes real, when all the while Richardson, the master forger, is creating his own world of authentic and forged letters. This is the world we readers are forced to enter.

Before we look at the way Richardson invented his own reality in his novels and letters, we must look at the ways he uses the letter to involve us in his novel, the ways he creates us as his readers. Through an intricate epistolary network, Richardson forces us into his fictional world. Barriers between life and art dissolve.

The concrete materials of correspondence help to convince the reader of the authenticity of the Richardsonian world. As we saw in Chapter Four, Richardson, master printer, always attended to the "minutiae" of his work. Documentation, footnotes, enclosed abstracts, abstracts of abstracts, and asterisked forgeries authenticate the fiction. Early in her letters, Clarissa encloses a "*Copy of the requested* PREAMBLE *to the clauses in her grandfather's Will.*"

(I, 30) [I, 21] Lovelace sends the "original" of Anna Howe's intercepted letter to Belford, since "it is too long to transcribe." He explains its unusual appearance: "Thou wilt see the margin of this cursed Letter crowded with indices [*]. I put them to mark the places which call for vengeance upon the vixen writer, or which require animadversion. Return thou it to me the moment thou hast perused it. Read it here, and avoid trembling for me if thou canst." (V, 30-31) [III, 1] Letters that are "too long to transcribe," their margins "crowded with indices," take on a life of their own.

To convince his reader that his letters are authentic, written by the trembling hand of Clarissa on her deathbed or by the dashing hand of Lovelace, Richardson keeps calling attention to the typography of his material.[2] "Don't you see how crooked some of my lines are? Don't you see how some of the letters stagger more than others?—That is when this Interview is more in my head than my Subject." (II, 335) [I, 468] Clarissa is writing Miss Howe from the "Ivy Summer-house," anxiously awaiting her fateful meeting with Lovelace. Again, from St. Albans, she apologizes for her narrative, so "dismally scrawled . . . owing to different pens and ink, all bad, and written by snatches of time; my hand trembling too with fatigue and grief." (II, 363) [I, 487] Finally, in his deathbed scenes, Richardson unashamedly exploits the difficulties Clarissa finds in even holding a pen; her writing is "much larger, and the lines crooked." (VII, 399) [IV, 298] She writes Mama Norton: "Twice have I been forced to leave off. I *wished* that my last writing might be to You, or to Miss Howe, if it might not be to my dearest Ma—*Mama*, I would have wrote— is the word distinct?—My eyes are *so* misty. If, when I apply to you, I break off in half-words, do supply them— The kindest are *your* due. Besure take the kindest, to fill up chasms with, if any chasms there be—" (VII, 405) [IV, 302] "Besure take the kindest" is hardly Miss Harlowe's most elegant sentence. She is offering us a small "chasm"; it is up to the reader to supply the word "to." A small task, to be sure, but one that forces us to enter into the novel. In the heavy-handed pathos of Clarissa's death-bed letters, Richardson boldly attempts to involve his reader fully in the preparations for her death.

In all of his novels, Richardson makes his readers aware of the physical nature of correspondence. His letters become real objects of weight, taking up actual space. Pamela's dress bristles with packets of letters, pens, and ink as she makes her clandestine deliveries under the sunflower plant. When B. threatens to strip her for her letters—"I never undress'd a Girl in my Life; but I will now begin to strip my pretty *Pamela*"—the sexual nature of correspondence becomes clear. (I, 321) [I, 208] Her letters have become part of her body. Since *Pamela* is a comedy, all ends well: to know her letters is to know the girl and make her Mrs. B. But Clarissa's situation is more desperate. Letters mean life for Clarissa; to cut her off from the sympathy of Anna Howe is to cut her off from her only contact with a reality that is apart from Lovelace. As Anthony Kearney suggests, to violate Clarissa's letters is to violate Clarissa.[3]

Like Pamela, Clarissa jealously guards her correspondence, filling her pockets and petticoats with letters from Miss Howe. Lovelace is as impatient to get at her letters as he is to get at her body, for letters mean knowledge, penetration, and mastery. In one scene, he attempts to snatch a paper lying at her feet while Clarissa sits, "huddling up her papers in her handkerchief all the time." Giving her "a more fervent kiss than ever I had dared to give her before," Lovelace scrapes up the letter and "whips" it into his bosom. Outraged, Clarissa makes "no scruple to seize the stolen Letter, though in my bosom." Lovelace in turn clasps her hand, "which had hold of the ravished paper." Lovelace not only ravishes the letter here; he ravishes Clarissa. His language becomes more explicitly physical: "Having gone thus far, loth, very loth was I to lose my prize—Once more I got hold of the rumpled-up Letter! *Impudent man!* were her words: Stamping again. *For God's sake,* then it was. I let go my prize, lest she should faint away: But had the pleasure to find my hand within both hers, she trying to open my reluctant fingers. How near was my heart at that moment to my hand, throbbing to my fingers ends, to be thus familiarly, though angrily, treated by the charmer of my soul." (IV, 51-53) [II, 271-72] Lovelace's consolation, apart from his throbbing fingers ends, is "that upon a greater offence," Clarissa's resentment "cannot be worse." Surely there can be no greater offense. More passion and engagement appears in Lovelace's description of the ravished letter than in his account of the rape itself.

Letters not only bristle and bustle, they exist somewhere—in the reader's brain, perhaps, or in the mind's eye of the writer—in handwritten state. In a scene from *Grandison* that McKillop appreciates as an example of Richardson's dramatic play with letters, one of Harriet's suitors reads aloud passages from a correspondent who is praising Harriet. He then recites further passages from his "copy" of his answer, lending the flattering copy to Harriet after "scratching out some sentences, but, it is added, only faintly."[4] Only faintly, because as Lucy Selby crows, "the ink I furnished him with happening to be paler than his, you will find he was not cunning enough." (I, 8) [I, I] More cunning is Richardson, who cleverly directs the reader to the scratched-over passage with a footnote: "The passages in this letter thus marked ("), are those which in the preceding are said to be scratch'd out; but yet were legible by holding up the letter to the light." (I, 10) [I, II] By this time, the reader is ready to hold his book up to the light to read the "hidden" passage.

When Belford assumes editorship of the novel known as *Clarissa*, we suddenly find ourselves in the process of reading letters that describe the making of the book we are reading. It is disconcerting to learn that plodding Belford has all along been directing our responses, arranging our fate as well as Clarissa's. The very idea of such a colorless character ordering our experience galls. Mowbray sends Lovelace a revealing description of his thorough methods. After Clarissa's escape nobody is "serene but Jack Belford, who is taking minnutes of exammninations, accusations, and confessions, with the signifficant air of a Middlesex justice; and intends to write at large all particulars, I suppose." (VI, 94-95) [III, 307] Serene, efficient, and judicious—the ideal editor. A bit ridiculous, perhaps. Lovelace never hesitates to puncture Belford's pomposity. But Jack Belford, scrupulously taking minutes, offers to vindicate Clarissa through Lovelace's letters. Truth matters more than friendship.

Through Belford, Richardson allows us to watch the Clarissa story, the official version, being created. Clarissa asks him to send her "a fair, a faithful Specimen from [Lovelace's] Letters or Accounts to you written upon some of the most interesting occasions," particularly "on or about the 7th and 8th of June, when I was alarmed by the wicked pretence of a Fire; and what he has written from Sunday, June 11, to the 19th." (VII, 67-68) [IV, 74-75] Clarissa has truly chosen a sample of "some of the most interesting occasions." Recalling the infamous events of June, the fire scare and the rape, which occurred June 12, Clarissa reminds *us* of our dual knowledge of the "interesting occasions." We remember the rape as told by Clarissa, in her rambling, agonized narrative of madness, so long withheld from the reader and Anna Howe, and we remember Lovelace's own cryptic version of the affair: "*Tuesday Morn., June 13*. And now, Belford, I can go no farther. The affair is over. Clarissa lives. And I am *Your humble servant*, R. LOVELACE." (V, 314) [III, 196] Richardson never lets us forget the form of his novel. Experience can be told, retold, and edited: the truth partly lies in the "fictional" telling. Clarissa's rape becomes a "fact" attested to by both participants in their letters, letters authenticated by Belford, the editor.

It becomes even more difficult to separate fiction from reality when we find ourselves accomplices to Lovelace in his attempts to seduce Clarissa. In the Tomlinson fraud, we are victimized along with Clarissa. But Richardson often includes his reader in the game. For instance, when Lovelace intercepts a letter from Anna Howe, a cryptic reference to Norris puzzles him: "She says in it, *I hope you have no cause to repent returning my Norris—It is forthcoming on demand*. Now what the devil can this mean! Her Norris forthcoming on demand!—The devil take me, if I am *out-Norris'd!*"[5] Characteristically, Lovelace plays with the word before dropping it, giving it his private definition, "to plot." "If such innocents can allow themselves to plot (*to Norris*) well may I." (IV, 188) [II, 364] But "Norris" baffles Lovelace; he never does learn what the reader is privileged to know—that Anna Howe sent Clarissa fifty guineas in her Norris's *Miscellanies*. As Miss Howe says, a stander-by may see more of the game than one that plays. When Clarissa and Lovelace test each other's inclinations about going to London for sanctuary—"This indifference of his to London, I cannot but say, made me incline the more to go thither," (III, 171) [II, 94] Clarissa reports—the reader soon learns the danger of Lovelace's "indifference" to London. "I saw she was frighted," he tells Belford, "and she would have had Reason, had the scene been London, and that place in London which I have in view to carry her to." (III, 178) [II, 99] "Honest" Tom Doleman sends Clarissa a list of suitable lodgings. Toying with her "power," she considers her choices. But first, "to try him (as in so material a point I thought I could not be too circumspect) I seemed to prefer those in Norfolk-street," (III, 196) [II, 111] but she relents to choose the Widow Sinclair's genteel house, as every reader warns her to desist. Too late, Lovelace exults: "Thou knowest the Widow; thou knowest her Nieces; thou knowest the Lodgings: And didst thou ever read a Letter more artfully couched than this of Tom Doleman? Every possible objection anticipated! Every accident provided against! Every tittle of it plot-proof!" (III, 199) [II, 113] Now we know as well the widow, the nieces, and the lodgings. Along with Belford, we have become Lovelace's unwitting accomplices.

Belford's prominence in the last quarter of the book may be disconcerting, even annoying, but it is necessary. He provides us with a way into Clarissa's suffering, and a way out of the guilt we are bound to feel over her rape. For we have, however unwittingly, helped to place Clarissa on the rack. As we read Lovelace's letters, we participate in her rape, peering through the keyhole alongside Lovelace to observe her sufferings. And so did Belford. Lovelace scornfully reminds him that he could have intervened on Clarissa's behalf at any time, but he stood passively by, allowing Lovelace to do his worst. "Thou knewest my designs all along," he taunts. Like a true knight-errant, Belford should have "stolen in when the giant was out of the way; or, hadst thou had the true spirit of chivalry upon thee, and nothing else would have done, have killed the giant; and then something wouldst thou have had to brag of." (VIII, 165-66) [IV, 455-56] But Belford only suffers his scruples silently, never even warning Clarissa of her peril. To make tardy amends after the rape, Belford becomes a trustee of Clarissa's memory. He redeems himself by memorializing her ruined innocence; we redeem ourselves by participating in her memorial. Clarissa's prolonged death, and Belford's even more prolonged testimony to it, give the reader the chance to reconstruct Clarissa's image as even more inviolate in death than in life. As spectators, we renew ourselves through her sacrifice. Ideally, the reader undergoes the emotional experience of the Christian approaching Easter. The grief of Lent follows the excess of Carnival, the rape. The death and apotheosis of the victim release guilt and purify the reader.

In memorializing Clarissa's death, Belford has two immediate goals: to alleviate his own sense of guilt and to save Lovelace. As editor of the correspondence and historian of Clarissa's last days, Belford labors to awaken Lovelace's sensibility: "Drive more spikes into thy hogshead, and roll thee down-hill, and up, as thou recoverest to sense, or rather returnest back to *senselessness*." (VI, 316) [III, 458] When he describes Clarissa's sordid surroundings, her physical weakness, her dependence upon strangers for comfort, he is putting Lovelace, and the reader, on the rack. "Upon every occasion that offers," he reminds Lovelace of his responsibility, underlining his guilt: "*The divine Clarissa, Lovelace—reduced to rejoice for a cup of cold water! By* whom *reduced! . . . Pause here a moment, Lovelace!— and reflect—I must!*" (VI, 277-79) [III, 430-31]

Belford's reasons for tormenting Lovelace are not purely benevolent. He enjoys tantalizing Lovelace, making him wait for crucial details. "Being obliged to give way to an indispensable avocation," he teases the impatient Lovelace: "I will make thee taste a little, in thy turn, of the plague of suspense; and break off, without giving thee the least hint of the issue of my further proceedings." (VI, 305) [III, 450] Belford even withholds Clarissa's posthumous letter to Lovelace, loftily explaining that "I will withhold this last till I can be assured that you will be fitter to receive it than Tourville tells me you are at present." (VIII, 17) [IV, 355] Belford decides that Lovelace does not deserve a lock of the dead woman's hair. Mowbry can "easily pacify him" with a lock of hair "near the colour, if he be intent upon it." (VIII, 52) [IV, 379] The final insult: "hair near the colour" for Lovelace, who wants to possess all of Clarissa, even her preserved heart.

Naturally, Lovelace chafes under such treatment, bitterly and humorously attacking his friend's heavy sentimentality. When Belford tells Lovelace that he regards Clarissa as "one sent from Heaven to draw me after her out of the miry gulf," (VII, 275) [IV, 214] Lovelace mercilessly undercuts the vision, comparing Belford to the monument of Dame Elizabeth Cateret in Westminster, "one clumsy foot lifted up . . . to ascend; but so executed as would rather make one imagine, that the figure (without shoe or stocken, as it is, tho' the rest of the body is robed) was looking up to its Corn-cutter." (VII, 331) [IV, 252-53]

Through Lovelace, Richardson makes some of his most telling attacks on the very sentimentality that he creates. Both Belford's unrelenting emphasis on the pathos of Clarissa's death and Lovelace's unrelenting resistance to that sentimentality occur at the same time. The reader shares both visions. "Poor Belton, I hear, is at death's door," Belford announces. "A messenger is just come from him, who tells me, He cannot die till he sees me." (VII, 137) [IV, 121] Lovelace cannot ignore such an opportunity for satire: "Methinks I am sorry for honest Belton. But a man cannot be ill, or vapourish, but thou liftest up thy shriek-owl note and killest him immediately." (VII, 140) [IV, 123] "Never," Lovelace complains, "did any mortal ring so many changes in so few bells. Thy true Father, I swear, was a Butcher or an Undertaker, by the delight thou seemst to take in scenes of death and horror." (VII, 439) [IV, 325] And Belford is annoying. Lovelace's satiric irritation defuses the reader's own anger at Belford's heavy moralizing and his macabre interest in deathbed scenes. Belford's sentimentality is a necessary channel of redemption for the reader. By vicariously suffering Clarissa's pain, the reader works out his own sense of responsibility for the rape. But the reader cannot suffer all the time; unrelieved sentiment creates resentment. By temporarily endorsing Lovelace's criticism of Belford, the reader finds relief from excessive pathos. Purged of resentment, and somewhat ashamed for identifying with Lovelace, we can continue our progress through the stations of the cross with Clarissa, to stand at last before her coffin in the Harlowe vault.

Belford reports the most extraordinary version of Clarissa's funeral. Unable to attend the ceremony, but moved by her cousin Morden's description by letter of the service, he imaginatively recreates the experience, crowding into the "awful Porch," descending "into the clammy vault," as "true Executor" to see her placed at the feet of "him whose earthly delight she was." With "averted face," he quits at last "the solemn mansion, the symbolic coffin, and for ever, the glory of her Sex," muttering memento moris. (VIII, 99) [IV, 411] Here we can see how the epistolary method allows Richardson to expand and multiply experience, to offer not one but two versions of the same event. We even have a third report of the funeral, Clarissa's own post-mortem instructions for her burial. After witnessing the hagiographic triumph of her death, we can only view her humility towards her remains as both pathetic and ironic. She requests that she be placed at the feet of her grandfather, but fears that "this last honour may be refused to [her] corpse; in this case," she wants to be buried in the parish churchyard "in the most private manner, between the hours of Eleven and Twelve at night; attended only by Mrs. Lovick, and Mr. and Mrs. Smith, and their maidservant." (VIII, 107) [IV, 416] Reading her bitterly humble request, remembering the triumph of her funeral, we recognize that she has truly prevailed. And as witnesses of her triumph, we are exonerated at last.

John Preston is uneasy about the way Richardson draws his reader into his novel, but into a position of little power.[6] The reader becomes similar in function to Anna Howe and Belford, correspondents who devote their time and energy to the conflict between Lovelace and Clarissa but play an "undistinguished" role, "emotionally involved, yet denied entry into the action." Preston's sense of frustration bears witness to the extraordinary amount of involvement the reader is made to feel with Richardson's characters. He objects to being placed "on the same footing" as the less distinguished Belford and Miss Howe, but the wonder is not that the reader is unable to "become" the more distinguished Lovelace or Clarissa (although to judge by Richardson's correspondence with such devotees as Bradshaigh and Cibber, many of his readers quite easily made the transformation), but that the reader is allowed to indulge in the fantasy of being "on the same footing" with *any* of the characters. Richardson grants his readers significant epistolary privileges, making them correspondents, letting them fill in the chasms, and giving them important information he has withheld from his other characters. The author would probably have applauded Preston's sense of frustration. He wanted his readers to become "undistinguished" Belfords, to apply the "lesson" of Belford's reformation to their own lives. In these fallen times, Belfordship does not appeal to many of us, but the sense of engagement we experience with Richardson's characters can be valued for its own sake, for the way it expands our own lives.

When Richardson allows us to "correspond" with his characters, he is exploiting the reader's belief that by understanding a person's style and by sharing his letters, one can understand the person himself. Richardson both encouraged and exploded this dangerous belief. Samuel Johnson, a great admirer of Richardson, distrusted personal letters. Examining Pope's correspondence, he decided that the common belief that "the true characters of men may be found in their letters," was wrong. "Very few can boast of hearts which they dare lay open to themselves," much less to their friends. No transaction "offers stronger temptations to fallacy and sophistication than epistolary intercourse. In the eagerness of conversation, the first emotions of the mind often burst out, before they are considered; in the tumult of business, interest and passion have their genuine effect; but a friendly Letter is a calm and deliberate performance, in the cool of leisure, in the stillness of solitude, and surely no man sits down to depreciate by design his own character."[7] As an artist experimenting in differ-

ent styles and different personalities, Richardson seemed to
share Johnson's distrust of the familiar letter even while he
exploited it as a vehicle of truth. Richardson's favorite
characters frequently experiment with style. Even Clarissa,
that determined recorder of the truth, wrote a letter "per-
sonating an anonymous elderly lady . . . to Miss Drayton's
Mother, who, by her severity and restraints, had like to
have driven the young Lady into the very fault against
which her Mother was most solicitous to guard her." (II,
82) [I, 295] Lovelace's "personations" are even more suspect. As he eagerly forges Anna Howe's letters, he breaks
our faith in the "truth" of the "friendly Letter."

"Personations" came easily to Richardson; he was accustomed to disguise himself to give unsolicited advice. Not
yet eleven years old, he assumed "the Style and Address of
a Person in Years" to chastise a scandal-mongering widow
"of near Fifty." But, he tells Stinstra, "my Hand-writing
was known. I was challenged with it, and owned the Boldness; for she complained of it to my Mother with Tears.
My Mother chid me for the Freedom taken by such a Boy
with a Woman of her Years: But knowing that her Son
was not of a pert or forward Nature, but on the contrary,
shy and bashful, she commended my Principles, tho' she
censured the Liberty taken."[8]

Ideally, style revealed rather than masked heartfelt emotion, the "soul" of the correspondent. Yet how could it
when so many deceivers could resort to the pen? Charlotte
Grandison wryly describes the fallacy of the personal letter
in her love affair with a bounder. Captain Anderson, who
appeared to be a man of sense, betrayed her with purchased
letters: "When he came to *write*, my judgment was even
still more engaged in his favour than before. But when he
thought himself on a *safe footing* with me, he then lost his
handwriting, and his style, and even his orthography. I
blush to say it; and I then blush'd to see it. . . . I could
not help *despising* him, when I found myself so grossly imposed upon, by the letters he had procured to be written

for him; and that he was not either the man of sense, or of learning, that he would have had me think him." (I, 407-408) [II, XXIX] There can be no greater sin in the Richardsonian world than resorting to a professional letter-writer—yet here Richardson was the main offender. His *Familiar Letters* were "published at the solicitation of particular friends, who are of opinion, that they will answer several good ends." Surely one "good end" was the opportunity they offered the semiliterate lover to write with assurance as "a respectful Lover to his Mistress" and receive a favorable reply. (*Familiar Letters*, pp. xxvii, 93-94) His letter manual would have been of great service to the despicable Captain Anderson.

Richardson's *Familiar Letters* were the logical outcome of his well-known early career as letter-writer and "early Favourite with all the young Women of Taste and Reading in the Neighbourhood." Directed "to chide, and even repulse, when an Offence was either taken or given, at the very time that the Heart of the Chider or Repulser was open before me, overflowing with Esteem and Affection; and the fair Repulser dreading to be taken at her Word,"[9] Richardson wrote for hire, learning love secrets in return for his labor. Samuel Richardson, letter-writer for "Women of Taste," was an early favorite, but Captain Anderson could be nothing but a reprobate. The artist can deceive with impunity, with a freedom withheld from the common man.

To return now to Richardson's youthful impersonation of the aged chider. The essential Richardson is already here. Executing his moral mission, he assumed a disguise. His mother, his first critic, "chid [him] for the Freedom taken by such a Boy with a Woman of her Years." The sexual connotation of Richardson's language here cannot be overlooked. To write to another of the opposite sex is to assume power over one's correspondent, to take liberties, to penetrate the veil of punctilio. But in spite of it all, Richardson's mother "commended my Principles, tho' she censured the Liberty taken." The tension between principles and liberty, bashfulness and boldness, never left Richardson. Writing gave him a way out of his "shy and bashful" nature. Mrs. Richardson, a well-meaning Christian woman, was able to commend the moral principles of young Samuel while censuring his liberty, but the two qualities cannot be separated so easily. Glorying in his creative license, Richardson managed to have it both ways, as moralist and rogue, "an early Favourite with all the young Women of Taste and Reading in the Neighbourhood."

Richardson retained his position as "early Favourite" until his death, especially in his productive years as a novelist. And he enjoyed his coterie of women, young girls like the coyly naive Miss Westcomb, young blues like Miss Mulso, old blues like Miss Sarah Fielding, and coyly naive old girls like Lady Bradshaigh. In his letters to his women friends, as we have seen, he tried out a number of roles and positions, baiting his intellectuals with paternalistic patter, defending polygamy to the monogamous Lady Bradshaigh, and playing "Papa" to the shy maidens in need of encouragement before they could drop their diffidence. In his letters, Richardson sought above all his correspondents' confidence. "But it is the diffidence I wish to banish . . . why the diffidence to such a one as I am!—a plain writer: a sincere well-wisher: an undesigning scribbler; who admire none but the natural and easy beauties of the pen: no carper: and one who has so just an opinion of the sex, that he knows, in a hundred instances, that the ladies who love the pen are qualified by genius and imagination to excell in the beauties of this sort of writing." But the diffidence, we know by now, was a necessary defense for the young maiden, and could only be dropped before the plain writing, sincere well-wisher.

Not many were around. Richardson's world was filled with deceivers (a Lovelace in every corner), and in the very paragraph before Richardson so grandly banished diffidence, he warned Miss Westcomb to guard against dangerous correspondents: "Writing to your own sex I would principally recommend; since ours is hardly ever void of design, and makes a correspondence dangerous:—Except protected by time, as in my case, by general character, by choice already filled up; where is the man that deserves to be favoured?" (*Letters*, p. 66)

Where indeed? Richardson alone was that deserving man. After creating a nightmare world of seduction and betrayal frightening enough to keep all but the most hardened of maidens locked tightly in their closets, Richardson attempted to break down the barriers with his mighty pen. He alone could pierce through the veil of decorum he publicly insisted upon. "And were there the least room to suspect that there was anything less than paternal in my views," he soothes, "I could not dare to urge the favour, or take the liberty."

Just as the young Samuel took "liberty" with a much older woman, so the elder Samuel took "liberty" with his young chits. How he loved it. He tells Miss Highmore that he has read part of their letters to her mother and father, adding wickedly that "I had beforehand, enclosed in hooks, [ ] what I thought you would not wish them, or anybody to see; with proper corrections, &c. so that the sense was not imperfect; and yet, to be sincere with you, I hinted, that there were two or three passages that I should not read, wherein I had treated our girl a little freely; and your good mama looked so pitiful for you—she sighed.— Then I wish not, said she, to see them." He adds, "I don't see that I can shew any part of your last favour, or of this my answer to it, to your insatiable, yet modestly curious, papa. Do you think I can? No, say." (*Correspondence*, vol. II, pp. 247-48)

"Dangerous" correspondence indeed. And what is there in the innocent letters that require hooks? Richardson not only enjoyed treating "our girl a little freely," but managed to obtain "insatiable, yet modestly curious" Papa's approval of his freedoms. He imagined that he had been

"more free with the sex than ever man was." (*Correspondence*, vol. VI, p. 224) Free with his pen, not with his
person. In personal conversation he was "always jealous of
suffering in the Opinion of my Readers." (*Letters*, p. 319)
Personal visits were difficult, he told Lady Bradshaigh: "I
never paid my personal Duty to your Ladyship, but I came
away half dissatisfied with myself, from the Diffidence I
have mentioned." (*Letters*, p. 319) To know Richardson,
one must attend to his writing. "In writing, I own, I was
always an impudent Man. But need I tell your Ladyship
that? . . ." There was, he feared, something wrong with
his personal appearance: "Something strangely forbidding,
of the hedgehog kind, must there be in my outward behaviour. What a supercilious creature must I be! I, who
in my heart, and with my pen, am the freest of all mortals." (*Correspondence*, vol. VI, p. 225)

Richardson appreciated the liberty his writing brought
him, the "artless freedom" of his letters. Yet even while
urging Miss Westcomb to give vent to her "every sentiment," he reveals an appreciation of the deliberation of
correspondence as critical as that of Dr. Johnson. Correspondence is "more pure, yet more ardent, and less broken
in upon, than personal conversation can be even amongst
the most pure, because of the deliberation it allows, from
the very preparation to, and action of writing." (*Letters*,
p. 65) Unlike Johnson, Richardson did not fear the deliberation, for deliberation protected purity—an odd thought,
but consistent with Richardson's fear of impulse. The young
girl had to be checked: what better place than in the privacy of her closet, where passion could be transmuted into
sentiment. Spontaneous deliberation became "writing to the
moment," a studied narrative technique. Harriet Byron
candidly describes her attempt to get everything down, to
recreate her experience for her readers. In an attempt to
capture the "supercilious looks and behaviour of Mr. Walden," she makes "mouths in the glass for several minutes
to try to recover some of Mr. Walden's, in order to de-

scribe them to you, Lucy; but I cannot for my life so distort my face to enable me to give you a notion of one of them." (I, 46) [I, XI] Writing to the moment takes some minutes, much practice, deliberation, and art. Richardson may have commended Miss Westcomb's "artless freedom," but his own literary freedom was demanding. "For the pen is jealous of company. It expects, as I may say, to engross the writer's whole self; every body allows the writer to withdraw: it disdains company; and will have the entire attention." (*Letters*, p. 66)

"The pen" allowed Richardson the freedom to learn about himself. In his characters and in his personal letters, he confronted motives and personality traits that seemed to escape him in his public life. When he wrote, he became so absorbed in his characters that he confessed to Lady Bradshaigh: "It is not fair to say—I, identically, am any-where, while I keep within the character." He is not any-where and he is everywhere, expanding himself beyond the limits of his conventional personality. (*Letters*, p. 286) Diderot praised Richardson's analytical powers in his famous remark that the author "porte le flambeau au fond de la caverne; c'est lui qui apprend à discerner les motifs subtils et déshonnêtes qui se cachent et se dérobent sous d'autres motifs qui sont honnêtes et qui se hâtent de se montrer les premiers. Il souffle sur le fântome sublime qui se présente a l'entrée de la caverne; et le More hideux qu'il masquait s'aperçoit."[10] Like most analysts, Richardson excelled in finding the hideous Moor in others; the Richardsonian hidden self is more difficult to reach. In his correspondence, where he enjoyed the freedom of role-playing with his ad-mirers, and in his characters, Richardson revealed his fas-cination with "unwind[ing] the mazes of the female heart." As I suggested in Chapter Five, Richardson, like Tiresias, explored women to understand himself. He told Stinstra that his early "Secretariship" to his lovelorn young women offered him a way into the minds of women, leading his "Enquiries, as [he] grew up, into the Knowledge of the

Female Heart. And knowing something of that, [he] could not be an utter Stranger to that of Man."[11] Exploration of the feminine heart led to an understanding of his own masculine self.

The pen provided Richardson with a way into the personalities of others, and ultimately a way into himself. To a certain extent we read *Clarissa* to understand the complex psychology not only of the characters but of ourselves. By recognizing the conflict between Clarissa and Lovelace, their struggle for dominance, and their mutual need to know one another, we can also recognize our own human connection to the conflict. When Belford tells Lovelace that he is laboring to make him "feel," he speaks for Richardson, who in turn speaks to the reader. The letters gave the novelist the freedom to enter the souls of his correspondents, to uncover their deepest thoughts and feelings, and to force the reader to "feel" his own discoveries about the human personality. Anna Howe speaks for Richardson when she demands "nothing less than the knowledge of the inmost recesses of your heart." (I, 275) [I, 188]

The epistolary method, as Leslie Fiedler notes, "is not merely an amateur's way out, as some critics have thought, but the analyst's way in, a way of rendering inwardness with extraordinary immediacy."[12] What better way in than through the personal letter, the testimony of the heart, as Lovelace would say. Yet that, of course, remains the problem. Lovelace would say it, just as he is preparing to deceive Clarissa through letters forged "from the heart." In his study of Richardson's correspondence, Malvin R. Zirker suggests that Richardson exploited his correspondents, using their letters as sources of information, "field work" for his novels: "As Joyce was to write to friends in Dublin for material for his novels, Richardson wrote to young ladies equally for the purpose of collecting data. His urging them to be frank, to write from the heart, is no more ingenuous than his asking Lady Bradshaigh to show him her diary or Miss Mulso to describe her rooms (she refused)."[13] More likely, Richardson was doing "field work" for himself, for in understanding the "minutiae" of Lady Bradshaigh's diary and Miss Mulso's rooms, he was unwinding the "secret mazes" of his own heart, exploring the feminine part of himself.

The Richardsonian self expressed in his work was a unified, completed self, both masculine and feminine, bold and diffident. Virginia Woolf's discussion of androgyny in art sheds light on the "undivided" Richardson. Woolf examined Coleridge's statement that great minds are androgynous, deciding that when the fusion between the masculine and feminine parts of the brain takes place, the mind is "fully fertilised and uses all its faculties." She warns that we must test our ideas of "what one meant by man-womanly, and conversely by woman-manly. . . . Coleridge certainly did not mean, when he said that a great mind is androgynous, that it is a mind that has any special sympathy with women; a mind that takes up their cause or devotes itself to their interpretation. Perhaps the androgynous mind is less apt to make these distinctions than the single-sexed mind. He meant, perhaps, that the androgynous mind is resonant and porous; that it transmits emotion without impediment; that it is naturally creative, incandescent and undivided."[14]

Virginia Woolf is raising a complicated issue here, for degrees of masculine and feminine tendencies are difficult, perhaps impossible, to measure. We can see, however, that there is a great difference between the way Mr. Richardson of Salisbury Court lived and the way he wrote. There were many sides to the man: Papa triumphantly teasing his chits; the painfully bashful visitor making his social "duty"; the benevolent man of charity befriending Mrs. Pilkington; and the outraged moralist scorning the "poison" memoirs of women like Mrs. Vane *and* Mrs. Pilkington, the wretch. In his life, Richardson repeatedly expressed his faith in a world of sexual differences, a world in which women had to follow their clearly defined roles. Yet in his art he created heroines who achieved success by transcending sexual and social boundaries. Both Pamela and Clarissa demand to be recognized as persons of worth and integrity, not as representatives of their sex or their class. In his work, especially in his favorite *Clarissa*, Richardson showed himself to be "naturally creative, incandescent and undivided."

Certainly, as Zirker suggests, Richardson, like all writers, used the stuff of daily experience for his art. He was quick to point out to Lady Bradshaigh that she was a very Anna Howe and a pert Lady G. His great interest in his correspondents' lives, however, and his desire to banish their diffidence came from his own need for both knowledge and freedom, the knowledge of the feminine side of himself and the freedom to invent his personality. In his letters, Richardson was playful, inventive, and creative, exploiting himself as he exploited his characters. Richardson told his Miss Westcomb the reasons a modest, diffident young woman should write, but considering Richardson's own diffidence, we can apply his remarks to himself: "Retired, the modest Lady, happy in herself, happy in the Choice she makes of the dear Correspondent of her own Sex (for ours are too generally Designers); uninterrupted; her Closet her Paradise, her Company, herself, and ideally the beloved Absent; there she can distinguish Her Self: By this means she can assert and vindicate her Claim to Sense and Meaning." (*Letters*, p. 68) The pen will show "Sense and Meaning"; indeed, it will invent meaning where none can be found. Richardson is advocating a self-sufficiency here, a happiness "in oneself." "Ideally," the correspondent's "beloved" is absent, for the presence of another would interfere with the fragile reality about to be created. It is far better to live in the mind than in the body, to shine in the privacy of the closet rather than the glare of the tea table, far better to enjoy the paradise within.

Richardson was always, as his biographers Eaves and Kimpel ably point out, a public man accustomed (however reluctantly) to society, not a modest young lady with nothing but silence to commend her.[15] But like his modest young lady, Richardson confessed to a sense of insecurity in the world, "a bashfulness, next to sheepishness."[16] He often complained of his inferior education. Perhaps he was projecting yet another role, that of the poor undesigning scribbler who never has had the time to read Spenser "at a heat, as I may call it," (*Letters*, p. 162) or Pliny. "As you say," he tells Miss Highmore, "I should never find time to read the book." (*Letters*, p. 160) "Alas! my life has been a trifling busy one," he confesses to Mr. Cave, apologizing for never having found the time to read all of the *Spectators*. (*Letters*, p. 165)

Poor Mr. Richardson may not have had the time to digest all of Addison, but he did find time to scribble— thousands of pages of prose, merely "busy" trifles, which he later edited and reedited, riddled and teased, reluctant ever to finish his work. Richardson, Mrs. Barbauld tartly observed, "never knew when to have done with a character." (*Correspondence*, vol. I, p. cxxi) For to quit a character, to finish a postscript, would be to return to the prosaic self. Better, surely, to remain very still in Clarissa's death chamber, or to perch expectantly in the "cedar-parlour" for news of the good man, better surely than to return to everyday life.

Richardson's fiction and his letters offered him a freedom he could find nowhere else. According to Mrs. Barbauld, he claimed that "my nervous disorders will permit me to write with more impunity than to read." (*Correspondence*, vol. I, p. cxci) "Impunity" is an aptly chosen word, for in his letters, he was exempt from the moral censor of everyday life. "What a rogue, as Lovelace says, is human nature," Richardson writes Miss Highmore, apologizing three pages later for his "freedom"—"let me desire you to excuse the freedom of my pen; I believe I have been very free." (*Correspondence*, vol. II, pp. 221-24) In his spider metaphor in the same letter ("But shall I not affront you if I compare you girls to spiders?") Richardson revels in his freedom. "This may not exactly quadrate to any particular case; but it came into my head and down it went." (*Correspondence*, vol. II, pp. 220-21)

"Down it went"—regardless of the consequences. Correspondence allowed a free field for invention, not merely for the collecting of data, the opportunity to play freely with images, characters, roles, to expand the self. Lovelace plays at being Tiresias, Clodius, Don Juan, and Don Quixote in his quest for secret knowledge, power, and freedom. And Richardson played at being Lovelace, Clarissa, Pamela, Sir Charles, always inventing a surer, "more perfect" self. In the paradise within, in the writing closet, Richardson enjoyed the freedom of his imagination, freedom with impunity.

Freedom dearly won. As we have seen throughout this study, to transform himself in his fiction, Richardson first had to transform his moral. And to transform a moral, the author first had to hold one, be it a warning against reforming a rake, an aversion towards "mannish" horsewomen, or the certainty that a servant girl in danger of being compromised by her master must come away "at once" lest she be corrupted. Diffident Mr. Richardson, so painfully self-conscious, could never have taken on the obsessive, compelling characters of his imagination without the moral license his didacticism provided. As he confided in his postscript to *Clarissa*, "under the fashionable guise of an amusement," he managed to "steal in" an investigation of the "great doctrines of Christianity." Just as surely, disguised as a didactic moralist, he managed to "steal in" ambiguous, complex characters of his own making, designed not only to perfect his readers but to complete himself. The act of writing, as process rather than as moral means to a higher end, became the perfectionism Richardson sought for so long.

"And indeed, my dear, I know not how to *forbear* writing," Clarissa writes to Anna Howe. "I have now no other employment or diversion. And I must write on, altho' I were not to send it to any-body." (III, 221) [II, 128] "Fresh cause of aggravation!" Lovelace rants. "But for this scribbling vein, or I should still run mad." (V, 28) [II, 525] I will allow Mr. Richardson the last word: "As to my health—I write, I do anything I am able to do, on purpose to carry myself out of myself; and am not quite so happy, when, tired with my peregrinations, I am obliged to return home." (*Correspondence*, vol. III, pp. 190-91)

Notes

Preface
1. Samuel Richardson, *The Correspondence of Samuel Richardson*, 6 vols., ed. Anna Laetitia Barbauld (London, 1804), vol. 1, pp. xcix, cii. (Hereafter cited in the text as *Correspondence.*)
2. Samuel Richardson, *The Selected Letters of Samuel Richardson*, ed. John Carroll (Oxford, 1964), pp. 66, 88. (Hereafter cited in the text as *Letters.*)
3. One of the most interesting approaches to *Clarissa*, William Beatty Warner's *Reading Clarissa: The Struggles of Interpretation* (New Haven, 1979), was published after I completed my manuscript. We differ markedly in method, yet in spite of Derrida and Nietzsche, we come to remarkably similar points of agreement about the self-consciousness of Clarissa and Lovelace, the fictive nature of Richardson's "reality," and the vengeful nature of Clarissa's forgiveness. Unlike Warner, I insist upon looking at Richardson's characters not only as creatures of rhetorical and strategic significance but as characters of "meaning." Warner and I share an appreciation of the gamester Richardson, the Lovelacian impresario playing with reader and character alike. However, I am also interested in discovering why the gamester plays.
4. For a more balanced approach to the Richardson canon, the reader is directed to Mark Kinkead-Weekes's *Samuel Richardson: Dramatic Novelist* (London, 1973), Margaret Doody's *A Natural Passion: A Study of the Novels of Samuel Richardson* (Oxford, 1974), and Cynthia Griffin Wolff's *Samuel Richardson and the Eighteenth-Century Puritan Character* (Hamden, Conn., 1972).

One. The Self-Made Saint
1. Richard Graves, "Trifling Anecdotes of the Late Ralph Allen, Esq., of Prior Park, near Bath," *The Triflers* (London, 1806), p. 68, as cited in *Samuel Richardson: A Biography*, by T. C. Duncan Eaves and Ben D. Kimpel (Oxford, 1971), p. 537.

2. Hester Thrale Piozzi, *Autobiography, Letters and Literary Remains*, 2 vols., ed. Abraham Hayward (London, 1861), vol. 1, p. 311, as cited in Eaves and Kimpel, *Samuel Richardson*, p. 535.

3. Matthew 5:48. "Be ye therefore Perfect, even as your Father which is in heaven is perfect." In *The Perfectability of Man* (London, 1970), a study of the history and philosophy of perfectionism, John Passmore finds this command from the Sermon on the Mount to be fundamental to an understanding of Christian perfectionism. (p. 68)

4. Samuel Richardson, *The Richardson-Stinstra Correspondence and Sinstra's Prefaces to Clarissa*, ed. William C. Slattery (Carbondale and Edwardsville, Ill., 1969), pp. 24-25.

5. J. S., *The Famous History of the Valiant London Prentice; Shewing His Noble Exploits at Home and Abroad. Together with His Love and Great Success: Very Pleasant and Delightful. Written for the Encouragement of Youth* (Newcastle, 1711).

6. Richardson, *Richardson-Stinstra Correspondence*, p. 27.

7. [Samuel Richardson], *The Apprentice's Vade Mecum: or Young Man's Pocket Companion*, ed. A. D. McKillop for The Augustan Reprint Society, nos. 169-70 (Los Angeles, 1975), p. v. (Hereafter cited in the text as *Vade Mecum*.)

8. Derek Jarrett, *England in the Age of Hogarth* (St. Albans, Herts., 1976), pp. 86-88.

9. On 23 November 1721, at the age of 32, Richardson married his former master's daughter, Martha Wilde, who was 23. She died ten years later after bearing six children, all of whom died in childhood. Richardson's biographers warn against mercenary interpretations of his first marriage: "It has been hinted that Richardson married his master's daughter, like a properly ambitious apprentice, for prudential reasons. But when he married, Richardson had long ceased to be the apprentice of John Wilde. Nor are there any grounds for thinking that Martha was very wealthy. She had £100 inherited from an uncle in addition to what her father left her, but her father was himself not too well off." Richardson told Lady Bradshaigh that he cherished "the Memory of my lost Wife to this Hour," and even after he married his second wife, Elizabeth Leake, "again the daughter of an old employer," Richardson still requested in his will that

he be buried with Martha. Eaves and Kimpel, *Samuel Richardson*, pp. 48-49.

10. M. Dorothy George, *London Life in the Eighteenth Century* (London, 1925; reprint ed., 1966), p. 225.

11. *Genuine and Authentic Account of the Life, Trial and Execution of Elizabeth Brownrigg . . . for the barbarous Murder of Mary Clifford, her Apprentice Girl . . . Together with The Sufferings of Mary Mitchell, and Mary Jones* (London, 1767), pp. 9-17. See also *An Appeal to Humanity in an account of the Life and Cruel Actions of Elizabeth Brownrigg* (London, 1767) and *Celebrated Trials and Remarkable Cases of Criminal Jurisprudence from the earliest record to the year 1825*, 6 vols., [compiled by George Borrow] (London, 1825), vol. 4, pp. 425-31.

12. "Sarah Metyard and Sarah M. Metyard for Murder, 1768," *Celebrated Trials*, vol. 4, pp. 432-36.

13. "Tryal of Elizabeth Wigenton for Whipping a Girl to death at Ratclyffe," *The True Relation of the Tryals . . . at Old-Bailey, 17th and 18th January, 16—*, listed in the British Library Catalogue as BM 515 L.2/7.

14. George, *London Life*, pp. 224-29.

15. Ibid., p. 271.

16. Ibid., appendix 4, "Apprenticeship Cases From the Middlesex Sessions and Records," pp. 420-21.

17. "Mrs. Barbauld, on unstated authority, tells us that [Richardson] used to hide a half-crown among the letters so that the first journeyman to arrive at work might find it, and that at other times he used fruit from his garden." Eaves and Kimpel, *Samuel Richardson*, p. 161.

18. Samuel Richardson, *Familiar Letters on Important Occasions*, ed. Brian W. Downs (London, 1928), p. xxvii. (Hereafter cited in the text as *Familiar Letters*.)

19. In his best writing Richardson avoided digressions. As Mrs. Barbauld argues, in *Clarissa* we "do not come upon unexpected adventures and wonderful recognitions, by quick turns and surprises: we see her fate from afar, as it were, through a long avenue, the gradual approach to which, without ever losing sight of the object, has more of simplicity and grandeur than the most cunning labyrinth that can be contrived by art." (*Correspondence*, vol. 1, p. lxxxiii)

20. See George Cheyne, *The Letters of Doctor George Cheyne*

to Samuel Richardson (1733-1743), ed. Charles Mullett (Columbia, Mo., 1943).

21. In *Samuel Richardson: The Triumph of Craft* (Knoxville, Tenn., 1974) Elizabeth Bergen Brophy also chooses to disregard the more inflammatory aspects of Richardson's novels. Taking the author's own artistic pronouncements very seriously, she argues, as he did, that the "warm scenes" served an edifying and artistic purpose. The novels "were designed to encourage emotional participation principally to make their moral message more telling, but also, as Richardson expounded to Lady Bradshaigh, 'to strengthen the tender Mind, and to enable the worthy Heart to bear up against the Calamities of Life.' " (p. 30) I first read Brophy after completing this manuscript, and was surprised to see how closely we follow the same line of investigation, and yet how far apart our conclusions stand. She argues, rightly and convincingly, that Richardson wrote consciously, not "in spite of himself," not "accidentally," but according to the precepts of a literary theory of his own making. Using his letters and novels, Brophy pieces together this theory, emphasizing the importance of verisimilitude and probability, the use of moral exemplars, the advantage of the epistolary style, and the need to involve the reader emotionally by writing "to the moment." A recovery of the fragments of Richardson's aesthetic philosophy is certainly helpful, but on its own it can also be misleading. Richardson himself often hedged, and often made broad statements of moralistic policy to elevate his own stature as one of the better writers. It is not merely his theory alone, which even Brophy admits was composed of ideas that were "already generally accepted commonplaces in his own time" (p. 108), but what uncommon things he does with his theory, how he contradicts and expands it, that matters. The tension between his moral and aesthetic principles, between his legitimate theories and his creative imagination, provides the power of his finest work.

22. Richardson, *Familiar Letters*, letters 153 and 160, pp. 200-202, 219-20.

23. Cynthia Griffin Wolff, *Samuel Richardson and the Eighteenth-Century Puritan Character* (Hamden, Conn., 1972), pp. 43-44.

24. Richard Cumberland, a sentimental dramatist who exploited the conventions of virtue in distress often enough in his

own work, regarded *Clarissa* as "one of the books, which a prudent parent will put under interdiction; for I think I can say from observation, that there are more artificial pedantic characters assumed by sentimental Misses, in the vain desire of being thought *Clarissa Harlows* [*sic*], than from any other source of imitation whatsoever. . . . I have a young lady in my eye, who made her will, wrote an inscription for the plate of her own coffin, and forswore all mankind at the age of 16." *"The Observer*, 27, 1785," *Novel and Romance, 1700-1800: A Documentary Record*, ed. Ioan Williams (London, 1970), p. 334.

25. Wolff, *Puritan Character*, pp. 52-53.
26. Passmore, *Perfectability*, p. 157. See John Dussinger's unpublished doctoral dissertation, "Richardson's *Clarissa*: 'A Work of Tragic Species' " (Princeton, 1964), for his discussion of Richardson's ideas of perfectionism. Chapter Two, pp. 68-119, is particularly helpful.
27. In "The Dark Night," St. John of the Cross explains the need for such suffering: "Because the soul is purified in this forge like gold in the crucible . . . it feels terrible annihilation in its very substance and extreme poverty as though it were approaching its end." *The Collected Works of St. John of the Cross*, trans. Kieran Kavanaugh and Otilio Rodriguez (London, 1966), p. 339.
28. Margaret Doody, *A Natural Passion: A Study of the Novels of Samuel Richardson* (Oxford, 1974), pp. 174-75. Doody cites Louis L. Martz's *Poetry of Meditation* (New Haven, 1965) in her discussion of the influence of religious works of the Counter Reformation on English poetry. Martz is generous in his definition of a "meditative tradition," noting that in their habit of meditating it is "possible to find a fundamental link between Vaughan, Marvell, Traherne, and even Milton." (p. 3) See Gillian Beer's "Richardson, Milton, and the Status of Evil," *Review of English Studies*, new series, vol. 19, no. 75 (1968), pp. 261-70, for a discussion of the connections between Richardson and Milton.
29. Wolff, *Puritan Character*, p. 46.
30. Two translations of *The Life of St. Teresa of Avila* were made into English by Roman Catholic exiles in the seventeenth century. *The Life of Saint Teresa of Avila by Herself*, trans. J. M. Cohen (Edinburgh, 1957), p. 19.

31. St. John, "The Dark Night," *Collected Works*, p. 316.

32. Ibid., p. 338.

33. *The Life of Saint Teresa*, pp. 229-30.

34. Ibid., p. 139.

35. St. John, "The Dark Night," *Collected Works*, p. 319. Psalm 72:22.

36. St. John, "The Living Flame of Love," *Collected Works*, p. 578.

37. Ibid., pp. 592-93.

38. In his discussion of John's use of the bridegroom metaphor, Passmore, *Perfectability* (p. 132), cites Zaehner's theory of the feminine aspects of the soul: "The soul, according to Zaehner, must realize that 'If it is to commune with God, its role can only be that of the bride, it must play the woman.' " R. C. Zaehner, *Mysticism: Sacred and Profane* (Oxford, 1957), p. 152.

39. St. John, "The Living Flame of Love," *Collected Works*, p. 593.

40. Robert T. Petersson, *The Art of Ecstasy: Teresa, Bernini, and Crashaw* (London, 1970), pp. 38-39.

41. *The Life of Saint Teresa*, p. 210.

42. George Cheyne, *An Essay on Regimen* (London, 1740), p. 25, as cited by Dussinger, "Richardson's *Clarissa*," p. 117. Here is an example of Cheyne's perfectionist prose: "You will fall away infinitely to what you are; every Atom and Fibre of your old Habit must be worn out; all must become new and you'll get to a moderate, Active, gay Temper and Habit and write Books without End, as I have done, and grow as rich as a Jew and settle all your Family to your Heart's Content." Cheyne, *Letters of Cheyne to Richardson*, p. 83. Elizabeth Bergen Brophy, *Triumph*, pp. 113-15, suggests that Richardson may have suffered from Parkinson's disease, a disorder of neurological rather than neurotic origin.

43. Tobias Smollett's Matthew Bramble claimed in his London letter of June 8 that London milk was made of "faded cabbage-leaves and sour draff . . . frothed with bruised snails . . . exposed to foul rinsings . . . spittle, snot, and tobacco-quids from foot-passengers." *The Expedition of Humphry Clinker*, ed. Lewis M. Knapp (London, 1966), p. 122. Dorothy George, *London Life*, pp. 340-41, cites an eighteenth-century cow-keep-

er's claim that because of the filthy habits of the retail milk dealers no "delicate person would possibly drink the milk."

44. Margaret Doody objects to "modern" interpretations of Clarissa's death as perversions of the "meaning" of Richardson's novel. She argues that to read *Clarissa* correctly, "it is necessary to understand what Christianity meant to the heroine and her author." *Natural Passion*, pp. 178-79. However, the "meaning" of religion for Richardson is difficult to fix, as it includes the tedious perfectionism Clarissa demonstrates in her carefully audited good works as well as the ecstasy of the mystic tradition. We cannot separate the erotic sensibility manifested in Clarissa's eager preparations to meet her "bridegroom" from the priggish piety manifested in her recorded daily works.

45. Cecil A. Moore, "The English Malady," *Backgrounds of English Literature, 1700-1760* (Minneapolis, 1953), pp. 205-206. See also G. S. Rousseau's discussion of the English malady and suicide in his chapter on science in *The Eighteenth Century*, ed. Pat Rogers (London, 1978), pp. 180-96.

46. Pierre Jean Grosley, *A Tour to London; or New Observations on England and its Inhabitants*, 2 vols., trans. Thomas Nugent (London, 1772), vol. 1, pp. 27-28. See also Jarrett on English melancholy, *Age of Hogarth*, pp. 176-80.

47. Verses 442-46, as cited in Moore, *Backgrounds*, p. 201.

48. Before her mysterious illness, Clarissa prided herself on her hardy constitution. She spent long hours in her "Ivy Summer-house," although it was "seldom resorted to by any-body else, except in the summer-months, because it is cool." (II, 303) [I, 447]

49. Samuel Johnson, *Johnsonian Miscellanies*, 2 vols., ed. G. B. Hill (Oxford, 1897), vol. 1, p. 297.

50. Emile Durkheim, *Suicide, A Study in Sociology*, trans. John Spaulding and George Simpson (London, 1970), pp. 42-44.

51. Ibid., pp. 225-26.

52. Levin L. Schucking, *The Puritan Family: A Social Study from the Literary Sources*, trans. Brian Bettershaw (London, 1969), pp. 155-56.

53. Paul E. Parnell, "The Sentimental Mask," *Restoration Drama: Modern Essays in Criticism*, ed. John Loftis (New York, 1966), p. 295.

54. John Dussinger, *The Discourse of the Mind in Eighteenth-Century Fiction* (The Hague, 1974), p. 115.

55. Samuel Richardson, *Works*, 12 vols., ed. Leslie Stephen (London, 1883), introduction, pp. xxxix-xl, as cited in Wolff, *Puritan Character*, p. 176.

56. Eaves and Kimpel, *Samuel Richardson*, p. 367.

57. Mark Kinkead-Weekes, *Samuel Richardson: Dramatic Novelist* (London, 1973), pp. 291, 294. Doody, *A Natural Passion*, p. 304.

58. "Memoir" of Richardson, *Ballantyne's Novelist's Library*, vol. 6 (1824), p. xlvi, as cited in Eaves and Kimpel, *Samuel Richardson*, p. 389.

59. Morris Golden, *Richardson's Characters* (Ann Arbor, 1963), p. 181.

Two. A Delicate Balance

1. John Traugott, *"Clarissa*'s Richardson: An Essay to Find the Reader," *English Literature in the Age of Disguise*, ed. Maximilian Novak (Berkeley and Los Angeles, 1977), p. 165.

2. T. C. Eaves and Ben D. Kimpel, *Samuel Richardson: A Biography* (Oxford, 1971), p. 557.

3. There have been many attempts to define the word "sentimental." R. F. Brissenden's *Virtue in Distress: Studies in the Novels of Sentiment from Richardson to Sade* (London, 1974) and George Starr's " 'Only a Boy': Notes on Sentimental Novels," *Genre*, vol. 10 (Winter 1977), pp. 501-27, are two of the most successful recent attempts. See Ann Van Sant's unpublished doctoral dissertation, "Masters of the Heart: A Study of the Uses of Sentimentalism in the Novels of Richardson, Fielding, and Sterne" (University of California, 1978), for her helpful analysis of sentimental values and attitudes in the eighteenth century.

4. See Golden's discussion of "punctilio" and social order. Morris Golden, *Richardson's Characters* (Ann Arbor, 1963), pp. 128-35.

5. Jocelyn Harris points out that Miss Barnevelt's mannerisms and remarks resemble those of Lady Mary Wortley Montagu. *Grandison* (I, 469).

6. Henry Fielding gives an extreme example of the dangers of the masculine woman in his pamphlet *The Female Husband: or, the Surprising History of Mrs. Mary, alias Mr. George Ham-*

ilton. Who was convicted of having married a Young Woman of Wells and lived with her as her Husband (London, 1746). Posing as Mr. George Hamilton, a doctor of physic, Mary Hamilton married Mary Price, an eighteen-year-old girl of "extraordinary beauty." "George" managed to satisfy his wife with "something of too vile, wicked and scandalous a nature, which was found in the Doctor's trunk"; at any rate, she made no complaints about her marriage. When her mother forced her to confess, the bogus husband was whipped publicly four times in four market towns in Somerset and imprisoned. The very evening of the first public whipping, apparently undeterred by her punishment, "George" offered her jailer money "to procure her a young girl to satisfy her most monstrous and unnatural desires." (pp. 20-23)

7. [John Brown], *An Estimate of the Manners and Principles of the Times* (London, 1758), p. 51.

8. Derek Jarrett notes that "as long ago as 1621 Robert Burton had quoted in his *Anatomy of Melancholy* the ancient proverb that England was a paradise for women and hell for horses." Derek Jarrett, *England in the Age of Hogarth* (St. Albans, Herts., 1976), p. 105. See also Edward Smith, *Foreign Visitors in England and What They Thought of Us* (London, 1889), p. 210, as cited in Gordon Rattray Taylor, *The Angel Makers: A Study in the Psychological Origins of Historical Change* (London, 1958), p. 293.

9. Henry Meister, *Letters Written during a Residence in England* (London, 1799), pp. 283-85.

10. *The Complete Letters of Lady Mary Wortley Montagu*, 3 vols., ed. Robert Halsband (Oxford, 1965-67), letter of 31 October 1723 to Lady Mar, vol. 2, p. 32.

11. *The Letters of Monsieur Cesar de Saussure to his Family: A Foreign View of England in the Reign of George I and George II*, trans. and ed. Madame Van Muyden (London, 1902), pp. 206-207.

12. In issue number 97 of Johnson's *Rambler, The Yale Edition of Samuel Johnson*, ed. W. J. Bate and Albrecht B. Strauss (New Haven, 1969), vol. 4, pp. 153-59, Richardson judges that "places of public resort . . . make home irksome," and predicts that "even fine faces, often seen, are less regarded than new faces, the proper punishment of showy girls, for rendering themselves so impolitickly cheap."

13. Masquerades were notorious in Grandison's time. In his *Survey of the Cities of London and Westminster*, 2 vols., ed. John Strype (London, 1754-55), vol. 2, p. 557, John Stow defines the masquerade as a place "where People disguise their Persons, and even their Sex, and mix with the Refuse of Mankind, where they see, and hear, and do such Things under the cover of a Mask, as the most Profligate would blush at in their proper Dress; this is an Amusement so universally detested and abhorred, that it needs no Remark." Sir Charles, of course, is no friend of the masquerade either; he prounounces that they "are not creditable places for young ladies to be known to be *insulted* at them. They are diversions that fall not in with the genius of the English commonalty." (I, 143) [I, XXVII] Harriet Byron will always regret her "presumptuous folly, in going dress'd out, like the fantastic wretch I appeared to be, at a vile, a foolish masquerade." (I, 168) [I, XXXIII]

14. James Peller Malcom, *Anecdotes of the Manners and Customs of London During the Eighteenth Century* (London, 1808), pp. 157-58.

15. E. N. Williams, *Life in Georgian England* (London, 1962), p. 51.

16. *The Ladies' Magazine: or Universal Entertainer* (London), see Saturday, 18 November 1749 and vol. 2, nos. 11-14.

17. Alison Adburgham, *Women in Print: Writing Women and Women's Magazines From the Restoration to the Accession of Victoria* (London, 1972), p. 106. This is a detailed and interesting study of the contents and style of women's magazines, with a helpful bibliography.

18. *The Complete Letters of Lady Mary Wortley Montagu*, letter of 10 October 1753 to Lady Bute, vol. 3, p. 40; letter of 19 May 1756 to Lady Bute, vol. 3, p. 106.

19. Doris M. Stenton, *The English Woman in History* (London, 1957), pp. 286-87.

20. Joseph Wood Krutch, *Samuel Johnson* (New York, 1963), p. 45.

21. *The Complete Letters of Lady Mary Wortley Montagu*, letter of 20 July 1719 to Bishop Gilbert Burnet, vol. 1, pp. 44-45. In 1753, however, she declared: "Nature has not plac'd us in an inferior Rank to Men, no more than the Females of other

Animals, where we see no distinction of capacity." Letter of 6 March 1753 to Lady Bute, vol. 3, p. 27.

22. Stenton, *English Woman*, p. 109.

23. Jarrett, *Age of Hogarth*, p. 106. See Jarrett's excellent discussion of women in eighteenth-century England, pp. 103-27.

24. John Langdon-Davies, *A Short History of Women* (London, 1938), p. 228, as cited in Richard Lewinsohn's *History of Sexual Customs* (London, 1958), p. 233.

25. William Alexander, *The History of Women, from the Earliest Antiquity, to the Present Time*, 2 vols. (Dublin, 1749), vol. 1, p. 106.

26. An anonymous eighteenth-century source cited in Georgina Hill, *Women in English Life from Mediaeval to Modern Times*, 2 vols. (London, 1896), vol. 1, p. 313.

27. [Fulke Greville], *Maxims, Characters, and Reflections: Critical, Satyrical, and Moral* (London, 1757), p. 127.

28. Alexander, *History of Women*, vol. 1, p. 403.

29. Pierre Jean Grosley, *A Tour to London; or New Observations on England and its Inhabitants*, 2 vols., trans. Thomas Nugent (London, 1772), vol. 1, p. 252.

30. Ibid., vol. 1, p. 243.

31. [Marquis of Halifax], *The Lady's New Year Gift: or Advice to a Daughter* (London, 1688), pp. 28, 32, 25-26.

32. Ibid., pp. 39, 43.

33. Adburgham, *Women in Print*, p. 34.

34. Philip Dormer Stanhope, Lord Chesterfield, *The Letters of Philip Dormer Stanhope, Fourth Earl of Chesterfield*, 6 vols., ed. Bonamy Dobrée (London, 1932), vol. 4, p. 1209.

35. Pat Rogers, *The Augustan Vision* (London, 1974), pp. 89-91.

36. G. E. and K. R. Fussel, *The English Countrywoman: A Farmhouse Social History* A.D. *1500-1900* (London, 1953), p. 112. "Women trained in the great houses made excellent wives for the farmers of the village that lived in its shadow. Some of them married the chaplain who had been employed in the same house." (p. 91) Mr. B.'s concern over Parson Williams is more understandable within such a social context.

37. Halifax, *Lady's Gift*, p. 25.

38. Eaves and Kimpel, *Samuel Richardson*, p. 557. See Law-

rence Stone, *The Family, Sex and Marriage in England, 1500-1800* (London, 1977), pp. 180-91, for a discussion of parental control and marriage in the propertied classes. His chapter on "Mating Arrangements," pp. 270-324, is most helpful.

39. G. E. Mingay, *English Landed Society in the Eighteenth Century* (London, 1963), p. 225.

40. Madame d'Arblay [Fanny Burney], *Diary and Letters of Madame d'Arblay (1778-1840)*, 6 vols., ed. Austin Dobson (London, 1904), vol. 4, pp. 325-26.

41. *The Autobiography and Correspondence of Mary Granville, Mrs. Delany: with interesting reminiscences of King George the Third and Queen Charlotte*, 3 vols., ed. Lady Llanover (London, 1861), vol. 1, pp. 23-28.

42. As cited in Eaves and Kimpel, *Samuel Richardson*, p. 174.

43. Curiously, Mrs. Delany's second husband, the Reverend Patrick Delany, upheld the rights of the parent over the child in matrimonial manners. In his *Sermons upon Social Duties*, he claimed that "as long as children continue a part of their parent's family, (which must be till they think fit to dispose otherwise of them,) they are absolutely in their parents' power, and have no more right to dispose of themselves than they have to dispose of the parents' fortune, or inheritance, or any of their goods." Although he warns parents not to "offer violence to their inclinations, by forcing them to marry against their will, he claims that "it were infinitely better, that perverse children should actually die in the disappointment of their inclinations, than that they should make both themselves and their parents for ever miserable, by an unfortunate and undutiful marriage." Reprinted in *Family Lectures* (1815), p. 706, as cited in A. D. McKillop's *Samuel Richardson, Printer and Novelist* (Chapel Hill, 1936), p. 135.

44. *Diary of Madame d'Arblay*, vol. 1, p. 257.

45. Ibid., vol. 1, pp. 233-40. W. Jackson Bate's account of Henry Thrale's infatuation with "the S. S." sheds light on this scene. Mrs. Thrale, well aware of the rival she found in Sophy, had reason for her malice. W. Jackson Bate, *Samuel Johnson* (New York, 1977), pp. 548-51.

46. See Sterne's description of his sentimental traveler's attempt to write a love letter:

"I begun and begun again; and though I had nothing to say, and that nothing might have been express'd in half a dozen lines, I made half a dozen different beginnings, and could no way please myself.

In short, I was in no mood to write.

La Fleur stepp'd out and brought a little water in a glass to dilute my ink—then fetch'd sand and seal-wax—It was all one: I wrote, and blotted, and tore off, and burnt, and wrote again— *Le Diable l'emporte!* said I half to myself—I cannot write this self-same letter; throwing the pen down despairingly as I said it."

Characteristically, Yorick undercuts his sentimentality with an ironically practical solution. He copies a letter La Fleur pulls out of his "little dirty pocket-book," written by a drummer in his regiment to a corporal's wife, "which, he durst say, would suit the occasion." Laurence Sterne, *A Sentimental Journey Through France and Italy by Mr. Yorick*, ed. Gardner Stout, Jr. (Berkeley and Los Angeles, 1967), pp. 151-52.

47. John Gregory, *A Father's Legacy to his Daughters* (London, 1775), pp. 87-88.

48. In this study, the sadist provokes pain, hurts people, and enjoys their suffering. The masochist values and even enjoys his or her pain. Ian Watt argues that sadism is "the ultimate form which the eighteenth-century view of the masculine role involved: and it makes the female role one in which the woman is, and can only be, the prey." Ian Watt, *The Rise of the Novel: Studies in Defoe, Richardson and Fielding* (Berkeley and Los Angeles, 1967), p. 231. William Lecky cites several examples of the eighteenth-century Englishman's more sadistic pastimes. Bearbaiting, boxing, and cockfighting were very popular. Ducks were hunted down by dogs in special ducking ponds. There was even a variation of cockfighting—cock-throwing—in which a cock was tied to a post "as a mark for sticks, which were thrown at it from a distance till it was killed." William Lecky, *A History of England in the Eighteenth Century*, 8 vols. (London, 1878-80), vol. 1, pp. 552-54.

49. Richardson published Hill's comments in the introduction to the second edition of *Pamela* (1741), eds. T. C. Duncan Eaves and Ben D. Kimpel (Boston, 1971), p. 19.

50. *The Art of Governing a Wife: with Rules for Batchelors. To*

Which is added, an Essay Against Unequal Marriages (London, 1747), p. 46.

51. Mrs. Mary Davys, "The Accomplished Fine Rake, or Modern Fine Gentleman," *Four Before Richardson*, ed. William McBurney (Lincoln, Nebr., 1963), p. 315.

52. Philippa Pullar, *Consuming Passions: A History of English Food and Appetite* (London, 1972), pp. 150-51.

53. Jarrett, *Age of Hogarth*, p. 113.

54. Mark Kinkead-Weekes, *Samuel Richardson: Dramatic Novelist* (London, 1973), p. 291.

Three. Down from the Pedestal

1. September 1818, p. 408, as cited in Gordon Rattray Taylor, *The Angel Makers: A Study in the Psychological Origins of Historical Change* (London, 1958), p. 277.

2. The Magdalen House was founded in 1758 to reclaim penitent fallen women. Richardson became one of the governors of the charity in 1760. The Magdalen House did not seem to be a controversial charity: Lady Bradshaigh, visiting the institution in 1759, wrote Richardson that she "thought [herself] in a congregation of saints." T. C. Duncan Eaves and Ben D. Kimpel, *Samuel Richardson: A Biography* (Oxford, 1971), p. 465. Jonas Hanway, however, at first declined to support the house, explaining that "for a man under forty to do so would be to call forth the comments of the unkind." Dorothy Marshall, *Dr. Johnson's London* (New York, 1968), p. 279. Richardson was safely over forty.

The Memoirs of Mrs. Laetitia Pilkington, 3 vols. (Dublin, 1748) tell her uneven history. She was frequently in financial distress. When Patrick Delany gave her twelve guineas in answer to one of her pleas, she received the money from his agent, Mr. Richardson of Salisbury Court, who generously gave her two guineas more, "with a Sweetness and Modesty almost peculiar to himself." (vol. 2, pp. 238-39) She later asked Richardson to supply her with pens, "gilt paper," and linen for her unfortunate child, who arrived at her door "big with child, naked and desolate." Eaves and Kimpel, *Samuel Richardson*, p. 178. In her sympathetic account of Mrs. Pilkington's trials, Virginia Woolf places her in the "great tradition of English women of letters. It is her duty to entertain; it is her instinct to conceal." Virginia Woolf, "The Lives of the Obscure," *The Common Reader*, first series (London, 1968), p. 161.

3. W. de Archenholtz, *A Picture of England* (London, 1797), pp. 302, 308.

4. Henri Misson, *Memoirs and Observations in his Travels Over England. With Some Account of Scotland and Ireland* (London, 1719), p. 60.

5. Pierre Jean Grosley, *A Tour to London; or New Observations on England and its Inhabitants*, 2 vols., trans. Thomas Nugent (London, 1772), vol. 1, p. 55.

6. Patrick Colquhoun, *A Treatise on Indigence, exhibiting a General View of the National Resources for Productive Labour* (London, 1806), pp. 38-43.

7. Leon Radzinowicz, *Cross-Currents in the Movement for the Reform of the Police*, vol. 3, p. 243 (1956) of *A History of English Criminal Law and its Administration from 1750*, 4 vols. (London, 1948-68).

8. *Tricks of the Town: Being Reprints of Three Eighteenth-Century Tracts*, ed. Ralph Straus (London, 1927), p. 23.

9. Ibid., p. 113.

10. Ibid., p. 189.

11. W. de Archenholtz, *England und Italien* (Liepzig, 1787), vol. 2, p. 257, as cited in Ivan Block's *History of English Sexual Morals*, trans. William H. Forstern (London, 1936), p. 100.

12. Sir John Fielding, *A Brief Description of the Cities of London and Westminster* (London, 1776), p. xxvii.

13. [Richard King] *The New Cheats of London* (London, n.d.), p. 25, and *Oxford Magazine* (1771), vol. 6, p. 82, as cited in J. Jean Hecht's *The Domestic Servant Class in Eighteenth-Century England* (London, 1956), p. 31.

14. Jonas Hanway, *Virtue in Humble Life*, 2 vols. (London, 1774), vol. 2, p. 223.

15. Dorothy Marshall, *The English Domestic Servant in History* (London, 1949), p. 12.

16. John Moir, *Female Tuition* (Dublin, 1787), p. 182, as cited in Derek Jarrett, *England in the Age of Hogarth* (St. Albans, Herts., 1976), p. 86.

17. Michael Ryan, *Prostitution in London, with a Comparative View of that of Paris and New York* (London, 1839), p. 173.

18. *The Complete Letters of Lady Mary Wortley Montagu*, 3

vols., ed. Robert Halsband (Oxford, 1965-67), letter of 1 March 1752 to Lady Bute, vol. 3, p. 9. Lady Mary speaks from experience here. When Edward Wortley refused to entail his property, Lady Mary's father rejected him as a suitor. Ready "to abandon all for him—Fame, Family, and Settlement," Lady Mary eloped with him in 1712. Robert Halsband, *The Life of Lady Mary Wortley Montagu* (Oxford, 1956), p. 24. After reading *Clarissa*, Lady Mary wrote to her daughter: "This Richardson is a strange Fellow. I heartily despise him, and eagerly read him, nay, sob over his work in a most scandalous manner. The first two tomes of Clarissa touch'd me as being very ressembling to my Maiden Days." Montagu, *The Complete Letters*, letter of 22 September 1755 to Lady Bute, vol. 3, p. 90. Halsband notes that the "aftermath of her elopement did not match Clarissa's. Wortley was no Lovelace; he lacked his charms as well as his vices." (p. 28) Indeed, Wortley's well-known meanness and his ambition to build up a great estate make him appear more like Solmes than Lovelace. When Wortley died, Lady Mary's bluestocking relative Elizabeth Montagu, estimating the size of his estate to be the "most notable sum" of £800,000 in money and £17,000 a year in land, wished that it might "make his heirs as happy and illustrious as the getting it made him anxious and odious." (p. 276)

19. R. F. Brissenden, *Virtue in Distress: Studies in the Novels of Sentiment from Richardson to Sade* (London, 1974), p. 185. Judith Wilt makes the "immodest proposal" that Lovelace never did actually rape Clarissa, arguing that when he reports to Belford that he can go "no farther," he is confessing his impotence. The women of Sinclair's house, versatile in the "breaking in" of young creatures, do the job. Wilt cites Clarissa's "visionary remembrances . . . of female figures flitting" before her and Clarissa's excessive fear of Mrs. Sinclair's "worse than masculine violence," claiming that Clarissa at last "learns the lesson Lovelace has insisted upon all along, the real enemy of woman is woman." "He Could Go No Farther: A Modest Proposal about Lovelace and Clarissa," *Proceedings of the Modern Language Association*, vol. 92, no. 1 (1977), p. 27.

20. "In the spring of 1775 a London tooth-drawer had his dead wife embalmed by a famous anatomist and placed in a glass case in his drawing room. 'Though she has been dead three

months she looks as well as when alive,' another wife told her husband in some wonderment." Jarrett, *Age of Hogarth*, p. 121.

21. A person convicted of a nonclergyable offense could not plead "Benefit of Clergy." "Originally, Benefit of Clergy meant that an ordained clerk charged with felony could be tried only in the ecclesiastical courts. But in course of time it entirely changed its nature. It became a complicated set of rules, exempting from capital punishment certain persons found guilty of certain felonies, which were not abolished till 1827. . . . Thus when a statute imposed capital punishment without benefit of clergy an offender found guilty of the relevant offence had to be sentenced to death." Radzinowicz, *A History of English Criminal Law* (London, 1948), vol. 1, p. 3.

22. Ibid., p. 632.

23. Ibid., pp. 440-42.

24. William Alexander, *The History of Women, from the Earliest Antiquity, to the Present Time*, 2 vols. (Dublin, 1749), vol. 2, p. 415.

25. William Blackstone, *Commentaries on the Laws of England*, 4 vols. (London, 1775), vol. 4, p. 211.

26. *The Poems of Jonathan Swift*, 3 vols., ed. Harold Williams (Oxford, 1958), vol. 2, p. 519.

27. Blackstone, *Commentaries*, vol. 4, pp. 211, 213-14.

28. *The Trial of Frederick Calvert, Esquire . . . for a Rape on the Body of Sarah Woodcock. . . . Taken in Shorthand by Joseph Gurney* (London, 1768), pp. 92-93, 230. The judge was Sydney Stafford Smythe.

29. Block, *Sexual Morals*, p. 283. "He fed the fat ones only with acids, the thin ones on a milk diet and beef-tea."

30. Philip Dormer Stanhope, Lord Chesterfield, *The Letters of Philip Dormer Stanhope, Fourth Earl of Chesterfield*, 6 vols., ed. Bonamy Dobrée (London, 1932), vol. 1, p. 176.

31. T. C. Muilman, *An Apology for the Conduct of Mrs. Teresia Constantia Phillips* (London, 1748), pp. 36, 38.

32. Chesterfield, *Letters*, vol. 1, p. 177.

33. E. Beresford Chancellor, *Colonel Charteris and the Duke of Wharton, Lives of the Rakes* (London, 1925), p. 5.

34. Ibid., p. 82.

35. *Some Authentick Memoirs of the Life of Colonel Ch——s,*

Rape-Master-General of Great Britain. By an Impartial Hand (London, 1730), p. 14.

36. *Authentick Memoirs*, pp. 37-40; Chancellor, *Charteris*, pp. 64-67. *The Proceedings . . . upon a Bill of Indictment found against Francis Charteris, Esq; for Committing a Rape on the Body of Anne Bond, of which he was found Guilty* (London, 1730).

37. Susan Brownmiller, *Against our Will: Men, Women and Rape* (New York, 1975), p. 28.

38. In the nineteenth century, Arthur J. Munby, civil servant, barrister, and minor poet, secretly married his servant after a clandestine relationship that had already been going on for sixteen years. Mrs. Hannah Munby, whose great joy was to show herself to her husband "in her dirt," preferred the role of servant to that of mistress, and refused to relinquish her lowly position, even sleeping in the kitchen occasionally after her marriage. She especially enjoyed cleaning "Massa's" boots, and frequently posed for his extensive photographic collection of working women, once blackening herself "from head to foot" and standing "almost nude" in "her noblest guise—that of a chimney sweep." On that occasion, Munby asked his diary, "Do I respect her less . . . because I allowed such degradation?" Munby reported with delight that after a genteel weekend in Southend at the Royal Hotel, where Hannah played "lady" in her "rich black dress" and "dainty gloves," she returned home happily to scrub the fender. "Her bare round arms were streaked and disfigured with soot and grime: but her face was soot all over—absolute blackness, so that not a feature could be distinguished." *Munby, Man of Two Worlds: The Life and Diaries of Arthur J. Munby 1828-1910*, ed. Derek Hudson (London, 1972), pp. 133, 360-61.

39. Andrew Moreton, Esquire [Daniel Defoe], *Everybody's Business is Nobody's Business; or Private Abuses, Publick Grievances: Exemplified in the Pride, Insolence, and Exorbitant Wages of Our Women Servants, Footmen, &c.* (London, 1725), pp. 4-5.

40. Grosley, *Tour*, vol. 1, p. 75.

41. *Tricks of the Town*, pp. 194-95.

42. Moreton [Defoe], *Everybody's Business*, p. 7.

43. *Prose Works of Jonathan Swift*, 14 vols., ed. Herbert Davis (Oxford, 1959), vol. 13, p. 57.

44. Richard Steele, *The Theatre*, no. 6, 19 January 1719-20, in the collection *The Theatre, to which are Added, The Anti-Theatre* (London, 1791), pp. 47-48.

45. Sir John Fielding, *A Brief Description*, pp. xxviii-ix; E. B. Chancellor, *The Annals of Covent Garden and its Neighbourhood* (London, 1930), pp. 56-57.

46. Thomas J. Barratt, *The Annals of Hampstead*, 2 vols. (London, 1912), vol. 1, p. 214. Stella Margetson, in *Leisure and Pleasure in the Eighteenth Century* (London, 1970), p. 58, records the "ups and downs" of Hampstead. Its reputation declined when the "riff-raff of the city, the gamblers and loose women of the town, found their way there," in the early half of the eighteenth century.

47. Captain Alexander Smith, *The School of Venus, or Cupid Restor'd to Sight* (London, 1716), p. A5.

48. [Ned Ward], *The Secret History of Clubs* (London, 1709), pp. 305-307.

49. Henry Meister, *Letters Written during a Residence in England* (London, 1799), p. 287.

50. Richard King, *The Frauds of London Detected* (London, 1770), pp. 13-14, as cited in Block, *Sexual Morals*, pp. 167-68.

51. Archenholtz, *England und Italien*, pp. 100-101, as cited in Block, *Sexual Morals*, pp. 66-67.

52. Block, *Sexual Morals*, pp. 189-90.

53. Georgina Hill, *Women in English Life from Mediaeval to Modern Times*, 2 vols. (London, 1896), vol. 1, p. 317.

54. John J. Richetti, *Popular Fiction Before Richardson: Narrative Patterns 1700-1739* (Oxford, 1969), p. 35.

55. Captain Charles Walker, *Authentick Memoirs of the Life, Intrigues and Adventures of the Celebrated Sally Salisbury with True Characters of her Most Considerable Gallants* (London, 1723), p. 8.

56. Captain [Christopher] Johnson, *The History of the Life and Intrigues of that Celebrated Courtezan, and Posture Mistress, Eliz. Mann* (London, 1724), p. 2.

57. Mary Davys, "The Accomplished Fine Rake, or Modern Fine Gentleman," *Four Before Richardson*, ed. William McBurney (Lincoln, Nebr., 1963), p. 372.

58. [Hugh Kelly], *Memoirs of a Magdalen, or the History of Louisa Mildmay*, 2 vols. (London, 1767), vol. 1, pp. 153, 155.

59. Ibid., vol. 2, p. 129.

60. Henry Fielding, *The History of Tom Jones: A Foundling* (1749), 2 vols., ed. Fredson Bowers (Oxford, 1975), vol. 1, p. 155.

61. Oliver Goldsmith, "She Stoops to Conquer," vol. 5 of the *Collected Works of Oliver Goldsmith*, 5 vols., ed. Arthur Friedman (Oxford, 1966), act 3, scene 1, p. 129.

62. Paul E. Parnell, "The Sentimental Mask," *Restoration Drama: Modern Essays in Criticism*, ed. John Loftis (New York, 1966), p. 289.

63. Richard Steele, "The Conscious Lovers," *The Plays of Richard Steele*, ed. Shirley S. Kenny (Oxford, 1971), act 5, scene 3, p. 375.

64. Richard Cumberland, "The West Indian," *Eighteenth-Century Plays*, ed. John Hampden (London, 1964), act 4, scene 2, p. 384.

65. Ibid., act 5, scene 5, pp. 400-401; act 5, scene 8, p. 406.

66. When Wortley tried to learn the size of Lady Mary's dowry, she denied knowing it: "People in my way are sold like slaves; and I cannot tell what price my master will put on me." Halsband, *Life of Lady Mary*, p. 16.

67. David Garrick and George Colman, "The Clandestine Marriage," *The Plays of David Garrick: Garrick's Own Plays, 1740-1766*, 2 vols., eds. H. W. Pedicard and F. L. Bergmann (Carbondale and Edwardsville, Ill., 1980), act 3, scene 1; vol. 1, pp. 295-96.

68. Pat Rogers, *Grub Street* (London, 1972), p. 143.

69. In a letter to Lady Bradshaigh, Richardson suggested that Belford "perhaps has too high Notions of her Excellencies," when he makes these remarks. (*Letters*, p. 107)

70. *The Lady's Magazine*, September 1818, p. 408, and *The Gentleman's Magazine* (1762), vol. 32, no. 1, p. 69, as cited in Taylor, *Angel Makers*, p. 277.

71. In "A Special Type of Object Choice Made by Men," *Sexuality and the Psychology of Love*, ed. Philip Rieff (New York, 1970), p. 55, Sigmund Freud argues that men love "harlots" because their infantile feelings have been fixated on their moth-

ers. When the male child learns that his parents indulge in the "ugly sexual behaviour of the rest of the world," he decides that the difference between his mother and a whore is not so great, since "at bottom they both do the same thing." Freud's argument can be extended to explain the difference between the saint (asexual mother) and the whore (sexual mother). Gordon Rattray Taylor also attacks the problem of the saint/whore split in *The Angel Makers*, applying his theory of parental identification to explain it. Relying heavily on Freud's theory of the Oedipus complex, Taylor divides the world into Matrists (uninhibited, romantic, and oral) and Patrists (repressed, classical, and anal).

72. See Ian Watt, *The Rise of the Novel: Studies in Defoe, Richardson and Fielding* (Berkeley and Los Angeles, 1967), pp. 144-46, and Lawrence Stone, *The Family, Sex and Marriage in England, 1500-1800* (London, 1977), pp. 380-86, on the social problems spinsters faced in the eighteenth century.

73. John Gregory, *A Father's Legacy to his Daughters* (London, 1775), pp. 87-88.

74. His argument directly relates to patrilineal descent. "Whereas a *naughty wife* often makes the children of *another man* heirs of her husband's estate and fortune, in injury of his *own children* or *family*. So tho' the crime may be equal *in other respects*, yet this makes the injury of the woman to the man, greater than *his* can be to *her*." (*Familiar Letters*, p. 63) Or as Samuel Johnson put it: "Consider, of what importance to society the chastity of women is. Upon that all the property in the world depends. We hang a thief for stealing a sheep; but the unchastity of a woman transfers sheep, and farm and all, from the right owner." James Boswell, *Journal of a Tour to the Hebrides, with Samuel Johnson, LLD*, ed. Allan Wendt (Boston, 1965), p. 250. See Stone, *Family, Sex and Marriage*, pp. 501-507, on the double standard.

75. "Epistle to a Lady," *Poems of Alexander Pope*, ed. John Butt (New Haven, 1963), p. 562.

76. "The Lady's Dressing Room," *The Poems of Jonathan Swift*, vol. 2, pp. 525-30.

77. See Leslie Fiedler, *Love and Death in the American Novel* (New York, 1960), pp. 29-42.

78. Joseph Wood Krutch, *Five Masters: A Study in the Mutations of the Novel* (New York, 1931), p. 159.

Four. Horrid Romancing

1. Iona and Peter Opie, *The Classic Fairy Tales* (London, 1974), frontispiece.

2. A. D. McKillop, *Samuel Richardson, Printer and Novelist* (Chapel Hill, 1936), p. 45. "The oft-repeated story of the good people of Slough, who gathered at the village smithy to hear *Pamela* read aloud, and at last went off in a group to ring the church-bells in honor of her marriage . . . is significant because it shows how *Pamela* took hold of what we may call the folk-imagination."

3. A letter by that "anonymous gentleman," Aaron Hill, published in the introduction to the second edition of *Pamela* (1741), complains that "Females are too apt to be struck with Images of Beauty; and that Passage where the Gentleman is said to span the Waist of *Pamela* with his Hand, is enough to ruin a Nation of Women by Tight-lacing." Richardson objected to this "too *tight-laced* Objection. . . . What, in the Name of Unshapliness! cou'd he find, to complain of, in a beautiful Girl of Sixteen, who was born *out of Germany*, and had not, yet, reach'd ungraspable *Roundness*," he wonders, neatly side-stepping Hill's point. *Pamela*, eds. T. C. Duncan Eaves and Ben D. Kimpel, (Boston, 1971), pp. 13, 16.

In *An Apology for the Life of Mrs. Shamela Andrews* (1741), Parson Oliver, Fielding's moral spokesman, objects to the instruction he finds in *Pamela*: "To look out for their masters as sharp as they can." The consequences: "If the Master is not a fool, they will be debauched by him; and if he is a fool, they will marry him." *Joseph Andrews and Shamela*, ed. Martin C. Battestin (Boston, 1961), p. 307.

4. When I talk about "reality" and the ways of rendering reality, I shall be using Ian Watt's definition of "formal realism": "the narrative embodiment of a premise that Defoe and Richardson accepted very literally, but which is implicit in the novel form in general: the premise, or primary convention, that the novel is a full and authentic report of human experience, and is therefore under an obligation to satisfy its reader with such details of the story as the individuality of the actors concerned, the particulars of the times and places of their actions, details which are presented through a more largely referential use of language than is common in other literary forms." Ian

Watt, *Rise of the Novel: Studies in Defoe, Richardson and Fielding* (Berkeley and Los Angeles, 1967), p. 32.

5. Samuel Richardson, *Clarissa: Preface, Hints of Prefaces and Postscripts*, ed. R. F. Brissenden for the Augustan Reprint Society, no. 103 (Los Angeles, 1964), p. 8.

6. T. C. Duncan Eaves and Ben D. Kimpel, *Samuel Richardson: A Biography* (Oxford, 1971), pp. 76-77.

7. Samuel Richardson, *A Collection of the Moral and Instructive Sentiments, Maxims, Cautions, and Reflexions, Contained in the Histories of Pamela, Clarissa, and Sir Charles Grandison* (London, 1755), pp. 8, 4.

8. Richardson, *Moral Maxims*, pp. vii, ix.

9. Roland Barthes, *Writing Degree Zero* (London, 1967), p. 9.

10. Hill's letter about his precocious servant boy, as well as his fear of Mrs. Jewkes, was included in the introduction to the second edition of *Pamela* (1741), eds. Eaves and Kimpel, pp. 18-19. Watt, *Rise of the Novel*, cites Hill's fears in his discussion of the "deep and unqualified identification" between Richardson's readers and characters. (pp. 200-203) In *Shamela* (p. 305), Fielding is actually transcribing the raptures of Aaron Hill, which Richardson included in his introduction to the second edition of *Pamela*: "If I lay the Book down, it comes after me.—When it has dwelt all Day long upon the Ear, It takes Possession, all Night, of the Fancy.—It has Witchcraft in every Page of it: but it is the Witchcraft of Passion and Meaning." *Pamela*, eds. Eaves and Kimpel, p. 10.

11. In his *Letters on Chivalry and Romance* (1762), Richard Hurd described the "revolution" in taste in the eighteenth century's "anti-romantic" bridling of fancy and the imagination. "What we have gotten by this revolution, you will say, is a great deal of good sense. What we have lost is a world of fine fabling." W. P. Ker cites Hurd in his essay on "Romance," *Pastoral and Romance: Modern Essays in Criticism*, ed. Eleanor Terry Lincoln (Englewood Cliffs, N.J., 1969), pp. 235-36. He goes on to suggest that the world of fables and romance was preserved in the nursery.

12. Arthur Johnston, *Enchanted Ground: The Study of Medieval Romance in the Eighteenth Century* (London, 1964), p. 35.

13. From *The Athenian Mercury*, 17 December 1692, as cited

in *Novel and Romance, 1700-1800: A Documentary Record,* ed. Ioan Williams (London, 1970), p. 29.

14. Johnston, *Enchanted Ground,* pp. 27-28.

15. Ibid., p. 30.

16. Ibid., pp. 32-33.

17. Ibid., p. 37. Richardson refers to the ballad entitled "The Lovers Quarrel: of Cupid's Triumph. Being The Pleasant History of fair Rosamond of Scotland. Being Daughter to the Lord *Arundel,* whose Love was obtained by the Valour of *Tommy Pots*: who conquered the Lord *Phenix,* and wounded him, and after obtained her to be his Wife. Being very delightful to Read. *London,* Printed by *A. P.* for *F. Coles, T. Vere,* and *J. Wright"* [?1675] as cited in Jonathan Swift, *A Tale of a Tub,* ed. A. C. Guthkelch and D. Nichol Smith (Oxford, 1968), p. 69.

18. Eaves and Kimpel, *Samuel Richardson,* pp. 11-12.

19. Ibid., p. 581.

20. Dieter Schulz, " 'Novel,' 'Romance,' and Popular Fiction in the First Half of the Eighteenth Century," *Studies in Philology,* vol. 7 (1973), pp. 80-83.

21. John Richetti, *Popular Fiction Before Richardson: Narrative Patterns, 1700-1739* (Oxford, 1969), pp. 175-76, 126-27, 125. See Ira Konigsberg's study of Richardson's own connections to the drama in *Samuel Richardson and the Dramatic Novel* (Lexington, Ky., 1968).

22. Henry Knight Miller, "Augustan Prose Fiction and the Romance Tradition," *Studies in the Eighteenth Century,* vol. 3, ed. R. F. Brissenden and J. C. Eade (Toronto, 1976), p. 249.

23. Johnston, *Enchanted Ground,* p. 40.

24. Opies, *Classic Fairy Tales,* p. 50.

25. Ibid., p. 117.

26. See Melvyn New's discussion of the providential aspects of romance under secular stress. The eighteenth-century novel unites two conflicting visions of life at the moment of an uneasy transition, partially reconciling romance and realism, providence and secularization. " 'The Grease of God': The Form of Eighteenth-Century English Fiction," *Proceedings of the Modern Language Association,* vol. 91, no. 2 (March 1976), pp. 235-43.

27. Miller, "Romance Tradition," p. 254.

28. Henry Knight Miller, *Henry Fielding's Tom Jones and the*

Romance Tradition (Victoria, B.C., 1976), pp. 40-41. Miller also discusses the importance to the romance tradition of the "monomyth," that controlling pattern of "Departure (or Exile), Initiation, and Return—or in one of its more significant variants, Fall, Suffering, and Salvation." (p. 23)

29. The Opies, *Classic Fairy Tales*, p. 11, do not consider the happy ending inevitable in the fairy tale. "Most events in fairy tales are remarkable for their unpleasantness. . . . in some . . . there is no happy ending, not even the hero or heroine escaping with their life." I suspect, however, that the common reader's tendency to "overlook" the unhappy ending reveals a desire for reconciliation stronger than the "reality" of the tale.

30. In *The English Novel: Form and Function* (New York, 1967), Dorothy Van Ghent's sensitive and influential essay on *Clarissa* introduces some compelling ideas about Richardson's use of myth. She maintains that myth "not only reflects the aspirations and ideals, the attitudes and customs of a large social group, but also seems to give to these attitudes and customs the sanction of some 'higher authority.' " (p. 69) However, many of her ideas about myth seem more pertinent to a discussion of *Pamela* than of *Clarissa*. Van Ghent claims that Clarissa "by her death" symbolically "makes great her class, giving supernatural sanction to its code," donating her "mana," and "making of it an embodiment of the order of the universe." (p. 74) But in her death, Clarissa leaves behind a society greatly dislocated, symbolizing chaos, not order. She elevates herself at the expense of the middle-class Harlovian society that has condemned her unorthodox actions. *Pamela*, on the other hand, uncritically celebrates the middle-class virtues. Her triumph rewards the "virtue" of her readers, and "reflects the aspirations and ideals, the attitudes and customs" of her class, granting them the sanction of the highest authority. God and Richardson smile on Pamela because she represents the proper virtues.

31. Mircea Eliade, *Myth and Reality* (London, 1964), pp. 5-6. In *The Uses of Enchantment: The Meaning and Importance of Fairy Tales* (London, 1976), p. 35, Bruno Bettelheim cites Eliade as saying that "every man wants to experience certain perilous situations, to confront exceptional ordeals, to make his way into the Other World—and he experiences all this, on the level of his imaginative life, by hearing or reading fairy tales."

32. G. K. Chesterton, *All Things Considered* (1908), as cited in Opies', *Classic Fairy Tales*, p. 9.

33. Bettelheim, *Uses of Enchantment*, p. 8.

34. Opies, *Classic Fairy Tales*, p. 11.

35. Ibid., p. 11.

36. See "Pamela's Clothes," by Carey McIntosh, reprinted in *Twentieth Century Interpretations of Pamela: A Collection of Essays*, ed. Rosemary Cowler (Englewood Cliffs, N.J., 1969), pp. 89-96.

37. Cited in Eaves and Kimpel, *Samuel Richardson*, p. 145.

38. Opies, *Classic Fairy Tales*, p. 15. In *The Fantastic in Literature* (Princeton, 1976), pp. 55-56, Eric S. Rabkin discusses the structural patterns dominating the fairy tale. He tests Vladimir Propp's theory of structural patterning against the plot of "Little Red Riding Hood." The first five structural functions Propp outlines are quite similar to the opening episodes of *Clarissa*:

1. One of the members of a family absents himself from home. [Clarissa was away from home when Lovelace first made his proposals to Arabella.]

2. An interdiction is addressed to the hero. [Lovelace's address to Clarissa is forbidden by her family.]

3. The interdiction is violated. [Clarissa continues to correspond with Lovelace clandestinely.]

4. The villain makes an attempt at reconnaissance. [Lovelace sets up an informant, Joseph, inside the Harlowe household.]

5. The villain receives information about his victim. [Lovelace learns about Clarissa from Anna Howe, Joseph, and even Clarissa herself.]

What complicates the structure, even in the first five episodes, is Lovelace's equivocal position. As both hero and villain, he will set Clarissa free from her family only to rape her, robbing her of herself.

39. Doody cites the two yew hedge passages to emphasize Clarissa's separation from her family, adding that the yew is "emblematic as well as realistic, as yew is an emblem of death." Margaret Doody, *A Natural Passion: A Study of the Novels of Samuel Richardson* (Oxford, 1974), p. 190.

40. Bettelheim, *Uses of Enchantment*, p. 144.

41. See Bettelheim's discussion of "The Frog King," *Uses of*

Enchantment, pp. 286-91. He connects the fear of the slimy, loathsome frog to the adolescent fear of the more unattractive, "slimy" aspects of sex.

42. Kinkead-Weekes's discussion of the rape and Clarissa's subsequent madness is especially sensitive to Richardson's presentation of the disintegration and reintegration of Clarissa's personality as expressed in her cryptic papers. Mark Kinkead-Weekes, *Samuel Richardson: Dramatic Novelist* (London, 1973), pp. 231-42.

43. José Ortega y Gasset, "A Short Treatise on the Novel," *Meditations on Quixote* (New York, 1963), p. 137.

44. Kinkead-Weekes, *Dramatic Novelist*, p. 269.

45. Northrop Frye uses these phrases to distinguish the hero in a discussion of the archetypal characteristics of romance. In romance, the hero is "analogous to the mythical Messiah or deliverer who comes from an upper world, and his enemy is analogous to the demonic powers of a lower world. . . . The enemy is associated with winter, darkness, confusion, sterility, moribund life, and old age, and the hero with spring, dawn, order, fertility, vigor, and youth." "Archetypal Criticism: Theory of Myths," *Anatomy of Criticism* (Princeton, 1957), pp. 186-87. We can see the way Richardson mixes these characteristics in Lovelace, giving us a villain vigorous and sterile, bright and dark, a youth who disguises himself as an old man, revealing his real identity while masked.

46. See Gillian Beer's "Richardson, Milton, and the Status of Evil," *Review of English Studies*, new series, vol. 19, no. 75 (1968) pp. 261-70. John Milton, "Paradise Lost," *Complete Poems and Major Prose*, ed. Merritt Y. Hughes (New York, 1957), book IV, lines 375-78, p. 287.

47. Watt, *Rise of the Novel*, p. 234.

48. Preface to *Sir Charles Grandison*, ed. Jocelyn Harris (London, 1972), vol. 1, p. xvi.

49. See Morris Golden's listing of the parallels between Richardson's works and the "pious" romance *Télémaque*, by Fénelon, a frequently translated favorite of both Clarissa and Pamela. Morris Golden, *Richardson's Characters* (Ann Arbor, 1963), p. 200.

50. Richardson, *Hints of Prefaces*, p. 5.

51. Golden, *Characters*, p. 27.

52. Tomlinson's real identity comes as no surprise to Richardson's ideally "attentive" reader, who consults the "Names of the Principal Persons," in which Tomlinson is listed as "the assumed name of a vile pander to the debaucheries of Mr. Lovelace." Richardson expects his reader to be ever vigilant, trusting no one, not even the author.

53. Ivan Block reports that "marriage by purchase continued in England up to the nineteenth century." It was especially frequent at the end of the eighteenth century, when he finds Archenholtz reporting that "never was the sale of women so frequent . . . as now. Scenes of this kind, once so rare, have become common. The sale of women among the common people is more frequent than ever." Often, "the husband led his wife with a rope round her neck, on a market day, to the place where cattle were sold, bound her to a post and sold her to the highest bidder in the presence of the necessary witnesses." Her price was seldom more than a few shillings. The "ordinary place in London where these sales of women were held was Smithfield Market, where . . . the cattle market was held." Ivan Block, *History of English Sexual Morals*, trans. William H. Forstern (London, 1936), pp. 54-58. Derek Jarrett cites the example of John Lees, a steel burner in Sheffield, who sold his wife in 1796 to Samuel Hall, a fellmonger, for sixpence. "Mrs. Lees was handed over to her new owner with a halter round her neck; but since the clerk of the market took fourpence for toll it is hardly likely that the purpose of this offensive pantomime was monetary gain. This was in fact the labourer's equivalent of divorce by Act of Parliament," Derek Jarrett, *England in the Age of Hogarth* (St. Albans, Herts., 1976), p. 120.

54. William Hazlitt, "On the English Novelists," *Lectures on the English Comic Writers* (London, 1819), p. 233.

55. New, " 'The Grease of God,' " p. 241.

56. J.R.R. Tolkien, *Tree and Leaf* (London, 1974), p. 59.

Five. A Lovelace in Every Corner

1. Mark Kinkead-Weekes, *Samuel Richardson: Dramatic Novelist* (London, 1973), p. 495.

2. Morris Golden's perception of the identification Richardson has towards his rakes remains critically significant; Morris Golden, *Richardson's Characters* (Ann Arbor, 1963), pp. 2-3. I

would place more stress, however, on Richardson's conscious, deliberate investment in his characters. To view his characters as passional, dramatically cut off from their moral and sociological context, is to discount what for me is the most interesting aspect of Richardson's novels, the tension between the moral and the aesthetic. Golden rightly points to Richardson's postured sadism in his letters and novels, as well as to the fantasy of dominance pervading his work. (pp. 6-23) I would only push the connection further, finding them a logical albeit convoluted result of the perfectionism that is always at the core of his writing. Richardson the man was always trying to remake himself. John Traugott seems the most sensitive critic on this point, paying strict attention to Richardson the man as he remakes himself into the artist. In his essay, *"Clarissa's* Richardson," *English Literature in the Age of Disguise* (Berkeley and Los Angeles, 1977), pp. 157-208, he attends to Clarissa's Richardson, "the perfected figure who interests us, for there he mastered the banal Richardson," (p. 173) This need to transcend himself, not necessarily to dominate others, seems crucial to an understanding of Richardson the artist.

3. The most enlightening records of rakes are Louis C. Jones, *The Clubs of the Georgian Rakes* (New York, 1942); E. B. Chancellor, *Lives of the Rakes*, 6 vols. (London, 1924-25); Geoffery Ashe, *Do What You Will: A History of Anti-Morality* (London, 1974); and Robert J. Allen, *Clubs of Augustan London* (Cambridge, Mass., 1933). William Lecky mentions the Mohocks in *A History of England in the Eighteenth Century*, 8 vols. (London, 1878-80), vol. 1, pp. 482-83. See also Donald McCormick, *The Hell Fire Club* (London, 1958). Ned Ward describes hell fire clubs in *The Secret History of Clubs* (London, 1709).

4. Jones, *The Georgian Rakes*, p. 95.

5. Information about the order is often contradictory and confusing. In *Sir Francis Dashwood: An Eighteenth-Century Independent* (London, 1967), Betty Kemp considers the order's infamous reputation to be part of a political smear campaign. (pp. 131-36) Much of the information about the order comes from an unfriendly source, John Wilkes, a former friar. Charles Johnstone added to Wilkes's account in his satirical novel *Chrysal, or the Adventures of a Guinea*, in which he reports supposed

orgies and blasphemies. See Ashe *Do What You Will*, and Jones, *The Georgian Rakes*, for extensive discussions of the order and the abbey.

6. Ashe, *Do What You Will*, p. 174.

7. John Traugott compares Richardson himself to Horner, the man of disguises and moral "guardian of the temple who unmasks to become its despoiler." "*Clarissa*'s Richardson," pp. 173-74.

8. "The Scowrers: A Comedy," *Works of Thomas Shadwell*, 4 vols. (London, 1720), act 2, scene 1, vol. 4, p. 328; act 4, scene 1, vol. 4, p. 372.

9. *Journal to Stella*, 2 vols., ed. Harold Williams (Oxford, 1948), vol. 2, pp. 508-9, 511-12, 509. We can find other contemporary references to the Mohocks in *The Spectator* papers, nos. 324, 332, 335, and 347. In 1709, four Mohock Indian Chiefs visited London to discuss a treaty with the government, arousing great interest. Jones, *The Georgian Rakes*, p. 19. John Gay mentions the Mohock exploits in *Trivia* and in his play *The Mohocks* (1712). Also see Lecky, *History*, vol. 1, pp. 482-83, and James Peller Malcom, *Anecdotes of the Manners and Customs of London During the Eighteenth Century* (London, 1808), p. 149.

10. After learning that Lovelace is a sober man, no gamester, has no financial obligations, and possesses a lively imagination and a surprising memory, Miss Howe still decides that "upon the whole," Mr. Lovelace is a "very faulty man." (I, 75) [I, 51]

11. Samuel Richardson, *The Richardson-Stinstra Correspondence and Stinstra's Prefaces to Clarissa*, ed. William C. Slattery (Carbondale and Edwardsville, Ill., 1969), p. 24.

12. T. C. Duncan Eaves and Ben D. Kimpel, *Samuel Richardson: A Biography* (Oxford, 1971), pp. 4-5.

13. Roy Pascal, *Design and Truth in Autobiography* (Cambridge, Mass., 1960). Pascal reminds us of Leslie Stephen's remark that "distortions of truth belong to the values of autobiography and are as revealing as the truth." (p. 62) See also pp. 176-78 for a discussion of the potential reality of invented situations.

14. Richardson, *Richardson-Stinstra Correspondence*, p. 25.

15. Eaves and Kimpel, *Samuel Richardson*, p. 30. See also

pp. 20-30. It is worth noting that the Reverend Edward Young, author of *Night Thoughts* and a good friend of Richardson, was another "moralist" involved personally with the Duke of Wharton. Young acted as Wharton's tutor until his sixteen-year-old pupil ran off to marry. When Wharton became a duke, he acted as Young's patron, once paying him £2,000 for *The Universal Passion*. According to Joseph Spence, when a friend of Wharton's commented on the large size of the gift, the Duke "smiled and said: 'It was the best bargain he ever made in his life, for he was fairly worth four thousand.' " Spence's *Anecdotes* (1858), p. 193, as cited in A. S. Collins, *Authorship in the Days of Johnson* (London, 1927), p. 139.

16. *Memoirs of the Life of His Grace, Philip, late Duke of Wharton. By an Impartial Hand* (London, 1731), pp. 4, 3.

17. "The True Briton," no. 25, *The Life and Writings of Philip, late Duke of Wharton*, 2 vols. (London, 1732), vol. 1, pp. 216-17.

18. Dr. Cheyne recommended that Richardson abstain from fermented liquors and from animal food in warm weather, and prescribed frequent vomits, cold baths, exercise, and chewing rhubarb. "He urged the virtues of a new machine called a chamber horse—some chamber horses had springs, but the one Cheyne describes is a chair set on a long board, which must have acted like a joggling board, supported at both ends and limber in the middle, with hoops to brace the arms and a footstool to support the feet, on which Richardson was to ride while reading or dictating." Eaves and Kimpel, *Samuel Richardson*, p. 63.

19. Max Byrd, *Visits to Bedlam: Madness and Literature in the Eighteenth Century* (Columbia, S.C., 1975), pp. 43, 54. In *Nightmares and Hobbyhorses: Swift, Sterne, and Augustan Ideas of Madness* (San Marino, Calif., 1974), p. 47, Michael V. DePorte also emphasizes the Augustan distrust of human singularity: "By drawing attention to the almost limitless possibilities for error, not to say madness, Locke, in particular, had made men both more conscious of human singularities and more distrustful of them." See also Michel Foucault, *Madness and Civilization: A History of Insanity in the Age of Reason*, trans. Richard Howard (New York, 1973).

20. The *Memoirs* of the Duke of Wharton describe a similar levity in the Duke, often resulting in manic practical jokes: "The

Poverty of his Circumstances prov'd a Fund of inexhaustible Humour; an empty Bottle was the Subject of many a dry Joke, and the want of a Dinner seem'd to whet more his Wit than his Stomach." (p. 32)

21. Ashe, *Do What You Will*, p. 103.

22. He asked Lady Bradshaigh to show him her diary and Miss Mulso to describe her rooms. See Malvin Zirker, "Richardson's Correspondence: The Personal Letter as Private Experience," in *The Familiar Letter in the Eighteenth Century*, eds. Howard Anderson et al. (Lawrence, Kans., 1966), p. 79.

23. Eaves and Kimpel, *Samuel Richardson*, pp. 537-38.

24. Watts suggests that Richardson "had a deep personal identification with the opposite sex which went far beyond social preference or cultural rapport. Such, certainly, is the implication of the fact that he was afraid of mice, or at least confessed to the future Mrs. Chapone, that he had 'ever had a kind of natural aversion to that species of animal.' " C. L. Thomson, *Samuel Richardson* (London, 1900), p. 93, as cited in Ian Watt, *The Rise of the Novel: Studies in Defoe, Richardson and Fielding* (Berkeley and Los Angeles, 1967), p. 153.

25. Christopher Marlowe, "The Tragical History of the Life and Death of Doctor Faustus," *The Works of Christopher Marlowe*, ed. C. F. Tucker Brooke (Oxford, 1969), p. 148, line 89.

26. Robert Halsband, *The Life of Lady Mary Wortley Montagu* (Oxford, 1956), p. 68.

27. James Boswell, *Journal of a Tour to the Hebrides with Samuel Johnson, LLD*, ed. Alan Wendt (Boston, 1965), p. 255.

28. Ivan Block, *History of English Sexual Morals*, trans. William H. Forstern (London, 1936), p. 133.

29. [Sophia Watson], *Memoirs of the Seraglio of the Bashaw of Merryland. by a discarded Sultana* (London, 1748), pp. 9, 28. Other rules were: "VII: No toasts to be drank, but the bashaw's health. . . . XIII: Not to sing, but in their respective apartments. . . . XIV: Every sultana to mend her own cloaths, and wash her small things. . . . XVII: No sultana to paint any part of her body but her face."

30. Ivan Block would find Lovelace to be suffering from the "English defloration mania. . . . For the Englishman, only the best is good enough. He must have something which can only

once, and by only one person, be possessed, and of which he can boast before others. This is the case as regards the virginity of a girl, which attracts the Englishman primarily as something select and unique," *Sexual Morals*, pp. 176-77.

31. Lovelace's grandiose scenario may not be entirely fantastic. In "The Tyburn Riot Against the Surgeons," *Albion's Fatal Tree: Crime and Society in Eighteenth-Century England*, ed. Douglas Hay et al. (New York, 1975), pp. 65-117, Peter Linebaugh discusses the folklore and ritual surrounding death on the gallows. Condemned malefactors frequently "treated the days of their hanging as a wedding." Three members of the Hawkhurst smuggling gang dressed all in white to be hanged. "Paul Lewis in 1763 went to his hanging in a white cloth coat, silver laced hat, white stockings and white silk breeches. George Anderson . . . hanged for stealing eight shillings' worth of silk ribbon . . . wore a white linen waistcoat and breeches trimmed with black ferret." Gentleman Harry Simms, hackney coachman and famous thief, was "cleanly dress'd in a White Fustian Frock, White Stockings, and White Drawers." Although it was not customary practice, maidens occasionally petitioned for the lives of prisoners. "Eighteen maidens dressed in white petitioned the King to spare the life of Edward Skelton, condemned in 1686, on condition that one of them would marry him," a possibility that Lovelace overlooks while planning his spectacle. Linebaugh reports several other virginal attempts, including the abortive mission of seven women from Honey Lane dressed in white, "carrying white wands in their Hands." (pp. 112-14)

32. Repetition is a favorite Lovelacian device: he pushes language beyond its limits. Listen to his description of a penitent Clarissa reduced to low fortune: "And thus may her *old* nurse and she; an *old* coachman; and a pair of *old* coach-horses; and two or three *old* maid-servants, and perhaps a *very old* footman or two (for everything will be old and penitential about her) live very comfortably together; reading *old* sermons, and *old* prayer books; and relieving *old* men, and *old* women; and giving *old* lessons, and *old* warnings, upon new subjects as well as *old* ones, to the young ladies of her neighbourhood; and so pass on to a good *old* age, doing a great deal of good both by precept and example in her generation." (V, 286) [III, 177]

33. It is interesting here to look at Lord Chesterfield's advice

to his son. A young gentleman "should be, for good purposes, what Alcibiades was commonly for bad ones, a Proteus, assuming with ease, and wearing with cheerfulness, any shape." Philip Dormer Stanhope, Lord Chesterfield, *The Letters of Philip Dormer Stanhope, Fourth Earl of Chesterfield*, 6 vols., ed. Bonamy Dobrée (London, 1932), vol. 5, p. 2025.

34. Gardner Stout, Jr., "Satire and Self-Expression in Swift's *Tale of a Tub*," *Studies in the Eighteenth Century*, vol. 2 (Canberra, 1973), pp. 325-26.

35. A. D. McKillop, "On Sir Charles Grandison," *Samuel Richardson: A Collection of Critical Essays*, ed. John Carroll (Englewood Cliffs, N.J., 1969), p. 125. Grandison did have his admirers. John Ruskin had difficulty choosing his favorite literary character—Sir Charles or Don Quixote. Eaves and Kimpel, *Samuel Richardson*, p. 391.

36. See Christopher Hill, "Clarissa Harlowe and her Times," *Samuel Richardson*, ed. Carroll, p. 120, on Richardson's ideas about polygamy.

Six. Created Selves

1. See Dustin Griffin's *Alexander Pope: The Poet in the Poems* (Princeton, 1978) for his illuminating discussion of the eighteenth-century preoccupation with the formation of the self. Citing Mr. Spectator's interest in "what it was that might be said to compose Personal Identity," and Shaftesbury's examination of "this thing of personality . . . how you . . . are you, and I am myself," Griffin investigates Pope's own concern with the attainment of selfhood. Less concerned about the perfectionism that attracted Richardson, Pope nevertheless viewed life as something to be harmonized and structured, offering opportunities to become, on a certain level, his best piece of art. (pp. 28-29) S. L. Goldberg also looks at the ways Pope worked at fixing an identity that he could "know," even though it "was continually at odds with his very capacity to know anything," in his essay "Integrity and Life in Pope's Poetry," *Studies in the Eighteenth Century*, vol. 3, eds. Brissenden and Eade (Toronto, 1976), p. 196.

2. See *Clarissa* (III, 201-2) [II, 115] for Lovelace's exploitation of Clarissa's "working mind."

3. In "Richardson's Pamela: The Aesthetic Case," *Samuel*

Richardson, A Collection of Critical Essays, ed. John Carroll (Englewood Cliffs, N.J., 1969), A. M. Kearney discusses the problem of Pamela's role as both narrator and character. He argues that although Richardson's "own inclination, and indeed talent as a writer, prompted him to release the (uncensored) contents of the mind in a flow of consciousness . . . at the same time, he is pulled away from the subjective pulse of experience towards the authorial and objective." This shift from subjective to objective is especially noticeable in Part II of *Pamela*, suggesting "a change of function for the heroine, a change which parallels her elevation from low to high life." (p. 32)

4. Leo Braudy, "Penetration and Impenetrability in *Clarissa*," *New Approaches to Eighteenth-Century Literature: Selected Papers from the English Institute*, ed. Philip Harth (New York, 1974), p. 203.

5. Ian Watt, *The Rise of the Novel: Studies in Defoe, Richardson and Fielding* (Berkeley and Los Angeles, 1967), p. 167.

6. See Anthony Kearney's discussion of the "compulsion and isolation" of Clarissa's world in "*Clarissa* and the Epistolary Form," *Essays in Criticism*, vol. 16, no. 1 (January 1966), pp. 44-56.

7. Irwin Gopnik, *A Theory of Style and Richardson's Clarissa* (The Hague, 1970), p. 77.

8. Ibid., p. 81.

9. Braudy, "Penetration and Impenetrability," p. 192. "Using Lovelace to define herself (as he uses her), Clarissa believes that she is a totally interior being, while he is totally exterior. The true self, as she defines it, is a purging of the external world—the theatrical role-playing definition Lovelace embodies—as well as the divisions he excites within her, her 'divided soul.' "

10. Ibid., p. 205.

11. Mark Kinkead-Weekes, *Samuel Richardson: Dramatic Novelist* (London, 1973), pp. 240-41.

12. Kearney, "*Clarissa* and the Epistolary Form," p. 54.

13. Gillian Beer, "Richardson, Milton, and the Status of Evil," *Review of English Studies*, new series, vol. 19, no. 75 (1968), pp. 261-70.

14. Brian Downs, *Samuel Richardson* (London, 1928), pp. 75-76. Downs argues that the only religious doctrine in Clarissa

is the "doctrine of future rewards." Richardson "substituted a
transcendental for a sublunary audit: and that was all."
15. A. D. McKillop, "Epistolary Technique in Richardson's
Novels," *Samuel Richardson*, ed. Carroll, pp. 147-48.

Seven. A Man of Letters
1. John Preston would disagree with this idea. In *The Created
Self: The Reader's Role in Eighteenth-Century Fiction* (London,
1970), he argues that when we recognize Lovelace's reconstruc-
tion of Miss Howe's letters, "the book begins to seem to be
about the literary evidence itself, letters rather than people." (p.
66) Richardson's emphasis on typography "is in fact a deliberate
reminder of the unreality of writing. It indicates how the characters in the book have become literary even to themselves." (p.
46) The documents begin to take on more meaning than the
action.
Surely a character can be "literary" and still remain "real."
Lovelace's delight in forging letters, the careful attention to the
minute particulars that makes his forgeries so convincing, help
to define and illustrate his character. His passion for letter-writing becomes part of his personality. Calling attention to the act
of writing and posting makes the characters more, rather than
less, convincing, especially to the passionate letter-writers of the
eighteenth century. Some fifty years after Clarissa, Miss Ellen
Weeton filled seven quarto volumes with copies of letters she
had sent and letters she had received between 1805 and 1825.
Her letters, vehicles for her "epistolary conversation," were "the
only expression of her genius (with the exception of her Journal,
sundry essays, poems, and Reflections), that her diffidence permitted her to produce." *Journal of a Governess, 1807-11*, 2 vols.,
ed. Edward Hall (London, 1936), vol. 1, p. xi.
2. See Preston's discussion of Richardson's use of the hiatus
and the dash, his deliberate disintegration of the sentence, *The
Created Self*, pp. 42-49. The convention of the disordered mind
reflected in the disordered sentence did not, however, originate
with Richardson. According to Robert Adams Day, readers of
epistolary novels before Richardson valued "an artificially disheveled style of incoherent exclamation derived from the sensationally popular letters of the Portuguese Nun and the heroic

drama." Robert Adams Day, *Told in Letters: Epistolary Fiction before Richardson* (Ann Arbor, 1966), p. 107.

3. Anthony Kearney, "*Clarissa* and the Epistolary Form," *Essays in Criticism*, vol. 16, no. 1 (January 1966), p. 48. "Any threat to Clarissa's correspondence becomes a threat to herself."

4. A. D. McKillop, "Epistolary Technique in Richardson's Novels," *Samuel Richardson, A Collection of Critical Essays*, ed. John Carroll (Englewood Cliffs, N.J., 1969), p. 150.

5. Margaret Doody, *A Natural Passion: A Study of the Novels of Samuel Richardson* (Oxford, 1974), p. 156, argues that Richardson used Norris's *Miscellanies*, a collection of poetry celebrating friendship and the "union of virtuous souls in Heaven," symbolically. Norris's most notable poems "deal with the mysterious parting of the soul from the body at the moment of death and speculate on the joys of eternity." Lovelace is truly " 'out-Norris'd' by Clarissa's joyful acceptance of death."

6. Preston, *The Created Self*, p. 59.

7. Samuel Johnson, "Pope," *The Lives of the English Poets: The Works of Samuel Johnson, LL.D.*, 9 vols. (Oxford, 1825), vol. 8, p. 314. See John Carroll on Richardson's theory of correspondence in *The Selected Letters of Samuel Richardson*, ed. John Carroll (Oxford, 1964), pp. 31-35. "When exalting the nature and value of correspondence Richardson ignores the psychological barrier against complete exposure of the self. . . . In forming his theories about letter-writing Richardson does not take account of the suppressions and evasions that may affect the style of the least designing of correspondents."

8. Samuel Richardson, *The Richardson-Stinstra Correspondence and Stinstra's Prefaces to Clarissa*, ed. William C. Slattery (Carbondale and Edwardsville, Ill., 1969), p. 26.

9. Ibid., pp. 26-27.

10. Denis Diderot, "Eloge de Richardson," *Oeuvres Complètes* (Paris, 1875), vol. 5, p. 215. The following translation is from Mark Kinkead-Weekes, *Samuel Richardson: Dramatic Novelist* (London, 1973), p. 486: "He carries the torch to the depths of the cave; it is he who teaches us how to discern the subtle, dishonest motives that are hidden and concealed under other motives which are honest and hasten to show themselves first. He breathes on the sublime phantom which presents itself

at the entrance of the cave; and the hideous Moor that it was masking, reveals himself."

11. Richardson, *The Richardson-Stinstra Correspondence*, p. 71.

12. Leslie Fiedler, *Love and Death in the American Novel* (New York, 1960), p. 41.

13. Malvin R. Zirker, "Richardson's Correspondence: The Personal Letter as Private Experience," in *The Familiar Letter in the Eighteenth Century*, eds. Howard Anderson et al. (Lawrence, Kans., 1966), p. 79.

14. Virginia Woolf, *A Room of One's Own* (New York, 1957), pp. 102-103. Woolf finds Shakespeare's mind to be "the type of the androgynous, of the man-womanly mind . . . creative, incandescent and undivided." Richardson also discussed the androgynous quality of Shakespeare, deciding that he knew the characters of women "best of all our writers. . . . he knew them better than they knew themselves." Richardson coyly denied that he knew women so well: "No, I say—I only guess at them: And yet I think them not such mysteries as some suppose. A tolerable knowledge of men will lead to a tolerable knowledge of women. Mrs. Shirley has said well, where she says that the two Sexes are too much considered as different species." (*Letters*, p. 292)

15. T. C. Duncan Eaves and Ben D. Kimpel, *Samuel Richardson: A Biography* (Oxford, 1971), p. 538.

16. Ibid., pp. 521-22.

Bibliography

Since my investigation into the world of Clarissa took me into areas far beyond my field of literary criticism, I have compiled a selected bibliography of the works most helpful to me in such strange territory. It is by no means an exhaustive one. The research of Judith Walkowitz and Stan Nash on prostitution should make future study of the fallen woman less difficult. I regret not having been able to use their work in my own research.

EIGHTEENTH-CENTURY ENGLISH LIFE

Barratt, Thomas J. *The Annals of Hampstead.* 2 vols. London, 1912.

Chancellor, E. B. *The Annals of Covent Garden and its Neighbourhood.* London, 1930.

Earle, Peter. *The World of Defoe.* New York, 1977.

Fielding, Sir John. *A Brief Description of the Cities of London and Westminster.* London, 1776.

George, M. Dorothy. *London Life in the Eighteenth Century.* London, 1925; reprint ed., 1966.

Jarrett, Derek. *England in the Age of Hogarth.* St. Albans, Herts., 1976.

[King, Richard.] *The New Cheats of London.* London, n.d.

Laslett, Peter. *The World We Have Lost.* London, 1971.

Lecky, William. *A History of England in the Eighteenth Century.* 8 vols. London, 1878-80.

Malcom, James Peller. *Anecdotes of the Manners and Customs of London During the Eighteenth Century.* London, 1808.

Margetson, Stella. *Leisure and Pleasure in the Eighteenth Century.* London, 1970.

Marshall, Dorothy. *Doctor Johnson's London.* New York, 1968.

Mingay, G. E. *English Landed Society in the Eighteenth Century.* London, 1963.

Rogers, Pat. *Grub Street.* London, 1972.

Rubinstein, Stanley. *Historians of London.* London, 1968.

Rudé, George. *Paris and London in the Eighteenth Century: Studies in Popular Protest.* London, 1974.

Shinagel, Michael. *Daniel Defoe and Middle-Class Gentility.* Cambridge, Mass., 1968.

Stow, John. *Survey of the Cities of London and Westminster.* 2 vols. Edited by John Strype. London, 1754-55.

Wroth, Warwick. *The London Pleasure Gardens of the Eighteenth Century.* London, 1896.

LETTERS AND JOURNALS

d'Arblay, Madame. [Burney, Fanny] *Diary and Letters of Madame d'Arblay (1778-1840).* 6 vols. Edited by Austin Dobson. London, 1904.

Cheyne, George. *The Letters of Doctor George Cheyne to Samuel Richardson (1733-1743).* Edited by Charles Mullett. Columbia, Mo., 1943.

Delany, Mary Granville. *The Autobiography and Correspondence of Mary Granville, Mrs. Delany: with interesting reminiscences of King George the Third and Queen Charlotte.* 3 vols. Edited by Lady Llanover. London, 1861.

Montagu, Lady Mary Wortley. *The Complete Letters of Lady Mary Wortley Montagu.* 3 vols. Edited by Robert Halsband. Oxford, 1965-67.

Munby, Arthur J. *Munby, Man of Two Worlds: The Life and Diaries of Arthur J. Munby, 1828-1910.* Edited by Derek Hudson. London, 1972.

Pilkington, Laetitia. *Memoirs of Mrs. Laetitia Pilkington.* 3 vols. Dublin, 1748.

Piozzi, Hester Thrale. *Autobiography, Letters and Literary Remains.* 2 vols. Edited by Abraham Hayward. London, 1861.

Stanhope, Philip Dormer. *The Letters of Philip Dormer Stanhope, Fourth Earl of Chesterfield.* 6 vols. Edited by Bonamy Dobrée. London, 1932.

Swift, Jonathan. *Journal to Stella.* 2 vols. Edited by Harold Williams. Oxford, 1940.

Weeton, Ellen. *Journal of a Governess, 1807-11.* 2 vols. Edited by Edward Hall. London, 1936.

TRAVELERS' IMPRESSIONS

Archenholtz, W. de. *A Picture of England.* London, 1797.

Fiennes, Celia. *Journey of Celia Fiennes.* Edited by C. Morris. London, 1947.

Grosley, Pierre Jean. *A Tour to London; or New Observations on England and its Inhabitants.* 2 vols. Translated by Thomas Nugent. London, 1772.

Meister, Henry. *Letters Written during a Residence in England.* London, 1799.

Misson, Henri. *Memoirs and Observations in his Travels Over England. With Some Account of Scotland and Ireland.* London, 1719.

Saussure, Cesar de. *The Letters of Monsieur Cesar de Saussure to his Family: A Foreign View of England in the Reign of George I and George II.* Translated and edited by Madame Van Muyden. London, 1902.

Smith, Edward. *Foreign Visitors in England, and What They Thought of Us.* London, 1889.

FAMILY, SEX, MARRIAGE, AND MORALS

Adburgham, Alison. *Women in Print: Writing Women and Women's Magazines From the Restoration to the Accession of Victoria.* London, 1972.

Alexander, William. *The History of Women, from the Earliest Antiquity, to the Present Time.* 2 vols. Dublin, 1749.

The Art of Governing a Wife: with Rules for Batchelors. To Which is added, an Essay Against Unequal Marriages. London, 1747.

Block, Ivan. *History of English Sexual Morals.* Translated by William H. Forstern. London, 1936.

Brissenden, R. F. *Virtue in Distress: Studies in the Novels of Sentiment from Richardson to Sade.* London, 1974.

[Brown, John.] *An Estimate of the Manners and Principles of the Times.* London, 1758.

[Fielding, Henry.] *The Female Husband: or, the Surprising History of Mrs. Mary, alias Mr. George Hamilton. Who was convicted of having married a Young Woman of Wells and lived with her as her Husband.* London. 1746.

Fussel, G. E. and K. R. *The English Countrywoman: A Farmhouse Social History* A.D. *1500-1900.* London, 1953.

Gregory, John. *A Father's Legacy to his Daughters.* London, 1775.

[Greville, Fulke.] *Maxims, Characters, and Reflections: Critical, Satyrical, and Moral.* London, 1757.

Habakkuk, H. J. "Marriage Settlements in the Eighteenth

Century." *Transactions of the Royal Historical Society*, 4th series, vol. 32 (1950), pp. 15-30.

[Halifax, Marquis of.] *The Lady's New Year Gift: or Advice to a Daughter.* London, 1688.

Halsband, Robert. *The Life of Lady Mary Wortley Montagu.* Oxford, 1956.

Hill, Christopher. "Clarissa Harlowe and Her Times." *Samuel Richardson: A Collection of Critical Essays.* Edited by John Carroll. Englewood Cliffs, N.J., 1969.

Hill, Georgina. *Women in English Life from Mediaeval to Modern Times.* 2 vols. London, 1896.

Hyde, Mary. *The Thrales of Streatham Park.* Cambridge, Mass., 1977.

Lewinsohn, Richard. *History of Sexual Customs.* London, 1958.

Moir, John. *Female Tuition.* Dublin, 1787.

Muilman, T. C. *An Apology for the Conduct of Mrs. Teresia Constantia Phillips.* London, 1748.

Pullar, Philippa. *Consuming Passions: A History of English Food and Appetite.* London, 1972.

Schucking, Levin L. *The Puritan Family: A Social Study from the Literary Sources.* Translated by Brian Bettershaw. London, 1969.

Sekora, John. *Luxury: The Concept in Western Thought, Eden to Smollett.* Baltimore, 1977.

Shorter, E. *The Making of the Modern Family.* New York, 1975.

Stenton, Doris M. *The English Woman in History.* London, 1957.

Stone, Lawrence. *The Family, Sex and Marriage in England, 1500-1800.* London, 1977.

Taylor, Gordon Rattray. *The Angel Makers: A Study in the Psychological Origins of Historical Change.* London, 1958.

Watt, Ian. *The Rise of the Novel: Studies in Defoe, Richardson and Fielding.* Berkeley and Los Angeles, 1967.

Whately, W. *The Bride Bush.* London, 1617.

Servants and Apprentices

Clark, A. *The Working Life of Women in the Seventeenth Century.* London, 1919.

Hanway, Jonas. *Virtue in Humble Life.* 2 vols. London, 1774.

Hecht, J. Jean. *The Domestic Servant Class in Eighteenth-Century England.* London, 1956.

Marshall, Dorothy. *The English Domestic Servant in History.* London, 1949.

Moreton, Andrew. [Daniel Defoe] *Everybody's Business is Nobody's Business; or Private Abuses, Publick Grievances: Exemplified in the Pride, Insolence, and Exorbitant Wages of Our Women Servants, Footmen, &c.* London, 1725.

[Richardson, Samuel.] *The Apprentice's Vade Mecum: or Young Man's Pocket Companion.* Edited by A. D. McKillop for the Augustan Reprint Society, nos. 169-70. Los Angeles, 1975.

S., J. *The Famous History of the Valiant London Prentice; Shewing His Noble Exploits at Home and Abroad. Together with His Love and Great Success: Very Pleasant and Delightful. Written for the Encouragement of Youth.* Newcastle, 1711.

Swift, Jonathan. "Directions to Servants." vol. 13 of *The Prose Works of Jonathan Swift.* 14 vols. Edited by Herbert Davis. Oxford, 1959.

RAKES AND FALLEN WOMEN

Allen, Robert J. *Clubs of Augustan London.* Cambridge, Mass., 1933.

Ashe, Geoffery. *Do What You Will: A History of Anti-Morality.* London, 1974.

Chancellor, E. B. *Lives of the Rakes.* 6 vols. London, 1924-25.

Davys, Mary. "The Accomplished Fine Rake." *Four Before Richardson.* Edited by William McBurney, Lincoln, Nebr., 1963.

Foxon, D. *Libertine Literature in England, 1660-1745.* London, 1965.

Johnson, Captain [Christopher]. *The History of the Life and Intrigues of that Celebrated Courtezan, and Posture Mistress, Eliz. Mann.* London, 1724.

Jones, Louis C. *The Clubs of the Georgian Rakes.* New York, 1942.

[Kelly, Hugh.] *Memoirs of a Magdalen, or the History of Louisa Mildmay.* 2 vols. London, 1767.

Kemp, Betty. *Sir Francis Dashwood: An Eighteenth-Century Independent.* London, 1967.

The Life and Writings of Philip, late Duke of Wharton. 2 vols. London, 1732.

McCormick, Donald. *The Hell Fire Club*. London, 1958.

Memoirs of the Life of His Grace, Philip, late Duke of Wharton. By an Impartial Hand. London, 1731.

Richetti, John J. *Popular Fiction Before Richardson: Narrative Patterns 1700-39*. Oxford, 1969.

Shadwell, Thomas. "The Scowrers: A Comedy." vol. 4 of *Works of Thomas Shadwell*. 4 vols. London, 1720.

Smith, Captain Alexander. *The School of Venus, or Cupid Restor'd to Sight*. London, 1716.

Some Authentick Memoirs of the Life of Colonel Ch———s, Rape-Master-General of Great Britain. By an Impartial Hand. London, 1730.

Tricks of the Town: Being Reprints of Three Eighteenth-Century Tracts. Edited by Ralph Straus. London, 1927.

Walker, Captain Charles. *Authentick Memoirs of the Life, Intrigues and Adventures of the Celebrated Sally Salisbury with True Characters of her Most Considerable Gallants*. London, 1723.

[Ward, Ned.] *The Secret History of Clubs*. London, 1709.

[Watson, Sophia.] *Memoirs of the Seraglio of the Bashaw of Merryland. by a discarded Sultana*. London, 1748.

CRIME AND THE LAW

Albion's Fatal Tree: Crime and Society in Eighteenth-Century England. Edited by Douglas Hay et al. New York, 1975.

An Appeal to Humanity in an account of the Life and Cruel Actions of Elizabeth Brownrigg. London, 1767.

Blackstone, William. *Commentaries on the Laws of England*. 4 vols. London, 1775.

Celebrated Trials and Remarkable Cases of Criminal Jurisprudence from the earliest record to the year 1825. 6 vols. [Compiled by George Borrow.] London, 1825.

Colquhoun, Patrick. *A Treatise on Indigence, Exhibiting a General View of the National Resources for Productive Labour*. London, 1806.

Genuine and Authentic Account of the Life, Trial and Execution of Elizabeth Brownrigg . . . for the barbarous Murder of Mary Clifford, her Apprentice Girl . . . Together with The Sufferings of Mary Mitchell, and Mary Jones. London, 1767.

Nash, Stanley. "Social Attitudes towards Prostitution in London from 1752 to 1829." Unpublished doctoral dissertation, New York University, 1980.

Proceedings . . . upon a Bill of Indictment found against Frances Charteris, Esq; for Committing a Rape on the Body of Anne Bond, of which he was found Guilty. London, 1730.

Radzinowicz, Leon. *A History of English Criminal Law and its Administration from 1750.* 4 vols. London, 1948-68.

Ryan, Michael. *Prostitution in London, with a Comparative View of that of Paris and New York.* London, 1839.

The Trial of Frederick Calvert, Esquire . . . for a Rape on the Body of Sarah Woodcock. . . . Taken in Shorthand by Joseph Gurney. London, 1768.

"Tryal of Elizabeth Wigenton for Whipping a Girl to death at Ratclyffe." *The True Relation of the Tryals . . . at Old-Bailey, 17th and 18th January, 16——.* Listed in the British Library Catalogue as BM 515 L.2/7.

Walkowitz, Judith R. *Prostitution and Victorian Society.* Cambridge, 1980.

PSYCHOLOGY OF THE SPIRIT AND BODY

Byrd, Max. *Visits to Bedlam: Madness and Literature in the Eighteenth Century.* Columbia, S.C., 1975.

Cheyne, George. *The English Malady: or a Treatise of Nervous Disease.* London, 1733.

————. *An Essay on Regimen.* London, 1740.

DePorte, Michael V. *Nightmares and Hobbyhorses: Swift, Sterne, and Augustan Ideas of Madness.* San Marino, Calif., 1974.

Durkheim, Emile. *Suicide, A Study in Sociology.* Translated by John Spaulding and George Simpson. London, 1970.

Dussinger, John. "Richardson's *Clarissa*: 'A Work of Tragic Species.' " Unpublished doctoral dissertation, Princeton University, 1964.

Foucault, Michel. *Madness and Civilization: A History of Insanity in the Age of Reason.* Translated by Richard Howard. New York, 1973.

St. John of the Cross. *The Collected Works of St. John of the Cross.* Translated by Kieran Kavanaugh and Otilio Rodriguez. London, 1966.

Moore, Cecil A. "The English Malady." *Backgrounds of English Literature, 1700-1760.* Minneapolis, 1953.

Passmore, John. *The Perfectability of Man*. London, 1970.
Petersson, Robert T. *The Art of Ecstasy: Teresa, Bernini, and Crashaw*. London, 1970.
Rousseau, G. S. "Science." *The Eighteenth Century*. Edited by Pat Rogers. London, 1978.
St. Teresa of Avila. *The Life of Saint Teresa of Avila by Herself*. Translated by J. M. Cohen. Edinburgh, 1957.
Zaehner, R. C. *Mysticism: Sacred and Profane*. Oxford, 1957.

Index

Hanway, Jonas, 107
Haywood, Eliza, 153-54
"heiress stealing," 109-10
Hill, Aaron, 198, 312-13
"Historical Faith": principle of,
146-47
Hogarth, William, 9, 11

Jarret, Derek, 9, 61
Johnson, Samuel, 153, 155, 220-
21, 277
Johnston, Arthur, 152

Kelly, Hugh, 122
Kinkead-Weekes, Mark, 49, 97,
254, 291

Lady Bradshaigh: correspondence
with, 76-77, 139-40, 207-208
Lady's Magazine, The, 130
Lady's New Year Gift (Halifax),
The, 63, 65, 71, 78
London Merchant (Lillo), *The*, 7
Lord Baltimore, 112-13, 115, 221
Lovelacian rake, 198-234 passim;
ambivalence toward, 229-31; as
artist, 208-14; Duke of Wharton and, 204-205; imagination
of, 220-28; madness of, 209-
11; as plotter, 210, 212, 222-
24, 227-28; roles of, 220

McKillip, A. D., 232, 258, 270
madness: eighteenth-century fear
of, 321; rake figure and, 209-
11
Malcom, James P., 57
Manley, Mary, 153-54
Marquis of Halifax, 63, 65, 69,
78
marriage, eighteenth-century: children and, 72-74; sexual stereo-
type and, 122-23; women and,
65-73
Marshall, Dorothy, 107

Martz, Louis L., 295
masculine roles: sentimental
woman and, 74-75
medieval romance: chapbook and,
155; eighteenth-century literature and, 152-53
Memoirs of a Magdalen (Kelly),
122
Miller, Henry Knight, 155-56
Milton, John, 184-85
Mingay, G. E., 70
Moir, John, 107
Montagu, Lady Mary Wortley,
56-57, 220, 305-306
moralism, 3-49 passim; artistic
method and, 236; fairy tale
and, 193-95; in *Familiar Letters*, 12-15; novel and, 16-49,
147, 150-51; *Vade Mecum* and,
5-8
*Most Pleasant History of Tom a
Lincolne, The*, 152-53
Munby, Arthur J., 308
myth, 315; in *Pamela*, 157-59

New, Melvyn, 194
novella: literary reaction to, 153-
54

Opie, Iona and Peter, 145, 155,
159, 161, 168

Pamela: character development in,
158, 237-45; Cinderella story
of, 157, 159; costume in, 165-
66; doctrine of virtue in, 19-
21; ending of, 166-67; epistolary method of, 235-37, 243-
45; ethical values in, 159; fairy
tale and, 145-46, 193-94; fallen
woman and, 100, 116, 136-39;
idea of "quality" in, 159-60;
melodrama in, 238-39; moral
maxims in, 150-51; mythic element in, 157-59, 315; notion of

Williams, E. N., 58
Wilt, Judith, 306
Wolff, Cynthia Griffin, 19, 25, 27, 29
woman, eighteenth-century: children and, 72-74; education of, 59-60; equality of, 58-62; fallen, *see* fallen woman; literary heroine and, 54-55, 123-28,

135-44; sentimental, *see* sentimental woman; submissive nature of, 62-67
Woodcock, Sarah, 112
Woolf, Virginia, 285
"writing to the moment": technique of, 282-83

Zirker, Malvin R., 284, 286

Carol Houlihan Flynn is Assistant Professor of English at New York University.

Library of Congress Cataloging in Publication Data

Flynn, Carol Houlihan, 1945-
  Samuel Richardson, a man of letters.

  Bibliography: p.
  Includes index.
  1. Richardson, Samuel, 1689-1761—Criticism and
interpretation.   I.   Title.
PR3667.F5   823′.6   81-47916
ISBN 0-691-06506-3   AACR2

DATE DUE

NOV - 7 2010			
DEC - 7 2010			

Demco, Inc. 38-293